5 Nov...

Thanks for being there &
in the "200 prd-tion."

Best,
R

SEYMOUR HERSH

Seymour Hersh
Scoop Artist

Robert Miraldi

POTOMAC BOOKS
An imprint of the University of Nebraska Press

∞

Library of Congress
Cataloging-in-Publication Data
Miraldi, Robert.
Seymour Hersh: scoop artist /
Robert Miraldi.
pages cm
Includes bibliographical
references and index.
ISBN 978-1-61234-475-1 (cloth: alk. paper)
1. Hersh, Seymour M. 2. Journalists—
United States—Biography. 3. United
States—Politics and government—
1945–1989. 4. United States—Politics and
government—1989- 5. United States—
Foreign relations—1945–1989. 6. United
States—Foreign relations—1989- I. Title.
PN4874.H473M57 2013
070.92—dc23   [B]   2013023619

Set in Lyon by Laura Wellington.
Designed by Nathan Putens.

To Mary Beth Pfeiffer, who understands
investigative reporting—and me.

Contents

Illustrations

Prologue

Chasing Sy Hersh

I have been chasing Sy Hersh, America's quintessential investigative reporter, for twenty-five years. He did not know it, however, until five years ago.

I first met Seymour Myron Hersh in the fall of 1985 when he was forty-eight years old. I had invited him to speak at my university, a small state college seventy-five miles from New York City near the Hudson River, where I taught journalism for thirty years. His controversial best-selling book, *The Price of Power: Kissinger in the Nixon White House*, had come out in the spring, and his speaking fee had doubled, from $2,000 to $4,000, although we got him at the bargain rate. (He now commands $20,000 a speech.) My office was located in a remote part of the 257-acre campus, and I hoped Hersh could find me. He was scheduled for an afternoon workshop with journalism students. He arrived fifteen minutes before showtime. "This is a tough place to find," he said. "Well," I answered, "I figured if you could find Calley at Fort Benning, you could find my office." He shuffled his feet in an "aw-shucks" manner, looked away, and said, "That was a long time ago." It had been sixteen years ago, actually, since he had tracked down the notorious William Calley who ordered the killing of nearly five hundred Vietnamese civilians in the village of My Lai in 1968. Hersh's exposé earned him the Pulitzer Prize in journalism and cemented his fame.[1]

As we walked across campus I told him how my wife, an investigative reporter, worried so much each time she published. "We all worry," he said. "We are out there alone." His book on Kissinger was bringing howls of protest from the former secretary of state's minions, and one minor participant in the plotline had sued Hersh for $50 million, although it ultimately was resolved in Hersh's favor.

At the workshop that afternoon I could not get him to discuss journalistic technique for the students I had asked to attend. Instead, he wanted to talk about the CIA, intelligence gathering, Richard Nixon, and Kissinger. The reporter did not want to talk *about* reporting—only what he had uncovered in the process of reporting. Like all the great journalists, his passion was reserved for the issues. Form and function were of little interest.

Before his evening lecture, the college president hosted a dinner at her home. The president invited vice presidents, deans, and local officials. This kid from Chicago, the son of immigrant parents, a law school dropout and former Chicago crime reporter, was a celebrity, "a fucking celebrity," as he called himself in a triumphant post-Pulitzer interview. One guest was Alan Chartock, a political science professor who was also a well-known personality on a network of National Public Radio stations he ran from the state capital in Albany. Hersh had a Washington DC neighbor whom Chartock knew. Hersh liked the man; Chartock did not. They proceeded to argue about him over dinner. When he left the dinner, Hersh said to me, "Who is that little prick?" I explained he is a considerably influential pundit in New York's capital. Hersh just uttered more profanities. Hersh seldom minces words or pulls punches, I came to learn. He goads and blusters and intimidates, leaving enemies everywhere he goes, from presidents to generals to secretaries of state. It is part of his style—and success.

The evening lecture went better. Nearly 750 people packed the college's largest lecture hall. Hersh had his notes on three small cards tucked into his pocket, but he spoke without them, fluently and passionately, assailing the immoralities of the Nixon era from Vietnam to Watergate. To many people in this university town, Hersh was a hero, and they applauded frequently. Hersh more than earned his fee. For Hersh, who had bankrupted himself as he traveled around the world to research *The Price of Power*, it was one of hundreds of talks to fill the coffers before the great investigative reporter zeroed in on his next target. He has had, in fact, two careers: the journalist who has produced hundreds of newspaper and magazine articles and nine books, and the public speaker who has crisscrossed the nation hundreds of times talking to crowds big and small in his breathless style, often saying more than he should and stirring controversy in the process. When the evening talk was over, and he had answered many questions and received a standing ovation, I escorted him back to his car. He was staying in a dingy hotel, courtesy of the college, outside of the village of New Paltz before heading home the next day. "I miss my family," he said as he left campus, referring to his wife Elizabeth and three children back in the nation's capital.[2]

I did not speak to Sy Hersh again for nearly twenty years as he produced five more books, all controversial, a few documentary films, and dozens of articles for the *New Yorker* magazine. That's when the chase began in earnest—to try to get Hersh to do what he despised—talk about himself. In 2004 I had decided to write his biography. He was sixty-seven years old, and I had filled folder after folder with old yellowed newspaper clips and bookmarked more websites with Sy Hersh profiles and commentaries than I thought my computer could hold. I sent him a registered letter to tell him my intentions. He had to walk to the post office in 102-degree Washington DC heat to pick it up. Not a great start. I had no clue if he would cooperate. He had long been intensely private and media shy, except when promoting a book or exposé for the *New Yorker* because then, after all, it was about the work. He had refused again and again to discuss his family or his upbringing. "God, this is all so tedious," he told one interviewer who made the mistake to ask about his early life. "What the hell does it have to do with anything I write?" One of the world's most famous investigative reporters did not think he was the story. Then again, at times there have been serious threats made against him, when a story touched a nerve, which may explain his reluctance to open his family life.[3]

When his older sister said she would love to talk to me, Sy vetoed the possibility. She knows little about my work, he insisted. I went back and forth with his twin brother, Alan, who also was willing to be interviewed. But we—Alan and I—could never agree on terms that assuaged Sy. Hersh's wife never answered my letter requesting an interview; Hersh had told me a long time ago I would not be able to interview her. Getting a lens on Sy Hersh through his family became impossible, which left, mostly, his work—the stories, the crusades, the endless controversies, the countless awards, and the long list of successes, victims, and enemies.[4]

Still, I was hopeful Hersh would talk to me, his first biographer. "Look," he said, in his famously rapid style when I first called him in 2004, "I am not dead yet." That the world knew. He had re-emerged on center stage that year, reporting on the aftermath of the 9/11 tragedy that had struck America. His exposé of the American torture of prisoners at Abu Ghraib in Iraq was groundbreaking. Awards poured in; he was profiled in magazines. While many applauded him, one Bush administration official called him "the terrorist of American journalism." From the press's point of view, he was back. Of course, he had never really left, as this book shows. From My Lai in 1969 to Abu Ghraib in 2004—logical bookends—he was remarkably productive, successful, and controversial. And, along with his longtime rival Bob Woodward, he has surely been America's most well-known investigative reporter. "You can't draw up a pantheon of American reporters that doesn't include Hersh," says author Thomas Powers. "If it's a pantheon of two, he's one."[5]

Over my years of research, Hersh has been polite but standoffish. "I just don't have time to sit down for long interviews," he said in one phone conversation. "Maybe when these sunavabitches are out of the White House," a reference to the Bush cast and crew. But when Barack Obama was elected, Hersh proved no more willing to talk about his life story. I should not have been surprised. Writers have been chasing him for four decades. His home and work phone numbers are publicly listed, and he answers his own phone, abruptly, with "Hersh." He will answer a few questions and then dismiss the caller with, "You've got enough. G'bye." The chase has been repeated dozens of times. David Jackson of the *Chicago Tribune* wanted to meet "the legendary investigative reporter" at an airport to talk with him as he came back to his hometown Chicago to receive an award. "Leave me alone," Hersh said. When Jackson met him at the airport anyway, Hersh acquiesced, and they drove together to his old neighborhood on the South Side. The result was a rare inside look. On another occasion, Hersh dismissed the Associated Press's Deborah Hastings after a few questions, saying, "I've given you more than enough."

When Scott Sherman wrote a profile of Hersh in 2003 for the *Columbia Journalism Review*, the closest he got was to watch Hersh take phone calls in his cubby-hole office, a scene that has been re-created by many journalists over the years. Joe Eszterhas, a magazine journalist who went on to write Hollywood screenplays, got the closest in 1975 when Hersh was riding high after his exposés of the CIA. Hersh sat for a long Q&A with Eszterhas for *Rolling Stone* magazine. But he could not get too close. "I don't want anybody reporting about my private life," he declared.[6]

Leonard Downie, who later became editor of the *Washington Post*, also got Hersh to talk in considerable detail in the mid-1970s, first labeling him the "scoop artist." Everyone else has mostly had to chase Hersh, a breakfast here, phone call there, a few stolen minutes in his office or before or after a speech. Marianne Szegedy-Maszak tried to write about him in 1991 for *Esquire*, but he kept saying to her, "But imnotgonnatell you a thing." She still wrote a story. His friend Robert Sam Anson interviewed Hersh for *Vanity Fair* just as his book on John F. Kennedy was coming out in 1997. The outcome may explain his shyness: his revelations about why he pursued Kennedy's sex life were thrown back at him by reviewers and enemies, and he *has* many enemies. I spoke to some, and decades after he wrote about them or someone close to them, they were still furious, still convinced they had been wronged. But there are others, to be sure, who insist Hersh is the man who speaks the truth, who cannot be stopped by government subterfuge, and who uncovers the hidden deeds that no one else can find.[7] You will find both those men in this book.

In 2008 journalist Wajahat Ali, who writes for *CounterPunch*, a biweekly muckraking newsletter, sought, as he put it, "to score an interview" with Hersh. The result was comic and typical. Reached by phone, Hersh said it was a bad time, that he had phone calls coming in all day. Undoubtedly true; he lives on the phone. Try me in two weeks when I will be back from traveling, Hersh said. Ali called back, a few days before Hersh was to return, thinking he could leave a voice mail. But the surly Hersh answered. "Why do you want an interview? Who are you again? Islamic what? Islamic? Listen, you know I did Jazeera right?" And on and on, concluding, more or less, with "I got a lot of reporting to do. I really don't like doing this. . . . I report the facts. I'm just a reporter."[8]

Ali had been treated to the famous Hersh brush-off. I pretty much got the famous Hersh treatment for five years. He was always polite. He answered my emails promptly but curtly. He gave a few phone interviews, and he promised on a few occasions to find documents he thought he had in his basement, but it never happened. He was too busy reporting, even now, at age seventy-six, finishing a big book on former vice president Dick Cheney. At times when I asked him questions about old stories, he simply could not recall. I seemed to know more about some of them than he did. Not surprising. He wrote hundreds of articles for the Associated Press and United Press International from 1963 to 1969, and then hundreds more for the *New York Times* from 1972 to 1979. Then more books and dozens of magazine articles for the *New Yorker*. When his "scoops" were newsworthy and controversial enough, which was often, he discussed his work with the press. He was on the record all over the place—from YouTube videos to interviews with Amy Goodman, Charlie Rose, and Jon Stewart, to countless short newspaper sound bites. And, maybe, in the end I was sort of glad to not have access. *Times* columnist Joe Nocera criticized Steve Jobs's biographer Walter Isaacson for being too close to his subject, with whom he met more that forty times. I never got close to Hersh. My view of him is, mostly, though his speeches, his "pimped" interviews, as he called them, his enormous body of work, and the ample comments he has made on that work for four decades.[9]

Some people who know him told me he would talk, that he has a very large ego. But an interviewer once asked him, how would you like people to remember you? He answered: "I couldn't care less. I don't believe in life after death." And while I do believe he cares, I think he cares about something else much more—being left alone so he can keep reporting. "The myth about me is that I am wildly abrasive, antagonistic, hostile," Hersh says. "I do very little to bother it, because the myth is a plus." He is crusty, crabby, and aloof—because it keeps people away and lets him do what he wants, which is to uncover more stories than any other journalist in the past forty years. It lets him be America's unrivaled "scoop artist"—and a great American journalist and character.[10]

Acknowledgments

Many people helped make this book possible. I am particularly grateful to Kelsey VanNorman, Robert M. Miraldi, and Mary Beth Pfeiffer. Various assistants aided me, including Ally Brisbin, Anthony Heim, James Audlin, Nina Schutzman, Alyssa Jung, and Marcy Velte. Marguerite Stein and Janet Graham Gottlieb helped me understand the Hersh family ancestry. Janet Gottlieb assembled the photographs. Gerald Sorin, David Krikun, and Susan Ciani all read important chapters. Various librarians at the State University College at New Paltz made my research possible. And the college gave me various leaves of absence and financial assistance. In particular, I thank Dean James Schiffer for his assistance. I am grateful for permission to use material from the *New York Times* Company records, A. M. Rosenthal papers, Manuscripts and Archives Division, New York Public Library, Astor, Lenox and Tilden Foundations; the Eugene McCarthy Papers at the University of Minnesota; and the Gerald R. Ford Presidential Library. I am grateful to the many people who talked to me about Seymour Hersh's work. My agent, Robert Wilson, believed in this work, as did my first editor, Hilary Claggett. And I appreciate the guidance offered by Elizabeth Demers and the careful editing of Joeth Zucco and especially Jane Curran. Helen Pfeiffer's support made this book possible. Lastly, thanks to the Schnellers—Sara, Quinn, Rocco and Lucas, who made me laugh.

SEYMOUR HERSH

CHAPTER 1

The Story No One Wanted

The Tip: "I Knew He Was a Tenacious Reporter"

Geoffrey Cowan was a twenty-seven-year-old Yale Law School graduate working in Washington DC in the fall of 1969. He had just helped start a public interest legal foundation that became an important force in representing civil rights groups, women's organizations, and labor unions. But Cowan was also following family tradition working part-time as a journalist, writing a column on politics for the quintessential alternative weekly newspaper, the *Village Voice* in New York City. His older brother, Paul, was a well-known progressive writer for the *Voice* who stayed in journalism his entire life. Geoffrey was only passing through on his way to a distinguished career as an academic, author, and director of the Voice of America. But in the tumultuous early fall days of 1969—just weeks after thousands celebrated peace and love at the Woodstock festival and just as Richard Nixon had secretly expanded the war in Vietnam into Cambodia—Cowan was coauthoring a Washington column, "The Seat of Government," that was making waves. Cowan and Judith Coburn had written one column that uncovered one of the war's darkest deeds, as least up until that point. They revealed details about "Operation Phoenix," the secret American intelligence program that ordered the assassination of Vietnamese civilians who were supposedly providing support for the Viet Cong and the North Vietnamese.

Probably because of that column, Cowan received a telephone call one day from a friend who had a secret source in the military. The friend said an American soldier was being charged with spearheading a massacre of a number of Vietnamese civilians. "The story won't be told. It will be covered up," the source said. Cowan tried to get the *Washington*

Post interested, but he had no luck. Cowan could have tried to publish it in the *Voice*, but he feared this well-known liberal newspaper would not be credible, and that the story was too important to be buried in a publication that might not be trusted. A lawyer working with Cowan at the Center for Law and Social Policy, Ben Heinenman, suggested Cowan call reporter Sy Hersh. Seymour Hersh. Seymour Myron Hersh. "I did not know him," Cowan recalled, "but from what I had heard I knew he was a tenacious reporter and he might run it."[1]

Indeed, although only thirty-two years old, Hersh had developed a reputation around Washington for his pugnacity. Born in Chicago to immigrant parents, Hersh had gone to the University of Chicago as a history major. Then he had drifted into journalism after failing law school. For a short period he published a weekly newspaper in suburban Chicago before working for the fabled City News Bureau. After a short stint working for the United Press International (UPI) in South Dakota, Hersh came east to cover the Pentagon for the Associated Press (AP), a time when he learned to ignore formal press briefings and wander the halls of the Pentagon, making friends with midlevel sources in the military's sprawling bureaucracy. His time with the AP ended when it refused to run a long series of articles he produced on chemical and biological weapons. His first book, *Chemical and Biological Warfare: America's Hidden Arsenal*, came out in 1968 to favorable reviews but small sales. "I knew his book," Cowan recalled. Many others did also since it played a key role in the Nixon administration's decision to ban the continued production of such lethal weapons.[2]

Hersh was also known in the journalistic community in Washington for another reason. He had left reporting for a three-month period in early 1968 to work on the antiwar campaign of Senator Eugene McCarthy of Minnesota as he sought to wrest the Democratic presidential nomination from Lyndon Johnson. This aberration in Hersh's journalism career ended when he had an argument with McCarthy. Now, in the heady fall of 1969, with thousands of protestors regularly amassing on the capital's lawns, Hersh was a freelance reporter. He was working on a book about the Pentagon—tentatively called *The Ultimate Corporation*—but he took Cowan's October 22 phone call and listened. "I've got a fantastic story,"

Cowan said. "There's a guy down in Benning (Fort Benning, Georgia) who is being held on a charge of murdering seventy to seventy-five Vietnamese civilians."[3]

Even though Cowan's source had gotten his information from someone whose name Hersh did not even know, Hersh declared: "I believed it instinctively." Hersh only knew the original source was in the military. "I still don't completely know why I believed my caller," he said. After all, Hersh, who makes sure his telephone number is publicly listed in Washington DC, gets calls from all sorts of sources giving him story ideas. "I am the clearinghouse for every tipster in the country," he said. And, he added, "I generally check out tips." This one just rang true because he knew—from his short stint working as AP's Pentagon correspondent—that many officers in the military "were as troubled as I was. Maybe it was that understanding, dimly perceived, that set me to work on Cowan's tip."

But part of the reason was Hersh's dislike for the war in Vietnam. He knew that "the full story of its nature was not known to most Americans." Having recently completed his book on military secrets in the stockpiling of chemical weapons, Hersh said he knew the U.S. Army could "court martial someone without anyone knowing." He also had to know that even if he could track this story down, it would be a tough sell to the public. "Americans simply did not believe such things went on in America," Hersh felt. And tracking the story was not going to be easy. Cowan was only minimally helpful. "I knew some pieces," he said, "and some of the names of the people involved." Although Hersh had a contract for his Pentagon book, his nose for news twitched enough that, he said, "I stopped all other work and began chasing down the story of the My Lai massacre."[4]

Turning a Tip into a Story

The summer and fall of 1969 make up one of the most head-spinning periods in American history. America was gasping at events—a woman dying in Senator Edward Kennedy's car when it plunged off a bridge on July 18; men walking on the moon on July 20. In August nearly a half million young people showed up near Woodstock in upstate New York to stage three days of unabashed frolic that translated into a cry for making love, not war. On September 24 the trial began of the so-called Chicago 7, a group of activists arrested at the riot-marred Democratic National Convention the previous summer. The defendants turned the trial into a political spectacle, the dissenters of America defying authority. On October 9 the National Guard was called in to control demonstrations outside the courtroom.

But those events that summer went beyond mere headlines; they represented a climactic closing to an era of unprecedented cultural and political tumult. Not since the Civil War had the nation been so split over basic values. The 1960s culminated with the forces of the counterculture—the hippies, the doves—clashing with the political establishment—the silent majority and the hawks. "We felt that the grown-ups didn't know what was going on. We were sure that it was the rule of the ignorant over the enlightened," explained David Obst, a twenty-three-year-old Californian who would soon hook up with Hersh in trying to find outlets for the reporter's work. What was driving the political opposition more than anything else, of course, was the Vietnam War.[5]

Richard Nixon was elected president in 1968 on two major platforms. He called for "law and order," attractive especially in the South, which suggested he would be tough on antiwar long hairs and civil rights protestors, "bums," he called them. Secondly, he vowed to end the war, implying he had a "secret" plan to hasten the withdrawal of American troops. When he took office, he and Secretary of State Henry Kissinger were convinced they could end the war in a year. But despite what Nixon said, he had no "secret peace plan" to end the fighting. His approach was not very different from Lyndon Johnson's. America would negotiate at the peace table in Paris, but if the North Vietnamese did not agree to mutual withdrawal of troops, Nixon would escalate attacks with massive bombing against the North. He had already secretly proven he could be tougher than Johnson, in fact, by sending American B-52s to bomb Viet Cong sanctuaries across the border in Cambodia, a tact Johnson had refused. The North Vietnamese were willing to absorb the new blows, hoping American public opinion would drive the president to end American participation. A key to Nixon's strategy thus became rallying Americans to support the troops and the continuation of the war. He could not afford another serious blow to American prestige, such as the Tet offensive of January 1968 when North Vietnamese troops mounted attacks that stunned American troops and startled domestic opinion.[6]

And that is why when 250,000 people showed up in Washington DC to protest the war on October 15, days before Geoffrey Cowan called Sy Hersh, Nixon was presented with a big crack in his attempt to control public opinion. Wearing black armbands to signify dissent and to pay tribute to Americans killed in the war—more than 47,000 soldiers—the demonstrators chanted, marched, and demanded an end to America's longest war. The demonstration was thought to be the largest in U.S. history with two million people involved nationwide. New York City's mayor ordered flags flown at half-staff. In Boston 100,000 people listened to Senator George McGovern, who would run against Nixon in 1972, lambaste the war. In England a young Rhodes Scholar at Oxford named Bill Clinton organized a large demonstration.

While demonstrators filled the streets, Nixon stayed in the White House, offering no comment. But General Earle Wheeler, chairman of the Joint Chiefs of Staff, more than likely spoke for the president when he called the protesters "interminably vocal youngsters, strangers alike to soap and reason." Nixon knew he had to fight back. Not only was the peace movement becoming emboldened, but the press was increasingly critical of the war effort. And Sy Hersh was about to become the leader of that pack.

Working in a windowless seventy-dollars-a-month room in the National Press Building in downtown Washington, the bespectacled, sandy-haired Hersh began to work his sources. In the breathless style for which he would become famous, he spent three days calling more than twenty-five people—in and out of the military, some retired. "I started making calls and I got nowhere," he said. Most reporters would have given up. One day in the kitchen of his home in northwest Washington, he told his wife, "I was really pursuing this mad story partly because I was bored to death and also I just wanted to pursue it."[7] Hersh went especially to pro-war conservatives who were likely to have been told about the massacre so that they would not have to read about it first in the press. Finally, an old friend on Capitol Hill, a staunch supporter of the war who worked for powerful conservative South Carolina Democrat Mendel Rivers, told

Hersh he knew a "few sketchy details." He urged Hersh not to write the story. "It'll hurt the Army, Sy," he said. "The kid was just crazy. I heard he took a machine gun and shot them all himself." Hersh disagreed and took a gamble. He called the public relations office at Fort Benning, where he was told those involved might be held. He asked for the names of any soldiers being held for court martial. The public affairs officer directed Hersh to a four-paragraph Associated Press story on the bottom of page 39 of the *New York Times* on September 7. The AP story, buried in a few other newspapers, said that William L. Calley, twenty-six, of Miami, had been charged with "murder in the deaths of an unspecified number of civilians in Vietnam in 1968." Hersh said the officer who talked to him was "courteous and helpful," but he seemed to know little. Hersh may have been wrong in this assessment. The Pentagon in Washington had in fact begun to develop a strategy for containing this story. When the AP story appeared on September 7, the military expected phones to ring off the hook with inquiries. Their strategy, in part, was to only release information when it was requested from Fort Benning as a way of keeping it out of the hands of the national press corps in Washington DC.

Winant Sidle, a general and chief of information for the army from 1969 to 1973, called the My Lai massacre "one of the most serious public relations problems faced by the army and the Department of Defense during the war debate." And while he later argued that the Pentagon needed to tell the public more about what happened in the tiny village of My Lai, when Hersh called in November Sidle was coy. When Hersh told the colonel "he had a news bombshell about My Lai," Sidle knew Hersh "smelled a rat." Sidle listened but did not take the bait. He wouldn't confirm Hersh's suspicions and provided little help beyond the original press release. "We simply hunkered down and awaited Hersch's [*sic*] action," Sidle recalled. Hersh's excitement was building. "It was hard to believe," he told his wife.[8]

The biggest challenge for the resourceful Hersh came next—to find the lieutenant who was soon to be at the center of an international scandal. "I was sure that Lieutenant Calley was the one accused of the mass murder," he recalled. But no one would even tell him how many murders had taken place, let alone where Calley was imprisoned. Hersh turned back to his Capitol Hill sources, pretending to know more than he did, employing what he called "the standard newspaperman's bluffing operation." While the tactic of lying to sources is debatable to journalism ethicists, it worked for Hersh, as did a number of other debatable tactics. His sources revealed that Calley was charged with the murder of over ninety civilians. Now Hersh wanted to find Calley's attorney to learn more. He returned to Cowan, his original tipster. Cowan took a day but came back with the name "Latimer." Nothing else. Hersh tried a few attorneys by that name in Washington, and one suggested Hersh might be looking for a well-known military attorney in Salt Lake City, George Latimer, a former judge on the Utah Supreme Court. Hersh called Latimer and hit pay dirt; Latimer was defending Calley. "I want to talk to you about this fellow Calley," Hersh said. "Oh, what a tragedy," he replied. "The government is making a tragic mistake." Hersh immediately asked if he could come to see the lawyer. "I wouldn't talk over the telephone to any potential source about the case," he said. He could get more information in person. He told Latimer he was on his way to California but could make a pit stop in Salt Lake City. This was a lie, but it worked. "Boy, if you want to come out here, that's fine," Latimer said. Hersh's only problem now was a very practical one. "I didn't have any money," he recalled. Nine months into the year 1969 Hersh had made only about $8,000. He turned to Philip J. Stern, a philanthropist and the grandson of Sears and Roebuck's founder. Stern had just started the Fund for Investigative Journalism, which promptly gave one of its first grants—$250—to Hersh. It enabled him to fly to Salt Lake City, and as Stern later bragged, the grant—another $2,000 would come later—allowed Hersh to "leverage a whiff into a colossal stink and contribute mightily to the change in how Americans viewed the war in Vietnam."[9]

On the night that Hersh boarded a plane to Utah, Latimer received a call from Lieutenant Colonel Douglas B. Tucker, an army public relations specialist who had first responded to media inquiries about the scandal in September. A friendly call, Latimer thought, one soldier to another. Whether they discussed how to handle Hersh's upcoming inquiries is unclear, but Latimer talked tough in regard to his client. He accused the army of making Calley a scapegoat for orders that came from higher authorities. And he implied that he was going to go up the army's channels to seek a dismissal. Certainly Latimer had the credentials to get to high places. He was a judge on the Utah Supreme Court until he was appointed by President Truman to a ten-year term as a judge on the U.S. Court of Military Appeals in Washington. In World War II, he spent three years in the South Pacific, rising to colonel. The army knew him well because he was already defending Green Berets who also had been accused of murder, a case that received considerable attention. Hersh, who has an uncanny ability to make friends with sources from both sides of the political spectrum, hit it off with Latimer. "He thought I was the nicest young man he'd ever met," Hersh recalled. Part of the reason was that he flattered Latimer by digging up documents from his most recent cases. "Now you could call it clever, you could also call it smarmy," Hersh said, but again it worked. His next gambit paid more dividends. He wondered how many people Calley had been accused of killing and doubled the number he had heard. "I said, 'I understand he was accused of killing 150 people.' A word for what I did—an actual word, it has three letters—it's called 'lie.'" Latimer responded, "What are you talking about, oh my God." He then showed Hersh a piece of paper, which indicated Calley was officially charged with killing 111 "Oriental human beings," words Hersh said "I'll never forget."[10]

When Latimer left the room, Hersh took notes on what the document had told him. Eventually he pried more details and confirmed facts. "It was a major step forward," he said. And then, oddly, he agreed to Latimer's request that he not print a word of this story until he called Latimer back when he was ready to publish. Journalists rarely allow sources to have what amounts to a veto over a story. "There was no reason for me not to make such a pact," said Hersh in what was to become a common practice of his—making deals with sources in exchange for information. Latimer told Hersh that Calley had been shipped back to the United States in midsummer after his third tour of duty. He was stationed at the largest army training base in America, Fort Benning near Columbus, Georgia. "Hell, I figured I'd find him. I decided to go blindly looking for him," Hersh declared. "I hot-dogged on the first plane out east." The army was not likely to look favorably on a reporter trying to find the man who held the key to unlocking the greatest scandal of the war. When Calley was told about the charges against him during the previous summer, he said at a military hearing, simply, "Yes, sir, I understand, sir." He saluted, and a colonel took him into an alley. "There is no need to publicize this thing," the colonel said. "The U.S. Army won't publicize it if you won't." Calley agreed.[11]

The Hunt for Calley

On November 11 Hersh flew from Washington to Columbus, Georgia, where he rented a car. And then the fun—and challenge—began. Hersh once said, "I like to write stories that make people jump up and down." But he also liked the adrenaline rush that comes with the hunt, the chase for a quarry that does not want to be caught. Fort Benning covers more than 182,000 wooded and muddied acres with the Chattahoochee River cutting down the middle. The total daily average population at the base is 107,998 with more than 75,000 soldiers training there and 55,000 working full-time. Finding Calley would be like finding a needle in a haystack. The traditional route to a source would be to contact public relations officers or to ask to see Calley's on-base lawyer. But just as Hersh knew that talking on the telephone was not the best way to get sources to be candid, he knew he needed to find Calley himself if he was to have any chance to get the real story. He began with the tried-and-true journalistic beginning point of contacting a telephone operator on base. But there was no listing for Calley. Dead end. "I was convinced the Army was hiding him somewhere in the base," Hersh said. "I figured a mass murderer like this has got to be locked up." The base had a dozen or so Military Police jails; Hersh visited them all, parking in front of the units, taking his briefcase and entering, saying to the sergeant on duty, "Hi, I'm looking for Bill Calley." No one asked who he was, and Hersh assumed they thought he was a lawyer. He did not correct them. After three hours, he had made no progress. He was not disheartened since Latimer had made clear that Calley *was* at Benning.

Next, Hersh said, "I made a reckless move." He went into the Judge Advocate General's Office since JAG would be prosecuting the case. He asked an elderly sergeant where he could find Calley. When asked, Hersh said he was a reporter, and the sergeant reached for a phone to call a colonel. Hersh walked out. "I'm not about to wait for any colonel," he said. "I want to be foot loose and fancy-free." Fort Benning is open to the public, so Hersh was not breaking any laws by wandering the base. But once the military knew he was hunting for Calley, Hersh understood Calley would be herded up and made unavailable. That explains, at least in part, why Hersh was consistently coy in announcing who he was as he walked the journalist's fine line between misidentifying himself and openly declaring his intention. The line grew thinner. Hersh visited Calley's lawyer, Major Kenneth A. Raby, but he was "visibly agitated" to see the reporter. Hersh briefly considered giving up, but he grabbed a quick and dismal lunch at a cafeteria and went back to the telephone operator. Reporters learn that second calls often produce new information. This time a listing under "new" soldiers turned up. Hersh hustled off to the main training unit for recruits where Calley was listed as living. It took him an hour to get there.[12]

Captain Charles Lewellen met Hersh with a big smile, the first he encountered all day, but that faded when he learned Hersh was a reporter looking for Calley. "I can't tell you anything," Lewellen said, and Hersh thought, "I knew I was finally getting close." Lewellen was the first soldier Hersh encountered who really could have told him something about My Lai. When the incident was taking place in March of 1968 and was being monitored in Vietnam by the army, Lewellen secretly turned on a recorder to tape radio messages. He did not know that his tape would become a live version of a massacre. But he chased Hersh away, saying, "If you've got any questions about Calley, take them someplace else." Hersh was enjoying the challenge. "The closer I got to Calley, the more chances I would take," he recalled. When Lewellen left, Hersh went upstairs to a barracks of mostly empty beds. One soldier was sleeping. Hersh—now getting brazen—kicked the bed, yelling, "Wake up, Calley." It turned out the soldier was off duty, detained while the army located his orders. "You mean that guy that killed all those people?" the soldier asked. Hersh later learned that hundreds of GIs knew what happened in March of 1968 in the village known to soldiers as either Song My or Pinkville. The soldier suggested to Hersh that a friend, another soldier, working in a nearby mailroom might be able to locate Calley. Hersh picked up the soldier in his car behind his barracks and drove to the mailroom. But he had to figure out how to get the soldier in the mailroom out to meet him. Again, Hersh bluffed. He straightened his tie, walked in, and with anger in his voice demanded to a sergeant: "I want to see Jerry outside in my car in two minutes flat." The sergeant smiled, figuring the soldier was about to get in trouble. A few minutes later "Jerry" appeared and told Hersh there was a lot of undelivered mail waiting for Calley. But no one knew where to locate him. The only way to get an address was to steal Calley's personnel file.[13]

After a pause Hersh said: "Well? Just do it. I promise I'll just look at it for a minute." Without saying so, Hersh was urging Jerry to pilfer the file. "I'll try, Mister." Moments later he returned with a sheet of paper that had Calley's local address in Columbus where he was supposed to be living in a house with other officers. Hersh drove over only to find out that Calley no longer lived there. But the officers—after he identified who he was and said what story he was working on—began to open up. And the story he and America would hear repeated many times began to emerge: civilians were killed at the village of My Lai, but the reason why varied. Hersh heard three explanations. The soldiers went wild, and what happened was simply aberrant behavior. Or, Calley and his company were just good soldiers following the chain of command. Or, war is hell, and this kind of thing happens, especially in a war where the enemy can't be readily discerned. And anyway, the other side was worse than America, committing more atrocities. The officers Hersh encountered off the base were angry about the treatment of Calley, who they felt was just following orders, participating in a planned battle. This was, after all, what the army had originally said happened at My Lai. In a press release the day after the March 16, 1968, incident, the army said 128 "enemy" had been killed in a "Vietcong stronghold." The assault "went like clockwork," the release reported.[14]

With no Calley in sight, Hersh returned to the base once more. Hersh said, "Goddamnit, what do you have to do to find this guy?" But now Hersh was told by another group of soldiers that Calley was living in a bachelor's quarters with fifty units. It was 7:00 p.m., and Hersh said he was "discouraged," but for the next two hours he knocked on every door, yelling, "Hey, Bill, are you in?" He recalled, "I wasn't about to quit. If need be, I thought, I'd stay at Benning and knock on the doors for weeks." Hersh added: "I'm a little bit of a madman I guess." He would only need another hour. Hersh's next tact was to stand in a nearby parking lot, stopping cars and asking if anyone knew where to find Bill Calley. One veteran officer, who was troubled by the direction of the Vietnam War, told Hersh he had just seen Calley. When he wondered why Hersh wanted to see him, the wily reporter knew what reason to give: "To give him a chance to tell his side, if he wants." The officer invited Hersh to join him for Scotch, and they drank for an hour. The officer said he was likely to meet Calley at a party later; Hersh could join them. More drinks followed. Hersh, exhausted and a little drunk, was about to find a motel, when the officer, standing outside with Hersh, said: "Hey, Rusty, come over here." Hersh wanted to beg off and go get some sleep. He did not know that William Calley's nickname was Rusty. "That's Calley," the officer told the reporter. "Are you Calley?" Hersh asked. "Yeah," he replied. "I am Hersh." "He's a good guy, Rusty," said the officer who introduced them. They agreed to go up to Calley's room to talk. Pay dirt.

On the face of it, Sy Hersh and Rusty Calley seem like oil and water. How could Seymour Hersh, son of immigrants who ran a dry cleaning store, educated at the University of Chicago, hard-nosed reporter who despised the war in Vietnam, who worked for the most prominent antiwar presidential candidate in the country . . . how could this person hit it off immediately with a twenty-six-year-old kid from Miami with no particular talents who had initially been rejected by the army at twenty-two and then worked as a short order cook, car wash worker, hapless railroad conductor, and investigator for insurance companies before being let in the army? But Hersh and Calley did hit it off, possibly because Hersh was a chameleon, but also because, as Hersh put it, "I was the last reporter with whom he would talk, and drink, for many months." Calley knew what the coming months would bring. So the two men went first to Calley's room and drank beers like frat brothers. "He reminded me of an earnest freshman," Hersh wrote. When the five-foot, four-inch 130-pound Calley took a shower and emerged nude, toweling himself off, Hersh could only think, "This is the man who shot and killed 109 people." The duo then got in Hersh's car, picked up some bourbon and steaks, and went to the apartment of Calley's girlfriend. She cooked them a great dinner. "It could have been a night with any old friend," Hersh said. But it was not. Lt. William Calley Jr. was an accused mass murderer, and now, as they sat in his girlfriend's living room, an alcohol glaze covering their view, the chain-smoking sergeant began to unfold for Hersh some of what happened on the awful day that helped change the course of the Vietnam War—and of Hersh's career.[15]

CHAPTER 2

The Scoop Heard 'Round the World

"Shoot Anything That Moves"

"It must have been a beautiful area, before the war," wrote Seymour Hersh about Quang Ngai Province. Beautiful, but also, he added, one of the most "dangerous regions in all of Vietnam." Fertile farmlands and green rice paddies were set in the foothills of the Annamese Mountains with the white sandy beaches of the South China Sea in the distance. But it was also a region filled with bitter and suspicious villagers, many of whom sympathized with the Viet Cong. And why not? Since the early 1960s their homes had often been burned by Vietnamese troops who wanted them to choose between the National Liberation Front Viet Cong and the U.S.-supported South Vietnamese government. Thousands of tons of bombs and napalm had made refugees out of 138,000 Vietnamese and destroyed 70 percent of the province's dwellings. William Calley's Charlie Company arrived in the province, which included the tiny village of My Lai, in the winter of 1968 to root out peasants who had gone over to the wrong side. In three months the company never had any direct confrontations with enemy forces, but booby traps and sneak attacks had taken their toll, killing five Charlie Company soldiers and injuring twenty-eight. And each time the Americans were attacked, the Viet Cong sneaked away.[1]

As Sy Hersh sat with Rusty Calley, some of the story of what happened on March 16, 1968, began to emerge. It is not clear how much Calley told Hersh—or how much of the horrible day he could fathom telling anyone. Undoubtedly his lawyers told him to be careful not to incriminate himself. But Hersh had also promised Latimer not to write anything until the lawyer had read his story. And he likely made promises to Calley that he would not convict the accused soldier in his stories. "I thought about how dumb he was. I could have really ripped him off," Hersh said. A year after the story came out, Hersh wrote: "To this day I have not written all that Calley told me."[2] But he learned enough to piece together what became the biggest news story of the year.

Angry, frustrated, and nervous, the men of Charlie Company, Hersh discovered, prepared a series of assaults on the enemy in an area known as Song My, which was a collection of rural hamlets including My Lai. For some reason it was labeled Pinkville on the army maps. Later testimony was mixed, but some soldiers recalled that they were explicitly told to kill anyone they encountered, young or old. "This was a time for us to get even. A time . . . when we can get revenge for our fallen comrades," recalled Sgt. Kenneth Hodges.[3] Early in the morning the men fanned out through the villages to flush out underground bunkers and small huts, looking for the enemy. All they found were old women and men, young mothers and children, and lots of animals. When they saw something move, the soldiers fired randomly into the surrounding fields and jungle, but there were no return volleys. It did not stop the assault, however. For reasons that would be unclear for quite some time—orders from above? a policy of leaving behind no survivors? the civilians were collaborators with the enemy?—the soldiers began to round up civilians. The killings began without warning. If the villagers did not come out of their houses, the soldiers threw in grenades. When they did come out, they were shot. At one point, Calley fired into the head of a monk who was praying over a sick old man and killed him. Soon after, Calley ordered three or four of his soldiers to push civilians—women, children, old people—into a ditch. When they tried to get out, Calley began shooting them. A lot of the women threw their bodies over the children, but the soldiers kept shooting. When some children tried to crawl out, Calley and his men shot and killed them. A two-year-old boy miraculously was unhurt and crawled away. Calley grabbed the child, threw him in the ditch and shot him.

"I guess you could say the men were out of control," one soldier said. It was an understatement. The shooting and killing and raping went on all morning. "Just like a nazi-like thing," one soldier said. In the end, perhaps as many as 500 Vietnamese civilians were dead, including, as a plaque in the village eventually reported, 182 women, of whom 17 were pregnant, 173 children (56 of them infants), and 60 men over sixty years old. No enemy soldiers were captured—or even encountered. The My Lai massacre was over before lunchtime. Hundreds of killings had taken place in different locations with many soldiers involved and many officers aware of what took place. No one, not even Calley, had any idea of the extent of the massacre. But Hersh now had enough information to know that a dastardly deed had taken place. Over the next five months he flew all over the country to piece together the full story, but for now he had a breaking story to tackle. "This wasn't an article for a journal of opinion," Hersh said, "it was hard news that should be written as such."[4]

Hersh flew out the next morning to return to Washington DC. On the plane he wrote a fifteen-hundred-word story that began in laconic fashion, saying that the army was completing its investigation into the role of the "boyish-looking" Rusty Calley in the killing of 109 Vietnamese civilians in the Viet Cong stronghold of Pinkville. "The army calls it murder," Hersh stated. Hersh said he interviewed the suspect, who was being held in secrecy at Fort Benning. He did not mention what he had to go through to find Calley, writing only that "his exact location on the base is secret." Much of the story is legalistic background, and eight of the ten sources are unnamed, which would become a Hersh trademark. Calley did not appear until deep in the story, saying, "I know this sounds funny but I like the Army." He did not say whether he—or anyone—had killed civilians. But others did. One anonymous Washington source told Hersh: "They simply shot up this village and (Calley) was the leader of it. When one guy refused to do it, Calley took the rifle . . . and did the shooting." Another high-ranking officer at the Pentagon, also unnamed, tapped his knee and said, "Some of those kids he shot were this high. I don't think they were Viet Cong, do you?" Calley declined comment. "With expressionless gray eyes and thinning brown hair," Hersh observed, Calley "seems slightly bewildered and hurt by the charges." But Hersh did almost as much in his story to defend Calley as to damn him. Latimer said soldiers in Vietnam couldn't tell who is an enemy and who is an ally. "Either they shoot you or you shoot them," he said. Others said Calley was a scapegoat just following orders. "The orders were to shoot anything that moved," an officer said. "And anyway in Vietnam, killing becomes nothing," said another officer.[5]

In the end, Hersh's story is a surprise: no gory details, no inflammatory quotations, and more information that is background or defending Calley than attacks on his alleged deeds. This was the cautious, almost conservative former Associated Press reporter, not the same reporter who bluffed and lied his way through Fort Benning. When he landed at Dulles Airport, Hersh called Latimer to read him the story and get his responses; Latimer suggested only one change that Hersh said strengthened the story. But now Hersh had his next problem: to find someone to publish the blockbuster. Getting a publisher would be difficult, he knew, because when he felt he had the story nailed down—and before he spoke with Calley—he had tried both *Life* and *Look* magazines. He first brought the story idea to a friend at *Life*, the nation's largest mass circulation magazine. "Out of the question," he was told. *Look* asked for a memorandum, describing what he knew, but they too declined. As big a story as My Lai seemed to be, "atrocity stories were not written because atrocity stories had not been written," points out British historian Kendrick Oliver, who has extensively studied the incident. "Journalists chose not to disturb the silence over the darkest aspects of the war effort." But Hersh made a different decision.[6]

Hersh thought that if he could lay out his facts for any major American newspaper, the story would be printed eventually—after the newspaper verified his information, used his sources, and then printed their own version. "I could respect this," he said, "but I simply wanted my story for myself."[7] So he turned to Plan B—his twenty-three-year-old antiwar tennis partner, David Obst, who had recently started the Dispatch News Service to get out stories about the war that no one else would produce. When he was a student in Berkeley, California, Obst often talked to GIs returning from Vietnam, and they all casually referred to killing "gooks." Obst was indignant, explaining: "We wanted people to know the truth. It was simple. We thought that if Americans really knew what was going down in Vietnam, the war would be over in a minute."[8] Obst described Hersh as a "good-looking bundle of energy" who scored poorly in the category of "works well with others" because he was "fiercely independent and unable to keep opinions or emotions to himself." And he was "the classic loner," but the loner was lured into telling Obst about My Lai between sets on the tennis court. "For the next week I was like a little kid pulling on his daddy's pant leg. 'Can I have it? Can I have it?'" Finally, Obst recalled, "on the court again the next day I could tell something was wrong because Sy's serve sucked and twice, after missing easy shots, he threw his racket. When he retrieved it the second time he pointed at me and yelled. 'Okay, it's yours. But don't screw it up.'" Obst didn't. He went to work trying to lure newspapers in America's largest cities by simply calling editors and telling them what he had—a risky approach that could have led to his being scooped. Hersh knew, for example, the *New York Times* was hot on the story. A *Times* reporter had been at Fort Benning at the same time as Hersh, but he did not find Calley. The *Hartford Courant* was the first to bite. Obst used this to bluff newspapers by lying to them that other newspapers were preparing to run the story. Many began to express interest. Meanwhile, Hersh was in "a rather agitated state," Obst said. He "didn't want to be bothered" with distribution until Obst told him what it would cost to send the stories to the newspapers via telex, a telegram-like system that predated the fax and allowed newspapers to easily send and receive stories. But it was expensive. Hersh had a fit. "Telex! How are we going to afford to send telexes! It'll cost a thousand bucks." Obst said he would send them collect to more than a hundred newspapers. "OK. Good idea," Hersh said. "Now leave me alone. I've got to finish this if we're going to have it" for the morning newspapers.[9]

A "Dark and Bloody" Day

Wanting more details and eyewitnesses, Hersh would have preferred more time before writing his first My Lai exposé. Moreover, not wanting to be seen as part of the antiwar movement, he hoped to wait until a massive demonstration scheduled for Saturday, November 15, took place. The Dispatch News Service was a risky home for Hersh. The syndicate was barely surviving, with about a dozen or so alternative newspapers carrying its stories. Hersh had written a few Sunday feature stories for Obst. But no one knew the Dispatch syndicate, which Obst described as "an antiwar news service devoted to telling the 'truth' about Vietnam." Hardly a ringing declaration of reliability. Obst, who later became the book agent for *Washington Post* star Watergate reporters Carl Bernstein and Bob Woodward, wrote a short biography of Hersh to accompany his first story. He sent a telex to a hundred newspapers, asking for a $100 fee. Hersh and Obst waited to see who took the story, going early the next morning to the National Press Building, which carried out-of-town newspapers in a top-floor library. "Sy and I stood in the stacks waiting. Finally, the out-of-town papers began to come in." Thirty-five newspapers had carried the story, including the *Boston Globe, Miami Herald, Chicago Sun Times, Seattle Times,* and New York's *Newsday.* "The story was out. The army could not cover it up any longer," Obst declared. The *St. Louis Globe Democrat,* which carried all five of Hersh's My Lai stories, declared on page one: "Lieutenant Accused of Murdering 109 Civilians." The newspaper's Washington correspondent, Richard Dudman, who eventually landed on Richard Nixon's enemies' list for his acerbic White House stories, read Hersh's work with interest. "I knew right away that it was a blockbuster," he said. Hersh felt right away the story would win him a Pulitzer Prize. "I just knew it," he said. "It's going to be an incredible story. The best story of anybody's life."[10]

But as historian Oliver has noted, it was not clear at the outset "that the massacre would evolve into one of the most momentous media stories of the Vietnam era . . . despite the publication of Hersh's report." For a few days, reaction to My Lai was muted as other news overshadowed the story. On the day the story broke, Vice President Spiro Agnew, at Nixon's behest, went to Des Moines, Iowa, and gave a speech that blasted the press coverage of the Vietnam War. He warned of a growing unelected concentration of media power in New York and Washington, with the implication that the Nixon administration might go after the three major television networks and maybe the other "liberal eastern establishment" print news outlets. "The day when the network commentators and even the gentlemen of the *New York Times* enjoyed a diplomatic immunity from comment and criticism is over!" Agnew declared to a standing ovation. The whiff of censorship was in the air, and the news world focused on it. On Saturday, November 15, five hundred thousand demonstrators showed up in the nation's capital to protest the war; Gallup reported that 58 percent of Americans thought the war was a mistake. And then on November 19, three astronauts landed on the moon, with a television camera allowing viewers to see them step onto its surface. Americans were entranced.[11]

Meanwhile, Hersh and Obst were angling for a follow-up story because Hersh knew he had only uncovered the tip of the iceberg. The idea for a follow-up came when he saw an article by *Washington Post* military writer Peter Braestrup on the day his massacre story appeared.[12] The *Post* had purchased Hersh's first article but then wrote its own story. A *Post* editor had called Hersh early in the morning on November 12 to grill him on his story. Legendary editor Ben Bradlee ran the meeting. "My story was passed around, read by all, and I answered some direct questions," Hersh recalled, adding that he was miffed because no one asked him if the story was true. But Hersh later learned that Bradlee told the group, "This smells right." Braestrup wrote in his story that the My Lai investigation by the army had been prompted by a letter from an ex-GI and Vietnam veteran, not a member of Calley's unit. Hersh did not have this fact; he reported only that many soldiers knew of the incident. The name of the letter writer, Phoenix resident Ron Ridenhour, surfaced finally in the *Arizona Republic*. On November 15 the Associated Press ran a short interview with Ridenhour, and UPI confirmed that it was his heartfelt letter—to the president, his congressman, and the Pentagon—that had made the army pay attention. "The kid! The kid! The kid!" Sy yelled, knowing that Ridenhour was the key to the next round of stories.[13] Despite the grisly nature of what happened at My Lai, there actually were a few heroes—and Ridenhour was one of them. He had heard about the incident while serving in Vietnam. "Oh man, did you hear what we did at Pinkville?" one GI asked him. He had not, and soldier after soldier whom he ran into repeated the massacre tale. "I was horrified," Ridenhour told a journalist many years later. So he began to compile information in a notebook. When he returned home to college in California, Ridenhour wrote a letter on March 29 that described a "dark and bloody" incident at My Lai, and he asked for an investigation. He also tried to get magazines interested in his version of events. Like Hersh, he failed.[14]

Hersh wanted to hear what Ridenhour knew—and especially who he had talked to. But he was out of money again. "Between us we barely had enough cash to cover airfare to California," Obst said. First Obst's father lent them money, and then Stanley Sheinbaum, a well-known progressive and a fellow at a California think tank, gave them more.[15] Hersh flew immediately to Claremont College and had lunch with Ridenhour. "He was a gold mine of information," Obst said. He knew who all the players were and how to locate them. Hersh got the phone numbers and addresses of soldiers scattered throughout the United States. Hersh was shocked that he was the first reporter to seek out Ridenhour. But he knew others were on to the story. In fact, in Vietnam soon after Hersh's story appeared, reporters descended on a shantytown of cardboard and tin shacks one kilometer from the massacre site. They searched long enough to find human bones. Hersh would have to hustle to stay at the front of the pack. He asked Ridenhour to allow him three days before giving the story to anyone else. "I was glad to," the twenty-two-year-old Ridenhour said. "He was the first person to respond."[16]

Hersh raced around the country, flying first on November 17 to Utah, renting a car, and driving to Orem, known as "Family City USA," in the north-central part of the state. He arrived after midnight at the home of ex-GI Michael Terry, who was sleeping. The sophomore at Brigham Young University was awakened and agreed to tell Hersh what he had already told army investigators: "They just marched through shooting everybody," he said. "Mostly women and kids." Near lunchtime, he said, the soldiers noticed some victims were still breathing. "So we shot them." The next day Hersh flew to Fort Dix, New Jersey, to interview Michael Bernhardt, a short, intense man who was completing his tour of duty. Bernhardt recalled that he arrived a bit later at the village. "As I walked in, you could see piles of people . . . all over." The soldiers were shooting women and children. "I don't recall seeing one military age male in the entire place, dead or alive," he told Hersh. He seemed relieved to be telling his story. As for Calley, "he killed a whole lot of people," Bernhardt said. The soldier also foreshadowed three major developments: First, he was told not to talk to anyone; the cover-up had begun. Second, although Calley was charged with killing 109 civilians, Bernhard said the body count was in the hundreds. The North Vietnamese were saying it was 567! And third, Bernhardt said, "some dude went along on the mission and shot pictures." In fact, unbeknownst to Hersh or the government, ex-GI Ron Haeberle was negotiating at that very moment with the *Cleveland Plain Dealer*, which purchased his photos of the massacre.[17]

On the plane ride back to Washington Hersh penned his story. "I was more than shocked at the details I was getting," he recalled. "I mean—I'd cry thinking about it. They were talking about shooting kids and executing people.... It was horrifying."[18] Meanwhile, Obst spent ten hours on the telephone lining up publication outlets. On November 20 the Dispatch News Service published Hersh's second installment. "Hamlet Attack Called 'Point-Blank' Murder," the *St. Louis Post Dispatch* headlined. This one was much more hard-hitting than the first account. Eyewitnesses would be difficult to refute; there were photos about to surface; and the army was trying to cover it up. Hersh led with the fact that three eyewitnesses—he did not name the soldiers—told him they either saw the murders or participated in the killings. "We just treated them like animals," the anonymous soldier said. For the first time the name of Captain Ernest Medina, the commander of Charlie Company, surfaced; he too was under investigation with Calley. The *New York Times* and the *Washington Post* were right with Hersh on the story. The *Times* had only one source, but the *Post* had three. Hersh was barely still out front, yet he was getting the lion's share of the credit for breaking the story.

More importantly, the My Lai story was reaching beyond America's shores because Obst was syndicating it abroad. The *London Times* put the story on page one with the bold headline: "We saw women and children killed, say U.S. soldiers." The conservative *Daily Mail* called it "The Story that Stunned America." And the tabloid *Daily Sketch* ran a front-page editorial that declared, "From today the war is over ... the president will have to pull out." A protest took place in front of the American embassy in London, and the incident was debated in the House of Commons. Back home, the outrage was palpable. A *Times* editorial called the incident "so shocking, so contrary to principles for which this country has always stood as to be beyond belief. The evidence mounts daily that something horrible did take place."[19] When Haeberle's explicit photos of piles of bodies—the women, the half-naked children—lying in ditches appeared in the *Cleveland Plain Dealer*, Secretary of Defense Melvin Laird told President Nixon, "There are so many kids just lying there; these pictures are authentic." Privately, Laird wanted to "sweep the whole thing under the rug." He told Secretary of State Henry Kissinger that he could understand a few random killings in war, "but you shouldn't kill that many."[20]

After a Senate committee looked at Haeberle's photos, Pennsylvania's Richard Schweiker described the affair as "a deliberate act of inhumanity—one of the darkest days in American history." Near tears, Ohio's Stephen Young called it "an abominable atrocity." *Time* magazine opined, "Only a shadow of a doubt now remains that the massacre at My Lai was an atrocity, barbaric in execution."[21] The hopes of the Nixon White House that this story could be covered up quickly disappeared. After Hersh's second installment, "the My Lai story now had a life of its own," Obst observed. Or, as historian Oliver put it, "the massacre was now out of the box, and there was nothing much that anyone could do to get it back inside."[22]

Nixon had hoped to end the war in Vietnam by first intensifying it. And to accomplish that he needed the media to be silent about the misery the war was causing for the people of Vietnam. Despite the growing criticism of the war after the Tet offensive of 1968, the press largely was compliant. Although there was a common belief that the media led the way, the media took a long time to jump in bed with antiwar protestors. Nixon was in San Clemente, California, when Calley was charged with the murders in September. He was warned about the dangers the accusation could pose to his war policy: "Publicity," one memo warned, "could prove acutely embarrassing to the United States. It might well affect the Paris peace talks, and those nations opposed to our involvement in Vietnam will certainly capitalize upon the situation. Domestically, it will provide grist for the mills of antiwar activists."[23] The Pentagon, meanwhile, was ready to do its part to muffle the story. The strategy was to downplay the accusations, but not lie. All comments would come out of Fort Benning in Georgia to keep the story as a purely local one. And then the public relations specialists would carefully monitor all inquiries about Calley. Each time Hersh called the public affairs office in Benning—and he did each time he wrote a story—the Pentagon in Washington was apprised. The Pentagon officer in charge of orchestrating the Pentagon response, Winant Sidle, later regretted the way it was handled. When he was initially shown the army press release on Calley's court martial, Sidle said, "I voiced reservations about its light tone since I was a believer in mistake admitting. But, I went along with it."[24]

And then as the Pentagon carefully managed information about My Lai, Sidle wished they would have provided more details, instead of letting Hersh dig it up. "We should have figured out a way to communicate to the press the enormity of the story. . . . this would have reduced almost certainly the impact of Hersch's [sic] story when it broke." Nixon's inner circle was split. Daniel Patrick Moynihan, a Nixon adviser before he became a U.S. senator, wanted a commission to investigate. "It is clear that something hideous happened at My Lai . . . I fear and dread what this will do to our society unless we try to understand it," he wrote Nixon. Nixon was inclined to open up the process more, telling his advisers he wanted a My Lai planning group to figure how best to control the problem. But Secretary of State Henry Kissinger, in particular, convinced him such a panel might open a can of worms into other alleged atrocities.[25]

For his part, the indefatigable Hersh was not done as he crisscrossed the country finding soldiers. Meanwhile, the television media now came full force into the story and—like the rest of the press—followed Hersh's leads. On the day his interview with Bernhardt was published, both CBS and NBC followed up that night, putting him on the national nightly news. Although Bernhardt largely repeated what he had told Hersh, now thirty million Americans heard the allegations.

Hersh next pursued an interview with Paul Meadlo, a twenty-two-year-old from New Goshen, Indiana, whom he described as a "tall clean-cut son of a coal mine worker." Meadlo had a special story: his foot had been blown off the day after My Lai, and he thought it was God's revenge. But finding Meadlo was not easy. Hersh recalled: "I'm somewhere in the West Coast. And I hear about Meadlo, and I find his phone. Somebody tells him, one of the kids I'm talking to in the unit, somewhere in Indiana . . . we didn't have Google; it was a lot harder then," but he found the phone number. He called and Meadlo's mother answered. "I said, 'I'm coming.' She said, 'I can't tell you he's going to talk to you.' I said, 'I'm coming, and you decide.' She said, 'Just come, but I can't promise.'" Hersh flew to Chicago and then to Terre Haute, Indiana, a city of fifty thousand that is seventy-five miles west of Indianapolis. "It took me forever, and I finally found this house,"

Hersh recalled. Meadlo lived on a chicken farm out of a Norman Rockwell painting. "It's poor, just chicken coops, no farm, no farmland, a bunch of shacks. That's the home," Hersh said. When he arrives, the mother greets him. "She's 50 maybe, weathered, no man around, looks 70. And I just say, 'Is Paul Meadlo in there? Is he around?' She said, 'He's in there.' I said, 'Is it alright if I talk to him?' She said, 'Okay,' and then she says, very angry and very low, 'I gave them a good boy, and they sent me back a murderer.'" For Hersh, it was clear, "The bottom line is, this is what war is."[26]

But Meadlo did talk to Hersh. He admitted that he had killed dozens of Vietnamese civilians at the orders of Calley, who, Meadlo told Hersh, said, "I want them dead." Sitting in Meadlo's house with his mother at his side, Meadlo told a grisly story of massacre and mayhem that had haunted him. He talked of seeing old men in the fields, "gooks," and shooting them as they begged to live. He grabbed one man out of a hut and shot him. "I just thought we were going to be murdering the Viet Cong," he said, but in the end he thought at least three hundred civilians had been killed, including women and children. "The women huddled against their children and took it. They brought their kids real close to their stomachs and hugged them, and put their bodies over them trying to save them. It didn't do much good." Hersh kept taking notes, knowing that the story just kept getting better—or worse. Meadlo's mother, Myrtle, shook her head, repeating, "I sent them a good boy and they made him a murderer." Once again, Sy Hersh had made a soldier and his family feel comfortable enough to confess and pour their hearts out. Maybe they were waiting for a chance at redemption, or maybe Hersh just knew how to make people talk. "I can be very personable," Hersh said. And Meadlo responded, shaking his head and telling Hersh: "The kids and the women—they didn't have any right to die." Perhaps Meadlo's testimony should have shocked Hersh, but by this point it did not. "So there it is," he said later. "The thumb sticking up. The cancerous fingernail of what's going on in Vietnam. This is what we do in Vietnam. Frankly I'd like to say it should have surprised me but it didn't," he said, recalling his reporting. In an odd reporter's way it actually excited him. "It's a moment you'll never forget. And I—no matter how much I write about it, I still think about it."[27]

When the interview ended, Hersh immediately called Obst. He was "terribly excited," Obst said. "We had the front page story of the world."[28] Obst knew he did not have to convince editors about the next installment. "I knew they'd run it," he said. Hersh had another blockbuster, and on November 25 he startled the nation again with Meadlo's story, syndicated once more by Dispatch News Service.[29]

With the few dozen names that Ridenhour had given him, Hersh knew there were more stories to tell. But he and Obst came up with another plan to move the story forward—and to make some money. Since the television networks had come so aggressively into the story, they decided to see if CBS's new televised magazine, *60 Minutes*, would be interested in Meadlo. This Midwest farm boy—so haunted, so earnest, so damaged physically and psychically by the war—would focus the nation's attention even more on the horror of My Lai. Meadlo was willing to talk, and for reasons that are unclear, he was willing to give Hersh "exclusive access" to him. In essence, he allowed Hersh and Obst to be his agents, to market him for interviews. *60 Minutes,* one year old in 1969, was the creation of producer Don Hewitt, who aimed to use star reporters to produce a combination of soft magazine features and hard-hitting investigative reports.[30] Soon, the formula would land *60 Minutes* at the top of the nation's television ratings as one of the most watched programs—and as the premier investigative reporting outlet on television. CBS called Obst to see if they had any soldiers who were willing to tell their stories. Hersh and Obst asked for money. "Hersh knew he had the kind of story he'd never have again," Washington attorney Michael Nussbaum recalled. "As a freelance he needed the money. He saw this as a rare opportunity to be compensated for extraordinary work." But CBS had a policy against "checkbook journalism"—the paying of sources for information with the reasoning that people would tell you whatever you wanted for money. So Obst called NBC and offered the competitor the story. An NBC producer "asked where I wanted the check sent," said Obst.[31] Learning the wiles of an agent, Obst called back CBS. He was offered $10,000 cash for Dispatch News Service to deliver the chicken farmer's son to New York City to be interviewed by Mike Wallace, the sixty-year-old newsman making his reputation as one of the brashest of the CBS team.

The night before Meadlo's nationally televised interview, Hersh slept on a couch at his house. "I remember he cried out a lot that night. Obviously,"

Hersh said, "my being there had provoked it." The next day, in front of a national audience, Wallace walked Meadlo through the shootings, getting him to repeat what he told Hersh. And then Wallace voiced what many were asking: "It's hard for a good many Americans to understand that young, capable American boys could line up old men, women and children and shoot them down in cold blood. How do you explain that?"

"I wouldn't know," Meadlo replied.

"Did you ever dream about this that went on at Pinkville?"

"Yes I did. And I still dream about it."

"What kind of dreams?"

"I see the women and children in my sleep. Some days . . . some nights, I can't even sleep. I just lay there thinking about it."

Barry McCaffrey, on his way to earning three Purple Hearts and becoming a general in the army, was a twenty-seven-year-old soldier recovering from serious injuries to his arm suffered in Vietnam. He was in Walter Reed Army Hospital in Washington DC. "Those of us on the ward were absolutely persuaded it didn't happen," he recalled. "We thought it was a complete fabrication. It was another attack by the press on us." But when Meadlo went on national television, McCaffrey, later to become a Hersh nemesis, was convinced otherwise. "I said, 'My God, they did it.'"[32]

One of America's foremost military historians, Stephen Ambrose, watched Meadlo tell his story. "I had a very, very hard time watching," he recalled thirty years after the broadcast. "And it was beyond my understanding that American boys could do this. Now, atrocities were certainly not beyond my understanding . . . but My Lai and the way it was presented on television just shook me to my roots. My Lai was the single most shocking thing to come out of the Vietnam War for me."[33] For his part, Hersh had mixed feelings on the Meadlo affair. "I don't claim this as the greatest day in my professional life," he said. "We sold Paul Meadlo, in effect. It was an incredible interview, and that, I think, turned the corner." But when Meadlo told Wallace, "I went in a village and killed everybody," Hersh knew he had the focus of the entire nation. And the reason was simple: "It was the CBS interview," Hersh declared. "Television was needed. Somehow, just relying on newspapers to sear the conscience of America hadn't been working."[34]

CHAPTER 3

Hersh Becomes a Target

Flying High

Sy Hersh and David Obst were flying high in late November. On November 25, the president announced that America would stop producing and stockpiling chemical and biological weapons. Although not widely known, it was a direct response to Hersh's 1968 book. Meanwhile, newspapers across the country were carrying Hersh's My Lai stories—with two more on the way—and the television networks were all following Hersh's lead. Suddenly, as Hersh told a group of newspaper editors, "the newspaper profession, in one of those collective changes of mind that can only be found in business, decided that each man's testimony was important to play all over the front pages." The once obscure Associated Press reporter was now getting his name known across the country. Syndicated columnist Mary McGrory wrote a profile of Hersh, saying it was difficult to capture the nervous energy of the "fast-talking fast-moving" reporter. Robert Walters of the *Washington Star* went to interview Hersh and Obst in their new offices in the National Press Building, but it was an odd interview: there was no furniture! "Obst and Hersh simply haven't had time for the luxury of setting up desks and chairs," he wrote, because they have been "single-handedly investigating" the massacre. An exaggeration, for sure; the press pack had descended on the story. But Walters saw the same thing as McGrory. Hersh's "non-stop style overwhelms observers even when he isn't working on something important," Walters wrote. Obst was particularly ebullient. "Now we have a little money to play around with," he chortled, referring to the $10,000 from CBS. "We're on our way." Showing the optimism of the young, and naive, Obst was convinced the atrocity stories would have a profound effect. "I really thought our story would end the war . . . . I couldn't imagine how . . . any rational person would let it go on."[1] But a counterattack on Hersh's work and motivations—and on the interpretation of what he was exposing—was about to begin.

The White House first commented the day after the Paul Meadlo interview appeared on CBS, a day a congressional committee also held a hearing to discuss the photographs in the *Cleveland Plain Dealer*, photographs that soon came out in *Life* magazine. The president's spokesperson called the incident "abhorrent to the conscience of the American people." But he assured the public that a full investigation was under way and that "illegal and immoral conduct" will be dealt with. Nonetheless, Ron Ziegler said, thousands of Americans had served with honor and courage, and this one incident should not reflect on them or the conduct of the war. "If Nixon's advisers had once hoped that the massacre could be held outside the horizon of public concern, that hope had finally faded," observed historian Kendrick Oliver. Hersh's work—and the press's follow-up onslaught—made sure of that. Nixon's strategy had always been to fight the press head-on. Vice President Agnew's attacks, secret plotting to take antitrust action against the television networks, and a plan to audit taxes of newspaper executives—all underscored his aggressive posture. "The greatest mistake we can make" in dealing with the press, he told his chief of staff H. R. Haldeman, "is to . . . slobber over them with the hope you can 'win' them. It just can't be done."[2]

In the midst of the My Lai stories the *Birmingham (Alabama) News* published a cartoon showing an enemy soldier presiding over an atrocity. Nixon urged his staff "to try to get this syndicated."[3] Secretary of State Henry Kissinger was urging that the administration take "some unified line."[4] Nixon adopted what became the common mantra: the other side is guilty of more atrocities than American soldiers. Overall, the Nixon staffers felt that the press was unduly blowing up the incident, for profit and for purely partisan reasons. When New Mexico senator Pete Domenici attacked Ron Haberle for selling his My Lai photographs, Nixon wrote a note, declaring, "Bravo!"

Profiteering was at the heart of the attacks against Hersh and Obst for bringing Paul Meadlo to CBS. Maine congressman Edward J. Gurney wondered if Meadlo could be believed if he was paid. "How much money changed hands?" Syndicated columnist John Chamberlain, longtime contributor to the conservative *National Review*, called Hersh "gluttonous," adding, "When 'idealists' cash in heavily on distributing what is conscience material, it is a bit offensive to those who are squeamish about making money out of blood." Hersh and CBS defended the interview. CBS news director Michael Silver said there was a written agreement that none of the money would go to Meadlo; it all went to Hersh and Obst. Washington attorney Michael Nussbaum met with Silver and wrote a handwritten contract to guarantee CBS exclusive access. "We needed to cover our expenses," Obst said. Hersh added, "The kid is getting absolutely zero." And that did not make Meadlo happy. He knew nothing about financial arrangements. "I feel I should be getting something out of it." All he got was a weekend in New York City and expenses, however.[5]

The Counterattack on Hersh

Two darker clouds were looming over Hersh. By revealing My Lai, was he an unpatriotic traitor, a communist dupe, a disloyal American? Even James Reston, the esteemed op-ed page columnist for the *New York Times*, raised that question. The day after Meadlo appeared, Reston wrote: "Whatever happened in the massacre, should it be reported by press, radio and television, since clearly reporting the murder of civilians by American soldiers helps the enemy, divides the people of this country, and damages the ideal of America in the world?" South Carolina congressman Albert W. Watson said, "this is no time to cast aspersions on our fighting men, the President and ourselves for that matter, as some members of the national news media and a few demagogs [*sic*] are doing."[6] And the Republican *Chicago Tribune* questioned the veracity of the reporting on My Lai. "Communists are experts at starting such rumors," they wrote.[7] Indignant, the newspaper then attacked Hersh and Obst for accepting $10,000 from CBS. For his part Hersh did not respond, but many years later he was still smarting. "There is always treason," Hersh said at a conference on war reporting, "but there is nothing that bars me from publishing something. There is no objective standard for treason. If I'm publishing something in the belief that what I'm doing is helping my country, it's going to be hard to convict me of treason." And Hersh believed his story served a vital purpose, public opinion aside. "We probably saved some lives which to me more than justified any question of pretrial publicity which has been waved in my face constantly since I began writing about this." When military sources told him not to print the story, Hersh replied: "It's your job to keep it secret and my job to find it out. If it's a just war and it makes sense, it's going to be reflected in the coverage. There was something wrong with that war."[8]

After three articles and with the media jumping on board, Hersh knew there were more soldiers' stories to tell if he was to make sure a full-scale army investigation took place—and if he was to stay at the front of the pack. And he needed to make sure his stories remained believable; credibility was vital. He wanted to delay his original November 13 story because of the antiwar demonstration in Washington. He was afraid of even the appearance of bias. "I didn't want the [My Lai] story to get con-fused with the activities of the anti-war movement," he said. But when he bumped into a reporter from the *New York Times* at Fort Benning, also in pursuit of William Calley, Hersh feared delaying. From Nixon's point of view, the war critics, Hersh included, needed to be discredited. Agnew had already attacked the bias he said was coming from the East-ern Establishment Press, as he called the *New York Times*, *Washington Post*, the *Boston Globe,* and national television networks. He attacked the TV anchors for lifting their eyebrows to influence a discussion. Agnew and Nixon—with help from speechwriter Patrick Buchanan, a White House aide and later a right-wing commentator and presidential can-didate—were beginning the assault on the press as an untrustworthy liberal institution.[9] By attacking Hersh's patriotism, financial motives, and neutrality, the negative effect of his My Lai stories could perhaps be limited. The press unwittingly helped the effort by regularly referring to the Dispatch News Service as "left-wing" or "decidedly New Left." A *Washington Post* story said Dispatch was affiliated with the "left-wing" Institute of Policy Studies, an early opponent of the Vietnam War. There was never any evidence of such an affiliation, yet that tag dogged Hersh and Dispatch.[10] The conservative John Lofton particularly lashed out at Hersh, writing, "When you ask Hersh about his biases and prejudices, he gives you a long song and dance about how he is a professional and how he can put his beliefs aside when he writes." But Lofton said it was absurd to believe this. After all, Hersh worked for Eugene McCarthy, he admitted he hated war, and even the establishment media said Dispatch News Service was politically left. "People with strong biases for or against certain subjects should not be assigned to cover those subjects," he wrote. Of course no one assigned Hersh—he ran after it without a publication backing him.[11]

When a British politician called Hersh a "leftwing kook," he reacted in angry fashion in an interview with McGrory. "Journalists, of course, have things they like and don't like, and they do their job," he said. "I think it's sad that more journalists aren't angrier today about the restrictions they have to put up with." Years later he was even more adamant, saying, "Terrible things always happen in war, [but] the responsibility of the press is . . . to find, verify, and publish the truth."

Hersh was actually a careful reporter from the conservative school of objectivity. His years with the Associated Press and United Press International had ensured that he carefully wrote facts only or allegations that were backed by reliable sources. It also ensured he worked hard to make sure the other side—Calley, his lawyer, or Pentagon spokespersons—were prominently featured. But this did not mean Hersh could not—and did not—have a point of view. "The My Lai stories reveal the problem of this war and a failed American policy," he commented to an interviewer, although he never wrote this. American soldiers "are doing exactly the things we went into the war to stop." Obst joined Hersh in balking at the left-wing label. "We have a point of view," he said, but he denied that Dispatch was "antiwar, antiestablishment or anti-anything. We're no more an antiwar news agency then the *Chicago Tribune* is a pro-war news agency." Obst and Hersh were simply young men angry at a war that had led good American soldiers to kill innocent men, women, and children. And they were also flat broke. Hersh was married and hoping to start a family. My Lai was a paycheck as well as, he kept repeating, a great story, a possible Pulitzer Prize–winning story, and a terrible injustice. Despite his denials, however, the tag "left-winger" would dog him—from My Lai to the present.[12]

"It Was Murder"

Criticism and controversy did not deter Hersh, however. He began to furiously crisscross the country in pursuit of more soldiers. The press's "indiscriminate use of eyewitness statements amazed me," Hersh later said. "I had carefully attempted to get some kind of 'feel' from each of my interviews before quoting them." Always a workaholic, Hersh was now obsessed with this story.[13] Work on his Pentagon book stopped, and he began to think about a book just on My Lai. He was planning a fact-finding trip to Vietnam but canceled it when the army announced on December 7, 1969, that it had impounded all pertinent field records; no documents would be available to journalists. Meanwhile, the army appointed William Peers, a plain-speaking three-star general, to begin a no-holds barred investigation into what happened. Hersh's exposé forced the government to act. But Hersh was bound and determined to beat Peers to the door of the witnesses. He flew fifty thousand miles over the next three months to find fifty eyewitnesses (thirty-five agreed to talk). He had to move fast. The military judge in Calley's court martial, fearing pretrial publicity, barred witnesses from talking to the press, and he was mulling a motion by lawyers that would put a prior restraint on the press. None of this stopped Hersh from writing or the soldiers from talking.

He zeroed in next on another all-American boy, a twenty-year-old Mormon from Portland, Oregon. He first met Gregory Olson on November 21 when he learned the tall square-faced young man had avoided killing civilians by shooting chickens and pigs instead. But Olson witnessed random and vicious killings in the days before My Lai. The soldiers had become "wild animals," he told Hersh. And then he revealed to Hersh a March 14, 1968, letter to his father in Portland. The massacre took place two days later. Hersh flew to Portland on November 26 to get permission to use the letter. "Why in God's name does this have to happen?" Gregory Olson asked his father. "My faith in my fellow man is all shot to hell. I just want . . . to come home." Scrawled in pencil on GI stationary, he told of how his friends, "normal guys," saw a woman working in the field and just kicked her to death and emptied their guns into her. "It was murder, and I'm ashamed of myself for not trying to do anything about it." Hersh knew instinctively he had located another reporter's gem. Olson's story established that wanton killings and soldier rage predated the massacre. The soldiers were just warming up. Hersh convinced the Olsons to let Dispatch copyright the letter; no one else could use it. Hersh's competitive edge was evident. On December 2 his article "Violence before My Lai" hit the nation's newspapers again.[14]

The nation had now heard from numerous American soldiers whom Hersh had located and convinced to talk. Reporters in Vietnam, meanwhile, had located survivors who told the awful tale from their point of view. And then, on December 5, *Life* magazine—which had turned down both Ron Ridenhour and Hersh when they sought to reveal the massacres—printed ten pages of photographs. Bodies on bodies lying in ditches in graphic color, all captured by former army photographer Ron Haberle and sold for $20,000 to America's largest circulating magazine. For the antiwar movement, the photographs were more proof of the war's insanity. One photograph was made into a poster with words from Meadlo's CBS interview superimposed on it. More than fifty thousand posters were distributed, and many were hung in subways in New York City. But for those who were supportive of the war, the reaction was markedly different. Many "sought refuge in denial," observed historian Oliver. One poll indicated more than half of America did not believe a massacre had occurred. But even if it did, it was understandable in a war where soldiers could not tell who the enemy was. If they killed innocents, it was the behavior of a few out-of-control, stressed-out soldiers. As Olson confirmed to Hersh, "The people I knew who did the shooting were not the most stable people." And anyway Calley and the boys from the farms must have just been following orders. This, of course, became the most hotly contested question over the next eighteen months in what Kendrick called "a painful and comprehensive national debate."[15] Were orders given to kill civilians? Americans were consumed by the story and the subsequent trial of Calley, but no consensus developed. And some turned their venom directly on the press for exposing the story and opening this national wound.

Richard Nixon had an easy explanation. "It's those dirty rotten Jews from New York who are behind it," he said.[16] It is not clear who he had in mind. Hersh is Jewish but he lived in Washington DC. Hersh did not know of Nixon's private comments, but he did feel the venom of anti-Semitism. On the way to writing her award-winning book about Vietnam, *Winners and Losers,* journalist Gloria Emerson asked Hersh if she could look at some of the letters he received. "She came by," Hersh recalled, "and read some of my old mail. She was very upset. A lot of the anti-Semitic stuff upset her very much." Hersh was nonplussed. "I can't get worried about somebody who's rational enough to write a letter, even a hate letter."[17] Nixon's staff, taking their cues from a president who despised the press, decided that Hersh was a dangerous character. When it was clear that he and Obst had profited from the Meadlo interview, Nixon told his staffers "to put a good news reporter" to work on a story about a possible lawsuit against Hersh for profiting from the story. Without Nixon's knowledge, however, someone from Henry Kissinger's staff decided to follow Hersh. As far as is known, the staffer trailed him one day on a bus ride and listened to his conversations, reporting back. Nothing else came of the surveillance. And Hersh moved on, writing one more story for Dispatch and then signing a contract with Random House to write a book. "Parts of this book will numb you," Random House proclaimed in advertisements. Hersh received $40,000 from syndication rights alone.

Nixon finally answered questions on My Lai on December 8, calling it "an isolated incident" and cautioning Americans to remember that the North Vietnamese use "atrocity against civilians as one of its policies." My Lai was clearly just an aberration. He promised an independent investigation if the military judicial process "does not prove to be adequate." He did not mention press coverage or Hersh, but ten years later in his memoir Nixon elaborated, writing, "I felt that many of the commentators ... who professed outrage about My Lai were not really as interested in the moral questions raised by the Calley case as they were interested in using it to make political attacks against the Vietnam war. . . . They had been noticeably uncritical of the North Vietnamese atrocities."[18]

But a close reading of Hersh's work on My Lai—five Dispatch articles, five magazine pieces, and an op-ed essay in the *Times*—belie any notion of partisanship. What comes through is a careful reporter, and not a commentator or polemicist. He is all business, all facts, albeit sometimes to the point of being too narrowly focused on just the facts. But that is hardly advocacy. Others would have to be indignant or demand an end to war. "A lot of reporting," Hersh declared, "is simply telling about things carefully and well. The idea is to collect so much damn information that you can be conservative."[19]

Hersh's early articles syndicated by Dispatch are pure exposé—laying out charges, finding participants and eyewitnesses, and raising questions about whether the killings were ordered by higher-ups. A cover-up of what happened lurks in the background. His May 1970 follow-up book, *My Lai 4: A Report on the Massacre and Its Aftermath*, is a more thoroughly documented exposé, but again it is wholly reliant on reporting, not commentary. He includes extensive endnotes, documenting sources in a manner more like a scholar than a reporter. A reader won't find Hersh emerging from between all the facts that make up this book. Wrote one reviewer, Hersh "did not try to make us understand. He just told it." In 1972, three years after he began his pursuit of My Lai, he drew a measured conclusion, writing, "There was no conspiracy to destroy the village of My Lai." There was simply and regrettably an earnest belief that communist sympathizers lived there, that a high enemy body count was possible that would boost careers, but army intelligence turned out to be incompetent. Thus, "a group of normally ambitious men" mounted "an unnecessary mission against a nonexistent enemy" and then found evidence to justify it—and cover it up. In interviews, as Hersh admits, he will at times go beyond his facts. But in print he was conservative, certainly not a "left-wing kook."[20]

When he had established what happened at My Lai, Hersh turned his attention to the Peers investigation that began eleven days after his initial story. William Peers set out to put together a minute-by-minute re-creation of the massacre. And on March 14, 1970, two years after the massacre and four months after Hersh's first exposé, Peers submitted a four-volume report—20,000 pages of testimony from 400 witnesses,

500 documents, 32 books of direct testimony. Thirty individuals were charged with participating in the killings or knowing about them and doing nothing to prevent or report them; it was recommended that the army charge fifteen individuals. But the report was kept secret. Ostensibly the reason was that to release details might prejudice trials. The reality was that Nixon knew the contents would bring more damage to the war effort and sought to stifle it. Hersh—still obsessed with this story—jumped in once more, even though, as he wrote, "the political furor over the cover-up died as My Lai 4 receded from the front pages." While the commission was doing its investigation, one of Hersh's anonymous military sources fed him the raw data coming out of Peers's interviews. In the end the source leaked to Hersh more than 30 volumes of the Peers testimony. "Twice a week a guy working on the report would meet me and we would Xerox another bunch of pages," Hersh explained. "This went on for a year." While Hersh's source is not known, it was likely someone cultivated from his days as a Pentagon reporter. "I don't go around getting my stories from nice old Lefties or the Weathermen," Hersh later commented.[21]

More than six months before the Pentagon Papers grabbed the nation's attention, Hersh was making headlines again with two articles in the *New Yorker* magazine. The *Times* treated Hersh like a newsmaker. "Journalist Who Disclosed the My Lai Story Now Charges U.S. Officers Destroyed Papers," the *Times* declared.[22] This was the start of a forty-year trend for Hersh of writing articles that were picked up as news by other media outlets. And the articles were newsworthy; Hersh revealed that the army had concluded that 347 civilians were killed at My Lai on one day alone, a total twice as large as it had conceded. The forty-eight-year-old two-star general in charge of the soldiers in Calley's division, Samuel W. Koster, and many of the officers under him came across as out of touch, living a lifestyle of shrimp and steak for dinner, more interested in inflated body counts and career advancement than winning a war. Haberle, who took the photos of the massacre, told Hersh: "My experience as a G.I. over there is that if something doesn't look right, a general smiling the wrong way . . . I stopped and destroyed the negative." And that, in essence, is what Hersh showed in great detail: the army knew about the massacre, looked the other way, and then tried to cover it up. Eventually in March 1972 Hersh brought out the Peers report in a book. A few of his instincts—both good and bad—are evident in this book. First, Hersh, the persuasive investigative reporter, gets what no one else could by cajoling a source to give him the secret documents that the army would not release. But then he wanted to show it off, by revealing the juiciest details, including what he indicates is another massacre in February 1970. Richard Hammer, who wrote a book on My Lai and another on Calley, pointed out that Hersh may "have overreached in his penchant for exposé." The second massacre had already been discussed by NBC, the *Times*, and Hammer. But "none of this," Hammer wrote in a book review, denigrates Hersh's efforts. His book "confirm(s) many of our suspicions and impressions about how the massacre was kept hidden for so long."[23]

And despite Hammer's contention that Hersh showed a tabloid side, the book again reveals his conservative side. What interested Hersh most was the army as an institution. He was not arguing against the war but how it was prosecuted, and how soldiers were trained—or not trained—to follow the Geneva Convention. He seemed to accept the war on its own terms, not arguing that it was unjust or racist or unnecessary, as so many did. He argued that if soldiers had been better schooled in the rules of the Geneva Convention, the My Lai massacre could have been avoided. Second, he implied that it was a war different from previous ones and that an updated version of the Geneva rules protecting the enemy—as well as civilians—needed to be constructed and enforced. And while Vietnam might have been the wrong war for America to fight, Hersh did not write this; he wrote that America's military simply fought the war without following international rules and its own internal guidelines. "The Army as an institution . . . made so much of My Lai 4 inevitable," he wrote. And it is a position he would hold onto even thirty years later when he convinced a former Pentagon officer to show him a report that had been buried in a military archive. The report detailed that the army knew of the inadequacies more than a year before My Lai but took no action. Even on the nation's premier page for opinion, the op-ed page of the *Times*, Hersh did not give his opinion. Once more he let the facts, a government report, speak for him.[24]

Journalism's Highest Honor

Ed Murphy was twenty-four years old when he returned from Vietnam in 1969. Growing up on Staten Island in New York City, Murphy had debated whether he wanted a life as a priest or whether to serve his country by going off to Southeast Asia as a soldier. He ended up in Vietnam, working in intelligence with Operation Phoenix, the secret government program in which American soldiers helped plot the assassination of Vietcong and North Vietnamese leaders—the enemy.[25]

Murphy came home scarred from doing things he has trouble talking about. But one of his assignments when he returned was to monitor the huge peace movement in Washington DC in the middle of November, just after Hersh's first story appeared. By day he did government surveillance. At night Murphy, who had turned against the war, joined protestors. The participants were all talking about what Hersh had revealed. "I was not surprised by individual atrocities but the size and organization of My Lai did surprise me," Murphy recalled. "The personal nature of what was done as opposed to remote killing from the air, it horrified me." But Hersh's exposé also emboldened Murphy. "I was already embarrassed by my own participation in the war and how I reacted in some situations," but when My Lai came out, Murphy said it made it possible for him and others to find an audience and help expose the Phoenix Program.[26] "The specific horrors of My Lai helped accelerate a growing consciousness that the war simply had to end," wrote cultural critic Carol Becker. Or as journalist Richard Boyle put it, "For me and for millions of my generation My Lai came as the final punch in the mouth, the end of our illusions. We could no longer say we didn't know. The day we learned of My Lai changed our lives." Sy Hersh and his reporting had altered the nature of the discussion.[27]

The long, slow move by America to disengage from Vietnam was not spurred by any one incident. Certainly My Lai was a key moment in America's longest war, but it would be exaggerated to call it the most important turning point in public opinion. But this is what many in the media implied when it happened. The *New York Times* said, "it may turn out to be one of the nation's most ignoble hours." And *Time* magazine called it a "graver phenomenon . . . far more crucial than the horror following the assassination of President Kennedy." Surely this is press hyperbole, although many years later historian Kendrick Oliver echoed this sentiment: "the My Lai massacre was a pivotal event not just in the history of the Vietnam war, but also in the history of the American nation as a whole."[28] And My Lai was momentous, creating a worldwide stir—and making Seymour Hersh an American celebrity. It did not, however, cause any great changes in the Nixon administration's approach. Obst and Hersh wanted the stories to end the war, and Hersh was convinced that his work did save civilian lives in the months following the exposure. But it is not likely it hastened the actual end of the war. What it did was further drive the wedge between America's political left and right. My Lai simply became another sharp divide between the hawks and the doves. In fact, it is one of the first cultural markers in the more than three decades of bitter fighting that followed between political and cultural poles in American life. And Hersh was one of the first journalistic lightning rods in that battle.

Although Hersh's exposés might be viewed as having a dividing effect, they also had other significant ramifications—on press coverage of the war and the long-term way that Americans viewed the conflict. By simply going after a story that the rest of the press ignored, that even reporters in Vietnam would not touch, Hersh set the agenda for the press corps. Max Frankel, who was the Washington bureau chief of the *New York Times*, later to become its top editor, admitted as much, writing: "I wouldn't doubt for a minute that the fact that Hersh was around town peddling the story gave it a competitive edge." The *Times* tried its best to stay close to Hersh, buying his Dispatch stories but then researching and writing their own stories. But they often could not reach Hersh's key sources, and he remained ahead of the pack.[29] After Hersh's account of My Lai filtered into newsrooms, "suddenly reporters were finding out that their newspapers were eager to print stories about the shooting of [other] civilians in Vietnam," as Hersh phrased it. On December 5, 1969, an AP reporter wrote about a killing spree he had witnessed four years earlier. On December 8, a separate AP account told about the withdrawal from Vietnam of a division because some of its troops indiscriminately killed civilians and then bragged about shooting a hundred Viet Cong every day. Hersh's reportage changed the tone of press coverage.

"From 1961 to 1967, for all the tension between the media and the government, and for all the mythology about the press as an adversary or watchdog of the state, the independence of the American news media was very limited," noted political scientist Daniel Hallin, who wrote the definitive book on Vietnam War coverage. Initially, the press stuck closely to "motherhood and apple pie" stories. And when they strayed occasionally, they paid the price. In August 1966 CBS correspondent Morley Safer showed video of soldiers burning down fifteen Vietnamese civilians' huts, with families still in the houses and women holding babies fleeing as soldiers torched their homes. The story caused a furor. The army initially denied it. And the day after it appeared, President Johnson called the president of CBS News and told him, "Your boys shat on the American flag!"[30] Four months later *Times* reporter Harrison Salisbury became the first American journalist to go behind enemy lines when he visited Hanoi. America had denied that it was bombing the capital city or hitting civilian targets. But Salisbury documented that a school was bombed and that residential areas were regularly targeted. Salisbury's reporting got him branded a traitor. The Pentagon labeled him "Harrison Appallsbury," and the *Times* was called "The New Hanoi Times."

Then came Hersh and My Lai.

Two questions beg to be answered about the My Lai work of Seymour Hersh. The first is why did Hersh get the story when so many other journalists, in both America and in Vietnam, did not? Why did Hersh choose to go well beyond the "grain of official truth" and stalk this story? And the second is, would the My Lai atrocity story eventually have come out if Hersh had not so vigorously pursued Calley and the eyewitnesses?

Kevin Buckley, a reporter for *Newsweek* who covered the war from 1968 to 1972, later observed that "My Lai was a shock to everyone but people in Vietnam." The atrocity was known to hundreds of soldiers and officers before a word was ever reported. Even Hersh acknowledged this fact. "My Lai was a bloody, bloody reprisal," he said. "After Tet, we really went bananas. You know, there were reprisals all over the country that weren't reported. I'm talking about murder. Things that weren't reported."[31]

And while there is no indication that any reporters in Vietnam knew of My Lai, certainly journalists knew of other atrocities. But they were not reported until after the My Lai story appeared.[32] Given that so many soldiers knew of the incident, it is possible it would have leaked out, but the war might have been long over when the public learned about the dark deeds. It was only when Ridenhour wrote his famous letter of March 29, 1969, that the army investigated, and that investigation led to Calley being charged. The army's hope was that by charging one lone soldier, who many viewed as a scapegoat, it could put the story and the incident to rest. So the Pentagon issued a short press release from the obscurity of Fort Benning. And their strategy worked. The *Columbus (Georgia) Journal* pursued the story, and AP and UPI wrote brief items. Some newspapers picked it up, but for the most part, the killings by an unknown sergeant from Florida remained a back-page story. The story had no legs and was, in reality, a nonstory. And that is when Hersh received his tip and began to go to work. Is it possible that the My Lai massacre, eventually the biggest story of 1969, would have just disappeared?

I posed this question to Kendrick Oliver, whose 2006 book is the most thorough and impressive analysis of My Lai. "I suspect that the story would have emerged in some form at some time," Kendrick replied. His reason was that the Calley proceeding was underway and would eventually lead to a public trial. The press could not and would not ignore a public event. He also felt the Haberle photographs and Ridenhour's persistence might have brought the story to light. But, he added, "it is possible to imagine the story becoming news without becoming a sensation." In other words, some coverage of the trial might have taken place. But that would be far different than the national and international sensation that My Lai became. It is also possible Calley might have taken a plea bargain offered to him, which would have eliminated the trial completely. Calley and his attorney might have gone away quietly. Thus, with no public event to cover, the press would simply have avoided a story that, before My Lai, was considered distasteful and offensive. The killing of nearly four hundred civilians in an obscure village in Southeast Asia would have been left to some historian to dredge up years later, in the same way that a massacre in Korea took more than fifty years to be revealed.[33]

But that still leaves unanswered the question of why Hersh—and no one else—pursued this story. Hersh's answer was simplistic. "It just smelled right," he said. But it had to smell right to other reporters also. No one else saw the magnitude of the story. Beyond that, other reporters had institutional obligations that prevented them from pursuing the story. Newspapers, with a family audience, connections to advertisers, and fears of offending conservative Americans, were leery about writing about a massacre. And while the AP and UPI, both of which Hersh had worked for, did not have the same constraints, they both tended to be cautious and careful to the point of bowing to some government desires. In part that is why Hersh quit the AP when they refused to let him write all he knew about chemical and biological weapons. Thus, Hersh's status as an independent made him, as Kendrick notes, "not subject to the institutional routines and daily deadlines" that were often "prompted by the activities of officialdom." Beyond this, Hersh simply had not acquired the concern of the mainstream press with matters of "taste." He was concerned about ruining Calley's chance for a fair trial, but he was more concerned that the public hear about the cold-blooded murder of innocents. Plainly put, he was indignant. And unlike the veteran reporters who had been stationed in Vietnam, he did not have any loyalty to the military, nor had he seen the day-to-day cruelties of war that might have made him more blasé about these killings. Many years later, he was clear what My Lai proved. The massacre "told us that we don't fight wars any better than the 'nips' and the 'krauts,'" he said referring to the Japanese and the Germans. "Nobody fights wars well—it's always brutal and it always involves a lot of abuses. These things happen in war, and to think otherwise is madness."[34]

There is one more factor to consider: although Hersh may be a conservative and cautious reporter, My Lai showed him to be something else—a brash, indefatigable, passionate, and indignant investigative reporter. When the army tried to hide the story, he became more determined than ever. When he could not find Calley, he would just not give up. He treaded in that gray area of investigative reporting, between breaking the law and using whatever means he could to corner his prey. When he located soldiers, he had the uncanny ability to make them talk, even at times when they should have kept their mouths shut. He knew when to push and when to console. His combination of anger and pathos, and a tad of ruthlessness, made him perfect to get this story. Oh, and one more thing. Not only did his nose for news twitch when he heard about the massacre. He smelled the Pulitzer Prize.

When David Obst was figuring out how to get Hersh's story sent to newspapers across America, he got a little help from a friend—Howard Simons, assistant managing editor of the *Washington Post*, later to become a key player in the *Post's* Watergate coverage. When it was over, and Hersh and Obst were basking in their achievement, Simons and Obst had lunch in early 1970.

"Did you send in your Pulitzer nomination for Hersh?" Simons asked. "The Pulitzer? You've heard of it, haven't you?" Obst looked bewildered.

"What am I supposed to do?" Obst mumbled.

"Jesus, you haven't done it yet?" Simons knew the deadline was that day because he was a judge on one of the panels. "Christ, Hersh is going to kill you."

Obst got into high gear. It was 3:00 p.m., and the application had to be postmarked by 6:00 p.m. He ran to the National Press Building, made copies of Hersh's five stories, bought a binder, and then tried to write the nominating letter.

"Everything I wrote sounded horrible," he recalled. "Finally I gave up and wrote in longhand that the stories spoke for themselves." He wrapped the nomination in Christmas paper and got it to the post office two minutes before closing. Months later, Simons called one afternoon and told him, "Your guy won the Pulitzer. It'll be announced tomorrow." Obst ran to Hersh's office to tell him.

"Sy you won it! You won the Pulitzer." Hersh jumped from his desk and rushed at Obst, picking him up and slamming him against the wall.

"Don't fuck with me," he yelled.

"I'm not, you idiot. Put me down. You won. . . . you won!"

Hersh calmed down and went back to his desk. "Yeah, well, they were great fucking stories."[35]

And back he went to work on his follow-up book on the Peers Commission investigation. Pulitzer Prize–winning reporter Seymour Myron Hersh, the kid from the South Side of Chicago, had just begun to scratch the surface on his way to becoming America's greatest reporter and "scoop artist."

CHAPTER 4

"Front Page" Lessons in Chicago

A Lucky Poker Game

The journalism career of Sy Hersh almost never got started.

The Chicago native stayed close to home when time came for college in 1954. Money was tight. His father, Isador, a two-pack-a-day cigarette smoker, diagnosed with lung cancer in 1952, died just as Hersh and twin brother Alan were getting ready for college. Sy chose a public university, the Chicago campus of the University of Illinois. Because many parents could not afford to send their children 140 miles south to the flagship campus in Urbana, Chicago residents had lobbied for a university in the city. The result: in 1946 a two-year undergraduate college opened on a 3,300-foot pier that extended into Lake Michigan, known as Navy Pier since it had originally been used by the U.S. Navy. For Hersh it was convenient—a few blocks from the family apartment and from their dry cleaning business—and a common academic starting point for children of immigrants.[1]

Hersh's passions were golf, baseball, and poker, but he encountered a professor at the university who encouraged him to follow more intellectual pursuits. Literature professor Bernard Kogan, thirty-four, in his third year at Navy Pier, took a liking to Hersh, possibly because they both loved baseball but also because, as Hersh said, "I liked to read books."[2] Kogan saw in Hersh a keen and almost electric intellect. He convinced Hersh to transfer to the University of Chicago, where he became a history major. Founded with money from John D. Rockefeller in 1890, it has long been one of America's foremost universities. But in the 1950s, the surrounding neighborhood of Hyde Park, where Hersh went to high school, had deteriorated, and crime rates were problematic. Applications to the university plummeted, and this may have helped Hersh gain entrance since he was—by his own admission—a "very mediocre student." He earned B and B minus grades. He liked to read the *New Republic* magazine and do the *New York Times* crossword puzzle. And he like to drink and party. After visiting one after-hours bar, he recalled, "We'd drink and stagger out . . . till seven in the morning. Drink martinis and stagger out puking."[3]

After completing his degree, he had no idea what path to choose. "I was going through all the things everybody goes through," he recalled. "Profound doubt, navel staring, insecurity about everything from your manhood to your brains." He tried selling Xerox machines and then strayed into the University of Chicago Law School. Since it is among the most highly ranked and selective law schools in the world, gaining entrance was impressive and no small accomplishment. But his entrance was happenstance and aided by friends. Hersh's best friend was David Currie, with whom he had played baseball. Currie's father, Brainerd, was a professor at the law school, and in August, shortly before classes were to begin, he helped Hersh gain admission. "I applied and was accepted in a week. Can you imagine doing that today?"[4]

The law school, originally housed on the campus's main quadrangle, relocated just as Hersh was entering, moving into a new building. Hersh did not have much time to learn his way around the D'Angelo Law Library or a new mock courtroom. The first year of law school is a demanding and regimented atmosphere for which Sy Hersh was not prepared. Moreover, law school might not have been prepared for Hersh. Rebels do not fit easily into the mold of law school. Whatever qualities of mind students may bring with them, they usually need to be set aside and given up in order to become a lawyer. The first year of law school is not just about taking courses in civil procedure, constitutional law, contracts, and torts. It is akin to boot camp; professors break students down into a shell of the free-thinking person they were. And then they rebuild each student as a person who "thinks like a lawyer." Hersh was not likely to be broken down—nor did he have the discipline to spend long hours poring over obscure legal cases just so that a law professor could nail him in class to give the facts or the arguments of the case. Mastering such discipline would have helped Hersh in his eventual journey into journalism, but it did not matter. Hersh earned decent grades at the start, but they got worse each quarter. "I had discovered golf, and I was playing a lot of good under-eighties golf in those days." Hersh flunked out of law school. "I hated it," Hersh said. "I just hated law." And it did not help that he did no work. Instead, Hersh would read Kafka at the library, placing the fiction inside the law books he was supposed to be studying. Hersh later admitted that part of his problem was a fear of failing. "I had fast-talked my way through college getting Bs but knowing nothing," he said. That would not work in law school. "So I got bounced out of law school," Hersh said. Twenty-two years old and out of work, he took a job in a Walgreen's Pharmacy selling beer and cigarettes. "I just bummed around," he said, but then he decided to give college one more try, enrolling in the university's business school. "Who knows why I did it. I didn't have any money." Business school lasted about a month. A class on statistics stumped Hersh. About business school, he said, "It was just so fucking boring."[5]

Hersh rented an apartment in Chicago that he could not afford, barely getting by while clerking at a liquor store in Hyde Park. The highlight was selling booze to the famous novelist Saul Bellow. He also sold Scotch to a former professor, Richard Stern, another famous novelist, who demanded to know why Hersh was wasting time selling liquor. Hersh moved to cheaper quarters, and a friend took his old apartment, also taking Hersh's telephone number. Hersh did not plan to be a store clerk for long, although, he said, "I didn't know what I was doing." A friend told him that Chicago's City News Bureau was hiring reporters; Hersh submitted an application. The City News Bureau was legendary in a city known for both its journalism hijinks and groundbreaking news traditions. It was a news-gathering collective, paid for by Chicago's five daily newspapers. Although it was the lowest rung on the journalistic ladder, it was also the place where scores of great reporters got their start, including Pulitzer Prize–winning columnist Mike Royko, novelist Kurt Vonnegut, and New York Times columnist David Brooks. And it was an entry-level place where cub reporters chased down murders, rapes, and muggings, working overnight shifts when the daily newspapers had few reporters available. There were no bylines, and sexy it was not. But Sy was out of work, and it would be a paycheck–$28.50 a week. He awaited a callback, but nothing happened for thirteen months.[6]

One night he was playing poker—at his old apartment. It was an all-night game, with, as Hersh recalled, "some serious money on the table." But Hersh lost. "You hang around till you get a good hand." But it did not happen, and by 2:00 a.m. he was broke. "I am sure I drank too much and then crashed on a couch," he recalled. At 9:00 a.m., the telephone rang, his old number, and he grabbed it by chance. "Hersh?" the caller asked. It was an editor for the City News Bureau. CNB editors were famous for getting a stack of résumés and just working their way down the stack in the order they arrived until they found someone available. The editor said he had a job for Hersh; he should come in Monday. Poker game over, career begun. Seymour Myron Hersh was about to enter journalism. "I had never written a thing in my life," he thought. But still, he was convinced, "I can write. I read a lot of books." And most importantly, "It's a great place to start," Hersh said.[7]

"Hard Street Work"

Mike Royko is a Chicago legend who won the 1972 Pulitzer Prize for commentary as an acerbic columnist for the *Chicago Daily News*. And like Hersh, he started with the City News Bureau, learning about both the streets of the Windy City and life in journalism. "In the beginning there was fear," he recalled. "Fear is something that a reporter has to learn. . . . Mean, tough cops who slam doors in your face. . . . politicians who can be hostile. Labor bosses can scare the hell out of you. So can generals and admirals and ghetto gang leaders. And presidents of giant corporations who threaten to get your job. Give them a chance, and they'll try to intimidate a reporter." Hersh had a lot to learn: it was his first journalism job, and he had no formal training. But being intimidated did not seem to be a problem. "He was very aggressive," recalls Casey Bukro, then a twenty-five-year-old editor who worked closely with the young Hersh. "He showed very early he does not back off from anything."[8]

Journalism is a highly competitive business in which big-city newspapers—there were five in Chicago in 1959—fight tooth and nail for readers and advertisers, often dragging each other into the gutter of "yellow journalism." But the City News Bureau was unique—a cooperative, created in 1890 to provide a shared source of local and breaking news. CNB reporters would track down stories and turn them over to the newspapers that paid their salaries. When events happened overnight the dailies knew they could rely on the bureau's cubs to cover the small stuff, the muggings and break-ins. CNB also assigned reporters to all the major municipal institutions, from the courts to City Hall. The dailies always knew they had coverage.

Still, the competition for stories at CNB was fierce. "It was a tough place. People literally punched each other fighting for stories," recalls Bukro. "Frantic, wonderful competition." Editors were demanding, especially the chief editor, Arnold Dornfeld, known as Dornie. "If your mother says she loves you, you check it out," Dornie would growl. And if the reporters balked, he added, "Spare me the bullshit, Laddie." Reporters worked weekends, nights, and holidays chasing down every body the coroner's office received and every fire in the city. "We were out all the time around the clock and every time we came across a really juicy murder or scandal or whatever, they'd send the big-time reporters and photographers, otherwise they'd run our stories," commented Vonnegut, later a famous novelist. Paul Zimbrakos, who worked at CNB for forty years, labeled it "hard street work . . . but important in the making of a good journalist." Added Richard Ciccone, "City News was the toughest boot camp in journalism."9

Hersh entered a world that was straight out of *The Front Page*, the hit 1928 Broadway play—written by Charles MacArthur, who had worked at City News—that was made into three Hollywood movies. MacArthur's wisecracking, cynical, hard-boiled reporters and editors captured what Hersh encountered—for better or worse. The dingy newsroom with its worn linoleum floors was on the twelfth floor of a Gothic skyscraper known as 188 W. Randolph Street, built in 1929, the last of Chicago's Art Deco breed. Eight typewriters supported a staff of thirty reporters who worked on cigarette-burned desks that had been handed down when the big-city newspapers were finished with them. Old fans whirled in the windows, and a police radio crackled. Editors barked out instructions and applied their changes to reporters's copy, which was then typed onto wax paper and put through a machine to make thirty-five copies, enough to be sent through underground pneumatic tubes to the city newspapers and radio stations. "Absolutely," declared Zimbrakos, "the place was just like *The Front Page*."[10]

Hersh, often wearing a pair of sneakers, spent his early months in the inglorious position of copyboy, helping City News make copies of reporters' stories so they could be distributed. "I worked eight hours a day doing that and getting coffee for the boys," he said. Soon enough, he was sent onto the streets of Chicago, a familiar place for the hometown boy. His first story came because all the reporters in the newsroom were drunk. He was sent to look into a fire. "An electrical fire in a manhole. My first story." The *Chicago Tribune* once described the life of a CNB rookie: "The West Side police reporter is expected to cover 12 police stations, three branches of municipal court, the county hospital, the morgue, the psychiatric hospital . . . the juvenile home and juvenile court, and the house of correction. In his spare time, he runs to fires and gets the verdicts at perhaps a dozen coroner's inquests." Sneakers would be fitting for a reporter who had to run, breathless, from place to place. Hersh worked at first with another reporter until he got his feet wet. Then he tracked down stories on his own and called them in to a rewrite man—an editor who takes the reporter's facts and assembles them into a story. Often that person was Bukro, a recent graduate of the Medill School of Journalism at Northwestern University, where he earned a master's degree. CNB, he said, "was not a place that suffered fools or mistakes." But Sy was good from the start. "Usually a new reporter would not make sense, but Sy could pull the story together and tell you what he had. Not everybody can do that." Usually Bukro would bark at reporters and tell them to call him back when they had it right. "I never had to do that with Sy. He was good at it and left out what was not important," Bukro said.[11]

Not that Hersh always knew what to do with the facts. He encountered his first murder one night when two cars crashed. "Smashed to shit," Hersh recalled. "Blood all over." The victims were two federal postal inspectors. Cops were all over, but no other reporters were around. It was a scoop. "Are they dead?" Hersh asked a cop. "Not until they are pronounced." But are they dead? The cop would not say, so Sy had to wait twenty minutes until the coroner pronounced the obviously dead bodies really dead. Then he called in the story; no one else had it. "I saw a lot of stiffs, a lot of dead bodies, a lot of corruption," he said about his seven months with City News. "You learned a lot" on the streets, he added, including how to get along with sources. Hersh played cards, smoked pot, and watched pornographic movies with cops at police headquarters. "That's just the way it was," Zimbrakos recalled.[12]

Along with understanding how to work his sources, another lifelong lesson Hersh learned: get facts and get them right. "Shithead was the nicest thing they could say to you if you got it wrong," said Bukro, who went on to a forty-year career with the *Chicago Tribune*. "You would be cussed out, humiliated, ridiculed for being inaccurate." CNB's editors taught reporters to check and double check. "You were not permitted to make mistakes," declared Bukro. "Checking it out" was the norm, Zimbrakos said. Reporters were "often told to call a source two or three times to get more information and make sure it is accurate." And once reporters got the facts, they were not permitted to insert their opinion into stories. Dornfield's mantra was, "Don't tell me what you think—tell me what you know."[13]

Editors ruled, whether reporters liked it or not. Once, in the middle of the Chicago winter of 1959, Hersh was sent out by editor Bob Billings to track down a story about a manhole cover that exploded. Billings, a hulking ex-football player, "was really antagonistic to me," Hersh remembered, adding that Billings saw him as "a punk Jew from the South Side of Chicago." Hersh nearly froze at the scene—"it was fourteen below," he said—as police told him there were no injuries and little damage. Hersh insisted to Billings there was no news, but he was told to file a story anyway. He grumbled and filed, but it was the start of Hersh's lifelong disdain for editors. Hersh clearly was "fighting some of the discipline," explained Zimbrakos. "He couldn't cope with a lot of the discipline."[14]

Hersh and Billings continued to butt heads, and it led Hersh into an unexpected encounter with Frank Pape, Chicago's most infamous detective. After a businessman jumped from a hotel window to his death, Billings sent Hersh to get details. He thought it was a simple suicide—but Billings wanted more. "You piece of shit, Hersh. How was he dressed?" A police sergeant gave Hersh the answer. What color was his tie? Billings asked. Hersh found out; it was red. Was he drinking, Billings asked. Hersh went back to the sergeant again but was told he would have to see Detective Pape to get the answer. Pape was a legend, Chicago's toughest cop who sent three hundred men to prison and five to the electric chair and bragged he never used his gun to fire warning shots, only to kill. He sent nine suspects to their graves. Detective magazines had published forty-nine articles about him. With his acne-scarred face and burly demeanor, he was intimidating. And the owlish book-loving Hersh was asking Pape a silly question about a dead guy's breath. He grabbed Hersh by the lapels, pulled him up to his face, and cursed him, adding, ""Do you think I smell the breath of every corpse that I discover?" Chastened and a bit scared, Hersh simply told Billings the police did not know if the dead man had been drinking.[15]

Lasting Lessons

The rigorous checking and rechecking of facts was good for Hersh, a lifelong lesson that became important later as his work elicited so much controversy. But he was also introduced to the seamier side of journalism—and may have picked up some disconcerting habits. The way the City News reporters gathered facts would have provided journalism ethicists with enough fodder and case studies for a textbook. There were few rules to newsgathering. The skittish managing editor, Larry Mulay, who ran the newsroom, recalled that when he was a reporter he interviewed a woman who reported a missing child. The woman would not let him in the house, he informed his editor. "Get in there if you have to burn the house down," the editor told Mulay. Soon after the fire department was called to the house because of a fire on the woman's front porch that Mulay had set. The fire fighters broke down her door, and Mulay followed them inside. The police found the bodies of the woman, who had committed suicide, and her dead child. And Mulay got the story.[16]

"In the end, whatever went into a story was accurate, but the methods might not have been ethical," conceded Zimbrakos. In those days it wasn't uncommon for a reporter to say he was from the coroner's office or the police department to get a source to hand over information. Reporters, Zimbrakos said, would "con" their way into someone's house and then steal a photo of a victim. And those tactics seem remarkably similar to what Hersh used in finding Lieutenant William Calley a decade later. The parallel was not lost on Zimbrakos, who commented in a book on the City News Bureau that it was no surprise that Hersh beat everyone to the My Lai story using "a few side-door tricks." It was the kind of story that a CNB staffer would know how to pursue—with or without ethics.[17]

The question of tactics did not seem to bother Hersh, but how City News treated race-related issues did. In 1953 a group of black families moved into a low-rent housing project on Chicago's South Side. Riots ensued. Hundreds of cops were sent to the scene; 250 people were arrested. Segregated Chicago got its first taste of riots. Some editors at City News felt they were partly responsible since they had fed the news to radio stations, and within moments hundreds of white protestors descended. City News was quite cautious after that on how it reported race news. Hersh recalled the day he was sent to cover a murder-suicide by a man who killed his wife and children then burned down their house. Firefighters wrapped the bodies in tarps arranged by size. "Like daddy bear, mama bear, and little baby bears—I'd never seen anything like that in my life," Hersh says. When he phoned the story to Bukro, a night city editor intervened. "Ah, my good, dear, energetic Mr. Hersh," the editor began. "Were the, alas, poor, unfortunate victims of the Negro persuasion?" Hersh said yes. The editor then said: "Cheap it out." Hersh wrote a one-paragraph story that said, simply: "Eight people, all black, were killed in a fire that raged through a house on the South Side today." Zimbrakos, however, with his four decades at City News, denies such a scenario was possible. "We not only sent out stories on every single murder, we also sent out stories on every violent death," he said. But Bukro was not convinced. When a murder story was withheld because of race, the newsroom argot was that CNB had "cheaped out." Bukro heard the phrase used. Zambrakos insisted City News "never cheaped out on a murder story." However, Hersh, who had grown up seeing his father regularly serving black customers in his dry cleaning store on Chicago's South Side, was not pleased. "I was really burned up," Hersh said. "I guess I was a boat-rocker even then." And, as

Hersh added, "I learned that African-American life wasn't the same as it was for whites on the North Shore."[18]

But the twenty-two-year-old Hersh had other worries. He feared the army would soon be knocking on his door. Since 1948 the United States had drafted young men to fill vacancies not being filled by volunteers. Even though the Korean War was over and Vietnam was three years away, Hersh did not want to spend two years in the army. He enlisted in the reserves, leaving City News after seven months, with the assumption they would take him back when he returned. But a final encounter with an editor may have doomed him. Every Friday night reporters—especially rookies—helped compile results of high school basketball games—sometimes as many as five hundred. These results were bundled and given to sports editor Phil Weisman. Hersh found the task onerous. "I don't think he liked the errands given to him," Zimbrakos observed. One day Hersh bought dozens of newspapers. He then pasted together hundreds of results from rugby, badminton and cricket games, and handed them over to Weisman—as a prank. Weisman was not amused. But it did not matter since Hersh was leaving for the army. He was assigned to Fort Leavenworth, Kansas, to begin basic training.[19]

CHAPTER 5

Selling, Publishing, Failing

Hersh, the Money Man

Fort Leavenworth, Kansas, is known more for its federal penitentiary than for the fact that it has the oldest active U.S. Army base west of the Mississippi. Occupying 5,600 acres and 7 million square feet in a thousand buildings, the base is sometimes known as the "intellectual center of the Army." But for Sy Hersh, Leavenworth was just a very hot place where he had to spend three months in basic training to avoid a two-year stint as a draftee. "It was 100 degrees every day," Hersh recalled, "And we had no money." So the soldiers, when not learning the basics of going to war and doing push-ups, drank liquor from local stills. "Homemade hooch," Hersh called it.[1] The hooch made the rigor of training easier and helped pass the time since his girlfriend, Elizabeth, was back in Chicago. Hersh's biggest challenge was learning a simple army rule: keep your mouth shut, never an easy task for a cocky young man whose mind and mouth were always working.

Nonetheless, Hersh was obedient and sober enough to make an impression. Knowing that he had worked for a news agency and had a university degree led the army to assign him to the public relations office at Fort Riley, Kansas, a huge base in northwest Kansas. "I think also that there weren't that many people around who could write," Hersh said. With 215,000 personnel at the base, Fort Riley was akin to a small city—and was a good place for Hersh to learn how information and people move around a military facility. It did two things—it gave him a primer on what the military does with people, allowing him to be prepared to tackle Fort Benning nine years later in search of Lieutenant William Calley, and it also gave him a glimpse of the military PR operation.[2]

The work likely surprised Hersh. The military was spending in the neighborhood of $20 million to promote itself, sending, for example, press releases to every hometown newspaper every time a local soldier was promoted. "Seymour Hersh, the son of Isador and Dorothy Hersh, of 835 E. 47th St., Chicago, has been appointed by the U.S. Army to the Public Affairs unit as an Information Specialist at Fort Riley, Kansas, the base commander announced yesterday." That kind of "news" release—or something like it—was then sent to every Chicago newspaper and all local weeklies. Often newspapers ran the releases in roundup columns on "locals in the military." Hersh learned how the army PR machine worked, and it was good insight to have for the time in five years when he worked for the Associated Press in the Pentagon.

When Hersh left the army he hoped to return to the City News Bureau. They would not have him, which was unusual, but his feuds with editors and his recalcitrance to do scut work came back to haunt him. So, even though he hated business school, he decided to try his hand at business as the owner and publisher of his own newspaper. After all, his father had run a small dry cleaner for years, and Hersh and twin brother Alan had helped around the store. Now he set out to publish a weekly newspaper in Evergreen, a suburban Chicago village of 3.2 square miles with fewer than twenty thousand people, most of whom were white. Hersh's partner, oddly enough, was Bob Billings, the burly editor at City News who had so gruffly pushed him around. They had become golfing partners and saw the chance to make money in this affluent southwest suburb. Billings "had the money," Hersh recalled, "and I had the energy." The *Evergreen Dispatch* seemed to fill a void—news about the library, schools, the Girl Scouts. Murder, mayhem, and the *Front Page* it was not. "I was used to rushing to shootouts at City News Bureau but this was more of the bake sale to benefit the library stuff," said Lee Quarnstrom, who was also at City News with Hersh and became a well-known columnist at the *San Jose (California) Mercury News.* Nonetheless, "we had a lot of fun," Hersh recalled. Paid circulation went up to 14,000, they were delivering 25,000 copies of the paper to 250 news delivery boys, and the paper began to attract national advertisers. "I could sell and I could talk," Hersh bragged.[3]

Hersh, the future hard-nosed investigative reporter, was the businessman, while Billings, the ex-jock, handled the editorial side. "It was local stuff, not hard-edged," explained Paul Zimbrakos, who came over with Hersh from City News to become part-time circulation manager. "They did not want to hammer potential advertisers." Billings was inspiring: "Young reporters wanted to be like him. Sy was kind of bookish, studious," said Quarnstrom who remembers Hersh asking him to write flattering stories about local businesses so they'd buy advertisements. "Sy seemed to be more interested in the business part of it, the ad sales, than news," Quarnstrom said. The staff recalled Hersh—fast-talking and breathless—writing down notes about advertisements and stuffing them in his pockets. Then, as deadline approached, he would dump out the notes for everyone to figure out.[4] Hersh was saddled with a lot of the drudge work. He had to pick up the newspapers in a truck and drop them off for newsboys to deliver. "Then I'd go back to the office and wait for mothers to call in and say their little Johnny is sick today," Hersh said. And then Hersh—future world-famous investigative reporter—became a delivery boy.

Short, Not-So-Sweet Stay in South Dakota

Mike Royko, later to become a famous columnist, did reporting for Hersh and *Evergreen*. "He covered school boards," Hersh said, adding that he remembers the paper doing "serious stuff." Quarnstrom disagreed, saying, "I don't recall ever going to the city council." Hersh and Billings clashed over the newspaper's editorials. "I wanted editorials about driving safely and things like that," Hersh said. Billings wanted to be "socially uplifting." "He wanted to urge them to do things like to see 'La Dolce Vita' and this was in a fine upstanding Catholic area, nearly all Roman Catholics." Hersh bemoaned that he was "struggling for dimes and nickels" while Billings was interested in high-brow culture. The *Evergreen Dispatch* lasted only about a year. "It was going great," Hersh said. But "one day I just woke up and said I just don't want to do this." Hersh was twenty-five, "almost a newspaper publisher, everybody's dream, but I realized that was not what I wanted to do." It is likely Hersh's heart was not really into the business of journalism. Also, however, the business was faltering perhaps more than Hersh remembers. "Got my paycheck one day and bank wouldn't cash it," Quarnstrom said. "They told me the paper was out of money." Julius Karpen, another City News colleague who later became the agent for singer Janis Joplin, came over to sell advertisements for Hersh, who, he said, "never kept money in his account." Hersh "had a money problem," he said. "He was always five minutes ahead of things." Karpen tried to cash one check, and it bounced. The bank said that as soon as Hersh deposited a check to pay his printer, the money would go to Karpen. It did, and soon after the *Evergreen Dispatch* went out of business. "I consider myself responsible for his success in journalism," Karpen said, laughing. But the Hersh who appeared for the six months that the *Evergreen Dispatch* was published was not the person who would show up later as America's foremost investigative reporter. "When I read about My Lai I had no idea he was a great journalist," said Quarnstrom. Hersh was no longer a publisher; he had to look elsewhere for work. Anyway, Hersh said, "I didn't want to be a suburban newspaper magnate."[5]

Reporters who worked at City News became members of a club, distinguished graduates who, as CNB alumni and novelist Kurt Vonnegut said, were a bit like "outlaws." They gained respect—at least in Chicago. "Working for City News was the only way you'd be able to get a job in a Chicago newspaper," Vonnegut said. "You had to start there." And it paid off for Hersh. When the *Dispatch* folded, he went to California, where his mother had moved, and played golf every day. When he tired of that a friend who was an editor at the United Press International agreed to hire him. Along with Associated Press, UPI was one of the most important and powerful news-gathering agencies in the nation as it fed stories to newspapers and radio stations. UPI was not the AP, but in 1960 it was a close second. Founded in 1907 by the famous Midwest publisher E. W. Scripps, it had six thousand employees and nearly five thousand subscribers, including a thousand newspapers. Most newsrooms had both AP and UPI tickers, usually side by side, as they pulsed out breaking news. The two agencies fiercely competed. Typical was the famous 1963 incident when Merriam Smith of UPI literally sat on AP's Jack Bell as Smith phoned in the first news dispatch that President John Kennedy had been shot. Smith won the Pulitzer Prize. Such a "war of seconds"—who could get it first—was perfect for the ever-competitive young Hersh. City News had trained him to live up to UPI's motto: "Get It Fast, Get It Right, Keep It Simple."[6]

Covering U.S. presidents was not in the immediate offing for Hersh. UPI assigned him to be their lone correspondent in Pierre, South Dakota, a small city on the banks of the Missouri River. A plum assignment it was not. "I was all alone," Hersh said, but he saw being "sent to Siberia" as an opportunity. Pierre was tiny compared to anything Hersh had ever known. Although it was the state's capital, Pierre had a population of only twelve thousand, the second smallest capital in the nation. But it was the center of South Dakota's small political world, and for Hersh a stepping-stone, part of the necessary apprenticeship on the road to investigative reporting. "I learned a lot," Hersh commented, including even how to punch a teletype machine to send his own stories.[7] Working for a news-gathering agency like the AP or UPI is odd because a reporter never quite knows who the audience is. A story of Hersh's might be picked up by a newspaper in Bismarck or Rapid City or in the Black Hills, and any client might make demands to check a certain story with hometown implications. Much of the work was routine—press conferences, press releases from the governor. Hersh did show some signs of the enterprise that later made him famous—and got him in trouble. One series of articles on the Oglala Sioux Indians, the largest tribe in the state, explored the poor conditions under which the tribe lived on reservations where they had been banished many years before by the U.S. government. "I was thinking of the bigger picture," he said. The stories landed in the *Chicago Tribune*, a fact Hersh recalled and was proud of years later. "That was a big deal for those of us who had never been east of Chicago," he observed.[8]

Hersh also began to learn to package his material. As the South Dakota legislature prepared for its 1963 session, he wrote a four-part series on what to expect. "South Dakota's 1963 legislators will earn more money, know more about every proposed bill and squabble just as much as ever," he wrote, but "don't expect many surprises. . . . South Dakota Legislatures just don't work that way." The articles reveal a very contemporary problem—expenditures were outpacing revenues, and the state had to decide whether to impose a sales tax. Hersh was careful not to weigh in, but he did not miss out on the biting nature of the racial divide in South Dakota in 1963. Civil rights activists were pushing for the state to adopt basic protections, but one skeptical legislator commented, "It has never been the job of the legislature to change what is in people's hearts." And the governor told him, "The outside groups will have to learn ... that you can't push South Dakota people around so easily." Hersh did not want to wait around too long to see how South Dakota solved its social problems, although he did follow up with another series, this time on the vexing problem of taxes. And a number of his feature stories went out over the national wire and were picked up by the *Chicago Tribune.*[9]

Hersh came to Pierre in late fall and parked his car, after which snow quickly covered it. "I didn't see the car again till late March," he said. Even though South Dakota was remote and far from Chicago, Hersh kept his nose in news and public affairs with voracious reading. He read *Harper's, Atlantic Monthly,* and *New Republic,* all progressive and thoughtful magazines that were models for his later reportage for the *New Yorker.* He dipped into Carl Sandburg on Abraham Lincoln and Arthur Schlesinger Jr. on Franklin D. Roosevelt. Particularly intriguing to him was the Vietnam reporting of the *New York Times'* David Halberstam, whose hard-nosed reporting on the war drew the ire of John Kennedy and offered another model for Hersh on resisting the government's view of events. Halberstam's model also reinforced for Hersh that he needed to get out of South Dakota. When the 1963 legislative session ended, he asked to be transferred to UPI's Washington Bureau. Said Hersh, "They said Omaha instead, so I quit—nicely and a little reluctantly—but I quit."[10] He headed back to Chicago to see if the Associated Press had a job opening for the City News Bureau graduate. Fate was on Hersh's side again. He was in the office five minutes when "some guy stood up and started tearing his hair out and quit. So they hired me a couple of days later." Right place, right time. The AP offices were on the second floor of 188 Randolph Street, the same building where he had started work with City News. Hersh was back home.

CHAPTER 6

From the "Front Page"
to the Pentagon

A Deadline Every Minute

Seymour Hersh entered a comfort zone when he returned to Chicago. Just to be in the same building where he had worked at City News must have put him at ease. And he was back covering the Chicago streets he knew so well from growing up on the South Side. But, on the other hand, working for the Associated Press was not the *Front Page*, and being in Chicago was not Pierre, South Dakota. This was the big time: the most important news-gathering agency in America in one of the nation's most important cities. The smarmy tactics that City News often encouraged would not be allowed at the premier news agency that supplied breaking stories to news outlets all over the Midwest, from the *Telegraph* in Alton, Illinois, to the *Daily Reporter* in Dover, Ohio, to the *Gazette* in Colorado Springs. Even the Department of Defense's *Stars and Stripes* picked up AP dispatches. The reach of the AP, including hundreds of radio outlets, was immense. "Accuracy, impartiality, and integrity"—those were the bywords of the AP, and Hersh had to learn the more rigid boundaries that came with establishment journalism. In the end he concluded, "The AP was good to me," but Hersh was never one to take kindly to rigidity and rules, so it was only a matter of time before the twenty-six-year-old would butt heads with editors. Not that the AP was going to allow him much room to roam when he arrived in the fall of 1963, shortly before the assassination of President John F. Kennedy.[1]

Going to work at the AP was akin to Sy Hersh's third tour of duty. City News was boot camp; then he served at Fort Riley in the real army. And finally came the AP, which Richard Pyle, Hersh's future colleague in Washington DC, described as "the Marine Corps of journalism." He said, "We take the beach and then everyone else comes in with the heavy artillery." Hersh, however, started out as a grunt, a foot soldier. His first assignment was to take stories written by other bureau reporters and rewrite them into short briefs to be read on the radio. "I began writing the whole nightly radio wire for Illinois stations," he said. "Rip-and-read" was a common tactic of radio stations. In 1964 stations were required by the federal government to provide news on the public airwaves, and instead of employing their own reporters, they relied on the AP to produce copy that could be read directly to the audience. Working the night shift, Hersh had to rewrite a thousand words an hour, "trying to make it lively," he recalled. The experience taught Hersh how to write tightly—always prized in journalism—and how to handle a range of news events. Ernest Hemingway once labeled journalism "cableese." "Isn't it a great language?" he mused.[2]

But it wasn't long before Hersh moved beyond "cableese." He thrived on the lonely night hours, taking stories written during the day and putting new leads—or beginnings—on the stories. "Once they realized I could turn a phrase," Hersh said, "they began to let me write stories." Hersh became a general assignment reporter, the glorious early stage of journalism when you enter the newsroom never knowing what will be on your plate. On one day Hersh was sent to a train crash where four died and forty were injured; on another day he was at the bedside of the ailing gospel singer and Chicago legend Mahalia Jackson; and then he was dodging bullets at the site of a racial riot in suburban Chicago.[3] From dangerously dwindling water levels in the Great Lakes to a gorilla on the loose in the city to union boss Jimmy Hoffa being sentenced to prison—Hersh was parachuted down each day into a new adventure. The challenge in this, of course, was mastering new issues every day and having to produce stories at lightning speed, at times six stories a day including one major one. There was a deadline every minute. And it is almost unfair to judge the prose produced under such time constraints. But produce Hersh did—almost a feature a day. Two things are evident: Hersh's early journalism reveals the heartbreak and tragedy that is life. And it shows Hersh to have the chameleon-like character so needed by a journalist, the "peeping Tom" of the heart characteristic that allowed him to cuddle up to so many different types of people. It was a characteristic that became one of his strongest attributes.[4]

The Softer Side of Life

In early February, as the biting cold hit the Midwest, Hersh traveled outside of Chicago to Northwestern University in Evanston, Illinois, to chat with Jacqueline Mayer, a twenty-one-year-old coed who had become Miss America in December. The other students, he wrote, "no longer stare when they see a book-laden brunette hurrying across campus in tennis shoes, slacks and a mink coat." The mink, a convertible car, and a $10,000 scholarship were the fruits of her crown. But at first, Hersh discovered, the "boys" were too scared to even look at her. Now, he wrote, her 36–22–36 figure does not seem to frighten them; she is a popular coed who is living a "Cinderella story." Little could Hersh or anyone know that seven years later, as she turned twenty-eight, Jackie Mayer would suffer a massive stroke and spend her days battling to overcome its debilitating effects.[5]

Five days later Hersh went uptown to visit the legendary Aragon Ballroom, once one of the most popular attractions in Chicago, hosting Frank Sinatra and Duke Ellington as couples swayed to the music. An underground tunnel supposedly connected it to an Al Capone speakeasy. But Hersh was there to mark the ballroom's last night. Anyone who knows the biting, politically charged work of the later Hersh would be surprised to see him writing about couples who "danced in Moroccan splendor under an artificial sky of twinkling stars and fleecy clouds." At times Hersh just ran into the odd and quirky characters who make up any urban locale. He found Richard C. Schroeppel, a sixteen-year-old who "likes mathematics, bowling, tennis, parties, the Beatles and girls. In that order." Which was not a surprise given that Schroeppel was the best math student in the United States. He went on to graduate from MIT at age twenty. And then there was "pistol packin'" Ann Soloman, twenty-one, a five-foot, one-inch owner of a leather goods store who wore a gun and holster as she waited on customers. "I just want to protect what I've got and I am mad," the modern-day Annie Oakley told Hersh.[6]

Acting a bit like television host Art Linkletter, Hersh told the sweet story of twenty-six first graders, "still learning how to print their names," who published a book of their drawings. One told him, "It's just make believe." More real was the prominent Joliet, Illinois, physician who was given a $5,000 fine and two years in prison because he avoided paying $35,000 in taxes on a Stradivarius violin by concocting a complicated fraud scheme. Wrote Hersh in a cutesy lead: "Ever since his youth, when he ushered at the Chicago Opera House, Bernard Mortimer has loved music—especially violin music." By hook or by crook, Mortimer was going to make the violin "sing again." And so he duped the government.[7]

At times he lurked around hospitals. In spring 1965, he followed sixteen-year-old football player Michael Koprowski as he was wheeled out of a hospital after delicate heart surgery, putting him back, as Hersh noted, "on the list of people with a future." It was a feel-good story. "We figured he was—at best—two months away from the end," said the surgeon who saved Michael's life. Responded Michael amid tears and cheers, "Just say I feel real good and I'm really grateful that they could do something like this." Also ailing was Mahalia Jackson, the Queen of Gospel singer. When she had a heart attack in October, Hersh reported the story, but she declined an interview, and doctors banned visitors. Five weeks later, on a Sunday afternoon, she gave Hersh a bedside interview, recalling that one day she woke up with flowers all over her hospital room, "and thought I was dead." The two-hundred-pound, fifty-year-old Jackson whispered, "I never knew so many people loved me, I never knew so many thought so much of my singing." She lived another eight years. Hersh indeed could turn a phrase, but he also knew how to cuddle up to sources.[8]

Slowly Hersh graduated to social issues that so typified the fights of the 1960s. As Chicago planned a vote on giving out contraceptives to married and unmarried women, Hersh waded in, finding an elected official, a Roman Catholic, who told him: "We give a bottle of pills to a 15-year-old girl and tell her she must not use this for fornication or adultery. We're now going to make it possible for anybody to become promiscuous." When the birth rate in Chicago dropped by 17 percent, he found sociologists who said the new popularity of birth control was the explanation. The Catholic Church declined comment. The story was noteworthy because it was Hersh's own enterprise that pieced it together, suggesting the beginning of the investigative reporter. But most of his stories were reactive, the result of events initiated by others. That's not to say that he was not learning how to be feisty and use various sources—named and unnamed—to make a point.[9]

In March 1965, for example, Chicago completed an $87-million downtown building that had the color of rusty metal. The hope was that when smog oxidized its outside, the building would turn an attractive color. On a Sunday afternoon, Hersh got a cop on the beat, a city official, and an executive of a cleaning firm—all unnamed—to say how ugly the building was right now and how it was unlikely to get better. One city official, deep in the story, defended the approach. But the criticism was clear with the use of what became a Hersh characteristic—unidentified sources. Most of his reporting was straightforward, however. He wrote stories on racial disputes and riots, on censorship, crime rates, affirmative action, gun sales, and migrant farm workers. And he got to dabble a bit in politics, presidential and otherwise: Barry Goldwater tested his Republican appeal in Chicago; Pennsylvania governor William Scranton was picketed when he came to town; and Senator Margaret Chase Smith of Maine blasted front-runner Henry Cabot Lodge. More to his liking perhaps was the rebellious and attractive black-haired Chicago housewife who fought the Chicago political machine—but lost her bid for office.[10]

Not all of Hersh's early work was so seamless. He did not pursue every story with the zeal he displayed later. A forty-seven-year-old newspaper reporter was missing for seven months, presumed murdered. Hersh diligently spoke with the family, but he showed no inclination to raise any of the nettling questions about her disappearance. Maybe the AP wanted only a one-day story.[11] And sometimes his stories fell short or came a bit late. Mayor Richard Daley celebrated his tenth anniversary as mayor in 1964, but it is unclear if he sat down with Hersh for an interview. More critics made it into the story than did Daley. He wrote a long, detailed, and well-researched story on the fact that the water level of the Great Lakes was at a record low in the summer of 1964. It was an impressive story, but the *New York Times* had written the exact story three weeks before. The AP was playing catch up, something Hersh had to do again a decade later when as a reporter for the *Times* he was asked to wade into Watergate.[12]

Hersh's habit of drinking and talking with night-owl friends changed a bit when, in 1964, he married Elizabeth Klein, whom he had met at the University of Chicago in 1958. Liz was a social worker who, one associate said, "had a calming influential effect on her unpredictable husband." But the rambunctious Hersh was not ready to settle down in the Windy City. He began to send out job applications, including to his top choice, the *Washington Post*. No one was interested, but the AP — seeing that he was an emerging star—came through. His stories often received prominent play in afternoon newspapers, and his work was noted regularly in the AP's in-house weekly log. "I was obviously hot shit," he said. So, in July of 1965 Hersh was rewarded with a transfer to Washington DC to work in the AP's capitol bureau. "I wanted Washington," he said. "AP wanted me to go. They were happy with it." Along with New York, Washington was the place all ambitious reporters wanted to be, a long way from the Badlands of South Dakota. The rambunctious Hersh had arrived—and he was eager and anxious to keep climbing.[13]

At War with the Pentagon

The Young Turks Chafe

Sy Hersh arrived in Washington with wife Elizabeth in the summer of 1965. Hersh was part of a remarkable group of young reporters who had joined the AP—James Polk, who won a Pulitzer Prize in 1974; Gaylord Shaw, a Pulitzer winner in 1978; Carl Leubsdorf, who became one of the nation's best known political writers; and Barry Schweid, who covered diplomatic and world events for the next four decades. But controversy was soon to follow these "young Turks" who, like Hersh, were impatient to make their marks on the world of journalism and to challenge the conventions of the profession that tied their hands in explaining an America on the verge of chaos and upheaval. But to do so they had three hurdles to overcome.

The first was to get off the mandatory overnight rewrite desk where all newcomers were lodged, and where they did little reporting and lots of revising of other people's stories. Hersh had not come to Washington from the powerhouse AP Chicago bureau to work for very long from 11:00 at night to 7:00 in the morning, poking around in the work of others. If they could get past the probationary rewrite desk, Hersh and his aggressive colleagues could then dip into the exciting public policy world that awaited them in the capital. Their reporting goal was simple: to write the kind of big stories that would be chosen to run on the AP's coveted "A" wire, the main feed to the nation's powerful daily newspapers. And once the "A" wire stories had made their mark, the prestigious capital "beats" that lured reporters to Washington in the first place would beckon—the White House, the Pentagon, the Supreme Court, the State Department, the Capitol. Unfortunately for Hersh, change did not come quickly at the

Associated Press, where many World War II generation reporters were not about to make room for the upstarts.

Hersh was "impatient," recalled Schweid, who worked at the AP for fifty years and came to Washington five years before Hersh. He was just "chafing at the snail's pace of change, at being confined, and at the lack of movement," Schweid added. "If you were patient, you had a chance." But Hersh was never known for his patience. Certainly it was understandable why he would want to move off night rewrite. Reporters mostly worked over other people's copy, getting it ready for the nation's afternoon daily newspapers by condensing, revising, and perhaps updating. The bureau centered around black teletype machines lined up in rows. All day and night they drummed out copy, like hypnotic music, pulsing out bulletins and updates as news filtered in from around the world. The goal, of course, was to get out the news before the arch-rival United Press International.[1]

Meanwhile, inside the room on Connecticut Avenue about a block from Dupont Circle, Hersh's goal was more limited—trim stories so Americans could get their news in digestible versions, an important task since the AP was the main source of information for much of what America consumed. But, to his chagrin, there was very little reporting, except for an occasional phone call to check a fact, if that was even possible at 3:00 in the morning. "When rewrites were done, you were on guard duty," said Shaw, who came to Washington about the same time as Hersh. "Guard duty" simply meant that you waited—and probably hoped—that some disaster might strike in the wee hours that would get you out of the office and into the real adventure of reporting. The mayhem of Chicago was much more exciting than rewrite. How could this be fun? "You were not reporting," said Leubsdorf, a colleague who worked at the AP for fifteen years and then became a political columnist in Dallas.[2]

Reporters only left the office to go out for "lunch," an evening ritual that often called for them to traipse around with night editor Joe Kane, who would fill reporters' heads with his wisdom on journalism. "Sy took one walk with Kane," recalled Shaw, "but never went again." He was simply not interested in kowtowing to an editor, especially one whose view of journalism was known to be cautious. Hersh often went alone to the famous Eddie Lawrence's Sandwich Shop and then hustled back in search of stories. Certainly Hersh must have understood the importance of the AP and the work—albeit drudge work—that he was doing on the night desk. Most of America was influenced by the AP's output. Their four thousand or so clients could not cover the sprawling bureaucracy of the capital; consequently the AP had to, and its reports dominated small-town America's press. Take, for example, Thursday, June 23, 1966, when a Seymour M. Hersh byline with a Washington dateline first appeared—in the *Ironwood (Michigan) Globe*. Ten stories were on the *Globe's* first page, and nine of them—from Vatican City, Santo Domingo, Saigon, Milwaukee, Benton and Lansing, Michigan—were written by AP reporters. Seven of the stories had the bylines stripped, but Hersh's remained.[3]

Entering the President's Office

Never bashful, Hersh bragged in this early story of an exclusive interview with America's most recent Medal of Honor recipient, a thirty-two-year-old lieutenant who, despite being wounded in a battle with Viet Cong, took over his detachment when the commanding officer was felled by bullets. "I just wanted to protect my men," the soldier said, adding: "We're fighting a just cause over there. The commies have to be stopped somewhere." There was no rebuttal from any war critics. The cautious AP editors in Washington and New York must have been pleased with Hersh's first flattering feature story about the military. This is not to suggest that Hersh was trying to curry favor. Far from it. "He never fit comfortably," suggested Kenneth Freed, an editor who worked fifteen years with the AP. "For one thing he came from Chicago, where they encouraged people to be aggressive." Hersh wanted immediately to be assigned a beat, a specialty area to cover. "He was eager to get off the desk," remembered Leubsdorf. So eager that Leubsdorf and Hersh would paw through the garbage pails of their editors to see what their memos were saying about their work. "He wanted to write his way off, to prove he could write," said Schweid. And, moreover, "with his plentiful energy, you were not gonna keep him on the overnight desk for very long," added Shaw. So Hersh began to find ways to work the night desk *and* write stories. And eventually to plot some schemes that would enable him to get certain stories past the eyes of wary editors. Quickly, some scoops came his way.[4]

In August he was able to get another exclusive interview, this time with Martin Luther King Jr., who was touring four big northern cities to measure the progress of voting rights for blacks. Hersh's interview came the day before Lyndon Johnson signed a historic voters' rights bill. King wanted to double the number of blacks registered, but he was not optimistic, telling Hersh, "I do not yet see the kind of vigorous programs alive in Northern communities that are needed to grapple with the enormity of the problems." Soon after, Hersh went to see Bayard Rustin, who organized the 1963 Washington march that drew 250,000 protestors. In a long interview, Rustin urged that more pressure be put on Congress to pass legislation. "Negroes are now on the threshold of attaining political power," he said. What is significant about this story, however, is that it reflected Hersh's enterprise—and his persistent interest in civil rights. The story was not hooked to any event; it did not have what journalists call a "newspeg." It was Hersh's initiative and his nose for newsmakers that made it happen, unusual for a young reporter. Some publications made it headline news.[5]

Having served his time on the night desk and—in theory—been schooled in the ways of the Washington bureau, Hersh was switched to general assignment after nine months. A beat still eluded him, but Washington is so chock full of governmental activity that some plum assignments awaited him nonetheless. And he began to carve out a niche, crusade on a few issues that he adopted, and develop his own style, including the use of numerous anonymous sources. And, of course, he began to butt heads with editors.

"Sy was high strung," observed Schweid. Walter Mears, a veteran AP reporter, was Hersh's golfing partner and competitor on the links where they would make small wagers. One day, Mears recalled, Hersh hit a first shot into a marshy area in front of the tee. A second ball also went into the lake. He turned to Mears and screamed, "Don't laugh." Of course, Mears burst out laughing. Hersh fired his club into the water, took off his shirt, and dove into the lake to retrieve it. He kept going under but never found the club. Hersh was a good colleague, Mears noted, but very competitive.[6]

Being competitive was a plus in reporting, and Hersh soon got the call to cover some secondary White House events. When Johnson's press secretary, George Reedy, returned from surgery, Hersh was invited in to talk—but only about the surgery. He wrote a feature story on Johnson's nominee for the U.S. Tax Court, who was blind. And on September 13 he went to the White House, into the president's office, and watched as Johnson honored Astronaut Charles Conrad in a playful afternoon ceremony when, as Hersh wrote, "the tow-headed Conrad boys stole the show. Three of them perched behind Johnson's desk, one sitting in the presidential chair. The fourth stood nearby watching a stenographer record what was said."[7] The Conrad kids might not have been the only giddy youngsters. Sy Hersh, twenty-nine, the kid from Chicago, the son of immigrant parents, was in the office of the president of the United States.

General assignment, as Hersh knew from Chicago, is a strange mix of life's oddities and events. Twice the University of Chicago history major had to play historian. He compared Lyndon Johnson's October 1965 abdominal surgery to the operation Dwight Eisenhower had in 1956, and then he described the nation's long concern and battle over civil rights, as the president moved his historic legislation forward. He reported a silly story on a report that said husbands usually win marital disputes over what household items to purchase, and he chronicled the adventures of a self-described "short, fat and grandmotherly looking" grandmother who was in a seven-year feud with the Food and Drug Administration to put more peanuts in peanut butter. He followed some of the president's activities—on new spending guidelines, civil rights, the war on poverty—and wrote roundup stories that simply gave an overview of events in the nation's capital.[8]

But little by little he got a serious focus, honing in when he could on civil rights stories. On Sunday, April 3, 1966, he went to Lafayette Park, across from the White House, where ninety homeless and jobless "Negroes" were camped out in small tents to urge the president to speed up $1.3 million in relief money for job training and housing. Hersh went into one tent and sat with Frank Smith, the group's leader, as five squirming youngsters slept alongside them and park police kept a close eye. "Hope we won't be here too long," Smith said. "We want to go home and start building homes." Added John Sylvester, who appeared much older than his forty-three years, "We're tired of living in tents." Two nights later Hersh returned as the protestors huddled on a cold spring evening. "Everyone thinks this is a publicity stunt but it ain't no picnic," declared twenty-one-year-old Eddie Robinson, standing alongside the manicured flower gardens of the park. Hersh tried to get government officials to say when money would be coming and seemed to be with the protestors in spirit, but it is not likely that his stories—or the protest—sat well with many of the rural newspapers that subscribed to the AP. They were way too "liberal."[9]

Crusading on the Draft

Young reporters on general assignment take most of their cues for stories from editors. As they develop specialty areas or become investigative reporters, they carve out their own assignments. So it is difficult to argue that in his early days at AP in fall 1965 and winter 1966 Sy Hersh was choosing his stories. But two issues do regularly emerge—race and the military. And many of them are follow-up stories, which usually means that the reporter, aside from taking assignments, has gone back to a certain story to pursue it. More than anything else, however, Hersh carved out a body of work and began his first crusades on issues related to the military—on inequities and problems in the military draft; on the shortage of military personnel to fight the growing conflict in Vietnam; and on the widening bombing of North Vietnam. In particular, his aggressive coverage of the Pentagon's air war in Southeast Asia led to conflict with his editors. But they also got him consistently on the "A" wire and landed him on page one of the *New York Times*.

Why Hersh turned his attention to the military in 1965 is unclear. Nothing in his background would have predicted an interest in military affairs. In fact, he went into the reserves to avoid being drafted. But it was a choice that shaped the rest of his career. Perhaps, like scholars often do, he found a niche—one that was being covered too passively by other AP reporters to suit him at a time when military issues were becoming paramount and protestors were taking to the streets about the Vietnam War. Or perhaps, like the young aggressive correspondents in Vietnam, he saw a vacuum. The World War II generation reporters were a different breed. "We thought the AP wasn't playing it straight down the middle," said Freed, a colleague and close friend of Hersh's at the AP. "We felt it was too supportive of the administration. Part was the age factor, part was institutional." Instinctively Hersh wanted news coverage that was more critical, more aggressive—and stories that would also push his career forward with "A" wire attention.

Hersh's slide into covering the military might have been pure serendipity. On December 23, 1965, as Christmas approached, General William Westmoreland, commander of U.S. troops in Vietnam, announced a controversial thirty-hour ceasefire; American bombs would halt. Hersh was in the newsroom and got the story. When he tracked down Hubert Humphrey at his home in Waverly, Minnesota, the vice president told him, "Let us hope the men in Hanoi will use these precious hours to come to the conference table." Hersh located four other Republican leaders, all home for the holiday break, and had them address the peace proposal. Peace was not to come for many years—and some believed the pause in bombing prolonged the war—but Hersh was off and running in his coverage of the Vietnam War.[10]

News coverage of Vietnam presented a dilemma for reporters. Objectivity had a long ascent in American journalism. In fact, the idea of independence for journalism had grown gradually for many years, dating to the era of the "penny press" in the 1830s. After the "yellow journalism" scourge of the 1890s and the crusading bent of the turn-of-the-century muckrakers, the industry turned to neutrality. By the early 1900s, led by the *New York Times*' fact-only balance, the news media etched out a credo: that reporters best served their audiences by keeping their biases muffled. Stay out of the story—that was the journalist's creed. By the 1950s objectivity had become a fetish by which the establishment press lived. At times it allowed them to be used by demagogues such as Senator Joseph McCarthy of Wisconsin. But voices in the culture—and in journalism—began to challenge the ideal by the mid-1960s, at a time when the press was grappling with how to cover a widening war in Southeast Asia. As historian Kathleen Turner points out, Vietnam "pressed correspondents to address the inadequacies of standard wartime reporting procedures to convey the intricacies of a limited conflict occurring in another culture."[11]

For Hersh, listening to emerging voices about journalistic activism would be difficult. He was trained from the get-go to stay neutral. At the City News Bureau, the mantra was, "No editorializing, no bias," noted long-time editor Paul Zimbrakos. At the UPI and the AP, opinion was anathema to its function which was to provide the first facts about the news, with the reporter staying out of the story. But Hersh quickly learned how to play with the rules without being labeled a sinner, how to meet the journalistic barometer of objectivity and still make the points he wanted. Hersh "had no agenda," insisted Freed, but nonetheless "Sy challenged all the assumptions."[12]

Take, for example, his first crusade—ten stories on the military draft over an eighteen-month period. When the government announced it would draft 36,450 men into the military—the largest draft since the Korean War—Hersh asked a pointed question: "Does the California surfer have a greater chance of getting drafted than the Alabama farmer? The surfer and the farmer would probably be surprised to learn that their draft chances depend very much on their fellow Californians and Alabamians." Hersh zeroed in on the tremendous latitude given state Selective Service boards and the inequity that resulted from not having national rules to decide who gets chosen from the pool of twenty-seven million eligible men. He spoke to forty-three of the fifty Selective Service directors (that is a lot of legwork for any story!) and concluded: "The states, guided only by a vague series of recommendations . . . have spawned the present helter-skelter pattern of educational and occupational deferments that has been so widely criticized." He wondered whether blacks and school dropouts were penalized by the system (adopted in 1951), while married men, college students, and those who chose the reserves were favored. He never mentioned, of course, the he had avoided the draft, although such a choice was perfectly legal. "One fact is indisputable," he concluded, "the present Selective Service system is unfair."

As the national controversy over the draft heated up and as Congress pursued the question, Hersh laid out options for reform—and predicted which ones Congress would take in 1967. Eliminating the draft or limiting American involvement in wars was not an option that Hersh raised. Congress, he predicted, will institute a national lottery, which it did two years later. Hersh's stories played an agenda-setting role in giving the draft reform debate a national audience. Stories in the AP always spur the television networks and national newspapers to pursue the topic. And on this story Hersh was a month ahead of the *New York Times*. His impressive package of stories, with solid sourcing and impressive statistics, lacked only some draftees to humanize the stories; his stories seemed desk- and telephone-bound. Nonetheless, "his research was always meticulous," observed Mears, the long-time AP writer who often edited Hersh's stories. "Once in a while he needed better sources or more sources, but he would go back when asked." What is also clear is that he became more emboldened as a writer as the package unfolded, especially in his use of anonymous sources. When he wrote his final story on the draft, it had few named sources. It is flecked with "sources said" and "informants" commented; even the quotations are from anonymous people. The aggressive and enterprising bulldog had emerged, but also the one with a plethora of unnamed people filling his stories.[13]

Hersh's daily schedule was way too busy for him to do much crusading for causes. A feature story on a school for dropouts; a congressman attacked in his office; Great Society money for the youth corps; a primary victory for Nelson Rockefeller; a Ku Klux Klan trial to cover—interspersed every now and then with a story on the military. But, finally, Hersh's hard work, resourcefulness, and productivity got him what he wanted. When senior correspondent Fred Hoffman was sent to Vietnam for six months, Hersh was moved into the number two slot at the Pentagon. This was like letting the fox loose in the hen house; he was about to start stirring the pot.[14]

CHAPTER 8

Fighting His Editors

Crusading for the Military

The Pentagon was the world's biggest military machine, but it also had the largest war public relations apparatus. The government spent more than $20 million a year in 1966 just to promote its activities—including the war in Southeast Asia—with three thousand people assigned to the Department of Defense PR staff. Many of the reporters who worked out of a small unglamorous Pentagon office were docile recipients of news doled out by the government. Fred Hoffman, although a thorough and reliable reporter, was a World War II veteran who was largely content with covering the stories that, to some degree, the Pentagon wanted covered. "There was a decided clash of culture," Hoffman said about the WWII reporters and Hersh's generation. "They accused us of being 'toadies,' but truly it did not happen. We had cordial relationships but there was a line drawn." Behind his back the younger reporters called him "Colonel Hoffman" because they felt he was soft on the Pentagon. Reporters grumbled that when the Pentagon wanted to get a message out, they knew they could rely on Hoffman. In fact, when he left the AP in 1984, Hoffman went to work in public relations for the Defense Department, a common merry-go-round. "Sy and Fred were like oil and water," said reporter Kenneth Freed. "Fred was a spokesman for the Pentagon. He probably had been there too long; he knew everything but did not see everything." Hersh, meanwhile, "was operating on the fringes." The sarcastic Hersh was a rumpled figure, his hair often askew, his shirt unbuttoned. "He was sloppy as hell as a dresser," recalled Freed, "but as a reporter he was resourceful and smart as hell."[1]

Hersh did not take long to jump in feet first as 1966 began. At first it was coverage as usual: Defense Secretary McNamara says the Vietnam War is at a turning point; the Soviets protest American nuclear testing; more planes ordered to fight the war; a Navy Cross for an officer known as "Mr. Vietnam." All were stories Hoffman would have covered. But Hersh wanted stories that did not come from the briefings or the press releases known as "blue tops" for their light blue coloring over a DOD insignia. "Many a determined young reporter," wrote *Washington Post* editor Leonard Downie, "had been worn down by the Pentagon's tight news-management producers and eventually became little more than an uncritical parrot of the military's pronouncements." It was easy to understand why.[2]

Reporters were cordoned off in a hallway known as Correspondents' Corridor. The large press room was across from the reporters' quarters. Reporters would troop in each day for a daily briefing at which a Pentagon spokesperson would deliver innocuous tidbits. Pulitzer Prize–winning journalist Sydney Schanberg called the military briefings "the five o'clock follies," because they often yielded little that was newsworthy and much that was PR bunk. Nonetheless, reporters were given so much information in reports and press releases and access to safe officials that they had no trouble coming up with stories—just not the stories that might reveal the inner workings of the military or of the war in Vietnam. Most correspondents—like the AP's Hoffman—learned to accept the restrictions set by the military. Hersh would not; he developed a *habit* of asking an impertinent question at briefings, and when it was brushed aside, he wandered the halls of the world's largest office building in search of sources and stories. Often he found high-ranking officers in their lunchroom—and they talked to him. The rumpled Hersh turned out to be a charmer—he readily convinced top- and mid-level Pentagon sources to talk. Pentagon officials began to call him "that little ferret," deriding the fact that he "broke every rule of bureaucratic journalism." Said Hersh in response: "I had more balls than most of the guys in the press room."[3]

In September Hersh found another crusade: Navy officials—including, anonymously, Admiral Clarence A. Hill Jr.—told him that there were not enough planes or qualified fliers to fight the intensifying Vietnam War. The story came to Hersh because, after getting a tip, he simply asked for documents that laid out the shortage that the Pentagon was trying to hide. When twenty-four fliers died in an accidental October fire aboard a carrier ship, Hersh used the incident to show the shortage was worsening. "It's pretty bad and getting worse," one source told him.[4] By early December unnamed sources told Hersh that McNamara had agreed to increase training for new fliers. "We've got a very severe shortage of pilots and it's going to become worse," a congressional insider said. By the end of December, a Senate subcommittee announced an investigation. Hersh's point was all but conceded—the war in Vietnam would take more resources, and the navy would get them. Hersh was not arguing against the war; he was in essence helping the military get what it needed to fight the war better.[5]

Exposing the Military

As 1966 drew to a close, Hersh had been right on target with two stories—the draft and the shortage of fliers. But another story—a very big one—came to his attention. The Johnson administration had been increasing American troop size in Vietnam. Hersh reported as 1967 began that the 473,000 troops now stationed in South Vietnam surpassed the 327,000 that had been in Korea. It was news that neither Johnson nor McNamara wanted the American public to hear; Hoffman might not have pursued it, but Hersh did, on his own, with no newspeg or governmental announcement. He just dug up and reported the statistics. It marked a decided turn in his reporting. "Sy was doing terrific stories on the Pentagon," recalled colleague Gaylord Shaw. "He had so much more energy than Hoffman. He had developed all these different kinds of sources." And it led, as Shaw said, to Hersh "breaking story after story."[6]

What caught his attention in particular was the bombing of North Vietnam. The Defense Department had repeatedly said it was only bombing military targets in the South. But in mid-December Harrison Salisbury, fifty-five, a veteran foreign correspondent for the *Times*, was granted a visa to enter North Vietnam—the first time an American correspondent had been allowed behind enemy lines. Salisbury sought to corroborate what the North Vietnamese had long asserted—that America was dropping bombs on nonmilitary targets and killing civilians. The Defense Department denied this, but never with much detail or vigor. As Salisbury moved around the North, American officials must have known he was inching closer to seeing that the U.S. government had been lying for nearly two years. Years later Salisbury learned, in fact, that Defense Department officials knew precisely what its bombs had wrought—that 31,300 civilians had been killed. Nonetheless, in Saigon and Washington the government made a proactive public relations strike. "The United States offered the world a flat denial today of North Vietnamese charges that American warplanes bombed inside the city limits of Hanoi Tuesday and Wednesday," Hersh reported on December 16 in a story that made front pages all across the nation. (The *Times* had a much vaguer and confusing story on the comments the day before.) Hersh expressed no skepticism or rebuttal to the American officials' statements, noting only that "outraged voices" from the Vatican and the United Nations might have prompted the "unusual detail" on the bombings. But his nose for news was whetted—and little did he know at that point that reporters covering the Pentagon had actually helped the government craft the denial![7]

Two days later Hersh gave the Johnson administration a full chance to buttress its assertion that any damage to downtown Hanoi was caused by the Communists' own anti-aircraft missiles, not American bombs. The proof was in what "reliable sources" told Hersh: more than one hundred 3,000-pound missiles were launched against U.S. aircraft, and four planes were shot down. "Informants" gave Hersh the story because they were "anxious to close the administration's credibility gap." Hersh was being used to get out the American side, something that Hoffman had been accused of doing, but that in reality is inevitably part of the job of the reporter.[8] Eight days later—Christmas Day—Salisbury's first dispatch from North Vietnam was published, the first of fourteen reports from Hanoi. From the Pentagon Hersh had to play mop-up on Salisbury's stories, which showed that America had indeed hit civilian targets and killed dozens of civilians; forays into the North were deeper and more damaging than anyone knew.

If you read the *New York Times*, you knew their correspondent was an eyewitness to the damage, but much of the rest of the country had to rely on Hersh's story—often placed on page one—that summarized

Salisbury's reporting and allowed the government to declare: while only military sites have been targeted, "it is impossible to avoid all damage to civilian areas." Salisbury's stories caused an international uproar. Even editors at the *Times* were queasy about his stories, and it is likely that Wes Gallagher, the AP general manager in New York, was hoping also that the bombing exposés would not go much further. They were angering the president, embarrassing the American government and the war effort, and perhaps damaging a chance for peace. Already, as Hersh reported, there would be no Christmas pause in the bomb assault this year.[9]

As 1967 began, Hersh dug in on the bombing story, despite the worries of editors. "He wanted to ruffle feathers," asserted veteran correspondent Walter Mears. And he was succeeding. Hersh's stories from the Pentagon had been causing him problems for a few months; he said editors in New York were heavily editing his dispatches. He blamed Gallagher, but colleagues doubted the AP's top editor was actually line-editing Hersh's copy. Nonetheless, Hersh believed that Defense Secretary Robert McNamara, the Pentagon's chief PR person, Arthur Sylvester, and Gallagher were meeting to discuss his work. "They wanted you to be on the team," he said. No one doubted that New York was keeping a watch on Hersh. As Gaylord Shaw said, "His stories always had an edge." Moreover, his use of anonymous sources had raised red flags. "People were somewhat annoyed that he had no or few names in so many of his stories," observed colleague Richard Pyle. Take, for example, a September 22, 1966, story on the fact that despite the opposition of the Soviet Union, the United States was exploding underwater nonnuclear bombs to measure earthquakes. His sourcing: officials, authorities, sources, one defense official. No one was named, and this was typical. The irony was that there were no hard and fast rules banning anonymous sources or, like today, defining when they could be used. It was just that Hersh was using unnamed people more than others. But it was also understandable that in the Pentagon environment anonymous sources were impossible to avoid. Even at the daily briefings for the press, Pentagon officials would insist they would not talk unless reporters agreed to not name them. Hersh had little choice. But it was also that his stories had a critical edge that others did not.[10]

Scamming His Own Editors

Eventually Hersh had to resort to a scam to get his stories past the watchful eyes of New York editors. Normally, when a reporter had an important story, he informed his editor, who would then decide whether to place it on the AP's "budget," a summary of forthcoming stories sent out early in the day to alert other editors. Then reporters would file those "A" wire stories by a 5:00 p.m. deadline. The budget stories were read closely by copyeditors. But Hersh, with the approval of his Washington editor Don Sanders, was omitting his stories from the budget. "In this way it would get past the desk." Hersh said. "By the time they realized, it was out and done." Hersh was beating the in-house censors, but he was also on a collision course. "You could only get away with this for so long," observed Jean Heller, another eventual Pulitzer Prize winner who came to the AP about this time.[11]

Harrison Salisbury's stories had caused a worldwide furor by the middle of January 1967. The United States was forced to slow down its air strikes of North Vietnam, Hersh's inside sources confirmed. When he asked the Pentagon to comment on what he had learned, a spokesman snapped at him: "We do not discuss targeting." Privately he was told that poor weather had caused a bombing slowdown, but Hersh mocked the response. When their heaviest bombing had previously taken place on December 12 and 13, fog blanketed the area, he argued. Public opinion was the real cause, not weather. Gen. Earle Wheeler, chairman of the Joint Chiefs of Staff, complained that the North Vietnamese "enemy propaganda complaints" should not be allowed to muddle the fact that bombing of the North was effective. But had America really bombed a school, hit water supplies, and unloaded on residential areas? Hersh kept working his sources and was able to get a definitive answer. He went to see a top-ranking military source, probably a general, but he had to be careful. Secretary of Defense McNamara, monitoring for leaks to the press, "kept a tough lid on these stories," Hersh said. Reporters had to sign in. So as to confuse McNamara, he signed in to see more than one general. There would be no way to trace his visit.[12]

The source told Hersh that new aerial photographs showed damage to civilian as well as military targets in North Vietnam. Here was the proof—the administration denials no longer held up. Hersh knew he had a big piece of the bombing puzzle to report. This was a story for the "A" wire. And when he sent it off in late afternoon, the *New York Times* was immediately interested. This was, after all, their story. Hersh received a call from *Times* reporter Neil Sheehan, the paper's Pentagon correspondent. It was Sheehan who four years later got the Pentagon Papers leak from Daniel Ellsberg. He had spent two years working for UPI in Vietnam, and his reporting, along with David Halberstam and Peter Arnett, was considered groundbreaking. Sheehan came to see Hersh. The *Times* never ran stories—even from the AP—without corroboration. In fact, usually, they took AP stories and then did their own version, as they would two years later when Hersh broke My Lai. Hersh was excited that his story had stirred the *Times*, and he took Sheehan to his source in the Pentagon, who repeated the information. What the *Times* really wanted, Hersh believed, was a story that would allow the Pentagon to simply deny the existence of the aerial photographs and debunk Hersh's stores. But Sheehan found that Hersh's reporting was on target, and he told the *Times* the story was worthy of its standards. It should be published. On January 21, on page one of the *New York Times*, Hersh's AP dispatch, "U.S. Photos Show Civilian Structures in North Damaged" appeared—without a byline. (Only *Times* reporters got bylines.) He reported damage to 228 civilian sites and 82 military structures. Five days later, citing the cumulative effect of the press exposés, he revealed that Hanoi was now off limits to American warplanes. The restrictions are "a result of everything that's gone into the press," a source said. "It shows we're taking into consideration what's being written." Indeed, so was much of America. Salisbury's reporting—and Hersh's help in spreading the story—got him labeled as a traitor, but the controversy they sparked undermined American and international confidence in the Johnson administration. It also decreased support for U.S. policies toward North Vietnam and put more pressure on Johnson to increase efforts toward peace.[13]

Hersh's "scoop" on the secret bombing won plaudits for the AP. And, Hersh said, "it probably bought me six more months of time" working there. Unbeknownst to his editors he continued to find ways to make the *Times* use his AP dispatches by sending out alerts marked "urgent" right around the *Times* 6:15 p.m. deadline. Sheehan would then call him to confirm the story. "We had a ritual," Hersh said. And they became friends. "He was impressed with my energy and ability to get the real truth out of the Pentagon system," Hersh said. He was clearly on the outs with AP's top brass. "Some of Hersh's problem with New York was that they had trouble with his personality," said Heller. "There were no good editors with Seymour." It only got worse when Fred Hoffman returned from Vietnam. Hoffman and colleague Hugh Mulligan had spent their time in Vietnam investigating reports of corruption. Their story became a runner-up for the Pulitzer Prize in 1967. Meanwhile, Salisbury's articles, believed by many to be the most significant of 1966, were snubbed by the Pulitzer board. A Pulitzer jury at first called them the best in the international reporting category, but the ruling board overturned their recommendation. "The editors who bestowed Pulitzer Prizes were not prepared to insult a president whose wrath was notorious," wrote historian A. J. Langguth.[14]

Salisbury left Hanoi knowing his stories had made their mark, that the world now knew America had lied while it killed innocents. But years later he observed, "I exaggerated the effect of my dispatches. They played a role, but a small one. . . . It would be a long time before the war would end." But he did gain respect for this up-and-coming AP reporter Sy Hersh—and more so when he broke the My Lai story two years later. In his memoir he wrote that "the words of the great investigative reporter Seymour Hersh . . . haunt me." No one, Salisbury wrote, "has done more to uncover the lies of war and peace, to bring reality to the public, to shoulder the responsibilities of the first Amendment" than Hersh. But what haunted him was seeing Hersh at a symposium on Vietnam in 1984. Asked if lying by government and duping of the public could happen again, he heard Hersh say, "It could happen again and probably would. The government would just lie."[15] Even way back in 1967, however, Hersh would not be a part of it, and his understanding of journalism—the reporter as gadfly and adversary—alienated some colleagues.

Hoffman was one of them; he felt that while he was away Hersh had done damage to his sources at the Pentagon. Hersh conceded he had a difference of style with Hoffman but called him a "good guy." For his part, Hoffman would not discuss Hersh, even many years later. No surprise. Their understanding of journalism represented a clash of approaches to journalism. A good look at this came by coincidence, when Hoffman and Hersh had stories side by side in the *Daily Reporter* of Dover, Ohio, on November 8, 1966. Hersh had an edgy story on the military draft that highlighted the slow pace of training reservists. Much of it was based on anonymous sources. Hoffman, meanwhile, stationed in South Vietnam, had taken a plane ride with a camouflaged jet firing deadly cluster bombs and napalm over Tay Ninh Province. "That was just great," a voice exults as bombs hit the ground, and "great sheets of red-orange flames engulfed trees. Tomorrow," Hoffman wrote, "it would be up to the infantry." The article, "All in a Day's Work!" could have been a military recruiting pamphlet.[16]

Hoffman defended his approach to journalism, implicitly criticizing Hersh. He said: "The herd took on this coloration—Vietnam is bad, cold war is bad and we oughtn't be nose to nose with Russians. They didn't concern themselves with the broad range of issues, just with who could sound tougher, who could score more points." Hoffman was likely still smarting—even many years later—from stinging criticism Hersh had made of him and other Pentagon correspondents in the *New Republic* magazine in 1967. Hersh jibed Hoffman because he sponsored off-the-record dinners with Pentagon officials and shut out reporters who did not "always toe the Pentagon line." Hersh rebuked the reporters who, he said, actually helped the Pentagon craft its denial that American bombs had hit civilian sites.[17]

Hoffman, however, fearing that an era of "gotcha" journalism was about to emerge, simply was speaking for a different generation. Hersh and his young colleagues wanted the AP to do more than observe and write with no coloration. Most of all, they didn't want reporters to act as agents of the government; they were adversaries. Hersh was influenced by the Vietnam reportage of Pulitzer Prize–winner David Halberstam, but he had also discovered the sage of Washington journalism, I. F. Stone, while he was covering the Pentagon. Izzy Stone, a small bespectacled sixty-year-old, was a legend in the capital, writing and publishing a small newsletter that took the Pentagon to task week after week. Stone's maxim that "all governments lie" was adopted by a legion of young reporters, including Hersh. One day in 1966, Hersh recalled, "this funny old man showed up there, introduced himself, and asked if he could look through the AP files." It was I. F. Stone, and Hersh let him look, but other reporters were miffed that Hersh let in this outsider. It was then that Hersh began to read Stone's *Weekly*. "He wrote some very good stuff exposing the Pentagon's lies," Hersh found.

Coincidentally, the AP boss in New York, Wes Gallagher, had already decided that cultural forces were forcing changes in the way the AP approached reporting. In 1966 Gallagher formed an investigative reporting unit, composed of his best reporters. As objectivity came under increasing criticism, the AP knew it needed to add enterprise to pursue issues and set the agenda for discussion, without waiting for government to act. It was not a rejection of the ethos of neutrality. But it was more in line with the kind of activist journalism Hersh and his younger colleagues wanted. Hersh, a good baseball player in his younger days, had made the all-star team—he was chosen for the investigative team. Joe Kane was picked as its editor, which was a bad omen. Kane was from the old school, cautious, and not likely to give his reporters room to roam. "He was a nice man," Hersh said, "but he did what the company told him to do." "Joe was afraid of his own shadow," noted Jean Heller, who later became part of the team and won a Pulitzer Prize in 1972. "Gallagher knew investigative reporting was legitimate and necessary," Heller added, "but they stepped into it gingerly because it was such new ground." Kane and Hersh soon butted heads.[18]

As Hersh made his way around Pentagon offices culturing sources, he developed relationships. "People trusted me, got to know me," Hersh said, "and so I'd get a heads up." One day he was told to pursue an overlooked story—a change in American policy about the possible offensive use of chemical and biological weapons. Moreover, the source said, this secretive area of the military would reveal all sorts of surprises and controversies. It was a big story, with huge implications, perfect for an investigation. The more he dug, the more he found—big government contracts with Fortune 500 corporations; scientists hidden on various payrolls; universities taking money to do chemical research. Most importantly, he found that the United States had piled up huge arsenals of some of the deadliest materials known with the potential to kill or maim thousands of innocents. And the public did not know. He found that America was moving toward reversing a policy dating to World War II — renouncing a no-first-use policy of chemical and biological weapons. It took him weeks, but he pieced the story together, his first serious investigation and multipart series of articles. But Kane and others had problems with the articles.

Kane was a "paper shuffler," Hersh said. "He didn't get it." He took Hersh's forty-five-page, seven-part series and turned it into one bland article. It begins: "The Defense Department is spending $230 million this year on a chemical and biological warfare program it describes as a vital deterrent as well as a standby weapons system." It is a classic balanced AP lead. It was not the lead Hersh wrote. When Hersh detailed how universities were complicit in this weapons buildup, the Pentagon got almost as much space to respond: "Research is necessary to assure the security of our country against surprise attack," a spokesman said. The response cried out for a Hersh rejoinder, or some further criticism of the policy. But it was left with a flat and straight response, as if Hersh was writing a breaking daily story. "There were two sides to every story," Gaylord Shaw said. "With AP you had to get response." But the article was so toned down that it was equal parts exposé and response. It is no surprise that it was mild enough for the military's *Stars and Stripes* newspaper to publish it. The hands of Kane and Gallagher are all over the story. Hersh was furious, lamenting, "If we lopped off 90 percent of the editors in the world we would be much better off." Reporter Walter Mears, an unofficial AP in-house historian, recalled the "aggressive" articles: "The AP felt he was going too far. Hersh was adamant he had documented it." Hersh lost. "That's when I decided I had to get out—nothing dramatic, no confrontation," Hersh said.[19]

Hersh tried to write the articles as a freelancer for other publications. But AP policy blocked him. Mears explained that "if you did the reporting on company time," the AP owned it. But Hersh's response was, "you don't want it anyway," so why can't it go elsewhere? The neutering of the series was the straw that broke the camel's back. Hersh's days at the AP were numbered. By April it was as if he had gone back to his beginning days as a neophyte correspondent—an article on Richard Nixon's handwriting, on a soldier who got the plague, on tactics used by the Israelis in desert warfare. He had no beat, no high-profile assignments. He was busted back to general assignment. "It was time," he said. "The AP was good to me. It was my apprenticeship. I learned the business from the bottom up. A lot of that stuff was invaluable in the shaping of my career." But, again, he had worn out his welcome. Big new stuff was around the corner, but so was more controversy.[20]

CHAPTER 9

Finding America's Hidden Arsenal

"Just a Drop Can Kill"

The-top-of-the-page banner headline was ominous: "U.S. Could Deliver Deadly Gases, Germs." Although pushed back to page four of the April 14, 1967, edition of *Stars and Stripes,* the independent newspaper that covers the military, the headline seemed to warn of ghastly American weapons with a searing exposé to follow. The byline was Seymour H. Hersh. Inexplicably, M for Myron was replaced with an H. Hersh might have been happy, however, if his name had been left off the article completely. The article was bland and muted. A subheadline took the bite out of Hersh's warning: "Research Is Defensive: To Deter Enemy," which was the government's contention, although Hersh's research showed otherwise. Editors at the Associated Press had taken Hersh's ten thousand words and compressed—he said "massacred"—them into a flat and conventional thousand words that only hinted at the dark and secretive nature of the weapons of mass destruction that America had been stockpiling ever since World War II.[1]

And Hersh was furious—not only with the editing but also because he knew a compelling story when he saw one. He knew it, in part, because as he scrambled around the country in pursuit of evidence, no one in the government would talk to him. "The military has consistently refused to make public many of the facts about chemical biological weapons," he wrote. And while secrecy was a way of life in the military, this one was extraordinary. "The secrecy over biological efforts has been almost an obsession with the military," he concluded. America's arsenal of gases, biological agents, and chemical bombs were as hidden as could be. "A secrecy curtain," Hersh called it, "cutting off the public's view." The facts, he wrote, "are cloaked in secrecy." Didn't the public deserve to know that nearly 10,000 civilians and 3,750 military officers in conjunction with seventy American universities were working nonstop at six military bases? Shouldn't they know that $300 million—a 30 percent increase in six years—was being spent to support these weapons? Most important of all, shouldn't they know that scientists had perfected "a massive array of deadly agents?" He posed the question that even many researchers and policy analysts were asking behind closed doors, "Can disease, once spread, be controlled?" And his inability to get an answer on the record from the Pentagon irked him most of all. "I hate secrets," he said. "I don't think there should be secrets. I'm awfully tired of people in Washington telling me something is secret in the name of national security."[2]

"The whole subject," Hersh wrote in words that were uncharacteristically dramatic for him, "has overtones of horror and revulsion that far outstrip the world's fear of a nuclear holocaust." It is "almost too horrible for rational debate," he added. And if these weapons are not controlled or eliminated, Hersh concluded, it might "set in motion a doomsday machine on the planet—striking down attacker and defender alike." These strong words, of course, did not make it into his AP dispatch. His article was produced for the AP's bold new investigative unit, but little or no reporter voice was allowed. "As for hard-edged investigative stuff," observed Pulitzer Prize-winner Jean Heller, "they wanted to tread very lightly in those early days." Hersh decided to move ahead on his own to tell the story. On May 6 he wrote an article about "secret work on gas and germ warfare" that the New Republic headlined "Just a Drop Can Kill." The article broke the AP's ban on outside work, and it did not sit well with his bosses.[3]

It was the first of six national magazine articles for Hersh—two in the New Republic, a well-known progressive magazine, two in Ramparts, a 1960s muckraking upstart, and two in the staid New York Times Magazine. Hersh could not know that his articles were making Pentagon insiders nervous and, moreover, were reinforcing the arguments of reformers—in both America and Britain—as they desperately sought to force the United States to re-evaluate its policies. In particular, as he noted in the opening salvo of his crusade, the United States had secretly made a major policy change from World War II, when Franklin D. Roosevelt declared the United States would never use biological or chemical weapons unless first attacked. But by the early 1960s, without any public acknowledgment, this policy had changed, as Hersh found by wading through congressional testimony and obscure language in military manuals. His first article was a jumble of information—on universities that were cooperating, on the history of weaponry, on a few isolated victims of gases being used in Vietnam. It can be difficult to read. But nonetheless it had alarming tidbits. Germ warfare is "just disease control in reverse," one researcher warned Hersh. "The gas from a single bomb the size of a quart fruit jar could kill every living thing within a cubic mile," a report indicated.[4]

No wonder the government did not want anyone to know.

When Hersh tried snooping around the 1,300-acre Fort Dedrick, fifty miles northwest of Washington DC, he made a wrong turn on an outlying road. An unmarked police car and two army jeeps with military policemen quickly surrounded the unassuming reporter with glasses. "They knew who I was, and where I was to go," he said, and so he was escorted without incident to a safe location—where he could not see anything revealing. Hersh was on to a very big and sensitive story. Bobbs-Merrill offered him a book contract—a $4,000 advance with $1,000 in cash. He left his $200-a-week AP job. "Screw it, I quit," he said. Given that he had moved into a new house in the Cleveland Park section of Washington and his wife was pregnant, this was a rash decision.[5]

Controversy and Criticism

Sy Hersh, the thirty-year-old fast-talking, manic hustler from Chicago, was neither afraid to take risks nor wade into controversy. And, indeed, chemical and biological weapons research, development, and deployment was fraught with worldwide controversy. Back in 1925 the world had, in essence, agreed to a complete ban on asphyxiating and poisonous gases, but the U.S. Senate had rejected the so-called Geneva protocols—a rejection that stood into the 1960s at the same time the United Nations was trying to tighten the world's consensus on controlling such weapons. In the meantime the United States has become the world leader in producing and stockpiling the outlawed weapons.

The big question, plain and simple: was it immoral to use gases and chemicals that could maim and kill people in slow and agonizing ways? "In ancient days, as today, the use of germs and gases was viewed as an especially abhorrent maneuver or threat," Hersh pointed out. But high-ranking military officers insisted that America could have saved lives in battles such as at Iwo Jima and that huge Chinese armies could be thwarted with weapons that would be cleaner than a nuclear bomb.[6]

The most pressing contemporary issue was Vietnam. Did this unconventional war, increasingly the target of protest, demand that napalm and tear gas—and maybe worse—be used to stop an unseen enemy? In 1967 alone the Pentagon purchased $60 million in defoliants and herbicides, enough to cover 3.6 million acres, half the farming land in Vietnam. No wonder, as Hersh pointed out, that the "most hated outfits in Vietnam"—known by the slogan "only we can prevent forests"—were the flying units that dropped these chemicals.

But critics, in and out of the Pentagon, were convinced that America's use of chemicals in Vietnam was a clear-cut violation of the Geneva ban. Even though the U.S. had refused to sign the treaty, it had abided by its spirit—until Vietnam. One Pentagon source told Hersh, "I'm ashamed now because of what we've done; we may have broken the barrier." The source added, "Why in the hell was it authorized in the first place?" It was a question the UN was asking also as it tried to toughen the Geneva language on chemical-biological weapons (CBW).[7]

And then there was the inevitable intervention of the Cold War. With a huge nuclear arsenal as a deterrent, weren't CBW still necessary to counter the Russians' secret and aggressive program? Didn't the United States have to stay at least even or ahead of its arch-enemy? While fourteen nations possessed these weapons, it was the arms race with Russia that drove American policy. What bewildered Hersh, however, was that "the Pentagon has done little to make the public actively aware of the Russian activity." The huge buildup came without a whiff of public knowledge. More importantly, if the American public was at risk, authorities had done nothing to prepare cities or people for how to respond to an attack. Meanwhile, "the weapons race has gone on," he wrote.[8]

Hersh located controversy in the question of whether American universities should be dirtying their hands taking federal money to help develop a weapon that was both deadly and inhumane? Hersh found college presidents who did not even know the extent of their universities' involvement in a CBW military-industrial combine that Hersh—and 1960s dissenters—found a growing threat. General Dynamics, General Electric, DuPont, Monsanto, Westinghouse—a "Who's Who" of corporate heavyweights—all heavily invested in CBW. In 1961 President Dwight Eisenhower first warned of the confluence of corporations and the military. To Hersh, the hidden Pentagon-big money cabal around this multimillion-dollar industry showed the dangers posed to a democracy that benefits the moneymakers more than the people.[9]

But Hersh was no ideologue; he was a reporter who avoided—to a fault—opinion and rhetoric in his writings. In March 1968 the army handed him the smoking-gun facts he needed when a national scandal erupted. In July he returned to Utah's Skull Valley, a barren salt desert eighty miles southwest of Salt Lake City where the army's Dugway chemical and biological testing facility is spread out over a million acres. He had visited the base—the nation's most important—as he prepared *Chemical and Biological Warfare: America's Hidden Arsenal,* a 354-page book that came out in September 1968. When he reached the base's entrance he was greeted with the sign: "Warning—dangerous instrumentalities of war are being tested on this post." And indeed the warning was borne out on the windy afternoon of March 13, 1968, after his book had been written but not yet published. But this was *his* story, the one he uncovered more than a year before anyone was talking about it, so he returned as the nation's eyes focused on Dugway.

The military needed to conduct airborne tests of nerve gas by spraying the chemical at low altitude while the wind blew at speeds of five to twenty-five miles per hour. The intention was to see how the gas would distribute in hopes of making an American attack—in response or otherwise—more predictable. When the test was over, researchers wearing protective suits would wander the area and inspect how vegetation and wildlife fared, although the result was predictable. A high-ranking military official said: "A tiny drop of the gas in liquid form on the back of man's hand will paralyze his nerves instantly and deaden his brain in a few seconds. Death will follow in 30 seconds." The tanks spraying the gas were supposed to open for only a few seconds. But something malfunctioned, and as the planes ascended the gas escaped higher than expected. One source told Hersh a lethal cloud went as far away as 394 miles. Highway 40, a main nearby thoroughfare, was spared—as were human lives—when the wind suddenly shifted directions.[10]

Early the next morning, the county sheriff was told there was trouble in Skull Valley; he quickly went up to see. "I've never seen such a sight in my life," he told Hersh. "It was like a movie version of 'death and destruction.'" Nearly 6,400 sheep were dead or dying from the nerve gas, known as VX. Reporters witnessed their drooping heads and twisted necks and spines, their heaving and kicking movements, patches of furry white, the sheep lying on the ground, for as far as the eye could see, gasping for life, but overcome by the gas. The army denied responsibility, a monstrous lie. But an army fact sheet distributed to Utah senator Frank Moss's office, and mistakenly sent to the press, revealed the chemical release. The army mounted an official investigation. Dugway was the U.S. Army's first major public mistake with a chemical weapon. Observed Hersh: "All the elements for a nationwide scandal were present: target practice with a lethal nerve agent; an incredibly obvious series of military lies, a heavy concentration of newspaper and radio-television reporters. Yet the sheep deaths led neither to congressional outcries . . . nor to a public debate about such weapons; nor did it even provoke any serious citizen reaction in Utah."[11]

The reason, Hersh found, was that the thousand civilians and the six hundred military personnel at Dugway feared that "too much investigating or talking about the incident might make the Army move its CBW base from Dugway." Hersh faced outright hostility as he tried to gauge public reaction and find the facts. "Some people here believe that pacifists would have a lot to gain—especially with articles like yours," said Jan Swanson, a twenty-five-year-old editor of the weekly *Tooele Transcript*. Some people actually thought the "pacifists" killed the sheep. Hersh did not respond. The state's top health official warned Hersh: "You have a terrific responsibility not to write anything that isn't going to do any good, something that will just upset people by telling them things they shouldn't know." Again, Hersh did not fire back. What he had run into was clear—everyone's livelihood was reliant on the military. "Everyone here has two cars, a camper, and a pickup truck," said the town sheriff. "They don't want to lose that." Even a doctor who was one of the few residents to publicly lambaste the military was realistic. "We've got a defense business bringing 35 million a year into the state; sheep bring in about 1/35th that amount. Which is more important for Utah?" he asked. Score one for the military-industrial complex—at least for the time being.[12]

The Voice of Disarmament—and the Enemy

Sy Hersh's crusade to reveal America's "hidden arsenal" had an odd and unconventional trajectory. First, he wrote what he thought would be a blockbuster series for the Associated Press, but his editors crushed it and ruined his chance of impacting public policy. Then he quit AP and quickly wrote two national magazine articles, which garnered widespread attention and led to his first book. Normally, for most authors, when a book is published, the story ends—it is a culmination. But, possibly because he needed a paycheck and also because the story was gaining momentum, like a good beat reporter and bloodhound, Hersh wrote four more articles. He was disappointed at the reaction to his first book. "I researched and wrote my ass off," Hersh said. Working in the small press room of the U.S. Department of Health, Education and Welfare, Hersh sometimes wrote all night, for twelve hours, trying to complete ten pages a day. He tackled the complex history, traced America's embrace of a first-use policy, detailed the different chemicals the government was stockpiling, and showed how Vietnam had become a laboratory for CBW. He concluded by wondering about the chances for disarmament.[13]

Bemoaning the U.S. efforts, he wrote, "It has moved very slowly in the field of CBW disarmament." In fact, he worried, "peace and disarmament groups may be in a futile race against time. Biological and chemical weapons are operationally effective in the United States today, and there is every reason to believe America's allies will soon have similar . . . capabilities." But beyond these rather weak statements about what needed to be done, Hersh was mum. What is clear in his first book is the reporter had not found his voice. He worked long hours and had done what one reviewer in the *New York Times* called "admirable work . . . a detailed examination," one that helped "inform lay readers of the horrors and intricacies of CBW."[14] But it was his reporting that impresses, not his conclusions. No explicit call for disarmament can be found, except by implication.

Over the years Hersh has developed a reputation as a plodding writer. It is in sharp contrast, for example, to Bob Woodward of the *Washington Post* and Watergate fame, whose books read like novels, even when about complex public policy. Hersh's first book can be a slog. He documents it with notes in the manner of a scholar, which means he is credible and definitive. But it often reads like an AP dispatch written from behind a desk. There are few anecdotes or people in the story. And he has difficulty finding a voice, which is no surprise. His training had been in a news genre that mitigated against reaching conclusions, sweeping or otherwise. The book may have suffered from another problem. Publishers are often wary of books that grow out of research for the daily news cycle and then are turned into books. They have a choppy feel that is difficult to overcome. And that was the case with Hersh's first book.

Nonetheless, the book was important enough that the opposition—the CBW proponents—felt the need to respond harshly to Hersh. The *Times* review offered only the mildest of criticism, in part because the reviewer, Daniel S. Greenberg, an editor at *Science* magazine, was in Hersh's camp, fearful of "the ravings of the CBW advocates" and the "loathsome consequences" of these weapons. However, a chemistry professor at the University of Amherst in Massachusetts was not so kind. Dr. Charles J. Thoman, viciously ripped into Hersh, calling him tendentious, arrogant, and "downright malicious." His biggest complaint—repeated for many years by Hersh's critics—was that the author's bias made it impossible for him to fairly evaluate reality. "To write an unbiased report of a prejudiced book is an impossible task," he explained. Thoman did not quibble with Hersh's facts but, he asserted, "obviously sincere attempts to explain the rationale behind CBW research and development are almost sneeringly brushed aside. On the other hand, facts and statements that support the author's thesis are greeted with rapture." One wonders, however, what book Thoman was reading, and if he was not guilty of exactly what he accused Hersh of doing. He concludes his review by stating that what is clearly needed is a CBW arsenal capable of deterring an attack, an adequate warning system to detect such an attack, and antidotes to minimize casualties. "The denial of the fact that an incapacitating agent would be a more humane method of dealing with enemy personnel than conventional weapons that maim or kill is sheer blindness," he wrote. To Thoman, disarmament was not an option. This was the university-military-industrial complex speaking. What was most unfair to Hersh is that his book regularly provided the chance for the proponents to argue their points. In fact, it often reads too much like a balanced news story, so much it bogs down the text.[15] But to Thoman, Hersh was the enemy, an implicit voice for disarmament—but a voice that was about to get louder.

Seymour Hersh's book gave him status as a knowledgeable commentator on the emerging weapons controversy. He quickly used the voice, writing a long article in the *New York Times Magazine* on "the secret arsenal." Oddly, he was bolder in the *Times* than in his book. Even the military was uncomfortable with these weapons, he asserted. "Use of gases and biologicals isn't manly," an unnamed officer told him. "It isn't the kind of warfare that cadets learn about at West Point: it's 'sneaky.'" There was growing consensus, he argued, that "the world never be exposed to the ravages of a chemical biological war" and that international disarmament was increasingly possible. And then, for the first time, Hersh wrote what amounted to an editorial, ending with a peroration. "What is desperately needed," he argued "is an open, rational public debate of the political and military implications involved. . . . But it cannot begin until more information is made available." Speaking like a true progressive optimist, Hersh declared, "If the world knew more about the potential horror of nerve gases and deadly biologicals, the drive for de-escalation and disarmament would be increased. And the United States, as one of the leaders of CBW research and development, would have an obligation to lead that drive."[16]

As Hersh's voice grew, so did his standing. The *London Times* called him "the Ralph Nader of America's chemical and biological armory," a reference to the man who championed reform of the American auto industry in the late 1950s. Nonetheless, Hersh was still disappointed at the reaction to his work. "Somehow it failed to make much of a mark at first," he said. "The public and the press simply did not want to believe that the United States was stockpiling nerve gas at army commands overseas."[17] Little did he know, however, that reformers inside and outside the military were paying attention to his work and that the results would soon be seen by the entire world.

CHAPTER 10

Speaking for Gene McCarthy

A Quixotic Campaign Is Born

Lyndon Johnson easily defeated Barry Goldwater in 1964 in one of America's largest landslides. Emboldened, the tall Texan pushed ahead on his Great Society reforms as Medicaid, Medicare, and civil rights legislation sailed through Congress. These were legacies and carryovers of John Kennedy's presidency, Johnson insisted, but so too was the gnawing war in Southeast Asia, which became Johnson's obsession—and folly. The French had failed in Vietnam, and America slowly but surely stepped into the vacuum, first with advisers under Kennedy. And then Johnson persisted, insisting on bringing the North Vietnamese to their feet, with thousands of troops and tons of bombs. But America had grown increasingly restive with the war as television captured the mounting casualties. "Wait until those coffins start coming home to the small towns in Minnesota, and you'll see the American people turn against this war," observed Minnesota senator Eugene McCarthy.[1] Hurt by successive summers of urban race riots and a faltering war, the Democrats took a severe battering in the midterm elections of 1966. By 1967 Democratic Party dissenters organized a "Dump Johnson" movement, unimaginable three years earlier. A cadre of antiwar liberals began to cast about for a candidate willing to take on a suddenly vulnerable sitting president.

The insurgents looked to the junior senator from New York, Robert Kennedy. But Kennedy feared a primary battle would wound the party and hoist a Republican—Richard Nixon, George Romney, or Nelson Rockefeller—to the presidency. And he feared he could not win. Eyes turned to McCarthy, a devout Catholic who was nearly Johnson's vice presidential choice in 1964. One credential made McCarthy most attractive—he firmly opposed the Vietnam War. "The central point," he said, "is what this war is doing to the United States . . . what it's doing to us around the world today, this draining of the material and moral resources of the country from our really pressing problems."[2] It was, McCarthy declared, a matter of conscience; the war had to be opposed. The insurgents threw their support to fifty-two-year-old McCarthy, although many still hoped Kennedy would jump in. McCarthy declared his intent in November 1967 to challenge Johnson in the April 2 presidential primary in Wisconsin, a progressive Minnesota neighbor. But his supporters convinced him to brave the snows of New Hampshire for the nation's first primary, March 12. McCarthy, the Irish Catholic poet who loved baseball and hockey, now had to put together a team for a quixotic quest for the presidency. "We were never quite a team," observed Curtis Gans, a young reformer who helped organize the "Dump Johnson" movement.[3] What actually emerged was more a guerilla uprising connected by an idea but with no central discipline. Nonetheless, it was destined to become part of American political folklore. A group of well-educated people, mostly liberal, jelled around a man who was like a nineteenth-century utopian poet. And although McCarthy was a loner who stuck to his own counsel, he still needed a campaign staff to run for office. Reporter Richard Stout, who covered McCarthy, observed that "a campaign staff began to develop, in much the way a pickup baseball game develops." And Sy Hersh—a baseball lover who hated the Vietnam War like Senator McCarthy—got a call.[4]

A Typewriter and an Insurgency

By early fall Hersh was awaiting publication of his book on chemical and biological weapons. He had also started his other career—hitting the campus lecture tour to tout the book and warn of these weapons of mass destruction. But the restless energy of the reporter, who glories in the crush of deadlines and pursuit of stories, still lurked in Hersh. He needed action. One of Hersh's golfing partners was Tim Clark, whose father Blair had been named manager of McCarthy's campaign. The Harvard-educated Blair Clark had been a CBS producer and once edited the liberal *Nation* magazine. Tim Clark told his father about Hersh. "I was interested simply because I didn't know much about McCarthy," Hersh said, adding, but "I liked his opposition to the war. He was somebody doing something and I was interested in that." Although Hersh largely kept his opinions to himself, privately he had grown to hate the conflict. "O.J.T.—on the job training," he said had turned him against Vietnam." I was covering the Pentagon," he recalled, "and I'd go to lunch with officers. And what they said was that you had to be a professional liar. It was all about body counts. That's how they measure success in the military. So they would lie about it. It turned me against the war." From Johnson to Defense Secretary Robert McNamara to the military's top officers, Hersh saw lying—and a foul war.[5]

Not sure he wanted to tackle the big Pentagon book, Hersh figured, "it was a good time to think about doing something else." Blair Clark called Sy for an interview. "It was a weird sort of talk," Hersh said. The urbane Clark, connected to high society and money but also with hefty experience in journalism, declined to look at Hersh's writing samples. This was a PR job; it called for handling reporters, not being one. "You're hired if we can get an OK," said Clark who ran Hersh's name by Jerry Eller, McCarthy's top Senate aide. McCarthy's wife, Abigail, objected. It is not clear why. "I didn't take it personally," Hersh said, not realizing that it was the beginning of feuding between McCarthy's long-time staff and the campaign staff. The final arbiter on Hersh's hire was his neighbor and friend, well-known liberal columnist Mary McGrory, who had McCarthy's ear. McGrory first revealed to the nation that McCarthy would challenge Johnson. She was part of his inner circle, which included Robert Lowell, the Pulitzer Prize poet. She told McCarthy to hire Hersh. In early January Hersh took off for wintry New Hampshire, where the first presidential primary was under way. He was about to cross over to what journalists often call "the dark side," the world of public relations. He would have to leave—at least temporarily—the chemical and biological weapons story and journalism.[6]

Why would Sy Hersh, age thirty, dogged reporter, become a press secretary? PR is, after all, a one-sided venture. Ostensibly, you lose your own voice as you become the spokesperson and advocate for your client. You need to convince the press—and the public—to elect your candidate. It means getting into the head of your client to articulate his or her point of view. The answer, in part: it was, as Hersh put it, "an opportune" time to do something else. He needed cash, although he had no expectation that working for McCarthy would make him serious money. For the independent Hersh the transition was not easy. And for Eugene McCarthy, not easily understood or particularly cooperative with his own staff, it was even more difficult. McCarthy "didn't like press secretaries," observed Peter Barnes, a writer for *Newsweek* who became a McCarthy speechwriter. Moreover, he said, McCarthy didn't really need a spokesman. He "resented them and served most of the time as his own press secretary—saying what he wanted to say, when he wanted to say it, and to whom he wanted to say it." And that, of course, made him a lot like Seymour Myron Hersh.[7]

Unbowed, Hersh headed to New Hampshire, not knowing what to expect. He was a political novice with no experience in public relations except watching PR flacks for eight years. Enter Richard Goodwin, a suave thirty-six-year-old star speechwriter, one of the bright young men who had worked for John Kennedy in his Camelot White House. A Harvard Law School graduate who clerked for the U.S. Supreme Court, Goodwin became a top adviser-speechwriter for Lyndon Johnson; he coined the label *Great Society* to describe Johnson's famous legislation. By 1966 he too had grown weary of the Vietnam War. "Military victory was impossible," he felt. The war was "morally and physically draining." And Goodwin said so publicly, splitting with his president and ending any relationship with Johnson. He returned to Massachusetts to teach at MIT. One morning, reading the newspapers, he saw that U.S. troops had burned a temple in the Vietnamese city of Hue. "That was the last straw," he said. "It was madness." And there seemed no limit to that madness. He told his wife, author Doris Kearns Goodwin, he was heading to New Hampshire to help McCarthy. "The hell with it, I am going," he said. "It's better than sitting on your ass in Boston."[8]

When Goodwin arrived he wanted to avoid being seen by the press. They would think that "Kennedy's man" had arrived. Seeing no familiar faces, he sought out press secretary Sy Hersh in his hotel room. He found Hersh disheveled—as usual—with his room cluttered with papers, but "Sy greeted me warmly, enthusiastically," Goodwin recalled. "It was my first encounter with a man who would be my constant companion for almost three months, whose frenzied energy, stimulated by profound commitment, was to provide the McCarthy campaign with much of its driving force." Goodwin got right to business.

Goodwin asked Sy, "What reporters are covering us?"

"None," he replied.

"Not a single one?"

"Not here; there were a few down in Manchester," Hersh said.

"We've got to make some news. If we make news then the reporters will come."

Goodwin suggested they draft a statement for McCarthy for a Senate hearing in Washington on the infamous Gulf of Tonkin incident Johnson had used to get carte blanche from Congress to send troops to Vietnam.

Said Goodwin, "Let's draft a couple of statements. We can show them to McCarthy in the morning. That'll make news, and bring the reporters."

"We don't have a secretary," Hersh said.

"Just a typewriter then."

"We don't have a typewriter," Hersh said.

They went to Goodwin's car to get his portable typewriter. "You, me, and this typewriter. Sy, together, we're going to overthrow the President of the United States."9 It was hyperbole, of course, but in the end Goodwin and Hersh and thousands of college students who descended on New Hampshire would have a profound effect on the 1968 presidential election—and the course of the Vietnam War.

Winning Trust, Feuding, Getting Chewed Out

Hersh was a work in progress as a press secretary. Journalism and PR are different. Goodwin knew the difference; Sy had to learn—if he could. On their first night together, Goodwin and Hersh prepared a statement for McCarthy at 3:00 a.m. After a few hours sleep they brought it to the senator at breakfast. The candidate must have been surprised to see Goodwin, whom he had twice asked to join the campaign. He approved the statement. Back at the motel, Goodwin instructed Hersh to call the television networks and major newspapers and ask why they were not in New Hampshire to cover McCarthy's statement on the Gulf of Tonkin.

"Don't tell them nobody else is up here either, just imply they're the one missing the boat," Goodwin said.

Goodwin was easy to work with, although later Hersh said he exaggerated aspects of their relationship and how important he was to the campaign. Like many others, Hersh said, Goodwin was "on the make," hoping to increase his own status and prestige—and angling for a position in a new administration. But he brought an important star quality, a veteran political presence and clout that made it easier for Hersh to get his memos and speeches in front of McCarthy. But Goodwin was never able to shed his image as Kennedy's man. Robert Kennedy, after all, was the first choice of the "Dump Johnson" cadre, and he always lurked in the background as a potential foe. Goodwin had to toss elbows with some of the McCarthy insiders, especially Senate staffers who feared being pushed out. It was worse for Hersh. He learned this quickly. Right after he came on board, McCarthy gave a major speech in New York. A reporter from a big newspaper approached him and said he had been waiting weeks to interview McCarthy; other reporters were in the same boat. Hersh went to Eller and asked about the interview. "I'll tell you what you do," he said to Hersh. "Wait until you get two hundred requests. And then, throw them over the wall, and we'll handle them." In other words, let McCarthy's inner circle handle it all. And Hersh thought to himself, "my God," his whole staff was an unmitigated disaster. Hersh quickly cornered the candidate and asked if he would do the interview. McCarthy agreed; it happened the next day. McCarthy was pleased, telling Hersh at a staff meeting, "Everybody thinks you're a great guy. You've got reporters sleeping in my bed, riding in the back of my car, and all that." Needless to say, however, Eller was not happy. And he and Hersh began to feud. "He and I would just tell each other off about every three days," Hersh said.[10]

In his first week on the job Hersh flew to California with McCarthy, a state the senator was eyeing for a June primary. Sy sat with him; they did crossword puzzles, and McCarthy talked about his twenty-year feud with the Kennedys, a bitter divide that had not healed. Hersh gave him a long memo on the recent indictment of famous pediatrician Dr. Benjamin Spock, charged with conspiring to violate the Selective Service Act by counseling young people to resist the draft. Hersh, an expert on the draft, told McCarthy why this indictment was unconstitutional. McCarthy glanced at it, and Hersh thought he did not read it. But at his first major speech at UCLA, McCarthy eloquently defended Spock, which Hersh called "brave." He concluded that speech writing for McCarthy "was rewarding." But at first not much else was. The press was largely ignoring McCarthy. The arch-conservative *Manchester Union Leader* in New Hampshire was obsessed with the Vietnam War—and Richard Nixon. Headlines in February blared: "Reds poised for big push," "Red tanks overrun camp." On February 21 the newspaper said Johnson had a 6–1 lead over McCarthy, whose candidacy was relegated to small back-page stories. The *Boston Globe* wrote some favorable stories, but the *New York Times* virtually ignored him; its editors felt McCarthy was not a serious contender. When reporter Ned Kenworthy did discuss McCarthy's insurgent campaign, he was dismissive. Even the senator's backers seemed "a little puzzled and disappointed because his whole performance struck them as half-hearted." And indeed McCarthy had the reputation as a lazy legislator, one who had a mind of his own on how a campaign should be run.[11]

"You couldn't push him," Hersh said. In the beginning Hersh wanted to "go slow" to win McCarthy's trust. What Hersh wanted was simple: "to get authority . . . to put out routine statements." In essence, he wanted to speak for the candidate. But neither the candidate nor his staff was very cooperative. Once, in New Hampshire, when Hersh could not reach the candidate, he released a statement without McCarthy's approval, and the senator became furious and demanded a retraction from his own campaign. "I didn't like getting on his bad list," Hersh said. But he also refused to play the role of sycophant. When McCarthy gave a flat speech one day—as he often did—Hersh refused to tell him it was a great speech. "He didn't like that," Hersh said. And at times they argued. Once, at a meeting, he asked who wrote his most recent speech. "Mostly mine," Hersh admitted. "Why," McCarthy asked, "do people write things you know I won't say?" "I was mad," Hersh recalled and he stormed out, slamming the door. McCarthy called ten minutes later and asked him to come back. "Come on down, let's work something out."[12] And they did. But the speech-writing remark hurt Hersh. He had read more than ten years of McCarthy's speeches; Hersh knew what he stood for and how he spoke.

Hersh had less luck with the candidate's wife, Abigail. She was a strong presence, especially in New Hampshire, where she stepped into a vacuum of leadership. Early on Hersh saw the secretaries in Blair Clark's office opening his mail and making copies of all correspondence. He asked why. They said all Clark's mail also had to be read by Mrs. McCarthy. Hersh was indignant, and he ordered them to stop. Mrs. McCarthy "hit the roof," he recalled. People told Hersh that Mrs. McCarthy was saying, behind his back, "We have to get rid of that Sy Hersh." But she never said anything to him. The staunchly Catholic Mrs. McCarthy was also offended by Hersh's constant cursing. *Time* magazine called Hersh "the unexcelled master of profanity." Hersh did not demur. "I mean, we all, I had to swear a lot." He even cursed the senator. "God damn him," was his common refrain, one he yelled in hotel hallways for everyone to hear. Mrs. McCarthy had other objections. Early in New Hampshire Hersh would paste up clippings of news articles for McCarthy to read. He regularly clipped the *Christian Science Monitor*, a fine newspaper, but one that some believed to be anti-Catholic, not a good thing for McCarthy, whose Benedictine background was well known. Mrs. McCarthy was livid that Hersh would use the *Monitor*. One day Hersh screamed at Mrs. McCarthy: "I'm not your press secretary. I'm your husband's."[13]

She began to accuse Hersh of being a spy for Lyndon Johnson, out to sabotage the campaign. "I am not hallucinating," Hersh said. "This lady has a few problems." Of course, Hersh did not know that the candidate was having his own problems with his wife. Their marriage was on the rocks, and McCarthy was seen often with two female reporters who were rumored to be his lovers. The *Washington Post* even warned him that it was being gossiped about widely, but they wrote no story. It was more than rumor. Right after the presidential campaign he split with Abigail, who refused to ever grant him a divorce. Hersh heard the rumors but did not think it relevant. All he knew was, "We really liked it when (Mrs. McCarthy) wasn't around because he was much nicer."[14]

The McCarthy campaign stumbled badly at the outset. January, Peter Barnes noted, "was a very bad month." The hallmark of the early campaign was disorganization and chaos. In the Washington DC offices of the campaign, Blair Clark had to run from room to room to take different calls because the telephone system had been installed improperly. It was comical. Eller told McCarthy that "a campaign centered on issues requires organization to an even greater extent than a personality contest." But McCarthy, who had made all decisions in his Minnesota senatorial campaigns, resisted the advice. "When it came to campaigning he had something of the mentality of a nineteenth-century capitalist—he would make the decisions and do everything almost alone." His staff warned him, "You've challenged the king in full view of the court. The penalty is death. You've got to have troops of your own." But McCarthy still resisted hiring schedulers and fundraisers. He acted like he was back in Minnesota. And no one was in charge. One party figure once remarked, "McCarthy's campaigns are run by the Holy Ghost." Theodore White, the famous chronicler of presidential campaigns, found it impossible to make a neat diagram of the organization of the campaign. The central nucleus, he wrote, was "the gravitational force of Eugene McCarthy's conviction."[15] But it led to embarrassing scheduling snafus on the campaign trail. The only constant was that the urbane and witty candidate spoke passionately about America's need to refocus its moral center, which had been lost under Lyndon Johnson.

External events, however, began to change the momentum and bail out McCarthy. On January 23, 1968, a Navy spy ship was seized by North Korean forces off the coast of Korea, with eighty-two crew members taken hostage and held for eleven months. It was the first time in over 150 years that a U.S. Navy vessel had been hijacked. And then, on January 31, eighty thousand North Vietnamese troops launched an assault on a hundred towns and cities in South Vietnam, the war's largest military operation. The attacks stunned American troops, and although the enemy was beaten back, the Tet offensive was a blow. It appeared American forces were reeling. McCarthy, reluctant to take advantage of the incidents, did not want to make the campaign against Johnson personal. He also knew he did not have to say much—events would do the job.[16]

Hersh, meanwhile, was doing his part to improve the candidate's standing with the press. Between 6:30 and 7:30 a.m. each day, after getting a few hours' sleep, Hersh wrote drafts of speeches and statements for McCarthy, who was often still in bed at 8:00 a.m. He would make a few changes, and then Hersh hustled out to distribute the material to set the press's agenda for that day—and hope even more that McCarthy would stick to the statements. Once, in February, Peter Barnes and Hersh put together a statement reacting to news out of the White House. McCarthy was not thrilled when Hersh brought it to him, preferring to address his own issues, not what the day's events dictated, but he agreed. When the campaign plane arrived in Chicago, all the major evening newspapers had it as their lead item. "McCarthy finally takes off the gloves and attacks Johnson." But Hersh said McCarthy "really didn't like that at all." It was not his style.

Hersh did pull off a minor publicity coup that helped humanize the icy McCarthy—and got national attention. Hersh and others convinced McCarthy to lace up a pair of ice skates at a rink in New Hampshire. Unbeknownst to McCarthy, the aides had snuck them along on the trip—even though the candidate had taken them out of his luggage!—knowing McCarthy had been a terrific hockey player. While the fifty-two-year-old senator took to the ice, Hersh rounded up reporters and photographers. When they arrived, the senator was briskly skating around the ice. It was a classic "photo op." McCarthy took three spins, and then Hersh escorted him to a changing room. He was puffing, somewhat angry, and barked at Hersh, "Why in the hell did you let me take that third turn, huh? You should have gotten me out of there before that." But the skating photos appeared across the country. It was much better than Lyndon Johnson showing reporters his stomach scars.[17]

Little by little, McCarthy's standing in the polls edged up. Hersh wrote to one of his sisters, "We're going to do over 40 percent!" Then the campaign's most important development took place: the "kiddies," as Hersh called them, began to arrive in droves to help their peace candidate—more college students than the campaign knew what to do with. They were given clear instructions—no beards, no miniskirts, no old blue jeans, no foul language. Following this "Get Clean for Gene" tactic, the students went door to door to make the pitch for the alternative to Lyndon Johnson. McGrory captured the spirit on March 5, a week before the primary: "What is happening is that violet-eyed damsels from Smith are pinning McCarthy buttons on tattooed mill-workers, and PhDs from Cornell, shaven and shorn for world peace, are deferentially bowing to middle-aged Manchester housewives and importuning them to consider a change of commander-in-chief." A curious alliance of old liberals and students emerged. "Hippies and housewives," *Life* magazine called it. And Hersh, the old newsman, knew a great story when he saw one. The national press came calling. "The kids were really marvelous for the national press," Hersh realized, and he immediately sent reporters to charismatic divinity student Sam Brown, the twenty-five-year-old leader of student volunteers. The story took off even more. They called it "The Children's Crusade." Hersh just had to play middleman. Goodwin was quotable as always. "I had never seen anything like it in politics," he observed. Hersh thought the role of the students was exaggerated by the press, mostly because it offered a great story line. "I was less enthusiastic about the kids," he said.[18] More important, he thought, was the fact that at 5:30 a.m. McCarthy shook hands with twenty thousand factory workers.

There was one more element the press loved—movie stars turned out for McCarthy. Blue-eyed Paul Newman was side by side with the candidate, drawing large crowds. Dustin Hoffman, Tony Randall, Robert Vaughn, Jack Paar, Lauren Bacall, Jason Robards, all hit the campaign trail in the final days. Student and star power were on display. LBJ was on no one's mind.

Amid the McCarthy tumult, Robert Kennedy called Goodwin, asking, "How do you think you're going to do?"

"We're going to get at least 40 percent, and if we had an extra ten days we'd be over fifty."

"How would I have done?" Kennedy asked.

"You would have won, sixty—forty."

But it did not matter, Goodwin recalled, because, even without Bobby, "I was now certain that whatever McCarthy's personal destiny, Lyndon Johnson would not be the next president of the United States."[19] He was correct, of course.

"The weekend before the New Hampshire vote, the momentum was dizzying," wrote *Newsweek*'s Richard Stout. "Newspapers, magazines, and television networks that had all but ignored the McCarthy story until then now sent in correspondents to catch up." Hersh was besieged by reporters asking the same questions and beseeching him to give them some anecdote, some personality quirk about McCarthy. It should have thrilled him, but he found it annoying. "I happen to be a damn good reporter," he said. "And I can't stand bad reporters. Why should I have to live with them?" But he did because they were telling his candidate's story. When Hersh woke up on March 13, McCarthy had garnered 42 percent; Johnson won with 49 percent. When absentee ballots came in, McCarthy had actually tied the president of the United States. "We had stunned the country. We had stunned ourselves," Goodwin said. McCarthy was, suddenly, "a shining knight from Minnesota assaulting the battlements of established power." On the night of the election McCarthy declared, "If we come to Chicago with this strength there'll be no riots or demonstrations, but a great victory celebration."[20] But the celebration did not last long. Kennedy immediately told the press he was re-assessing. One McCarthy worker said, "We woke up after the New Hampshire primary, like it was Christmas Day, and when we went down to the tree, we found Bobby Kennedy had stolen our Christmas presents." McCarthy was bitter. "That Bobby; he's something isn't he?" McCarthy said privately. "He wouldn't even let me have my day of celebration, would he?"[21] Hersh would have liked to wake up the day after and repeat McCarthy's message that America needed to become the world's moral leader again. But instead the press was clamoring for reaction to Kennedy. Pulitzer Prize–winning columnist Murray Kempton, a McCarthy supporter, wrote that Kennedy "was like a man who comes down from the hills after the battle and shoots the wounded."[22]

A Fight over the Ghetto

Hersh immediately looked ahead to the next primary in Wisconsin where nineteen delegates were at stake. Reluctantly, he approached the candidate at lunch the next day. He was laughing with Paul Newman and Mary McGrory at a hotel in Manchester. Hersh waited until they were done. He told McCarthy that the *Chicago Sun-Times* wanted to do a long cover-page profile to run two days before the Wisconsin primary. Hersh knew the *Sun-Times* circulated extensively in many of Wisconsin's working-class Polish neighborhoods. The reporter needed an interview and would ride that day in the car with McCarthy. "Reporters think interviews are important," Hersh knew. "I think you ought to do it." McCarthy did not answer. Hersh's pitch was met with stony silence. Then, McCarthy said, in front of everyone, "Why, Sy? To make you happy?" More silence as Hersh squirmed, embarrassed by being cut down. "I felt like stabbing him," Hersh recalled. "It was a brutal thing to say."[23] Maybe the Kennedy entrance into the race irked him, or maybe he was tired of the press. Hersh put away the insult and McCarthy did the interview, but it did not bode well. McCarthy's status had changed; Hersh had his hands full handling requests. Hersh also resented the sudden influx of financial fat cats entering the picture, people not seen in New Hampshire, now trying to run the campaign.[24]

But Hersh had his own press operation to run. His top assistant was Mary Louise Oates, an energetic young woman who had been an award-winning UPI reporter. "Oates spoke softly only when conditions demanded, in the middle of a funeral mass, for example," Richard Goodwin recalled. When she first met Goodwin she shouted: "You're Dick Do-goodwin. Come in and meet the teeny-boppers." Later on she told the press he was "Che Guevara with teenyboppers." Oates was Sy's assistant, but Goodwin described her as "his confidante, therapist, and guru." Oates had the charm to talk with reporters when they seemed lost. "Her candor and bluntness made her credible, while her passionate, nearly coarse, humor-tinged enthusiasm endeared her . . . to reporters who realized they're dealing with a rare blend of idealism and toughness."[25] She and Hersh made a good team—independent, voluble, like-minded. It may not have endeared them to everyone. They called the campaign's two biggest financial backers "the Gold Dust Twins" and made jokes about them. Neither backer was very pleased. Money became an issue and almost led to a fistfight in Wisconsin a week before the primary. Hersh and his staff had prepared packets of publicity material for weekly newspapers. Since their deadlines were a week before the vote, it was urgent to get them material by special delivery. But Hersh's staff had no money. They went to Howard Stein, the president of the Dreyfus Fund and an early financial supporter, and Ted Warshafsky, a lawyer and treasurer of the Wisconsin campaign. Warshafsky declined. At the end of a long day, Hersh, Warshafsky, Stein, and movie star Newman were having drinks in a hotel room. "I want you to know your kids came looking for a hundred dollars today and I told them to go to hell," Warshafsky said to Hersh. "That's great, Ted," Hersh replied. Twenty minutes later, after he spoke to his staff, he learned that the denial of the money meant they could not mail the packets in time for the election. Hersh was furious. He came back to the room, recalling, "I was ready to kill him." He charged into the room, and Newman, who had played a prizefighter in the movie *Somebody Up There Likes Me*, had to jump up and intercede, stopping Hersh from attacking Warshafsky. "I was insane," Hersh admitted. No punches were thrown, but they missed the mailing deadline.[26]

Hersh's was a close-knit unit. "It was almost like a love cult we had," he said. "Everybody working very hard, terribly loyal to me. They all really liked me." The loyalty was tested. Hersh and Oates had to leave Wisconsin for a short time, and they returned to find staffers crying. Mrs. McCarthy had told them Oates and Hersh would not be around much longer.

In Wisconsin getting attention from the press was not a problem. Now there were too many reporters; Hersh had trouble finding accommodations. When reporters had to double up in rooms, or when McCarthy threw out the prepared text of speeches reporters had been given, they yelled at Hersh. Setting and making policy for McCarthy, however, was more problematic. And the issue that brought simmering tensions of the campaign—the idealists versus the pragmatists—to boil over was race relations. "The central issue in the 1968 campaign was race, not Vietnam," explained Dominic Sandbrook, a McCarthy biographer.[27] America had gone through three tumultuous summers of race riots with forty-three deaths in Detroit and twenty-five in Newark. But the third worst city was Milwaukee, Wisconsin, where four died. Race polarized the state. And many of the Polish and German working-class neighborhoods of Milwaukee were angry about black protestors, blaming the influence of outsiders and communists. Of course, contentious battles over civil rights legislation had taken place all over America. Militant alternatives to non-violent protest, such as the Black Panthers, had sent a shiver through the country. America was as much polarized over race as it was over Vietnam. On February 19 race came further into focus as the Kerner Commission warned of "two societies, one black, one white—separate but unequal." It urged a "commitment to national action—compassionate, massive, and sustained." McCarthy was one of the first national figures to support the findings, in part because Hersh had urged it in a long memo. Race was important to Hersh. He had seen this polarization close up—growing up on the South Side of Chicago and as the AP's special correspondent on race issues.

Hersh and his siblings grew up in an apartment on East 47th Street in Chicago, a neighborhood primarily white and immigrant that had seen many Jewish entrepreneurs start successful businesses. The neighborhood changed dramatically after World War II as African Americans moved in increasing numbers out of what was Chicago's black neighborhood, Bronxeville, into Hyde Park, where Hersh's father operated Regal Cleaners, a dry cleaning store. Many whites fled to wealthy suburbs. The Hersh family stayed, and Isador Hersh served a large black clientele. At the end of the day Sy Hersh would bring the day's earnings to a local bank. One afternoon he noticed a young black man following him. He was scared, thinking he was going to be robbed. But he soon realized that the husky man, known simply as "Piggy," was actually shadowing Sy to make sure no one bothered him. "It later dawned on us—he was protecting us," Hersh recalled. His father's commitment to the neighborhood had won friends for the Hersh family.

When Sy went to work for the AP he was assigned to cover race issues. Chicago was tense. In August 1964 a black woman allegedly stole a $2.60 bottle of gin from a liquor store in Dixmoor, an integrated but predominantly black suburb two miles south of Chicago. When the owner beat the woman, word spread, and crowds of blacks set fire to the store. Riot police—and Hersh—came to the scene. Fights broke out as young whites taunted the protestors. Rocks were thrown at cars of white-driven vehicles. Ten gunshots rang out, and at one point police pushed Hersh down, screaming, "Get back! They're shooting at us!" A black teenager told Hersh: "If they start it, we're gonna finish it." Before it was over at 2:30 a.m., 39 people were injured and 31 arrested as 225 cops and tear gas were needed to quell the disorder. Hersh had seen a race riot.[28]

As the April 2 primary approached, Hersh had more authority than ever in dealing with the press. But he also found access to McCarthy increasingly limited. After a trip to Oregon with McCarthy, Hersh came back to Washington to find he could not even telephone the senator. He had to walk to his Senate office to see him. Once it almost resulted in a fistfight with Charlie Callanan, McCarthy's personal assistant, who had been told to keep Hersh away. Hersh's relations with McCarthy were also tense. Once, while a group sipped martinis, McCarthy inspected a speech Hersh had written. "This is the worst stuff I've ever read," he said. "Lord, I can't believe how bad this is." Finding the remark demeaning, Hersh thought he was supposed to get on his knees like a slave and say, "Well, yessah, I'll go wan 'an fix it up for ya, sah."[29]

A bigger problem was the sparring with the Senate staff, which was still feuding with the campaign staff, but it was also due to the growing influence of Curtis Gans, who did not trust Hersh. But the feeling was mutual. Hersh described Gans as "second rate" and repeated the joke that Gans "had slept through the Kennedy assassination" when he was a UPI reporter in Dallas. This was true, but since Gans had worked the night shift and was sleeping, it was hardly a fair comment. But Gans was a pragmatist, and on the issue of race he butted heads with Hersh.[30]

Hersh not only wanted McCarthy to focus on civil rights—he wanted him to campaign in the ghetto of Milwaukee. Gans disagreed. It would inflame blue-collar workers and conservative Democrats whom McCarthy needed. "The Senator's problem lies where the votes lie in the teeming urban centers," wrote Ned Kenworthy in the *Times*. "And here the Negro vote in a close contest can be crucial."[31] Kennedy was not running in Wisconsin, but the next primary was in Indiana, with a heavy black vote. And eventually California would hinge on getting the minority vote. A Milwaukee organizer for the campaign realized there was no literature on McCarthy's stand on civil rights. He made some, but Gans and Goodwin vetoed it. Student canvassers were told to avoid race. "It amounted to a cold political judgment that seemed slightly out of kilter with the pristine nature of the new politics," wrote Stout. To Hersh, it was just "a dumb thing," orchestrated by Gans. "There was no sense in deemphasizing the ghetto. If we won in the state by 65 percent it would not make a God damned bit of difference if we did poorly in the ghetto," Hersh said.[32]

And it came to a head the night of March 25 when nearly forty staffers—Hersh and Oates included—jammed into Gans's hotel room in Milwaukee to demand that race be a focus. The *Times'* Kenworthy called it a "spreading discontent" and a "staff tempest." Their demands were turned down. The candidate would stay out of black neighborhoods, and race would be underplayed. Soon after he had addressed a crowd of fifteen thousand in Madison, McCarthy said, "I have no problem on civil rights." And, in fact, some felt his record on race was better than Kennedy's. But his demeanor belied that. "He wasn't very good with the blacks," Hersh observed. "He certainly was no bigot, (but) he didn't show soul."[33]

"I was sort of his black man," Hersh explained. On a few occasions Hersh was assigned to accompany McCarthy to secret meetings with blacks in various cities because Hersh was comfortable with people of color. "It would depress me," he said. "They would want to go for him but he wouldn't demonstrate that he had a psychological commitment to the cause." McCarthy was a cold fish, and it was just not his style to display his empathy. But it hurt, and it came to a boil after the meeting in Milwaukee. Hersh and Oates struck back. The prepared a letter of resignation, and Oates apparently leaked it to the *Times'* Kenworthy late in the evening after the meeting.

The resignation caused a huge flap. For three nights in a row the resignations were highlighted in the Huntley-Brinkley NBC news broadcast, the highest-rated news program. The Associated Press called it a "mini-revolt" in the "Children's Crusade." The *New York Times* placed the story on page one, with Kenworthy framing the issue in terms of McCarthy's reluctance to accept how "white racism" was a factor in American cities. The *Milwaukee Journal* also put the story on page one, calling the race factor decisive. Some said to Hersh, "I didn't know a press secretary was so important." Well, Hersh replied, "we're not, but there just wasn't much news being generated." McCarthy was none too pleased. "I don't know why they were unhappy," he said. "I don't have perfect peace and harmony in my campaign. No one does in a campaign." And then he snapped at the reporters, "Most of you fellows are frustrated campaign managers." Goodwin tried to calm the waters, calling it a "tempest in a teapot." But Stout, covering the campaign, insisted the resignations "plagued (McCarthy) throughout the rest of the primaries." McCarthy said nothing could do as much damage as the Hersh resignation story had done.[34]

Some were pleased to have Hersh exit, and Gans said Hersh would have been replaced after Wisconsin. "They were running up and down the halls complaining about McCarthy," Gans said. "We could not have him saying these things. Sy Hersh is not a quiet person." But he did go home quietly even though the biggest bombshell of the campaign was about to come. Two days before the Wisconsin primary—which McCarthy won easily—Lyndon Johnson shocked the world. After a speech on the progress of the Vietnam War, Johnson slipped in the now immortal words, "I shall not seek, and I will not accept, the nomination of my party for another term as your President." Lyndon Johnson was out. The McCarthy campaign had done the unthinkable—the president would not run again, setting up a Eugene McCarthy–Bobby Kennedy showdown. But Sy Hersh would not be a part of it. He was exhausted and fed up, and he returned to Washington DC. "I went home and slept for about a week," Hersh said.[35]

CHAPTER 11

Stunning Triumph over Germs

The End of "Dirty" Politics

Leaving the McCarthy presidential campaign was not easy for Seymour Hersh. "I can hate him and I can love him," Hersh said about the senator, but, mostly, "I love him." Hersh had grown used to dealing with elected officials who left much of the policymaking to staff members. But McCarthy was different; he was smart, and Hersh felt strongly about him, declaring, "I think he would have been a good president," better than Robert Kennedy—and certainly better than Richard Nixon. Hersh also had guilt at how he had left the campaign, with a midnight resignation letter. It was not his style. "They could have gotten me out by simply asking," Hersh said. "I was dying to get out of the job. I hated it. I believed in the campaign but I just couldn't stand the job." The night he resigned, Hersh wanted someone to talk him out of it, but campaign manager Blair Clark was weak and out of touch. And the "inane backbiting" from the old Senate staff and Mrs. McCarthy had worn him down. Hersh knew he could be easily replaced, but he felt the press operation would fall apart quickly when he left. Indeed, the event that followed almost immediately proved that.[1]

Surprised by the adverse reaction to avoiding civil rights, McCarthy's staff made an about-face. Four days after Hersh left, McCarthy's Wisconsin director announced the senator would visit Milwaukee's black neighborhood. "There is not one iota of truth that Senator McCarthy has ducked the civil rights issue," a staffer told the *New York Times*. To prove this a bus filled with reporters accompanied the senator to Milwaukee. It was the type of event McCarthy hated—a spectacle with little meaning beyond symbolism, an event more for the press. And he was uncomfortable wading into crowds. As the *Times* predicted, the senator's reception in the Negro area was "subdued." One McCarthy staffer called it sadly comical. The senator went on a street corner, and groups of blacks—seeing a busload of white people—ran the other way. McCarthy walked quickly though the neighborhood, shook a few hands, and then got back on the bus. He did his duty, but it was not an event that would win him black votes in the Indiana primary.[2]

Although Hersh thought being a press secretary was an "awful job . . . a disgraceful way to spend your life . . . a glorified travel secretary . . . [with] no cerebral thought at all," he actually toyed with returning. In planning for Indiana McCarthy asked, "Can we get Sy to get involved in that?" Hersh entered a negotiation for returning. He met personally with McCarthy. "We'll work you in, Sy," McCarthy told him. And, Hersh said, "I was going to come back," perhaps as a policy analyst. But it did not happen; it was over, or so it seemed. He received dozens of requests to be interviewed and lucrative offers to write a kiss-and-tell account. "I didn't talk to anybody about it," he said. Hersh turned his attention—by necessity—back to his freelance writing, and especially to the issue of chemical and biological weapons disarmament. Just as he was leaving the campaign, *Chemical and Biological Warfare: The Hidden Arsenal* came out in serial fashion in the *New York Review of Books*, a left-leaning publication read by intellectuals. Hersh was on the map, and when the book came out in September, he took to the lecture circuit mostly at college campuses. After a dozen speeches in a few days, he was more sympathetic to McCarthy, who became cranky during the campaign. "I was exhausted," Hersh recalled.[3]

September brought another possibility. Robert Kennedy was assassinated on June 5, the night he won the California primary. Although he felt the campaign was over after the assassination, McCarthy stayed in the race in a showdown with fellow Minnesota senator Hubert Humphrey, who eventually won. The Democratic convention in Chicago, of course, was a debacle, with out-of-control police attacks on demonstrators turning McCarthy's dream of a triumphant march by antiwar partisans into a nightmare of brutality. When it was over, McCarthy took his family to France to recuperate. But some antiwar political activists were not done. The choice of Humphrey, a defender of the war, and Richard Nixon, a lifelong hawk, was a bleak one. Kennedy speechwriter Adam Walinsky contacted Hersh to discuss a new political party with McCarthy at the top of the ticket. He asked Hersh to bring the senator to a meeting, and he did. In September they huddled with Richard Goodwin, Jesse (Big Daddy) Unruh, a powerful California kingpin maker, and a number of Kennedy supporters. McCarthy felt he could win Wisconsin, Minnesota, New York, and California, but he feared the election might go to George Wallace, the conservative southerner who was far riskier than either Nixon or Humphrey.

In the end the idea of a fourth political party went nowhere. And Hersh was done with politics. Journalism had its seamy sides, but politics, he thought, was all "so scurvy . . . so dirty." His foray to the "dark side" was over. But his opponents—and they would become legion as the years passed and as My Lai awaited him—would always use it as proof that he could not be trusted to be anything other than a liberal. Humphrey never recovered from the debacle of Chicago, even though Nixon beat him by only about five hundred thousand votes. On the night of the election, at 4:00 o'clock in the morning, Hersh sat on the front porch of Mary McGrory's Washington home, along with the *Boston Globe's* Robert L. Healy, who eventually ended up on Nixon's enemies list. "I got drunk," Hersh said. "We were all very drunk." Richard Nixon was now the president. The only good news, Hersh said, was he promised so little that any crumb Americans got would be welcome. Nixon had more than a crumb awaiting Hersh, however.

A Stunning Triumph

Sy Hersh had little reason to expect progress from Nixon on chemical and biological weapons. In the 1960 election Kennedy proposed bringing the weapons under international regulation with a view toward their elimination, but Nixon called their continued development essential to defense. When Nixon was elected, he asked the Joint Chiefs of Staff to reassess the weaponry. Little happened, however. Nixon's concern was more with freezing the number of missiles in the Soviet Union's arsenal, which led to the first Strategic Arms Limitation Treaty (SALT) treaty.[4]

But Nixon's priorities changed when he took office. Unbeknownst to Hersh, Nixon's secretary of defense, Melvin Laird, a Wisconsin congressman who vowed to serve only one term, was determined to move aggressively to eliminate chemical and biological weapons (CBW) from the U.S. arsenal. Laird had seen budgets for biological weapons go up through the 1960s as the military argued it needed to keep up with an aggressive CBW program by the Soviet Union. Despite this argument, Laird thought it was time—as did Hersh and many scientists—to seek a ban. It made political sense because it would help deflect protest over American use of herbicides in Vietnam. "I felt the time had come to take action," Laird said years later. Even though the issue was of little concern initially to Henry Kissinger, Nixon's key foreign policy adviser, Laird was adamant that a comprehensive review was needed. "It is clear the Administration is going to be under increasing fire as a result of numerous inquiries," he wrote in a classified memo to Kissinger in April 1969. The inquiries were coming from Congress—but also from the continued work of Hersh, which meant the new administration was under both internal and external pressure. Kissinger went along, writing, "I share your concern." On May 28 he ordered a far-ranging policy analysis that covered everything from the nature of the CBW threat to a review of defoliants being used in Vietnam. The scope was sweeping, even asking for a recommendation on whether the U.S. should finally ratify the Geneva Protocol of 1925, which prohibited chemical and biological warfare and to which most of the world had agreed.[5]

As a policy review got under way, Congress took an interest, spurred in part by Hersh's articles in the *New York Review of Books*. Richard D. (Max) McCarthy, a congressman from Buffalo who was eying a U.S. Senate bid in 1970, took the lead against what he called "the ultimate folly." He was watching television with his wife when NBC aired a documentary on chemical and biological warfare. McCarthy's horrified wife asked him what he knew, and the answer was very little. McCarthy and his staff began to talk to Hersh, who, in essence, briefed them on the problem, which is not surprising given the expertise he had developed. What Hersh found odd was that McCarthy, when he went public, "would repeat things I'd say as his findings. And everybody would say how wonderful it is." Hersh had become a source on the CBW story, and eventually he would be reporting what McCarthy had said, which was really what Hersh had said. Hersh saw the fine line between reporting and creating news and the insider games that get played out in Washington. Nonetheless, Hersh needed Max McCarthy to keep his story moving.[6]

After receiving a special briefing from the Pentagon in March, Max McCarthy made a major speech on the House floor on April 21, attacking the contradictions in the government's statements. Representative Gerald Ford accused him, God forbid, of advocating disarmament. McCarthy followed with public hearings that raised more questions than answers. Hersh chronicled it all in a June article in the *New Republic*, focusing on four congressional probes that were pressuring Nixon to address the growing cloud over this "hidden arsenal." Hersh's story suddenly had legs. "The Pentagon," he wrote, "has constructed in secret a vast CBW network, almost a miniature of the military-industrial complex." America spends four times as much on these weapons as it does on cancer research. And a few weeks later, in the more radical *Ramparts*, Hersh made a leap, pointing to the military's accidental killing of more than six thousand sheep at Dugway, Utah, as "a microcosm of what's wrong with America, of what's really meant by the phrase 'military-industrial complex.'" Lots of money from a government-corporate cabal established "the kind of atmosphere in which operations such as chemical and biological warfare can prosper with no question asked."[7] These were the kinds of words the new administration did not want to hear, worrisome rhetoric that might further inflame protestors who had flooded the nation's campuses in the spring of 1969 in opposition to the war. While Nixon had announced he was bringing home sixty thousand troops, he had also widened the war by secretly dropping bombs on Cambodia. The president did not need a controversy over chemical and biological weapons to get in the way of his dual plans—end the war, his way, and negotiate an arms treaty with the Soviet Union.

Meanwhile, America's staunchest ally, England, put more pressure on Nixon in July, right after Hersh's two articles appeared. At a UN arms control forum in Geneva, the Brits proposed a total ban on the production and stockpiling of biological, but not chemical, weapons. Then, on September 19, America's arch-enemy added to the emerging debate when Soviet foreign minister Andrei Gromyko gave a major speech on CBW policy to the United Nations, calling for a comprehensive ban on both chemical and biological weapons and the destruction of existing stocks. The CIA, as Hersh reported, believed the Soviets were talking publicly about disarmament but privately moving ahead furiously. Nonetheless, events were moving at lightning speed. What would the United States do? The week after Gromyko's speech, Hersh weighed in again in the most prestigious news forum in the country, the *New York Times Magazine*. Clearly, people inside the Pentagon and the White House were now talking to Hersh. Still, he complained, "the secrecy over biological efforts has been almost an obsession with the military." The government won't even acknowledge "that America is heavily involved in a biological research and development program" or that it is "fully capable today of mounting an effective attack with biological warfare." Only Congressman McCarthy is single-handedly mounting a challenge to U.S. policy, he declared.[8] But Hersh's sources were not all that good. Hersh picked up Laird's softened position on CBW, but he did not know that inside the White House Laird was aggressively pushing a ban. Nor did he know that shortly before his article appeared the administration's top science adviser had produced an internal report that urged destroying all existing stockpiles, which, he argued, were unreliable for a military attack and, moreover, ran the risk of mutating into an uncontrollable disease. No final decision had been made, with some military officials adamantly arguing that the Soviets were ramping up their CBW program.[9]

The various options had not yet been put before the president, but pressure on Nixon came from all directions, including Hersh, who was now journalism's foremost expert on this worldwide issue. His voice was still a bit shaky, however, and Hersh the reporter is more evident than the advocate, at least in the early part of his long *Times* September 28 article. He relies on McCarthy to make allegations. One in particular is interesting. McCarthy says a reliable source told him the United States was close to using biological weapons against Cuba in the early 1960s. That unnamed source was Hersh. Hersh mainly relies on scientists and Pentagon insiders to present the "doomsday" possibilities that a spread of bacteria could present. As the article nears its conclusion, Hersh's voice grows stronger. "The need for a biological disarmament agreement has been long overdue," he declares, repeating what he only implied in his book a year earlier, before Britain, the Soviet Union, and Laird came on board. Britain, he points out, may be the world's leader in research and expertise, but "the biggest culprit—in terms of perpetuating a CBW arms race—has been the U.S. military." And therefore, he concludes, "The burden, clearly, for the future control of biological warfare is on the United States, the nation that is the world leader in the development of biological weapons."[10]

Less than two weeks after Hersh's *Times* article, the White House convened a meeting of Nixon, National Security Adviser Kissinger, Secretary of State William Rogers, Secretary of Defense Laird, Joint Chiefs Chairman General Earl Wheeler, Arms Control Agency Director Gerard Smith, and CIA Director Richard Helms. Nixon, well prepared, asked a number of cogent questions as he listened to a debate on a ban. The group agreed that chemical and biological weapons needed to be discussed as separate classes of weapons. And no one argued that chemical weapons should be banned. Banning biological weapons, however, had the support of everyone but the Joint Chiefs. Nixon expressed no preferences; when he returned to his office, however, he quickly signed an order to ban biological weapons from America's arsenal and to destroy stockpiles, a startling change in American policy dating back to 1943—one that had cost $726 million.

For Nixon, morality was not the issue—politics and image making were. Nixon knew that germ warfare was unpredictable and might do more harm than good; that America's nuclear arsenal provided enough deterrent that an enemy was unlikely to risk a biological first strike; and that banning biological weapons might discourage hostile nations from acquiring a "poor man's atomic bomb" that could serve as a military equalizer. More than anything, however, "Nixon wished to be seen as a 'man of peace' at a time when the Vietnam War was provoking strong opposition both at home and abroad," observed scholar Jonathan B. Tucker, an expert on the decision.[11] Added to Nixon's woes was that on November 13 the first installment of Hersh's My Lai articles had made national headlines. The White House needed to shift the focus.

The administration wanted to make a big international splash with its announcement. On the morning of November 25 Kissinger met with reporters in the kind of background session for which he later became famous—or infamous. No attribution or quotes; the spotlight would be on the boss, who would make the announcement. "Yes, we are giving up a means of retaliation," he told the press. "But when we considered the long-term effect of bacteriological warfare, what would be involved in using it, we concluded . . . the consequences would be too uncontrollable."[12]

Later in the day the president made his announcement. "Mankind already carries in its own hands too many of the seeds of its own destruction," he said. "By the examples we set today, we hope to contribute to an atmosphere of peace and understanding between nations." The next day the headline blared across the top of the *New York Times:* "Nixon Renounces Germ Warfare."[13] Foreign leaders praised the initiative. Max McCarthy and others complained that the president did not go far enough and that by avoiding chemical weapons, the United States could still use defoliants in Vietnam. But the criticisms were minor. After all, the achievement was significant and marked the first time that a major power had unilaterally renounced an entire category of weapons of mass destruction.

It would be easy to give credit for this major policy change to Seymour Hersh's two-year effort. And he deserves considerable credit—for breaking ground with a story no one else wanted. For being his usual dogged self, digging deeply into places where he was not wanted. And for going out on a limb—as investigative reporters do—to stake out a position that had not yet been reached by policymakers—or the public. But his role is more complicated. What credit does Hersh get for this triumph? I posed this question to Dr. John Ellis van Courtland Moon, a scholar who was working on a book on American biological weapons and an expert on the subject's history. Hersh's book and articles were being read by scientists and the military. But, Moon said, "he was preaching to the choir." The CBW reformers were already looking for disarmament, a halt to production, and stricter international regulations, led especially by Harvard professor Mathew Meselohn, who first briefed Kissinger. But Moon also noted that when Hersh's work appeared, it buttressed the beliefs of disarmament advocates who, until Hersh came along, had no public voice. Laird was comfortable taking an aggressive stance in the White House because

Hersh's book made it easier, and when the *New York Times* gave voice to the story, it became legitimate. Hersh was painting a scary picture that aroused both reformers and antiwar dissenters. He gave voice to what even those inside the military were saying. His conferral of status to the need for disarmament made it easier for everyone—from Nixon to Max McCarthy—to take a public stand against continued production. No doubt, Moon said, "it had an impact."[14] Later, in assessing how one become knowledgeable on the issue of chemical and biological weapons, one scholar said: "One must study Pulitzer Prize–winning Seymour Hersh's seminal work, *America's Hidden Arsenal*."[15]

Without Hersh's work biological warfare disarmament may have gotten done anyway—but it is not certain. His lone journalistic voice made the issue impossible to ignore. It was a stunning triumph for the thirty-year-old Hersh, one that gets lost because as Nixon was announcing the ban, Hersh was off tracking down the My Lai scandal. Nonetheless, he had his first great victory in hand.

CHAPTER 12

Scoop Artist Meets the Viet Cong

"God Will Punish You, Calley"

Winning the Pulitzer Prize changes a reporter's life. Legendary columnist Mike Royko, who worked briefly for Sy Hersh when he ran a suburban Chicago newspaper, won his Pulitzer in 1972. When a colleague earned the prize, Royko summed up what it meant: "Congratulations, you've just written the first line of your obituary." No matter what else he did for the rest of his career, Hersh would be known as the man who won the Pulitzer Prize for uncovering the My Lai atrocity. As 1982 Pulitzer winner John White observed. "It's the dream everyone has—it's like going for the moon and reaching it." And that's how it was for Sy Hersh. He and David Obst, who had syndicated the My Lai stories, moved into a three-room suite of offices in the National Press Building in Washington. Hersh got himself a New York agent to handle his affairs. "A good agent," he said, "who made sure I made as much as I could if I were a top-flight reporter for one of the big newspapers."[1]

The Pulitzer led to a book contract with Random House from which the newspaper rights alone earned Hersh $40,000. As he crisscrossed the country in search of evidence on the cover-up of My Lai, Hersh became a college campus sensation. The notoriety of My Lai and the antiwar fervor on campuses put him in great demand, and his speaking fee rose to $1,500. Similar to a politician who develops a stump speech when he campaigns, Hersh perfected a moving My Lai message.

In early 1970, for example, Hersh visited a State University of New York college in the small village of New Paltz, seventy miles north of New York City. The college of five thousand students was a hotbed of radicalism as students took over an administration building. Hersh's visit packed seven hundred into the college's largest auditorium. The often unkempt Hersh was dapper in jacket and tie. He carried note cards but, typically, rarely glanced at them. "He uses old-fashioned free association," commented Robert Katz, Hersh's booking agent for twenty years. Hersh's mind works at lightning speed as he jumps from thought to thought, although always with an overall theme. "He doesn't prepare his talks," offered David Jackson, a reporter with the *Chicago Tribune* who watched Hersh get ready to speak. "His mind just starts going." This night in New Paltz, "it was a My Lai talk but the framework was American foreign policy," recalled Gerald Sorin, a history professor who attended. Sorin said Hersh told the audience: "America is not innocent. It was a broader framework than just My Lai." But within the framework Hersh wove some of his most startling massacre anecdotes.[2]

He explained how Charlie Company, William Calley's unit, lost soldiers on patrols. "Everyone would talk in terror of their private parts being blown up," he said. "They were increasingly angry." Finally they were told that the next day they would encounter the "enemy" face to face. That night, "the kids did what those kids did: they toked up," and he put his hands to his face as if he were smoking a joint. At 3:30 in the morning "they got on a chopper" and went to the village of My Lai, "to kill or be killed." But they met only old men, women, and children making morning tea. So, "they put 'em in ditches and shot and shot and shot," Hersh said matter-of-factly. "What I am telling you is empirical." He would know—he spoke to sixty-two of the sixty-seven soldiers involved. It was the white soldiers who did most of the shooting, he said. Twenty-five black and Hispanic soldiers "shot, but they shot high. It just wasn't their war. If the whitey wants to go do this . . ."

And then, as the audience sat silently, he said a Vietnamese mother who was dead had cradled her small child to protect him. When the shooting was done the boy crawled out and ran. "Plug him," Calley told Paul Meadlo, the soldier who went on national television. Meadlo refused. "Calley, with this great show of bravado, ran behind the kid in front of everybody and shot him in the head," Hersh said. "Big man on campus." More silence. Hersh, barely pausing, said the next day Meadlo stepped on a land mine and lost his right leg. They called in helicopters to get him to a hospital, and with soldiers surrounding him, he said to Calley, "God has punished me, Calley, and God will punish you." The soldiers could not stand his taunts, "Get him out of here, get him out of here. They didn't want to hear it." Concluded Hersh: "The kids who did the shooting were as much victims as the people they shot." There was spontaneous applause. "But a pocket of the audience sat still, scowling, mostly faculty 'patriots' who did not like his message," remembered Sorin. "They were not happy." But they were clearly in the minority. When it was over, Hersh received a standing ovation.[3]

Hersh was constantly on the go. He did fourteen talk shows on a trip to Chicago, mixing Vietnam with talk about sex and women's issues. Sometimes, at the colleges, he took chances, often beginning his talk by asking if there were any Vietnam vets who had manned helicopters. When there were, he said: "Tell the audience about the skids." And the soldiers told how helicopters flew low and struck Vietnamese farmers or peasants with the craft's skids. "I discovered the quickest way to demonstrate not only the depth of savagery in Vietnam but also the widespread knowledge of it among the military," Hersh explained.[4] In his low-key reportorial way, Hersh was a hit. He packed the house one night at the University of Minnesota. "The students gave me a standing ovation—fifteen minutes—I'm a fucking celebrity," he declared. Never one to be modest, he commented after an appearance on CBS's *60 Minutes*, "They told me I was great—I'm stupendous on television—never get rattled." He did a segment for NBC's *Today* show and concluded, "Boy, I was good. Sensational."[5] The touring enabled him and his growing family—he now had two children—to move to a larger Washington house. Despite his newfound celebrity, Hersh's focus was still on My Lai.

Hersh's newspaper articles and his My Lai book established clearly what happened. He then turned to a formal government inquiry that began eleven days after his initial November 13, 1969, exposé. The Peers Commission report (described in chapter 3) charged thirty individuals with participating in or knowing about the killings and doing nothing to prevent or report them.[6] When the report was leaked to Hersh, he turned it into two long articles in the *New Yorker*. And the *New York Times* put his revelations on page one.[7]

Hersh's My Lai fame was now worldwide. He turned down considerable money from someone who wanted to make a film out of the atrocity, even though over the years he has been accused of profiting unduly from the massacre incident. The European press wrote about his new revelations, and the Soviet Union authorized newspapers to print a serial version of the cover-up book. And the North Vietnamese, thinking either that he was an honest broker or that he could be used, twice invited him to see how they were treating American prisoners, one of the war's most contentious issues. Nearly 1,500 American soldiers had been lost, and about 500 were likely still alive in North Vietnam's dozen prison camps. "Some people I really trusted [told] me there were some serious signs of trouble" in the treatment of POWs, Hersh said. Despite how harshly the *Times'* Harrison Salisbury had been treated for his 1967 trip behind enemy lines, Hersh accepted. *New Yorker* editor William Shawn asked Hersh to write about POWs, and he discussed also filing stories for the *Times*. The kid from Chicago was now a foreign correspondent.[8]

Hunting for POWs

Hersh intended to visit Vietnam in early 1970, but when the Peers investigation began, the army closed access to all sources. However, the North Vietnamese promised him special access to places that had been kept out of sight. He waited for weeks in Vientiane, Laos, for a visa. He arrived for a two-week visit in March, staying at the luxurious Hotel Metropole, a 1901 landmark where Jane Fonda stayed, but which was now virtually deserted in wartime Hanoi. His hosts, who initially did not remember he was coming, dropped him off and insisted he take a nap after his long journey. "Of course, I didn't," Hersh said. "I was full of piss and vinegar." He immediately wandered into a small park where children, just out of school, greeted him in impeccable English. The next day he got to work but—to his disappointment—the North Vietnamese had a rigid agenda. "They pretty much gave me the standard tour," he said. Not that he was the standard visitor. "Everybody knew who I was. I was sort of a culture hero there," he said. "The gentleman who told the truth about the war," was how workers greeted him. It bothered Hersh enormously. He told them, "Look, I'm not somebody here who's going to make a statement for you. I'm a journalist." March 16 marked the four-year anniversary of the My Lai massacre, and he talked to a number of survivors. The North Vietnamese wanted Hersh to go on radio to talk, but he refused, saying, "I just didn't think it was my business to go on the air." He would not let himself become "Hanoi Jane."[9]

The Vietnamese took him to a Hanoi museum that depicted the rout of South Vietnamese troops at a battle in Laos. They called it the biggest victory of the war since the 1968 Tet offensive and said it proved Nixon's policy of Vietnamization—turning the war over to the South Vietnamese—was a failure. "Whether that judgment is right cannot be assessed adequately from here," Hersh wrote in the first of more than 250 stories he would write in the *Times* over the next nine years.[10] But the Vietnamese had to be more pleased with this story than the Nixon administration, which was secretly negotiating a trip by the president to communist China, a shocking diplomatic foray for the longtime Cold Warrior. Nonetheless, Hersh had his first byline in the *Times*. "Ah, the 'by-line,'" wrote Max Frankel, later to be the *Times* top editor. "Your name immortalized in the world's greatest newspaper, in bold type atop your own prose."[11] Three days later Hersh described how the Vietnamese were making use of virtually all material retrieved from shot-down American planes—and there were hundreds. "The claim of destruction of American aircraft may be impossible to verify, but there is no question that aircraft wreckage has become a part of the culture," Hersh pointed out. Hersh dampened the propaganda tour, however, when he insisted that his hosts describe in detail the fate of one soldier, Everett Alvarez Jr., the first American shot down in 1964 and held captive for eight years. His hosts accommodated, describing the day Alvarez's plane was shot down. "There was a great cheer," Hersh was told, and then the villagers came with bamboo sticks intending to hurt him, but his captors protected him. "He was swooping down to do terrible things but now he had no way of harming us," Hersh's guide said. Alvarez was sent to one of the North's many hidden prisons, where he remained for eight years. A year after Hersh's visit, Alvarez was released. But Hersh never got to see him.[12]

In fact, if Hersh's goal was to find out about American prisoners, his two weeks were a flop. He returned each night to his hotel, where he would eat in a private restaurant. But he was isolated. "I was lonely," he said. One night, Hersh recalled, he talked to a bunch of monkeys. Some evenings, accompanied by interpreters, he wandered nearby streets. He talked to many wounded soldiers who, to his surprise, spoke glowingly of how the Americans fought. "They were very tough fighters," one told him. When he wrote this, his hosts were not pleased. "It caused a hassle," Hersh wrote, but he was never censored as he filed his stories from Reuters' Hanoi office for a dollar a word. The North Vietnamese were reading his stories carefully. In one he quoted an official as saying American flyers had avoided bombing a key bridge where dozens of American planes had been shot down. Not until Hersh's last day did they permit it to be published—with a clarification; the official did not mean to criticize the Americans. They knew Hersh's stories were being dissected by American intelligence. He filed a few sensitive stories after he left the country.[13]

Finally, on March 15, Hersh met two American prisoners, and he wrote the one dispatch that landed on page one. The Vietnamese dismissed the POW issue as a smokescreen concocted by Richard Nixon to avoid negotiating peace. "The prisoners are only a small part of the war as a whole," the editors of North Vietnam's official newspaper told Hersh. Hersh did not disagree. "I knew [the POW situation] was very much politicized by the Nixon administration," he said. He met the prisoners under what he called "sad conditions." They appeared healthy but were restrained, offering little to give any real sense of how POWs were being treated. More than likely they had carefully rehearsed their answers to avoid any problems when they returned to prison. North Vietnamese officials "did not seem to realize that interviews with a few carefully selected pilots in a less than open atmosphere fell short of demonstrating the adequacy of treatment," Hersh wrote. But he let them describe some of their experience. Colonel Edison Miller of Tustin, California, told Hersh that his wife "knows that I love her and that I miss her," but the "Vietnamese have suffered much worse than I have." Hersh did not do much to pierce the world of the POWs. "I was very disappointed," Hersh concluded. "I wanted to go into a camp. I didn't like the fact they didn't let me." And although some prison camps were known to be in Hanoi, Hersh never got to one. Working the phones was easier than working the streets in an enemy country.[14] Hersh wrapped up the tour with fifteen hours of interviews with two high-ranking North Vietnamese officials who had a pointed message: if North Vietnam triumphs—not that victory is close—it will not impose socialism, nor will it let America impose its will on the country. "You can say that we have not fought 720 years," one official said, "to let the South come under neo-colonialism."

Reporter Sy Hersh in North Vietnam was more a water boy—carrying messages to the United States—than the scoop artist who uncovered My Lai. He also was hoodwinked. He did not know the Vietnamese were about to launch—soon after he left—the Easter offensive, a massive invasion of the demilitarized zone between the two countries to seize territory for leverage at peace talks. "I felt like I'd had my pants pulled off," he said. "I'd gone down there and I'd never even smelled it." He flew home disappointed, but he also was thinking his freelance career was about to end. After his third article, the *Times* removed the short italic note describing him as a freelance writer. They simply began to use his byline as with full-time correspondents. "That's essentially how I figured out Abe had offered, or was going to offer, me a job," Hersh said.[15] He was correct. Despite Hersh saying "fuck you" to Abe Rosenthal in a phone conversation three years earlier, the *Times* ambitious editor knew he needed to add a top-flight investigative reporter, someone less concerned about "the news that was fit to print" than about the news no one else could get. Hersh was the man.

CHAPTER 13

The *Times* Calls

A Tip Leads to a Crusade

The *New York Times* is the most well known and highly respected newspaper in the world. As the Bible of the intelligentsia, a must-read for everyone in government, finance, and academe, its foreign news and diplomatic coverage is as closely watched as is the State Department or the United Nations. Former *Times* reporter Gay Talese described it as "a cathedral of quiet dignity." Said Seymour Hersh, "The *Times* is the best newspaper in the country. No question about it. Every budding journalist wants to work for the *Times*." In fact, Hersh wanted to join the newspaper as far back as 1970. Pulitzer Prize–winning *Times* reporter John Darnton recalled being at a journalism convention soon after Hersh had won his Pulitzer Prize. "Hersh was a superstar," Darnton said. "Everyone talked about him." When he gave his talk, Hersh said his goal was to work for the *Times,* which thrilled Darnton, who saw it as vindication that, despite the counterculture tone of the day, his own decision to work at the establishment *Times* was a good one.[1] Hersh was not bashful in approaching the *Times.* "How about a job?" he asked Rosenthal just before he left for North Vietnam. "I am anxious to do some writing about other aspects of American life . . . . I've had it with mass murders."

The *Times* had been vetting Hersh for two years. In 1970 Washington bureau chief Max Frankel located seven of Hersh's Dispatch News Service stories—including his My Lai articles—and sized them up. He was worried because, he wrote Abe Rosenthal, "some people have borne vague suspicions that Hersh is given to editorial axes." The *Times* had heard the rumors: he was an untrustworthy lefty! "I came with the mark of Cain on me because I was clearly against the war," Hersh said. But Frankel found

Hersh to be "a reporter first of all. He has mastered the techniques of marshaling factual evidence and avoiding the crusader's instinct. I think we should not let him walk by." But they did, and a year later, when his name resurfaced again, Frankel called Hersh "first-rate" yet concluded, "We do have a number of good investigative reporters." Hersh had to wait until he proved himself with his trip to North Vietnam; he was offered a job in April 1972. He was eager to get started. "I'll be forwarding a long list of story ideas—some of which I have been working on for years," he wrote Rosenthal assistant Peter Millones.[2]

Despite its star-studded cast of reporters—Hersh was joining a newspaper with five Pulitzer Prize winners, including Rosenthal—the *Times* did not have a reputation as an investigative paper. Sassy *Times* reporter John L. Hess observed that "muckraking . . . tended to make the Times brass nervous." In fact, he added, "truly investigative, questioning, skeptical reporting was practically unTimesian." But Rosenthal knew that smaller publications—*Philadelphia Inquirer, Boston Globe*—were winning Pulitzers, and that the *Washington Post* was outpacing the *Times* in the nation's capital. He knew also the *Times* revenues and circulation were flagging, putting the newspaper in serious financial trouble. The *Times* needed to catch up with a trend that was catching fire. "They hired me to be an investigative reporter," Hersh said.[3]

But his first assignment was of a different sort. Hersh barely had time to unpack when the *Times* sent him to Paris, where the Vietnam peace talks were unraveling. His high-level contacts with the North Vietnamese were put to work. An anonymous North Vietnamese official insisted to Hersh that Nixon's bombing of the North must halt before talks could resume. "No matter how disastrous the bombing is for our people, it brings about no change in our attitude," the official said. In his first big story for the *Times,* Hersh was allowed to use an unnamed person to yell at the Americans. A day later the head of the Vietcong delegation gave Hersh a ninety-minute interview at a villa near Paris. His long article deftly wove demands the United States was making with candid views of the other side, a rarely heard voice in the American press. The peace negotiations were especially troubled since, the day before, the United

States had placed explosives in Haiphong harbor, where Hersh had just reported how the key port had withstood years of bombing.

In his third story for the *Times* Hersh wrote a "news analysis" on the delicate dance that the negotiations presented. Veteran reporters, such as Hess, who was covering the talks in Paris, must have been miffed at the latitude given the thirty-five-year-old Hersh. It was one thing for heavyweight columnists like James Reston and Anthony Lewis to weigh in on the op-ed page, but for the new kid on the block to be given such privileges was remarkable. Nonetheless, covering diplomacy was not what Hersh was hired to bring to the *Times*.[4] Hersh returned to the *Times* moribund Washington bureau, looking for a topic he could sink his teeth into. He did quick hits on familiar topics. Someone leaked the final version of the Peers Report, and Hersh hit page one with news that forty-three officers—including two generals—were charged with covering up the killings. It was news he had already reported in the *New Yorker*.[5]

And then his telephone rang with a call from Otis G. Pike, a six-term congressman from Riverhead, New York, and a member of the House Armed Services Committee. Since they did not have a previous relationship, Hersh was unsure why Pike called. But the congressman told him, confidentially, he should look into the case of General John David Lavelle, fifty-five, who had just been mysteriously relieved as commander of all air force activities—including bombing missions—in Southeast Asia. Something was terribly amiss, Pike said. The military first said Lavelle was ill, but then it conceded that "irregularities" caused his dismissal. "The Air Force did not tell the truth," Pike told Hersh. Hersh wasted no time. He tracked down Lavelle on a golf course. "He conned me into meeting him," said Lavelle. And, as he did with William Calley's lawyer, Hersh bluffed, telling the general he had information that President Nixon personally ordered him to make unauthorized attacks. "I told [Hersh] the report was full of inaccuracies," recalled Lavelle, who died in 1979. After Hersh, an expert golfer, gave lessons to two of Lavelle's sons, the men went inside to talk. Lavelle said Hersh "just dreamed up" stuff to get him talking. But Hersh's ploy worked again. "He got out of me," Lavelle conceded, "more information than I should have given him."

Lavelle advised him not to write a story before congressional hearings, but two days before they began Hersh told him: "My editor has made the decision; we are going to publish." Lavelle said Hersh removed any inaccuracies, but the incident and the fact that Hersh tricked Lavelle into talking with his bluffing made him angry. "I never did talk to the press again," he said.[6] Many years later the Lavelle family was still angry at Hersh's coverage.

On June 11 Hersh was on page one, tapping his military and congressional sources—all anonymous—to report that Lavelle was ousted because he had ordered repeated unauthorized bombing attacks on North Vietnam. These came before the North had launched a March 30 invasion, which led Nixon to order retaliatory attacks. The Lavelle-ordered bombings—as Pike suggested—raised two serious questions. Did Lavelle's superiors—Defense Secretary Melvin Laird, Joint Chiefs Chairman Thomas H. Moorer, and Vietnam commander General Creighton T. Abrams—order the attacks? Hersh wasted no time in asking, "Who authorized such missions?" At the time of the attacks it was well known the White House carefully controlled bombing. And if Lavelle's superiors did not know, then an even more "grave" question was: "Is it possible for a battlefield commander to grossly violate operational orders and not be detected for three months?" A. M. Rosenthal was tickled pink. His investigative reporter was already paying dividends. As Hersh mounted his first crusade for the *Times,* the squirming in the White House began—and would get worse. Laird secretly told Pike that too much poking around into the Lavelle affair could jeopardize the president's reelection.[7] Pike refused to be silent—and he kept calling Sy Hersh.

Hersh the "Troublemaker"

The newspaper crusade—much in decay today—is an old-fashioned journalistic tool, perfected by publishing giants Joseph Pulitzer and William Randolph Hearst in the 1890s. It combines reportorial exposé with editorial advocacy, and the result of documenting abuse and demanding action is often social change. The *Times,* however, has never been a crusading newspaper; it is the paper of record. But the *Times* has what Reston labeled a "ripple" effect. When it legitimizes an issue, everyone follows.

Hersh quickly learned this. Over a six-month period—as the White House became increasingly anxious—he mounted a thirty-one-story crusade that spurred investigations by the U.S. House of Representatives and the Senate and forced the Nixon administration to plot a cover up that was a trial run for Watergate.

Events moved fast in what became known as the Lavelle Affair. The reason, in part, was that Hersh kept finding pieces of a puzzle that had Washington abuzz. Pike called a hearing on June 12 to question Lavelle and his superior, General John D. Ryan, the air force's representative on the Joint Chiefs of Staff. Hersh wrote an advance story the day of the hearing, giving Pike the chance to raise the key questions. "I don't honestly know if General Lavelle is a hero or a villain," he said, but the Pentagon is "trying to sweep a scandal under the rug. All I've gotten is curves thrown up at me."[8] The question was about complicated military rules of engagement. Ever since Lyndon Johnson halted bombing of Vietnam in 1968, planes accompanying reconnaissance flights over enemy territory could bomb surface-to-air-missile sites that had fired on them first. This was called "protective reaction." Did Lavelle use the cover of protective reaction to bomb North Vietnam without approval, a violation of the complex rules? The government said he did, and sought to force his retirement, busting him to lieutenant general, the first time a general has been asked to retire at a lower level.

The war of words heated up the first day as Lavelle and Ryan quarreled. Lavelle insisted the bombings had been approved by Creighton Abrams, commander of troops in Vietnam who was being considered for reappointment. Lavelle said he was told to liberally interpret the "protective reaction" rules to permit bombing, but Ryan said Lavelle was removed because of "irregularities" in 28 bombings by 147 aircraft. Lavelle ordered records falsified to cover up unauthorized air strikes, Ryan said, which Lavelle heatedly denied. Lavelle's denial looked weak the next day when Hersh reported that an air force sergeant—whose name was not revealed—had sent a letter to his senator, Harold Hughes, and complained that "we have been reporting that our planes have received hostile reactions whether they have or not." The sergeant didn't know who ordered the falsification. Still, it begged the question: did Lavelle order the bombings and cover-up on his own? "There was a high command officer involved," said Hughes.[9]

Unbeknownst to Hersh or Congress, on that same day, June 14, Nixon, considerably agitated about the emerging scandal, met with Secretary of State William Rogers and National Security Adviser Henry Kissinger. "That damn general is going to cause you a lot of trouble; that Lavelle," Rogers said. Nixon replied: "What the hell is that all about? And is he being made a goat? If he is . . . it's not good. I don't believe in it." Presumably the president meant "scapegoat." Kissinger blamed Laird for removing Lavelle soon after the sergeant's letter went to the secretary of the air force, whose investigation discovered falsified documents. Aggravated, Nixon asked, "Why did he even remove him? You, you destroy a man's career." Later, Nixon returned to Lavelle. "We all know what protective reaction is. I don't want a man persecuted for doing what he thought was right. I just don't want it done." Nixon then asked, "Can we do anything now to stop this Goddamn thing." Growing more furious, Nixon said, "Why the hell did this happen?" Laird, Nixon said, "knows Goddamn well, that I told him, I said it's protective reaction. He winks, he says, 'Oh I understand.'" The president was remembering a February 3 conversation with Ambassador to Vietnam Ellsworth Bunker during which the president ordered that American fighter planes should not have to wait to be attacked before firing back. Expand the definition of "protective reaction," he demanded. "Who the hell's gonna say they didn't fire?" And "if it does get out . . . he says it is a protective reaction strike. . . . we can bomb the hell out of a lot of other stuff."[10] But now it *was* out, and Lavelle was getting the blame—for the time being.

When Hersh bluffed Lavelle, saying the president ordered the bombing, he had no idea how close he was to the truth. "I did not know Nixon was involved," Hersh said years later. But the rest of the press began to smell blood in the water. "This is the largest contingent of press I've seen here since the My Lai situation," said Representative Charles Gubsen of California. The day after the first public hearing the *Times* ran five stories, including a column by Reston and an editorial that demanded punishment and a closer look by Congress. Reston lamented that the White House always wanted to blame "troublemakers" like Seymour Hersh and muckraking columnist Jack Anderson. Who is really responsible for this mess, Reston wondered.[11] Two days later, by the way, the White House's other "mess" began. Six men were captured at the Watergate Office complex and charged with breaking into the headquarters of the Democratic National Committee. Cub reporter Bob Woodward of the *Washington Post* went to the burglars' arraignment.

"Troublemaker" Hersh was clearly in charge of leading the media inquiry as he widened the story past General Lavelle. First, he located four former air force analysts who told him that in 1970 they regularly used "protective reaction" to cover up unauthorized bombing missions over Vietnam and Laos. A former air force captain called protective reaction "very much of a joke," adding it "allowed us to go out and bomb North Vietnam all the time." Another airman said it was a euphemism "to bomb the hell out Vietnam." Those were Nixon's exact words in the Oval Office. No wonder, columnist Tom Wicker wrote, the North Vietnamese snicker at Nixon's "peace proposals. "The other side does not trust our word, and has little reason to do so." The Pentagon would not respond to Hersh.[12] But the government got testy the next day when Hersh reported the number of "protective reaction" strikes was three times the twenty-five that had been publicly conceded. "It was a constant joke . . . an excuse to hit," said a former intelligence officer. Hersh stated the obvious: "the controversy over protective reaction has spread." Especially so when one airman reported that Admiral John S. McCain, father of the future presidential candidate, was regularly told of the attacks. The Pentagon's terse reaction: "If those men say whatever they say, that is their problem." Hersh called the scandal "the most potentially significant of the air war."[13] Hughes insisted on a Senate investigation: Are others guilty beside Lavelle? Has Nixon lost control of the air war? Did Gen. Abrams know?

Hersh did not wait for the Senate to come up with answers. He found six defense specialists who concluded that control over the military was much less restrictive under Nixon than under Lyndon Johnson. One concluded the "protective reaction" gambit had been going for three years, but, another added, there is "no big conspiracy here." These are just "the rules of the game." Of course, the reader had no way of knowing who was talking. All six remained anonymous. But it was alarming enough for the

Times to editorialize again, comparing the Lavelle affair to My Lai and questioning whether Creighton Abrams should be reappointed commander of military operations. And the Senate Armed Services Committee agreed. Mississippi senator John Stennis, a pro-military Democrat who headed the committee, called for hearings. He wanted to hear from Abrams, Lavelle, and the sergeant whose letter started the affair. Hersh began his exposé with a tip from Representative Pike, but now Senator Stennis also became a regular source. "We would talk on the phone nearly every morning, early," Hersh said. The ultra-conservative Stennis got along just fine with the liberal reporter. Even though Hersh's congressional sources were impeccable, he did not know about another White House meeting that took place soon after Nixon had a chance to see Hersh's June 19 story.[14]

Kissinger urged the president to stay clear of the Senate inquiry. "Frankly, Henry," Nixon said, "I don't feel right about our pushing him [Lavelle] into this thing and then giving him a bad rap! You see what I mean?" Kissinger was vague, but he knew serious matters were about to be aired that could be damaging. Who ordered the bombings? Had Nixon lost control? Should Admiral Moorer not be allowed to stay as the top military official on the Joint Chiefs? Careers were on the line. "I want to keep it away if I can," Nixon said, "but I don't want to hurt an innocent man."[15]

Nixon could have easily put the matter to rest that day. The unauthorized bombings—twenty-nine out of approximately twenty-five thousand flights—were logical responses to the constant use of radar that jeopardized American reconnaissance missions. And they came at a time when it was clear the North Vietnamese were building up for a massive invasion of the South. But Nixon did what became his modus operandi—he chose to cover up what was a logical bending of the rules of engagement, one the public would have understood. Privately, even the air force was asserting: "There was ample room for disagreement" about the rules of engagement; a court martial against Lavelle would never hold up. Nonetheless, Nixon held a nationally televised press conference that night and, when asked about Lavelle and his ordering of the bombings, took Kissinger's advice: "It wasn't authorized," and thus "it was proper for him to be relieved and retired."[16]

Inside the Beltway, all eyes focused on the Senate hearings. In "The Private War of General Lavelle," *Newsweek* described a "widespread conspiracy" in which "scores of pilots, squadron and wing commanders, intelligence and operations officers, and ordinary airmen were caught up in the plot." The *Washington Post* said, "What Lavelle did—taking a war into his own hands—has obviously grave implications for the nation in this nuclear age." "Was Lavelle the only bad apple?" asked National Public Radio's Nina Totenberg. Hersh let others make definitive declarations; he simply kept reporting. September 8: The Pentagon knew of at least one of the raids. September 9: Similar raids in Cambodia killed civilians and hit a school bus. This allegation irked the government. It came from a letter to Senator William Proxmire from four intelligence sergeants who released the letter only to Hersh. "We don't know if it's true or not," the air force declared.[17] Exclusive information was becoming Hersh's forte.

The whistleblower who began the scandal with a letter was about to testify. No one had talked to him. But before the hearing Hersh flew to Orlando, Florida, to meet with Lonnie Franks, then twenty-three, spending four hours with him in his small apartment. Still in the air force, he hoped to be a career officer. Many saw the Cedar Rapids, Iowa, Franks as a hero, revealing misdeeds at the peril of his own career. He would speak only to Sy Hersh. "He talks too fast and too loud and doesn't pronounce his words correctly," Franks said, but "he really is a guy who was trustworthy. He listened." Franks detailed how he and many others took three hours to doctor bombing reports after the pilots returned. They had to make it appear the plane had been fired on to justify the dropped bombs. "Everybody knew we were falsifying these reports," he declared. What impressed Franks most was that Hersh insisted on getting names of people who could verify his story, and he called them all. "Lonnie Franks came forward when others didn't," Hersh said. "He wanted the right thing to happen and did what few people would do. Franks told the truth." Hersh hit page one once again. "He was just banging on this story every day," observed Patrick Casey, a lawyer who eventually became counsel to the Lavelle family.[18]

Meanwhile, Lavelle testified behind closed doors that he had neither violated his orders nor overseen a cover-up. Still unresolved was the key question, Hersh wrote: "Did General Lavelle act alone?" It took Hersh only one day to get "well-placed sources" to reveal Lavelle's secret testimony. And the general pointed the finger at Joint Chiefs chairman Moorer and Vietnam commander Abrams. Senator Stuart Symington of Missouri actually left the hearing room on day two and sought out Hersh to tell him: "I am convinced that a lot of people below [Lavelle] and a lot of people above him knew of the attacks." "The Air Force is trying to make a patsy out of him," an unidentified source told Hersh.[19] When the hearings were completed, Hersh reviewed all the conflicting testimony and the status of the probe. But it all led back to one simple conclusion: "Somebody higher up must . . . have known what was going on." He just could not prove it. The hearings continued, but the mountain of facts produced by Congress and the news media could not resolve the diverse accounts. Of course, Nixon and Kissinger could have, but they remained silent while Lavelle was left to sway in the breeze. Lavelle's critics—some wanted him court-martialed—thought he had gotten off too easily. His supporters thought he had been singled out for unfair treatment. Both sides thought there was more to the story than had been told. And Hersh kept trying to uncover more. But after nearly five months, the story ran out of steam. The Lavelle Affair was just about over. The Senate could not find enough documentation to blame General Abrams. As Senator Stennis explained, "There was no testimony that put a hand on him or laid a speck on him." The Senate approved Abrams for another term in Vietnam. And if the scandal did not touch Abrams, it did not touch Moorer. The higher-ups—Abrams, Moorer, McCain—all got their rewards. As the scandal waned, Nixon said he was tired of "all of this goddamn crap about Lavelle!" but he added, "I feel sorry for the fellow because . . . we did tell him . . . if they hit there, go back and hit it again. Go back and do it right. You don't have to wait till they fire before you fire back."[20]

Not a Rogue After All

John D. Lavelle died on July 10, 1979. He was sixty-two and deeply wounded by the attacks on his character, which hastened his death. His family—seven children and wife Mary—all suffered with him during the six months of allegations and public hearings. Seymour Hersh's reporting angered the family, even though Hersh tried to follow the scandal up the ladder and away from Lavelle. The general was not the only one hurt. Lonnie Franks had to leave the air force because his whistle blowing prevented advancement. His commanding officers did not like a tattletale. He remained bitter forty years later when an odd set of coincidences made the story resurface.

Patrick Casey, a Pennsylvania attorney, and his father decided to write a biography of four-star general Jerome F. O'Malley, who served under Lavelle and was a pilot in the unauthorized raids. While researching the book, they retrieved seven hundred pages of White House tapes from 1972, when Nixon discussed the bombing. As the tapes reveal, in February he enlarged the definition of "protective reaction" to allow more punishment of North Vietnam, hoping to bring it finally to its knees.

Defense Secretary Laird then flew to Vietnam and personally told General Lavelle to be aggressive in air strikes and liberally interpret the rules. Laird said the administration will support your efforts. When Lavelle's planes dropped bombs, it was known and scrutinized by various commanding officers. His superiors criticized him only for not being aggressive enough. Lavelle knew the strikes were necessary for two reasons—the North was massing for its March 1972 Easter offensive, and the enhanced radar capability of the Vietnamese had made preemptive strikes vital to preventing planes from being shot down. When radar locked in on the planes, they had to react to survive. Previously only the actual firing of missiles would elicit a "protective reaction." So when flyers returned and said they had fired without prompting enemy fire—meaning no one shot at them before they bombed—the rules of engagement technically did not allow them to retaliate. Radar locking in, Lavelle told his staff, is a reaction. But a radar alert did not qualify on the bureaucracy's paperwork. And thus Franks and others began to change records to indicate the planes had been fired on. They felt that Lavelle has ordered such falsification. When Franks wrote his letter, and the air force found the altered documents, Lavelle immediately ordered the practice stopped. He said he did not know it was taking place.[21]

What became clear to attorney Casey was that Lavelle had authorization for the bombings, and he had not knowingly ordered documents falsified. When he wrote a long article in *Air Force Magazine* in 2007, Casey was contacted by the Lavelle family and then gave the White House tapes to Seymour Hersh, who promptly wrote a *New Yorker* article. Hersh recounted the events, but did not unequivocally clear Lavelle. "The Lavelle incident," he wrote, "has a special resonance: in the midst of a disastrous and unpopular war, a President and his closest confederates authorized actions in violation of both the rules and their own stated policies."[22]

The Nixon tapes were enough for the secretaries of defense and the air force to conclude in 2007 that Lavelle deserved to have his military rank restored. President Obama made that recommendation to the Senate Armed Services Committee in 2010. Only Henry Kissinger still defended the Nixon White House, saying the strikes were not ordered by the president. "That argument is totally false, demonstratively false," he said. But the *New York Times* wrote a rare editorial correction thirty-eight years later. Lavelle, it declared, "was not a rogue officer waging his own 'massive, private air war.'"[23] Hersh still believes the general did authorize that documents be falsified. As this book went to print, the U.S. Senate had not yet cleared Lavelle. And the Lavelle family, forty years later, declined to discuss Seymour Hersh.

CHAPTER 14

Digging into Watergate

Missing the Greatest Story

In August 1972 Robert M. Smith, a thirty-two-year-old reporter in the Washington bureau of the *New York Times*, took the acting director of the Federal Bureau of Investigation, L. Patrick Gray, out to lunch at a fancy French restaurant. Smith had written three page-one stories about Gray, who succeeded J. Edgar Hoover; Gray had taken a liking to the Harvard-educated Smith. In a room crowded with diners, and with Smith unable to take out his reporter's notebook, Gray leaned in and confided. People in very high places in the White House—including the former attorney general, John Mitchell, then heading Richard Nixon's reelection campaign—were involved in the break-in at the Watergate complex that took place on June 17. And the president? Smith asked. "He looked me in the eye without denial—or any comment," Smith said. "In other words, confirmation." The director of the FBI had just implicated the President and the former top law enforcement officer in the country in the yet-to-emerge Watergate scandal.[1] Smith slumped in his chair, shocked, his appetite gone. The FBI director had just laid out the Watergate scandal before anyone—including the *Washington Post's* Bob Woodward and Carl Bernstein—had the story. Unfortunately for Smith, it was his last day. He was leaving the *Times* and going, the next day, to Yale Law School, although Gray did not know that when they scheduled lunch—or when he leaked his news. Smith raced back to the *Times* office and grabbed the news editor, Bob Phelps, insisting they go into Phelps's office. "This is incredible," Smith said, as he tape-recorded his recollection of the conversation while Phelps took notes. "There we were with leads from the acting director of the FBI," Phelps recalled, indicating the president was involved in Watergate, long before anyone suspected, and that it was part of a large-scale White House espionage effort.[2]

With Smith leaving, Phelps had to figure out what to do with the tip. But somehow the story just died. "Why we failed is a mystery to me," said Phelps, who finally disclosed the missed story in 2009 when he was eighty-seven years old. It would have been logical for Phelps to turn to his crackerjack staff of thirty-five reporters. "We had one of the world's finest new bureaus at anytime," observed Smith. The *Washington Post* feared Walter Rugaber more than any other reporter; his early "beats" rivaled Woodward and Bernstein, but Tad Sculz, who had broken the 1961 Bay of Pigs invasion, correspondents Robert Semple, James Naughton, Christopher Lydon, John Crewdson—all good reporters—were also nibbling at the story. And then, of course, there was the thirty-six-year-old Sy Hersh, who the *Times* hired specifically to be their ace investigative reporter. He was the most logical candidate to be given the Gray leak. "I never knew about the conversation," Hersh said.[3]

Smith, still angry about the bumbled opportunity three decades later, observed: "I do not know what happened. I assumed the paper, for some reason, could not confirm it. It was tremendously shattering. Why didn't Phelps do anything with it?" The week after debriefing Smith, Phelps and his wife went on a month's vacation; he thought he gave the notes and the tape to a reporter or editor. When he returned, he never followed up. "It defies any sense," Smith said. "He wasn't a stupid editor." But some wondered if the hands of bureau chief Max Frankel or even powerful columnist James Reston had entered the mix. Hersh was sure that Frankel had talked to Secretary of State Henry Kissinger, who assured him the break-in did not reach the Oval Office. But Phelps said if Frankel was told the story had no merit, he never passed it on nor did anything to call off the staff. "From the top editors on down we all shared in the blame," Phelps said.[4] Which didn't convince an angry Smith and a dubious Hersh.

On one level it is easy to see how the *Times* could miss the story. It was a police story, a break-in, burglars caught red-handed, albeit in the headquarters of the Democratic Party, wearing surgical gloves. The *Washington Post* was a local newspaper; DC was its town. Reporters knew cops and courts and had sources on a beat the *Times* did not cover. The *Times* was interested in the White House and the federal agencies—not cops and robbers. And although it emerged early that the burglars had connections to espionage, no one could nail down the White House connection to the break-in. "From the beginning we saw the possibilities of Watergate as an important story, although certainly not in the dimensions that eventually surfaced," Phelps said. But Phelps simply did not think the scandal could possibly reach into the White House. He and Frankel both asked their reporters to check out the early reporting of Yale graduate Woodward, twenty-nine, and the long-haired, twenty-eight-year-old Bernstein—"snot-nosed" kids, he called them—to see if anyone trusted their findings. The *Times* concluded that the *Post* was "headed down the wrong path," said Frankel, who was Washington bureau chief and eventually became executive editor. Unfortunately, Frankel bemoaned later, the *Times* relied on reporters with "vested interest in bureaucracies, not rookies" with no predispositions.[5]

The forty-two-year-old Frankel was a career *Timesman*, rising from the metro desk to foreign correspondent. In February 1972 he accompanied Richard Nixon and became friends with Kissinger on their historic trip to China; Frankel won the Pulitzer Prize for his coverage of the trip. In May he accompanied Nixon to Moscow to for the signing of a historic arms treaty. Frankel was getting ready to leave Washington to become the paper's Sunday editor in New York. "My involvement with any of the Watergate stuff was so marginal," he said. If anything, Phelps noted, Frankel "wished he had taken a more active role."[6] But Frankel might have ignored the story because he simply could not believe it had sinister implications. "Not even my most cynical view of Nixon had allowed for his stupid behavior," he wrote. "There he sat at the peak of his power; why would he personally get involved in tapping the phone not even of his opponents but only a Democratic Party functionary? For once, my habit of hypothesizing my way through a story slowed me down." Ben Bradlee, editor of the rival *Washington Post,* did not bother to hypothesize. Watergate, he said, "hit you in the face. Five guys in business suits . . . wearing surgical gloves . . . carrying tear-gas fountain pens . . . and walkie-talkies."[7]

Sy Hersh agreed, but he also saw the story very early with a larger frame. When he joined the bureau in 1972, "I was telling him [Frankel] about really big things in the White House," Hersh recalled, saying he and Frankel exchanged memos on the story. Hersh's sources in the White House warned him about the "enemies" mentality of the Nixon administration and the tactics they were plotting. The break-in was not the story. But Frankel turned Hersh down on his Watergate suggestions. "I was not Max's guy," Hersh said, which was odd because it was Frankel who urged Rosenthal to hire him, saying, "His ability would bring us great reward."[8]

And now the biggest reward of all—"the greatest story in a generation," as the *Times* later called it—was at the newspaper's fingertips from Hersh's contacts and the Gray leak. Hersh was so angry at Frankel that he nearly quit soon after he was hired. "I think I would have done the story," Hersh said about Watergate, but Frankel had helped confirm his growing belief that editors were useless. "I always think that they're all mice training to be rats," he said. In fact, he threatened to quit a number of times, Phelps recalled, explaining: "With his reputation . . . he knew he could land a good job. So the threats were not idle. Yet he knew that the *Times* gave him the greatest impact. He told me once that even though he could write endlessly for the *New Yorker,* a much shorter piece in the *Times* had greater effect with policy makers."[9]

Instead of Watergate, Hersh turned for the next ten months to General John Lavelle and Vietnam. "I had deliberately continued writing about Vietnam, staying as far away from Watergate as possible," Hersh said.[10] It would take a drubbing from the *Times'* biggest rival to bring Hersh back to Watergate.

New Sweaters, New "Beat"

Before they won the Pulitzer Prize and became part of American folklore, Bernstein and Woodward were bottom-of-the-rung reporters on the *Washington Post* metropolitan desk. Woodward, a navy veteran whose Republican father was a judge, had scored some triumphs for a suburban newspaper before coming to the *Post.* Bernstein was another story—a pot smoker and college dropout who grew up in various newsrooms. But he could write, and he knew the streets of DC. They were an odd couple—Peck's Bad Boy Bernstein and Ivy League Woodward. But the duo grabbed hold of the Watergate story and, as Frankel later wrote, gave the *Times* "a humbling reminder of the essence of great reporting: dogged detective work that confronts and badgers sources until they cough up the clues that transform suspicion into evidence."[11] Given the chance, Sy Hersh would have surely matched them. Commented Hersh: "If you ask me whether I think I would have cracked Watergate by myself if I had been on it from the beginning ... I'd have to say yes." But he stayed away. When editors beseeched him to join the reporters desperately trying to catch the *Post*, Hersh showed them all the other stories he was working on. Sy was free to pursue whatever he wanted, Phelps noted. He resisted pressure to join the story.[12]

Meanwhile, early in 1972 before the presidential election, Woodward and Bernstein—and ten other *Post* reporters—solidified their hold on the story by coming up with three scoops in succession. The showed that money from the Nixon campaign had gone to one of the burglars; they revealed that Mitchell controlled a secret stash to pay for off-the-books activities; and they learned that the administration and the Committee to Re-Elect the President had a spying scheme to disrupt the campaigns of Nixon challengers. This story went well beyond a mere "third-rate burglary," as the president's spokesman called it. It was the "White House of Horrors," said Mitchell. Woodward and Bernstein were showing that Watergate was really about officially sanctioned criminal activity, serious abuses of presidential power, and eventually obstruction of justice.[13]

The *Times*, although in hot pursuit, always lagged behind. *Post* editor Bradlee chortled: "There are many, many rewards in the newspaper business, but one of them comes with reading the competition quoting your paper on its front page." News editor Phelps employed a Washington taxi driver to pick up the early "bulldog" edition of the *Post*. During Watergate, reporter Jim Naughton recalled, "We all dreaded having the night duty and having to scramble to match whatever the *WashPost* had in its bulldog."[14] Hersh never had to pull the night shift.

The gnashing of teeth in the *Times* New York offices was palpable. From the *Times* point of view the natural order was the landmark 1971 Pentagon Papers story when Daniel Ellsberg leaked the hidden history of the Vietnam War to *Times* reporter Neil Sheehan. Only after the *Times* was restrained from publishing did he turn to the *Post*. Now the shoe was on the other foot. "The story of Watergate triggered another heated competition between the *Times* the *Washington Post*. Only this time the *Post* ran well ahead of us," recalled Frankel, who said the *Post* was outreporting the *Times* five to one. Rosenthal was impatient. He hired investigative reporter Denny Walsh, who won a Pulitzer Prize in St. Louis, telling him: "We don't want this to happen again." Walsh was assigned to Watergate. But Rosenthal also ordered his new Washington bureau chief, Clifton Daniel, to tell Hersh he had to put aside all other stories and get on the Watergate beat. "I read the papers," Hersh said. "We were suffering."[15]

Hersh felt comfortable with Daniel, who was married to President Harry Truman's daughter. Daniel called Hersh "a dynamo of a reporter. He could remember a hundred telephone numbers, punch out any one of them faster than the eye could see, relentlessly grill a news source, cajoling, threatening and wheedling, and extort more information than any newspaperman I have ever seen—mostly on the telephone." Daniel, who wore London-tailored suits, also thought the rumpled Hersh needed sprucing up. Around Christmas he bought Hersh a box of Brooks Brothers shirts and sweaters. "He did not think I was up to the *Times*' dress standard," Hersh said, "and told me that I was henceforth assigned to Watergate." After Nixon was reelected with more than 60 percent of the vote, Woodward and Bernstein were stumped on where the story should go next. "There was a vacuum after the election when Carl and I really weren't concentrating," Woodward recalled. "We had taken some time off and were working on our book [*All the President's Men*] and traveling around making speeches. Hersh moved right into the vacuum."[16]

Journalism was never a nine-to-five job for Sy Hersh. He starts early in the morning calling sources at their homes. He keeps up the phone calls into the evening and on weekends. When editors at the *Times* wanted to talk with Hersh, they would send instructions to the switchboard to order all calls to Hersh stopped. Otherwise they could not talk to him. He was alternately brusque, charming and threatening to sources. To be good at journalism, he said, means "BSing people, reading their minds."[17] What stuck out in Rosenthal assistant Arthur Gelb's mind was his interviewing prowess: "His ability to make people cower on the phone was unbelievable. Cajole, threaten. He scared the hell out of half of Congress." But the

Watergate beat was new territory for Hersh. He had to find sources deep in the White House, Justice Department, and Congress. He feared Woodward and Bernstein "were too far ahead, and too conversant with White House officials whose names I didn't even know." But he had once told Rosenthal, "I am anxious to do some writing about other aspects of American life." Now he had his chance to tackle a threat to the Constitution.[18]

Hersh's first big Watergate scoop came partly by chance. He saw an outline from his publisher, Random House, in which the shadowy figure Andrew St. George indicated he would partner with burglar Frank Sturgis, then on trial, to tell the inside story of Watergate. Hersh called St. George, threatening to write about his book unless he put Hersh in touch with Sturgis. St. George protested—even calling Rosenthal—but he delivered Sturgis. Hersh learned that four of the five burglars were receiving $400 monthly payments—"hush money." Hersh had "sources close to the case," but only Sturgis was named. Hersh's sources reported the White House had an espionage effort that went beyond the Democratic National Headquarters, and Mitchell knew it when he was attorney general. That allegation touched a raw nerve. The Committee to Re-elect the President said to Hersh: "If the Times chooses to publish these unsupported statements, it would be a serious act of journalistic recklessness and irresponsibility." The story ended up on page one January 14, but not before Hersh tangled with his own editors. After two months of work, he wrote a five-part series; his editors chopped it to one story. They put a lead on the story that Hersh did not like. So after the story was read by all editors, he resorted to a trick he learned at the AP. He called the copydesk in New York right before deadline and said he had to put a new lead on the story. He substituted his original lead: "At least four of the five men arrested last June are still being paid by persons as yet unnamed, according to sources close to the case." No one asked a question.[19]

It was a big scoop. As Hersh explained, until Sturgis "told me about the money . . . it did not occur to me or anyone else to change our focus from what they did before and during the break-in to what happened afterward—the cover-up." Everyone followed Hersh's story. The night the story came out, Woodward and Bernstein received calls at home, telling them the *Post* had been badly scooped. Woodward said he was glad, that Hersh's debut actually helped their efforts. Bradlee realized the significance, remarking how Hersh "dropped a beauty on us and the world with a detailed account." However, he added, "I hate to get beaten on any story, but I loved that one by my pal Hersh because it meant the *Post* was no longer alone in alleging obstruction of justice—as long as we didn't get beaten again." But it was not to be. Sy Hersh had pulled into town, and as *Washington Post* editor Leonard Downie wrote, "The competition between [Woodward and Bernstein] and Hersh, which helped speed the unraveling of Watergate, had begun."[20]

The stories came fast and furious. Over the next year Hersh wrote more than forty articles on Watergate, most appearing on page one. "In effect," said Hersh's editor Phelps, "he practically took the story away from the *Post*." It was, he said years later, "a remarkable display of investigative skill." John W. Dean, the president's counsel whose televised testimony made him a national celebrity, said that in 1972 it was the *Post* that emboldened prosecutors to pursue the investigation. But later on, in 1973 and 1974, he said, "the most devastating pieces that strike awfully close to home" were written by Sy Hersh.[21]

Two weeks after his first scoop, Hersh went after the thirty-three-year-old Dwight Chapin, the ambitious appointments secretary who ordered payments to Donald Segretti, the man behind the White House's "dirty tricks" operation. "I got Chapin's resignation," Hersh bragged. The next day he revealed that the FBI failed to investigate Segretti, although they knew of his activities. His information came from a White House source who called Hersh. "People were coming to *me* now," Hersh said. Then, on February 9, in further proof that Hersh had become an important player, the chief federal prosecutor, Earl J. Silbert, ended a ten-day silence and gave Hersh an interview.[22] All of the break-in defendants would be called back before a grand jury, he declared. Had the defendants pleaded guilty, the Watergate scandal could have stopped right there. But Hersh—and the emerging press stampede—was digging in.

Watergate was not an easy story. Sources on the inside had to be developed and their motives assessed to ensure they were not leaking information for their own purposes. This happened once to Hersh when he wrote two stories about John Dean, using unidentified sources who said Dean met with Nixon forty times to discuss various matters, including Watergate. This was many more times than prosecutors knew, but it turned out the source—possibly Dean or his attorney—was simply trying to make Dean more attractive to prosecutors to avoid prosecution. Hersh later defended his story. "That story wasn't completely wrong," Hersh insisted. "It never said that Dean never could implicate Nixon. It just said that he hadn't yet in his interviews with prosecutors."[23]

Years later critics would use Hersh's mistakes as fodder for vicious attacks on his reliability.

A bigger issue for reporters was to understand what they were actually learning and not just churn out "scoops." With leaks pouring out and bits and pieces coming from so many media outlets, readers could be very confused. For example, on February 24 Hersh wrote—with more unnamed sources—that Nixon had refused to order prosecution of a navy official who had stolen classified documents from the White House and passed them to the chairman of the Joint Chiefs of Staff. In effect, one arm of the government was spying on another. What it all meant was unclear and difficult to fit into the Watergate story. "One closely involved source" said the president told his top aide, John Erlichman, "John, if you prosecute this you'll blow the whole thing open." But no one knew what the "thing" was. Hersh would make it clearer eventually. But the *Columbia Journalism Review* recognized the problem: "a perpetual scramble of names, jumble of cases, mélange of hearings . . . a mere blur to almost all but those professionally or criminally connected with the stories." Hersh's work could be dense. Wrote one critic, "Reading Seymour Hersh is typically like reading a laundry list that ticks off carefully accumulated details and quotes as if they were a dry enumeration of socks and tee-shirts. The power of his work comes from his dogged work as a researcher who tracks down bits of information that nobody else finds."[24] But it was not always an easy read.

Rugaber, the most active *Times* reporter on Watergate, said, "Give Sy great credit for coming into the story when it was well along and breaking the stories he did." Denny Walsh was more effusive, saying, "Sy walks the razor's edge day after day and produces good stories without once getting nicked." Editor Phelps was thrilled that Hersh was now leading the way "with a remarkable display of investigative skill." But some editors were wary of Hersh's persistent use of unnamed sources. Abe Rosenthal decided to issue a "Seymour Hersh Edict" on sources.[25]

Controversial Secret Sources

Journalism's rules on anonymous sources are unwritten, variable, and changing. The *Times* certainly had no prohibition on using them, but it was assumed they would be minimized. The *Post*, of course, had developed a key source known as "Deep Throat," who remained anonymous for another thirty-three years! In fact, use of anonymous sources was one reason *Times* editors distrusted the *Post's* early Watergate reporting. Phelps said even if the *Times* pursued the Gray leak, it would have needed two confirming sources. "Our credibility was too precious to sacrifice," he declared. But then Hersh entered the story. Anonymous sources dominated his reporting, as perhaps they should have since in Watergate very little was on the record and less was happening publicly, except a trial of seven burglars. Nonetheless Hersh challenged the *Times* standards. Typical of his early Watergate reporting were these usages: sources close to the case; a source who has provided reliable information in the past; well-informed government official; one closely involved source; one reliable source; one insider; military officials; Pentagon sources; one official. He does have named sources also, but anonymous people, complained his editor Rosenthal, "walk ghost-like through Mr. Hersh's stories."[26]

By early February Rosenthal had had enough. He wrote a memo saying he warned Hersh about "a certain technique that I found improper. . . . that was ascribing long, colorful pejorative comments in direct quotes to anonymous officials." Anonymous sources are permitted, but "it was entirely another to allow those sources to denounce this person or that person or to be quoted as to their own interpretation." Rosenthal added, "Sy apparently has not gotten the point. . . . Get it across to him and make sure that the practice stops fast, hard and totally."[27]

Rosenthal was dreaming. As his top aide Gelb put it, "He would take no bullshit from no one." Perhaps Rosenthal was mollified that while Hersh briefed Clifton Daniel each day on his stories, only Rosenthal knew his secret sources. Hersh did not trust the well-connected Daniel; he gave his sources different names when talking to the bureau chief. "Otherwise," he said, "they would have been all over town." Little seemed to change in Hersh's reporting style, however. In fact, he needed anonymous sources more as Watergate moved to various grand juries. The *Times* policy had always been to avoid testimony given to grand juries, secret proceedings to gauge if there is evidence to charge someone with a crime. Fairness dictated not naming targets since the suspicions might be bogus. But Hersh changed the *Times* policy as he revealed what was being said in grand jury rooms. On April 22, for example, he described John Mitchell's testimony that he approved paying the Watergate burglars but did not see it as a bribe for silence. The grand jury was probing if top aides had gotten Nixon's OK to pay the burglars. Someone was leaking to Hersh immediately after the grand jury, leading Hersh to comment, "I had extraordinary access."[28]

Jokingly, Hersh said, "If I happened to be standing next to the urinal with somebody who knew something about the grand jury, it was in the *Times*" the next day. But Denny Walsh explained, "Nobody was second guessing. Whatever it took to get going on Watergate, that's what they were going to do." Some editors felt using grand jury stories "was crawling in the gutter," Hersh remembered. But "who crawled into the gutter first," the reporter asked rhetorically, "we or the White House?"[29]

By April Bernstein and Woodward were increasingly nervous about Hersh overtaking them. "The more we've written the more we have found our role is lessened," Woodward told editor Howard Simons, who tried to calm him. "Don't diminish your own role," he said. But he quickly added, "Those guys at the *Times* are good, they're really good." Hersh, in particular, he said. Simons, who had urged Obst to submit Hersh's Pulitzer nomination in 1968, called Hersh "good but not good. There is the good side and the bad side. Sy does some things I wouldn't tolerate on my newspaper. Blackmail . . . . that's not my idea of what professional journalism is all about. And yet I like Sy and I've liked him for a long time." Simons knew how Hersh had carved into the *Post*'s exclusive hold on Watergate. "I don't know whose nose he had a ring in but . . ."[30] He didn't finish the sentence. They all wondered, who was Sy Hersh talking to?

The *Post* reporters decided it was time to meet Hersh, who didn't know the rookies. They knew of Hersh, however, long before Watergate. He was a famous Pulitzer Prize winner. "If there was one reporter who was not likely to be taken in by White House manipulations," they later wrote, "it was Seymour Hersh." Enter again David Obst, Hersh's My Lai agent. By 1973 he had reinvented himself as a successful book agent; he was, coincidentally, the agent for Carl and Bob for *All the President's Men.* "I kept wanting to get Woodward and Bernstein together with Sy because it was driving me crazy," Obst remembers. "One of them would run a story and my phone would ring and they'd say something like, 'Tell your friend Mr. Hersh he's way off on this.'" On April 8, 1973, they met in Virginia so no one would see them. "It was like watching the World Series of Poker, it was so much fun," Obst recalled.[31]

Hersh showed up in old tennis shoes, a frayed pinstriped shirt, and rumpled khakis. "He was unlike any reporter [we] had ever met," they wrote. He called Henry Kissinger a war criminal and criticized a colleague for writing "lies." He made clear his view of Nixon. "I know these people," he said. "The abiding characteristic of this administration is that it lies." But Hersh also made clear what his journalistic scruples were—no cheap shots. About one Watergate suspect, he told them. "I'd really love to get that son of a bitch . . . but . . . either I get him hard, with facts, solid information, evidence, the truth, or I don't touch him." He might have been talking about Bob Haldeman, who he said he disliked most, partly because of his crew cut. And while the four reporters discussed Watergate in detail, they did not help each other with sources—even when Hersh and Bernstein smoked a joint, no one revealed sources.

"We're drinking and having a good time," Obst said. As the dinner was ending near 11:00 p.m., Woodward asked Hersh what story was next. "Just a little something," Hersh teased. Woodward then called the *Post's* city desk. He came back white-faced and said to Bernstein, "We're out of here." They just walked out, with no goodbye. They hustled back to their office to find the early edition of the *Times.* Hersh reported that burglar James McCord had told a federal grand jury that the Committee to Re-elect the President had funneled money to the burglars to buy their silence. It was the first confirmation the committee was involved—another breakthrough in the unraveling scandal. McCord confirmed his testimony in a telephone conversation with Hersh.[32] "Sy falls off the couch, laughing," Obst said. He had outraced Bernstein and Woodward to the key sources—and a big scoop.

Two weeks later Hersh reported that the Watergate case had been "broken open," an exaggeration. But his story indicated that "Congressional and Administration sources" were now saying that evidence had been amassed to implicate Mitchell, Dean, and the president's personal attorney, Herbert Kalmbach, as well as the President's chief fund raiser, Maurice Stans. "We know the whole story now," an anonymous administration source told Hersh. Rosenthal was beaming from New York, sending Hersh a short note: "I think you are doing a hell of a good job. The paper needs people like you who will go after a story no matter what and no matter who." Sy's reply: "It's been a pleasure working for this paper. . . . Haven't even had a story cut." Which was a fabrication. However, he added, he wanted a "substantial pay raise." Daniel supported Hersh, calling him "the outstanding performer in the bureau in the biggest story of the year."[33] But the stress of catching up on Watergate—he called the competition "horrific"—took its toll on the thirty-six-year old Hersh. The strain began to show.

Henkel, Paul: A Cappella, St. Council, Pythagoreans, Euclideans, Track, Capt. Jr. Swim Team, Capt. Var. Swim, Letterman, Eng. Honor, Hallguard.

Hersh, Alan: Jr. Math Honor, Sr. Math Honor, Hallguard, Hydeparker Agent, Box Office, Var. Track, St. Council.

Hersh, Seymour: Pythagoreans, Euclideans, Intramural Golf, Sigma Epsilon, Intramural Basketball.

Higashiuchi, Joan: Leaders, GAA, French Club, Pep Club, St. Council, Sr. Girls, SE, Div. Chairman.

Hirn, John: Jr. Math Honor, Chess Club.

Holland, Charles: Hallguard, St. Council, Annual Agent.

FIG. 1. Seymour Hersh, top right, and his twin brother, Alan, are pictured in the 1954 yearbook of Hyde Park High School in Chicago. (Courtesy of Hyde Park High School)

FIG. 2. Bodies of men, women and children are piled in a ditch in the village of My Lai where American soldiers massacred hundreds of unarmed Vietnamese civilians in 1968. (Ron Haeberle / TIME & LIFE Images / Getty Images)

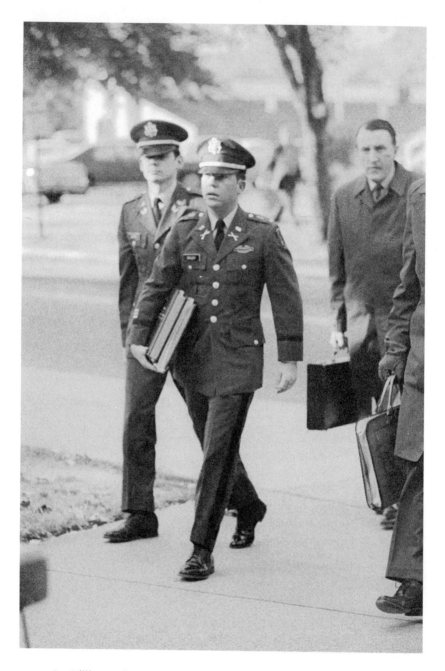

FIG. 3. Lt. William Calley Jr. leaves his trial after Hersh's stories identified him as the twenty-five-year-old American soldier who ordered and assisted in the killing of nearly five hundred civilians in My Lai. (AP Photo)

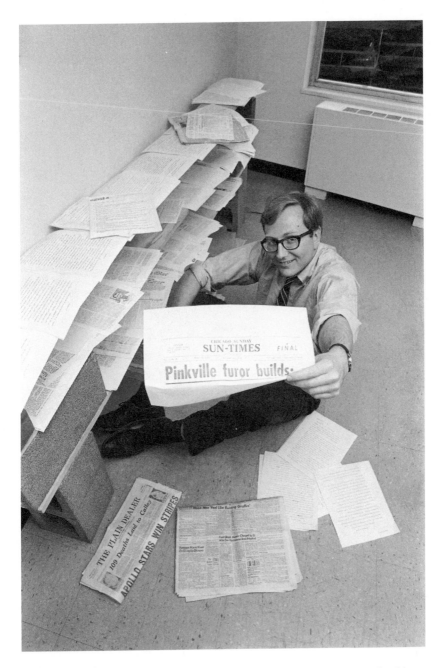

FIG. 4. The thirty-two-year-old Hersh smiles as he holds up a newspaper that blares the headline of one of his five stories about the massacre in My Lai. (AP Photo / Bob Daugherty)

FIG. 5. Hersh huddles with Eugene McCarthy in 1967 when he acted as the senator's press secretary as he ran for the Democratic presidential nomination against Lyndon Johnson. (University of Minnesota Libraries)

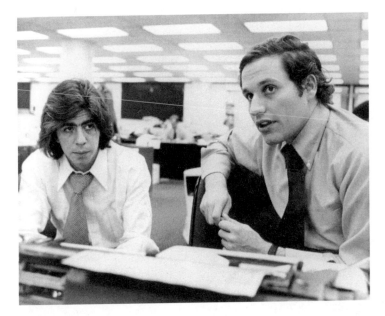

FIG. 6. After Hersh went to work at the *New York Times* in 1972, he dove into the story of the Watergate scandal and engaged in a fierce competition with Carl Bernstein, left, and Bob Woodward of the *Washington Post*. (AP Photo)

FIG. 7. Photographer Annie Liebovitz, on assignment for *Rolling Stone* magazine, captured Hersh in 1975 in a rare photo with his family, Matthew, left, and wife Elizabeth holding Melissa. (© Annie Leibovitz/Contact Press Images)

FIG. 8. Hersh relentlessly works his government sources with the telephone and he is caught here by *Vanity Fair* photographer Jonathan Becker in 1997 as the magazine readied an article about Hersh's controversial book about John Kennedy, *The Dark Side of Camelot.* (© Jonathan Becker)

FIG. 9. By 2004 Hersh was famous enough that Roman Genn drew this caricature of him for conservative magazine *National Review*. (Roman Genn)

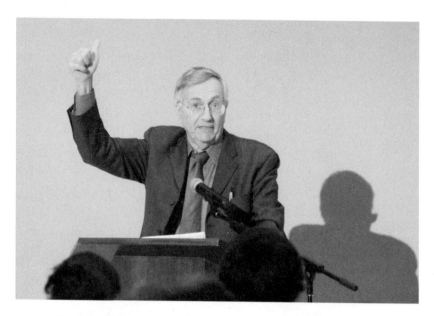

FIG. 10. Ever since he won the Pulitzer Prize in 1970, Hersh has crisscrossed the country giving speeches. Here he gestures in a speech on foreign policy at the University of North Carolina in 2011. (Photograph by Katie Sweeney / The Daily Tar Heel)

FIG. 11. Yoko Ono gave Hersh the LennonOno Peace Prize in 2004 for his groundbreaking work on the scandal at Abu Ghraib prison in Iraq. (AP Photo / Kathy Willens)

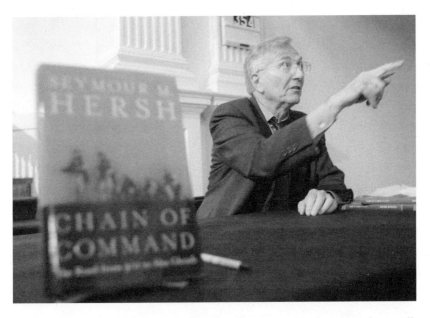

FIG. 12. When his 2004 book, *Chain of Command*, came out, Hersh went on the TV talk show and book-signing circuit to promote his ninth book which spent some time on the best-seller lists. (Alex Wong/Getty Images News/Getty Images)

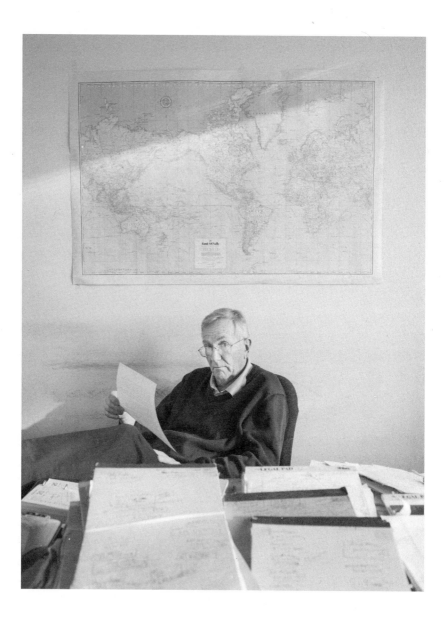

FIG. 13. Even after four decades of reporting, Hersh immerses himself in documents and reports as he sits in front of a map of the world in his tiny two-room office in Washington DC. (Mark Mahaney)

CHAPTER 15

Cambodia, Bombs, and Impeachment

Feeling the Stress

When Sy Hersh, Carl Bernstein, and Bob Woodward met for dinner in April 1973, Woodward refused to toke on the marijuana they passed around. He knew the White House was looking to cut the credibility of the *Post* reporters. "These Goddamn cannibals," Nixon said in an April 27 meeting with press secretary Ronald Ziegler. "Hell, they're not after [Bob] Haldeman or [John] Erlichman or [John] Dean; they're after me, the President." Nixon was working with Ziegler on a speech that he would give right after the resignation of his top aides; he wanted it to be aggressive. "We aren't going to take this crap," he declared. "They can attack the President's men, but they must not attack the President." Then, he asked Ziegler, "Hersh, can you talk to him?" No, no, Ziegler replied. He needed to "hit on" Clifton Daniel, the bureau chief, or Scotty Reston, the columnist. Ziegler rehearsed his pitch. "Can't run a story like this in the *New York Times* . . . on speculation about the President of the United States. You have an obligation as a major newspaper and so on . . ." And while such an approach might make inroads with Daniel or Reston, he knew it had no chance with Sy Hersh.[1]

For his part Hersh was able to keep hammering away because his sources in the Justice Department were so good. Mark Feldstein, biographer of muckraking columnist Jack Anderson, felt Hersh had a leg up on Woodward in developing Justice Department sources. Seymour Glanzer and Earl Silbert, both Jewish, were more comfortable with Hersh than the Waspy Woodward, he argued. In mid-May someone leaked a document just to Hersh indicating that burglar James McCord was told by the White House to say he was working for the CIA when he led a team into Democratic headquarters. He refused. And then, on May 10, Hersh reported that federal prosecutors felt that John Dean, the president's former counsel, had no evidence to link Nixon to the break-in or cover-up. The story was wrong; Hersh had made his first mistake. But inside the White House the Dean story hit close to home. Haldeman and Nixon met the morning of Hersh's story, trying to figure out if Dean had anything on the president. They fretted over a safe Dean kept with national security documents, and worried that Hersh would find out. "Seymour Hersh—he's got a good line into there," Haldeman said about Hersh's connection to the prosecutors. "He's been accurate on everything he's printed."[2]

That assessment turned out to be false, and perhaps to make up for his error, Hersh pushed the Dean angle hard, reporting next that the lawyer tried to set up a spy ring to infiltrate protestors at the upcoming Republican National Convention. Then on June 3 Hersh contradicted his initial Dean story, reporting that Dean told Senate investigators he huddled more than forty times with Nixon, who showed "great interest" in the Watergate matter.[3] The White House was indignant, charging that the story was "part of a careful, coordinated strategy . . . using innuendo, distortion of fact and outright falsehood. We categorically deny the assertions." But Hersh rebutted the denial. "We're all scared to death by this guy," said an unidentified source with close connections to top White House officials. "We don't know what he can or can't prove." And the anger was not just in their prepared statement. Meeting with Nixon on June 5, his new counsel, J. Fred Buzhardt, called Hersh's story "very careless," adding, "I think Woodward and Bernstein wrote it accurately."[4]

While both the *Post* and the *Times* had an army of reporters covering Watergate, it was Hersh and Woodward and Bernstein who were dueling daily for scoops. "There was a lot of pressure on Hersh," Woodward said. "When we beat him, the people would have a fit at the *Times*. They'd call him up late at night to get him to confirm our story and do better." Once, Woodward wrote a story that indicated that Nixon had bugged his own brother, Donald, to make sure he wasn't doing anything to embarrass the president. Hersh was furious at being scooped. He called Woodward and yelled, "You fucker, you fucker!" It wasn't the only time that Woodward and Bernstein angered him. In *All the President's Men* they described him as pudgy. "Do I look pudgy to you?" Hersh fired back. "I'm much more of an athlete than either one of them. . . . What they didn't say in the book was that we were all sitting around getting high and putting down everybody. I didn't see them put in the book what they were saying about Ben Bradlee [*Washington Post* editor] that night. Damn cheap shot artists." Yet Hersh also called their competition "admirable."[5] But he and Woodward in particular knew what was up for grabs: Who was America's greatest investigative reporter?

Woodward and Hersh "became particularly fascinated with each other," wrote Leonard Downie, a top *Post* editor. After the initial meeting, they became tennis partners (Hersh won but never paid for the court), and they met weekly for a pizza dinner. "We never traded hard information," but sometimes Woodward said Hersh tried to get him to reveal sources, "but I wouldn't play. He tried to milk me in a manipulative but good-natured way. It was tricky sometimes but fun—absolute fun." Hersh said he "knew little about Woodward and Bernstein's sources, and nothing about Deep Throat," their famous secret source, W. Mark Felt, the number two man in the FBI. "I thought that Felt was a source for a colleague of mine at the *Times* on at least one story," Hersh said. "But Woodward and Bernstein had many excellent sources."[6]

Clearly they were on each other's heels. "I suspected that they were talking to many of the same people I was," Hersh noted. Once a source asked to see Hersh, but he declined. The source said, "Well somebody else is coming," meaning Woodward. Hersh then demanded to see the source immediately. Too late. Woodward left him a note: "Kilroy was here," which was their code for each other. "They're terrific reporters," Hersh said. What worried him most, however, was that they knew how to deftly work their sources. "They were friendly, kidding, joshing. People liked these two guys. That used to make me very nervous."[7]

Although playful, the competition was also stressful for Hersh. "It's no fun picking up the *Post* and seeing a story you knew nothing about on page one," he noted. And while he might have seemed unshakable in his confidence, the pursuit of Watergate physically affected him. He suffered from rashes and severe dandruff. "But I don't allow it to interfere with my work," he declared. "I'll go anywhere any time to meet anybody who may have information."[8]

Just as John Dean prepared to face the U.S. Senate and a mesmerized national audience in late June, prosecutors kept wagging their tongues to Hersh about Dean's testimony. Hersh tried to wheedle even more out of the White House. He telephoned Buzhardt, the president's lawyer, and, bluffing, told him he had evidence indicating Dean was a big spender on diamonds and boats. "He asked us, did we know," Buzhardt told Nixon and General Alexander Haig in the Oval Office. "Did we know all this from our investigation?" "Oh, he got it?" Nixon asked. "He got it," Buzhardt answered. "We put it together, but he got it from somebody else." "Good," the president replied. Buzhardt was gleeful that Hersh seemed ready to write a critical story on Dean. But Hersh was just trying to see if the White House would concede they were investigating the former Nixon lawyer. "Does Hersh understand this?" the president asked, wondering if the reporter was going to slam Dean. "Yes, sir, yes, sir, Hersh understands . . . very clearly, and we didn't tell him." But Nixon must have been disappointed because Hersh's resulting story was a mild rebuke of Dean, saying he had used $14,000 of campaign money to help pay for his wedding but paid the money back. No mention of luxurious purchases.[9]

Hersh saved his ammunition for Nixon. On June 17 he predicted Dean would implicate the president, saying the order to break in to the offices of Daniel Ellsberg's psychiatrist came from the Oval Office. When Dean told the president what he knew, he was so startled it brought him "out of his chair," Hersh reported. The president, a source told Hersh, had never realized there were all these people involved. "He could see the tracks leading right up to the oval office," Hersh wrote. Once more, Hersh was bringing the public right up to Nixon's door. His next discovery, however, would bring them on to Nixon's lap—and help bring down the President.[10] Hersh was ready to move from Watergate (about which he wrote nearly fifty stories) to a story he could truly claim as his own.

Illegal Bombs Away

Hal M. Knight was a thirty-three-year-old graduate student at the University of Memphis in 1973 when he read Sy Hersh's *Times* stories on the unauthorized bombing allegations against General John H. Lavelle. Major Knight had supervised radar crews in Vietnam, but after being passed over for two promotions, he resigned in 1972. Reading Hersh's stories startled Knight: he realized the Senate "was unaware of what had taken place while I was out there." General Lavelle, he said, was being "disciplined for doing the same thing on a small scale that I was doing on a big scale."[11] His conscience gnawing at him, Knight wrote a letter to Wisconsin senator William Proxmire, revealing that he had been involved in illegal bombing of neutral Cambodia in 1969 and had then covered it up. "It always begins with a letter," Hersh wrote, recalling that My Lai began with Ron Ridenhour and Lavelle with Lonnie Franks. And someone always leaks that letter to Sy Hersh, thus precipitating Hersh's next *Times* blockbuster—two dozen stories that culminated in the president of the United States being charged with violating the Constitution. The allegations came a whisper away from being added to the bill of particulars Congress eventually drew up in its attempt to impeach Richard Nixon.

How Hersh got wind of this story is unclear, but its roots surely were in his pursuit of a completely different White House scandal. Sources told him in mid-May 1973 that the president had authorized wiretaps on the telephones of a dozen employees of Henry Kissinger's National Security Council. The taps started in May 1969 when the *Times* revealed that Nixon had bombed Vietcong sanctuaries in Cambodia. Lyndon Johnson had refused to do this; Nixon did so quickly but wanted it kept secret for fear of unleashing the antiwar movement. The leaks infuriated Kissinger and Nixon. "The President's motives [in bombing] were honorable," a source told Hersh, adding that the "blabbermouths had to be stopped." Deep in Hersh's May 16 page one story in the *Times*, Morton Halperin, a Kissinger aide whose phone was tapped, put his finger on Nixon's discomfort. "They were mad at the leak because they were trying to keep from the American public that, while the administration was claiming it was withdrawing, in fact it was escalating the war." They also were trying desperately to keep it secret from Congress and, of course, from the press.[12]

In hot pursuit, Hersh went the next day to the White House to meet General Haig, Kissinger's top aide. An in-person interview was odd for Hersh, who mostly worked the telephone, prompting one of his editors, Bill Kovach, to comment: "In Sy's hands the phone was an improvised explosive device." But Haig likely wanted to intimidate Hersh with the gravity of the White House—and call him off. Haig urged Hersh to abandon the story; the wiretapping was legal, necessary, and not newsworthy. When Hersh balked, Haig warned the reporter the story might lead to Kissinger's resignation, something no one wanted since he was the guidepost of foreign policy during the turbulent Watergate scandal. Finally, Haig took a new tact. "You're Jewish, aren't you, Seymour?" Up to that point Haig had always called him "Sy." Hersh was indeed Jewish. "Let me ask you one question, then. Do you honestly believe that Henry Kissinger, a Jewish refugee from Germany who lost thirteen members of his family to the Nazis, could engage in such police-state tactics as wiretapping his own aides? You owe it to yourself, your beliefs, and your nation to give us one day to prove that your story is wrong."[13]

On May 17, the day after the Haig plea, Hersh wrote another page one story. Kissinger, he charged, had given the names of his own aides to the FBI for wiretapping. His role was "far more extensive than previously reported," and contradicted what he told Hersh the previous day—that he never approved such wiretaps. Kissinger, in Paris, did not respond, but one official told Hersh: "Henry wanted some of these guys bugged himself. They were disloyal . . . giving him real problems."[14] Halperin, who later sued Kissinger and won a civil lawsuit, said flat out about the wiretaps, "They were clearly illegal." But why, Hersh wondered, were Kissinger and Nixon so upset to resort to unprecedented wiretaps? Surely more than just leaking of information—a way of life in the capital—worried them? The *Times* had missed Watergate; Hersh was not going to miss this story.

Back to Hal Knight, whose letter was passed by Proxmire to the Armed Services Committee, where Hersh's sources were superb from his Lavelle coverage. The weekend before he was to offer explosive public testimony, Knight talked to Hersh; he wanted to spill the beans. "I didn't take an oath to support the military," he said, "I took an oath to support the Constitution." What Hersh revealed was that in early 1970 American B-52s dropped tons of bombs on Cambodia as Knight went through a daily cover-up ritual, entering fake bombing coordinates into computers. A courier hand-delivered the real sites to be bombed, sanctuaries where enemy soldiers were thought to be hiding. Then, at dawn, Knight burned the orders in a special bin after which he called Saigon to say, "The ball game is complete." It was part of an elaborate scheme to hide the raids at a time when America officially recognized the neutrality of Cambodia. Knight once fell asleep and did not make his phone call. "All hell broke loose," he said.[15]

Knight tried to learn who was giving orders for the cover-up, but he was told, brusquely, to mind his own business. Knight's dilemma: "I wasn't a dove," he told Hersh. "I was all for what we were doing [bombing the sanctuaries]. I knew the way we were doing it was wrong." And on July 15 Iowa senator Harold Hughes agreed, saying, "I want to determine who gave the orders for the bombing and why the public wasn't told." The Pentagon was tight-lipped: "We're just not going to talk about it." But one day later Hersh's revelations hit pay dirt as the government made a remarkable turnaround when Secretary of Defense James Schlesinger admitted in a letter that in 1969–70 the United States had flown 3,630 B-52 raids over fourteen months, dropping a hundred thousand tons of bombs on Cambodia. Because of the "sensitive operational and diplomatic situation, special security precautions" had to be taken, Schlesinger said. How widespread, Hersh wondered, was the falsification of documents? More importantly, can the military provide assurances that policies designed to protect nuclear-armed B-52s are working?[16]

In the White House Kissinger was feisty over Hersh's exposé. "What do we care if the New York Times clobbers us now if it helps us end the war sooner?" he asked Nixon, who agreed. But surely they felt otherwise as their embarrassment mounted, and as they engaged in a tricky dance over Cambodia. The communist Khmer Rouge guerrillas, who turned out to be brutal oppressors, were slowly marching toward the Cambodian capital Phnom Penh, their path helped by America's 1970 invasion of the country and the persistent bombing. Times correspondent Sydney Schanberg was chronicling the Cambodian war in what led to a Pulitzer Prize for him after almost being killed by the guerillas. The illegal bombing, he said, "was known for some time." And it "did draw a lot of attention because [Hersh's stories] provided the details we hadn't known before and caused great embarrassment at the Pentagon and the White House."[17] Tired of the war, Congress was demanding that the bombing stop by August 15, challenging the president's constitutional authority.

Hersh's stories—revealing a duplicity that rivaled Watergate—did not help the president's case to continue the war in Cambodia.

The Watergate of Foreign Policy

On July 19 the Pentagon said ex-secretary of defense Melvin Laird and the president both approved the secret bombing, but Senator Hughes insisted the Senate was lied to. The next day Laird told Hersh he never ordered that documents be destroyed, and the military's former top official, General Earle Wheeler, was aghast, saying, "I cannot understand why files were burned. The whole thing makes no sense." It also clearly violated military rules and was illegal. Who ordered it? An anonymous source at the Pentagon said to Hersh, "Somebody somewhere had to know about this." Hersh was on a roll as he sought to find who gave the orders. "He's one of a kind," observed Pulitzer Prize–winning editor Gene Roberts, who had just left the *Times*. "He is just relentless in the pursuit of a story." And the story was leading to Kissinger, who gave a rare telephone interview to Hersh, insisting that he "neither ordered nor was aware of any falsification." He added, "I think it is deplorable."[18]

The story got juicier when the Pentagon got caught in a bald-faced lie, having to admit that just a month earlier it concocted a "cover story" to hide the bombing and gave Senate investigators false documents. "Obviously it was a blunder of some magnitude," said Pentagon spokesperson Jerry Friedheim. Many years later he admitted he should have known better when dealing with Hersh. "We all knew what kind of reporter he was," Friedheim said. "He was hard working" and only attended press conferences the day after he exposed a story to see if the Pentagon would react. Hersh was always fair, Friedheim recalled, saying, "We treated each other as pros." But when he called, Friedheim observed, "You knew enough to be careful. He had his sources. You never knew exactly what he was working on." What Friedheim failed to anticipate was that Knight would talk to Hersh about "Operation Menu," the secret Cambodia bombing. Still, there was not much the Pentagon PR staff could do, because, as Friedheim pointed out, Cambodia was "a Henry [Kissinger] policy that we couldn't talk about."[19]

In late July Hersh summed up the state of the scandal and then moved to widen the story. His revelations prompted a thirty-year-old airman to say that on six occasions he was directed to bomb hospitals in North Vietnam, a violation of international law. "It was one of those things I wasn't too proud of," he said. A former Green Beret called Hersh to tell him he participated in numerous secret missions—kidnappings, ambushes, attacks—during which hundreds of soldiers were killed. It was all kept secret. "Dammit, these people put their lives on the line. Don't they at least deserve to have their families told that they are dead?" The Pentagon admitted that eighty-one soldiers were missing in Cambodia and Laos. The Laos mention hit a nerve; Hersh discovered the Senate believed the secret bombing extended to hundreds of air strikes over the Ho Chi Minh trail in Laos.[20]

All the while, recriminations and squabbling among top government officials mounted. The former secretary of the air force, the highest civilian in the service, said he knew nothing. The second-highest-ranking military official in the air force said his office was kept out of the loop. Someone leaked to Hersh three-year-old secret testimony of Secretary of State William Rogers, who declared: "Cambodia is one country where . . . our hands are clean and our hearts are pure." Hersh's reporting made that statement laughable. In eight days of public hearings the Senate tried to determine who gave the orders. A deputy secretary of defense testified that Secretary Laird had signed a memo that approved misrepresenting the bombing. But Laird, again, demurred. The whole matter, he insisted, was discussed and approved "at the highest level of government." And that meant Kissinger and Nixon. Hersh was again so close to fingering the two most influential men in the government. The influential *Times* columnist Tom Wicker expressed his disgust with the whole business. "The proper word for the Cambodian bombing story," he wrote, "is lying."[21]

The Cambodia story had moved with remarkable speed as Congress sought a halt to all bombing. In less than a month Hersh's exposé and the Senate's swift investigation had made it the Watergate of foreign policy. "Although no such talk has yet been heard in public, some members" of Congress," Hersh wrote in a news analysis, "are convinced that the secret bombing of Cambodia will emerge as another, perhaps more danger-ous, facet of the Watergate scandal." As with Watergate, no one, Hersh wrote, has taken responsibility. "The personal role of Mr. Nixon in all of this is not known," he pointed out, but surely a "Watergate-inspired Congress" will ask, what constitutional basis did the president have for bombing a neutral country and not telling the Senate? Does any secret military campaign justify falsified reports? Only in the era of Watergate when the president was so under siege and only with a reporter who was given remarkable authority could a journalist pose such bold questions. Of course, Hersh's sources were also asking those questions. Ohio Republican representative William Saxbe told Hersh there is more reason to impeach Nixon on Cambodia than Watergate. "I think they were getting their orders from the Commander in Chief," he said, adding, "If the charge is serious enough, there's impeachment."[22]

On July 31, 1973, the retired chairman of the Joint Chiefs of Staff, General Earl Wheeler, pointed blame directly at the president, saying he received a half-dozen orders from Nixon to falsify documents. It was the first public acknowledgment of what many suspected: this was a Nixon-Kissinger policy to avoid public scrutiny. Massachusetts Democratic representative Robert Drinan had heard enough. While the Senate pursued the facts, he introduced the first impeachment resolution in Congress—dealing not with Watergate, but Cambodia. Drinan's appeal did not get much attention. But the editorial writers were, like Hersh, beginning to connect the lawlessness of Watergate with Cambodia. Anthony Lewis, a thoughtful liberal columnist in the *Times*, observed that "men who wage war in secret find it easy to tap telephones, and justify burglaries. . . . A decent government . . . does not embrace lawlessness as policy." Georgia senator Sam Nunn, a conservative pro-war Democrat, stated, "We have created a monster here with this false reporting."[23]

Finally, because of Sy Hersh's crusade, Richard Nixon was forced to respond to the furor. Appearing before a friendly Veterans of Foreign Wars audience in New Orleans on August 20, he said the bombing was "absolutely necessary" to protect American soldiers. He denounced "the great anguish and loud protest from the usual critics," presumably the same Sy Hersh who he had only weeks before tried to use to plant favorable Watergate stories.[24] Nixon never mentioned the falsification of records, which was the heart of the controversy. Nor did he mention that the bombing did not accomplish its primary goal—to clean out the sanctuaries in Cambodia. And, of course, he did not address the allegations that the bombing actually aided the Khmer Rouge guerillas in their eventual takeover of Cambodia.

Hersh could have gloated, but he remained very much the reporter. On September 21, when the Defense Department issued a report on Cambodia, a report full of glaring holes and discrepancies, he meticulously analyzed the document. It is impossible to find anything that resembles opinion or advocacy in his long news analysis. The closest he gets is asserting that the document "did not answer the crucial questions." Hersh understood his role and was simply not comfortable in taking any liberties beyond that of activist observer.[25] He had done his work with his exposé. Others would have to take it to the next level. And Congress tried.

The House of Representatives considered impeachment of Nixon a year after the Cambodia story ended. One of the twenty-nine proposed impeachment items dealt with Cambodia. It charged, in part, that the president "authorized, ordered, and ratified the concealment from the Congress of false and misleading statements concerning the existence, scope and nature of American bombing operations in Cambodia in derogation of the power of the Congress to declare war . . . and by such conduct warrants impeachment and trial and removal from office." A defiant Nixon told an aide: "They can't impeach me for bombing Cambodia. The president can bomb anybody he likes."[26]

Whether Nixon was correct was not resolved. The resolution did not survive the House's scrutiny. In the end only three specific impeachment charges were leveled against Nixon; Cambodia was not one of them. But some congressmen were angry that Cambodia was dropped. Representative John Conyers declared: "The manner in which the Cambodian bombing was initiated, conducted, and reported clearly exceeded the constitutional powers of the presidency, and presented indisputable evidence of impeachable conduct." Others felt that the war powers question was too murky to risk in impeachment.[27]

But Washington and the journalism community knew what Hersh had done—taken a hidden scandal and forced Congress to grapple with another instance of a presidential administration that knew few boundaries. The next year Seymour Hersh was awarded his first George S. Polk Award, one of the premier prizes in journalism. The award is given for original investigative and enterprise work that requires digging and resourcefulness—and brings results.[28] It was Hersh's work on Lavelle that prompted the whistleblower who exposed the bombing to come forward. It was Hersh's page one stories in the *Times* that forced the Senate to begin hearings. And it was his aggressive coverage and crucial questions that planted so many doubts in congressional minds that by late summer of 1973 the president had no choice but to stop any effort to continue its bombing campaign and the war in Southeast Asia. Certainly, this was not Sy Hersh's doing alone, but he played a mighty role in it all. What could he possibly do for an encore?[29]

CHAPTER 16

Hunting the Coup Plotters

A Dandelion in a Windstorm

By the fall of 1974 Sy Hersh was the Golden Boy of the *New York Times*, but he had his share of flubs and missed stories. As he pursued Watergate and wider corruption in the White House in late 1973, one source filled Hersh's ears with sketchy details about some sort of taping system in the Oval Office. Something about the president bugging his own conversations. Hersh was getting nowhere on the story until the source hooked him up with a Secret Service agent. "Secret Service guys rarely want to see reporters," Hersh pointed out. This one did. He brought Hersh to a crowded noisy discotheque, where he took Hersh on the dance floor. "We did not dance," Hersh said. The agent told Hersh the president was sitting in his office listening to tape recordings of his conversations. "It's the craziest thing," the agent said, "the President just sits in his office all day listening to tapes. He's got hundreds of tapes." Nixon was trying to figure out what evidence his own conversations would offer investigators about Watergate.

Hersh returned to his office to work the phones. He called Nixon's counsel, J. Fred Buzhardt, who declared, "Come on, I'd know about a taping system." Hersh turned to top Nixon aide John Erlichman, who "swore up and down there was no taping system." Erlichman "often didn't tell me the truth," Hersh said, "but he never lied to me." Finally Hersh went to "The Big Lying Machines," Press Secretary Ron Ziegler and three other inside sources. They all denied it existed. And they were not lying; they did not know. So Hersh dropped the story. The tapes were not revealed until congressional testimony by Alexander Butterfield on June 25, 1973, shocked the nation. "It was probably good that the story came out later," Hersh said. "We might still have Nixon."[1]

Hersh missed another major story. John Darnton was a novice thirty-two-year-old working in the *Times* New York office in early 1973, years before he won a Pulitzer Prize for his dispatches from Poland. A source told him that that Vice President Spiro Agnew was accepting bribe money from the U.S. Small Business Administration. Darnton did not know what to do with it or how to track it down. An editor told him to call Hersh and turn it over to the ace investigative reporter. Hersh returned Darnton's call. In his staccato style, he asked, "What you got?" Darnton told him. Hersh asked a series of lightning quick questions. And then declared, "It doesn't sound right. Not a story." Darnton and Hersh moved on, the Agnew story ignored. On October 10, 1973, Agnew resigned and pleaded no contest to federal income tax evasion for failing to report $29,500 in income that was, essentially, bribe money he received while he was governor of Maryland. Hersh missed the chance to bring down a vice president.[2]

A few misses did not affect Hersh. He was nonstop in pursuit of scoops. "He rarely completes a sentence and is almost continually on the telephone," noted a story in the *Times* archives that called him "as active as a dandelion in a windstorm." He was an amusing figure in the DC office. His sandy blonde hair was parted on one side, looking, one observer said, like it "sees a comb just once a day." Black horn-rimmed glasses sat on a sharp nose, and three brownish moles were visible on the left side of his chiseled jaw. He wore button-down collar shirts, the sleeves rolled up, and a tie that was always open at the collar. His three-sided desk was adjacent to a window. A typewriter sat on one side. The rest was piled high with manila folders stuffed with notes and newspaper clippings, legal pads, a Rolodex, and a small calendar. Thick government reports, half open, sat awaiting the reporter who knew that talking to people was not enough. He had to read everything.[3]

But the phone was still his key weapon, crooked in his neck like an appendage. Like all reporters, Hersh was always coy about his sources. Once he told me, "I don't discuss sources," but strictly speaking that was not true. At times he would be clear that a certain person was not his source or that a story did not emanate from a certain official. But he never divulged his sources. He aggressively sought out new government insiders. When people retired from the CIA or the Pentagon, he would find their names and call, declaring, "Hi I'm Sy Hersh and you probably want to talk to me." Retired generals, in particular, liked to hear from him. No one else was calling. But his sources in the Congress, culled carefully from his Watergate and Lavelle work, paid off again in the fall of 1974. Someone brought him a seven-page letter written on July 18 by thirty-eight-year-old liberal Massachusetts congressman Michael Harrington, who had twice read secret testimony given to a Senate committee by CIA director William Colby in April 1974. "The Spymaster," soon to become a Hersh phone mate, told Congress the Nixon administration had expended $8 million to help oust Salvador Allende, the elected socialist president of Chile who died in a September 11, 1973, coup d'état. Harrington, indignant at the CIA's role, wanted a full-scale investigation, but he was bound by congressional rules and could not reveal the testimony, even though he was able to distribute it to other congresspeople. And then, not surprisingly, someone leaked the letter to Hersh, who always denied Harrington was his source. No one believed him or Harrington.[4]

On Sunday, September 8, less than a month after Nixon's resignation and on the day that Gerald Ford pardoned the former president, Hersh exploded on the *Times* first page: "CIA Chief Tells House of $8-Million Campaign against Allende." Harrington's letter, "a copy made available to the Times," said the CIA — with the approval of the secretive "40 Committee" headed by Secretary of State Henry Kissinger—had tried to "destabilize" the government by influencing unions, political parties, and media in an effort to oust Allende, who was nationalizing American companies' $1.5 billion in investments. A Marxist in the U.S. hemisphere could not be tolerated. The story offered minimal detail on how the money was spent—that would come later—but Kissinger clearly was Hersh's target. One unnamed official told Hersh that well before the coup, the 40 Committee—"which is Kissinger and nobody else"—was determined to oust Allende. "Henry," a source said, wanted him out quickly, with force if need be. Kissinger declined comment. But Hersh was setting himself to head in two directions. Kissinger had told Congress that the United States had nothing to do with the Allende overthrow; the evidence might now point to perjury. And secondly, lying aside, the use of the CIA to influence the internal politics of foreign governments, often quietly acknowledged, could now be brought before both Congress and the public. Unlike Watergate, Hersh was in front on this story. The *Washington Post*'s ace foreign affairs reporter, Laurence Stern, had to play catch-up. He wrote a story similar to Hersh's on the day Hersh broke the story, but Stern was not able to get the Harrington letter. Hersh's sources continued to pay rich dividends as he zeroed in on Kissinger. With the *Post* and *Times* both pursuing the story, "a public furor ensued," observed Nathaniel Davis, the U.S. ambassador to Chile during the coup.[5]

Columnist Tom Wicker acidly asserted: "The real need is to face the fact that gangster schemes, bribery, violence and even assassination are being carried out in the name of the great American people." These were serious charges. Could Hersh prove them? More was at stake than simply showing that the Nixon White House had intervened in another government. Chile was a special case. "The fall of the Allende government became a judgment on the viability of the democratic road to socialism," observed Davis. Allende was promising to transform the landscape without violence or authoritarianism. The progressive world wanted Allende to succeed. The military coup was "traumatic," Davis wrote, adding, "The sudden end of the Allende government lighted up the night sky . . . exposing a stark landscape we might rather not have seen." Hersh was now threatening to show what many had suspected: the coup plotters had American help. He did not know exactly where the story would lead, however.[6]

Going after "Henry"

By the time Hersh dug into Chile, he was a veteran at mounting crusades. But this time it was different—he was gunning for the powerful and iconic Kissinger from the start. Remarkably the rest of the *Times* editorial staff—from the columnists to the editorial writers—were immediately on board in agreeing that something very wrong had occurred, before any official investigations commenced. "Who gave the United States the right to make such a judgment in opposition to a free Chilean election?" asked Wicker. Quickly, many congressional leaders joined the angry chorus. Everyone just accepted that intervention—legal but morally suspect—had taken place. The immediate acceptance probably was because so many suspected all along that something was amiss in Chile.

"There was widespread surmise of U.S. involvement," commented the United Press International's Martin Houseman, the most well-connected American reporter in Chile. But none of the correspondents could ever pierce the CIA veil. The man who came closest was muckraking columnist Jack Anderson, who in March 1972 first revealed the connections between the International Telegraph and Telephone Company (ITT) and the CIA, both of which wanted to protect the giant company's Chile assets. Anderson's stories caused a furor, prompting a Senate probe that saw CIA director Richard Helms deny U.S. involvement, a lie that eventually got him convicted of perjury. "Those of us who had watched United States policy at the time [1970–73] felt in our bones that [the U.S.] was intent on establishing the climate for the overthrow" of Allende, wrote Laurence R. Birns, a professor of Latin American studies, "but we lacked the proof." Hersh set out to deliver that proof.[7]

Harrington urged Congress to begin investigations, but Colby's assurances that the CIA had nothing directly to do with the Allende coup—a bending of the truth, at the very least—quieted the legislators. The day after Harrington's leaked letter was published, Hersh scurried to his Beverly, Massachusetts, home, where Harrington talked freely. Congress will not investigate, Harrington charged, because they "fear that they'll run into Kissinger."[8] The powerful Arkansas Democrat who chaired the Senate Foreign Relations Committee, Senator William J. Fulbright, will not take on the secretary of state, he added, "because it would mean exposing the fact that Kissinger himself was the man who controlled and directed the policy of using covert action to make it impossible for Allende to govern." The next day the State Department defended their wounded boss, saying that testimony given to Congress showed the United States was not involved in the Chile coup. Hersh's reporting refuted the State Department's denials. He learned that the CIA had deleted 168 passages from the book manuscript of ex-agents John D. Marks and Victor Marchetti's *Cult of Intelligence*. One censored passage quoted Kissinger in 1970 as saying, "I don't see why we need to stand by and watch a country go Communist due to the irresponsibility of its own people."[9] Kissinger would not respond, only authorizing a spokesman to say decisions regarding Chile were approved by all members of the proper government committee.

An "incensed" senator Frank Church of Idaho vowed, "I'm not going to let this matter slide by." Hersh learned that another Nixon administration official, Daniel Patrick Moynihan, then U.S. ambassador to India, was equally indignant. He wrote an angry cable to Kissinger (promptly leaked to Hersh), saying that Prime Minister Indira Gandhi feared that her country would be the next target of American intervention. Harrington, meanwhile, called a news conference to demand that Kissinger explain U.S. actions in Chile. Hersh's crusade was on.[10]

In typical *Times* fashion Hersh kept out of his stories. Journalistic rules of objectivity, of course, would not let the reporter visibly weigh in. Years later Hersh made clear what he was thinking, writing that "official distortions and lies about Chile reached a point equaled" only by Watergate. To Hersh the hand of Henry Kissinger was all over the Chile operation.[11] The ambassador to Chile during the early stages of the CIA's intervention was Edward M. Korry, who had been a well-known journalist. He was already under a microscope since columnist Anderson had written two years before that Korry was closely linked to the attempt by American businesses to block Allende's election. Korry's relationship to the CIA would become controversial and embroil Hersh in a journalistic imbroglio over his fairness and research tactics. But sources were filling Hersh's ears with Korry's alleged complicity. Hersh, logically, sought him out. According to Korry's son and his wife, Patricia, Hersh said: "I need your help in getting Kissinger. If you don't help, I will nail you." Korry balked and complained to his friends at the *Times,* but nonetheless he did talk to Hersh—consistently, on the record—over the next two months as the plot thickened.[12]

Hersh did not really need to give his opinion in the fall of 1974 because the rest of the *Times* team was using his facts and then weighing in. Wicker called it a "sordid story of indefensible American intervention." A *Times* editorial called the use of American money for intervention "appalling"; even worse was the lying to Congress. Liberal columnist Anthony Lewis called on Congress's "old-boy network" to shed its penchant for "covering up for the dirty tricks of their friends in the national security business."[13]

It was Wicker who first raised the Kissinger question publicly when he asserted on September 13 that the secretary of state "appears to have been a principal force in this covert intervention." Two days later Hersh tried to prove that was true as "well informed government sources," including former Nixon administration staffers who had read secret testimony, laid out for Hersh how Kissinger had masterminded the economic sanctions that punished Allende's government and how he pondered tougher measures, including armed invasion. The sanctions differed from the CIA activities, but, Hersh wrote, Kissinger controlled both "with great secrecy." It was explosive stuff that, for the first time, came very close to the secretary of state, the last man standing from the Nixon years. "There was set in motion a carefully planned program led by Kissinger," a source said. He chaired weekly meetings and was involved in all the minutiae of the distribution of money to foment anti-Allende activities. Kissinger was mum. Hersh noted, almost gleefully, how the secretary of state was coming under increasing criticism—and Hersh was the reason. The *Times* asked in an editorial the next day, "And what of the role of Henry Kissinger in this sordid affair?" Undoubtedly Kissinger was seething. And Hersh and the rest of the press had stirred the pot enough that the people at the top now had to act.[14]

Kissinger told the press aboard Air Force One, as President Ford returned from speaking at the United Nations, that the president would brief leading members of Congress about the American role in Chile. The Senate Foreign Relations Committee, after a long closed-door meeting, decided it must mount an investigation. Senator Fulbright told Hersh and other reporters waiting outside the meeting room that "the involvement of the CIA in other countries has been well known for years. There's not much news in that." But nonetheless the Senate would ask questions. Fulbright was piqued, however, at something else. Someone was leaking secret testimony—to Hersh—and the senators were so angry they almost refused to open a probe. "The commotion over the leaks almost wiped the whole thing off," one source said.[15] Truth was that Fulbright, an early opponent of the Vietnam War, was worried about the press's "new inquisitorial style. " Months later he wrote: "It seems to me unnecessary at this late date to dredge up every last gruesome detail of the CIA's designs" against Chile. The American people, he said, "need and desire . . . restored stability and confidence." Hersh was just a dangerous muckraker. It was a familiar refrain, one first heard in 1906 when President Roosevelt coined the word *muckraking* as a pejorative, asking the soon-to-be famous magazine journalists—Upton Sinclair, Ida Tarbell, Lincoln Steffens—to stop their revelations about American government and business. Fulbright represented the voice of the establishment decrying the post-Watergate muscle flexing of in the press. For his part Hersh was not listening. It was full steam ahead, mostly in pursuit of Kissinger, with some collateral targets—and damage—along the way.[16]

Details on how the United States tried to undermine Allende became clearer on September 20 when Hersh's inside sources asserted that the majority of the American millions of dollars went to a black market to support union groups being urged to take to the streets. Strikes by truckers, taxi drivers, and shopkeepers—as many as 250,000 people in the streets—made a violent overthrow of Allende inevitable. Hersh's sources insisted that Kissinger merely wanted the money to prevent Allende from becoming a one-party dictator, which, of course, is what his eventual successor, Augusto Pinochet, did become. The following day Hersh used congressional sources to make clear that when Kissinger testified in secret he never mentioned support of the unions. Hersh was taking Kissinger head on, in part, because no one in the Congress seemed to want to. As he later reported, when Kissinger came to testify, "The Senators rolled over and played dead. It was his celebrity status." Hersh was not so impressed. He was quickly becoming, as one magazine put it, "Henry's nemesis." His colleague Tony Lewis conceded that Kissinger was a brilliant negotiator, but he operated alone and without constraints of law or oversight. Added Wicker, someone needs to clarify Kissinger's role in this "reprehensible" act.[17]

The president was finally forced to respond. Amid the controversy over the Nixon pardon, he sought to defend the CIA's action in Chile, arguing that covert activity to prevent communism was perfectly acceptable. Howls of protest began. Ford had revived what many thought was a dead issue: Is it "proper for a democracy, using its intelligence agencies, to intervene in the internal affairs of other countries?" asked *Times* Washington bureau chief Clifton Daniel. Ford answered that "such actions are taken with the best interests of the countries involved." Senator Church demurred, as did many others, saying that Ford seems to respect "no law other than the laws of the jungle." Hersh came close to straying from his neutral position when in the *Times* "Week in Review" section—which gave reporters more leeway—he concluded that "the good old days are now gone," the days of promoting coups in the Congo and killing Che Guevara in the jungles of Bolivia. The CIA's "dirty tricks" department is in trouble, Hersh wrote, almost wistfully, noting, "These are hard days for the men who run the CIA." One third of its employees and perhaps half its budget go toward clandestine activities. But Congress is knocking at the door. Some now believe, Hersh declared, "that unless the intelligence service begins its own house cleaning, the Congress will." Wicker was more militant, asking, "Cut the CIA in half, or kill it altogether?"[18]

Hersh was running out of fresh material for his crusade. But one more source whom he cajoled into talking fostered another Kissinger controversy. Ray S. Cline, who had been director of the State Department Bureau of Intelligence, became the first insider to flatly contradict the White House's version of events. Cline alleged there was considerable opposition to the White House's strategy. However, "either Nixon or Dr. Kissinger—or both—decided to push the program," he told Hersh. Former Chile ambassador Davis said Cline's comments "enraged" Kissinger, who ordered his top deputy, Lawrence Eagleburger, to find a newsman he could trust and refute Cline's version. Eagleburger met with CBS's Daniel Schorr, who had reported on the CIA, to show him various documents undercutting Cline. The documents had Cline's handwritten comments, indicating he was at the very least not hostile to the actions.

Hersh confronted Eagleburger and wondered if it was legal for him to show classified documents to a newsman. Eagleburger said that he only told Schorr about the memos. But Hersh was able to take the documents' contents and use them against Kissinger, showing that American money had gone to support right-wing groups. The Cline story caused a ruckus. Kissinger, of course, was angry that his parrying with Hersh went poorly, and Cline felt he had been misquoted. He asked for and received a correction. He never said that union groups had directly been financed by the United States, only that they had benefited from American money. It was a minor discrepancy. But for Hersh it was clear his work was now under a microscope. The man people thought to be his initial and chief source, Representative Harrington, was being bullied by the House of Representatives. "They'll do whatever they forcefully can to make an example of me," he said, although he was later cleared of being the leak to Hersh. More importantly, Ambassador Korry, pilloried by the Senate, Wicker, and *Times* editorials, began to call all over town to demand that the Golden Boy set the record straight. It led to the closest scrutiny of Hersh's work that he had ever undergone—from the outside and from inside the *Times* itself.[19]

"Trashing the Ambassador"

Edward M. Korry was a Horatio Alger story.

Born into poverty in Manhattan, Korry became an award-winning foreign correspondent and eventually American ambassador to two foreign countries under three presidents. After graduating from a small Virginia college, he worked for NBC before joining United Press International, which made him chief Eastern Europe correspondent in 1947. He was the only U.S. reporter behind the Iron Curtain at the controversial treason trial of anticommunist Roman Catholic Hungarian priest Cardinal Josef Mindszenty. From 1954 to 1960 he was European editor of *Look*, a must-read mass circulation magazine. In 1962 he began a career in government. In 1963 President Kennedy appointed him ambassador to Ethiopia, where he helped bring about the release of captive U.S. diplomats. President Johnson named him ambassador to Chile in 1967; in 1969 Nixon asked him to stay on, even though he was identified with the Democrats.[20]

Ambassador Korry was unhappy when, in 1970, Allende was elected with a narrow thirty-thousand-vote margin, not enough to be formally declared president. The Chilean legislature would thus have to decide the election, which presented American policymakers their big chance to sway the outcome. When they failed, and Allende was certified as president, Korry sent a cable that read more like a magazine piece, writing: "There is a graveyard smell to Chile, the fumes of democracy in decomposition. They stank in my nostrils in Czechoslovakia in 1948, and they are no less sickening today." Korry did not want to see the Marxist Allende elected; Hersh's sources knew it and filled his ears with Korry's

Cold Warrior words. How far did Korry go in supporting the Kissinger-Nixon maneuverings to block Allende's election and the ousting of him from the presidency? Korry was a sideshow to Hersh's goal of showing how Kissinger was behind the Chile coup. But for Korry, his reputation, career, and livelihood were on the line, and partly in Sy Hersh's hands.[21]

Ambassador Korry surfaced early in Hersh's Chile stories. He and two other State Department officials had testified the previous year about the allegations—made first by columnist Anderson—that ITT money went to the CIA to influence the election. Anderson tied Korry to the ITT money, writing that he "ran the U.S embassy virtually as a branch office for ITT." As Hersh probed the Nixon-Kissinger-Chile axis, Korry logically came under suspicion because of his harsh anti-Allende rhetoric, even though behind the scenes he was negotiating to recover assets for American companies being nationalized. Korry adamantly denied involvement in giving money to opposition candidates, having any contact with the military, or attempting to bribe legislators. But CIA director William Colby's testimony—as Hersh read it—seemed to belie this, and the chief counsel of a Senate subcommittee looking into the matter told Hersh, pointedly, Korry was "not candid" and "in substance and spirit" his "intent was to deceive." A State Department spokesman denied the allegations. For Korry and Hersh it was the beginning of a long dance. The ex-newsman knew how journalism worked, and he understood that journalists often had to repeat what seemingly reliable sources told them, but Korry insisted to Hersh he had no knowledge of what led to Allende's overthrow, even though he did not want to see the socialist elected. Hersh did not believe Korry, plain and simple. People he trusted were telling him otherwise, and the cables he saw showed a bellicose anticommunist. "I like Ed Korry," Hersh said. "I didn't believe his account of what happened." Patricia Korry, his widow, however, insisted that early in their interviews Hersh told Korry: if you help me get Kissinger, I will clear your name. Mrs. Korry said her husband was outraged. Reporters did not blackmail sources; either he was innocent or not.[22]

On September 10, two days after Hersh's initial Chile exposé, he called Korry twice, looking to dig deeper. Korry was angry. The previous day Hersh quoted a Senate lawyer as saying Korry had lied before Congress.

Hersh could not reach Korry since he called him at an office where he had not worked for five months. NBC did find him. "Simple justice and journalistic ethics should have dictated a serious effort . . . to contact me prior to dissemination of such defamatory allegations," Korry wrote to Hersh's boss, Abe Rosenthal. Korry and Hersh then yelled at each other, with Korry charging that the CIA influence in Chile began during the Johnson years, before his time, but Hersh failed to mention that. His implication: Hersh—and the Senate—were covering up for the Democrats, noting that Hersh's story was based on a leaked letter from a Democrat. After all, Hersh had been Democrat Eugene McCarthy's press secretary! Hersh scoffed. According to Korry, Hersh then revealed his real motive: "This time we are going to nail Kissinger," he said, adding that he needed Korry to not "clam up" when Kissinger's name was mentioned. The conversation grew more heated when Korry complained that the *Times* was not printing his version, hinting at a "plot" against him. Hersh called Korry "paranoid." But Korry countered that Hersh was "guilty of extortion—abusing his power as a representative of the *Times*." Korry said Hersh then repeated he was out to get Kissinger and that unless Korry helped, "I could expect what I had gotten from him." Hersh was shouting at Korry and told him to look into the reporter's background to see what sort of man he was before he made such assertions. "He was terribly angry," Korry recalled.[23]

But so was Korry, who became obsessed with clearing his name. He eventually called two good friends at the *Times*, editor Rosenthal and Sunday editor Max Frankel. When Frankel reported from Europe as a novice foreign correspondent in the 1950s, the Korrys befriended him. Korry also helped Rosenthal, urging him to take the *Times* offer to be their correspondent in Poland, where he won a Pulitzer Prize in 1960. But Frankel could not help; it was out of his jurisdiction, and, he said, Hersh was a lone wolf who could not be controlled.[24] One wonders if either editor really cared to get too concerned with what was a minor official involved in a story with a much larger frame—the involvement of the White House in the overthrow of a foreign leader. But Hersh did keep pecking away at Korry, depicting him as desperately not wanting to be seen as the man who let Chile fall into the hands of a Marxist. In that sense he echoed President Nixon, who feared Chile would become his Cuba. The Anderson revelations of two years earlier had been even more damning than anything Hersh wrote, but although nationally syndicated, his column was often buried on back pages. Hersh was writing in the *New York Times.*

Hersh "knew what he could do," Patricia Korry said, still angry at him thirty-five years later. "He had a powerful tool" in the *Times.* Her husband wrote to Rosenthal about the "unlimited power" of the press and the "irreparable damage" to his reputation by "repeated unsubstantiated defamation." It may already "be too late to repair the damage," the fifty-three-year-old lamented, which turned out to be true as friends deserted him and disappeared. "A denial never catches up with the accusation," he added. Finally, Rosenthal gave Korry a chance to explain his side. On September 12 veteran reporter Peter Kihss went to the Korry's home north of New York City to spend four hours with the ambassador. Korry explained in detail that there was no "hard line" taken by him against Allende, that he had tried to negotiate, but that he also had been very frank—if Allende nationalized American property, "not a nut or bolt would be allowed to reach Chile under Allende."[25] A photo of Korry wearing sinister-looking dark glasses accompanied the story, which upset him. "I have not worn dark glasses for years," he muttered. He got more upset, however, when Wicker wrote a column the next day charging that Korry lied. When Hersh called again, fishing for information on Kissinger, Korry was prepared. He took notes while his wife listened on an extension, and he told Hersh he was sending the summaries to Rosenthal. "I don't know that I like that," Hersh said. Politely, Korry responded that he did not like the *Times'* "smear campaign" against him. "Are you aware of the damage you and the *Times* had done and were doing?" Hersh, unbowed, kept trying to see if Korry knew that the CIA had helped provoke strikes in Chile. Absolutely not, he replied, which turned out to be true. Why would you even ask me that, he wondered. Laughing, Hersh replied, "I did it just to provoke you." As usual Hersh was bluffing, trying to get a source to talk. "Mr. Hersh was friendly and I was courteous," Korry wrote, but he was seething at the *Times,* which he called "so egocentric, so self-righteous, so bureaucratic" that it can only "back gradually into the truth by finding new victims."[26]

By this time Rosenthal was worried about Hersh's reporting. He asked reporter John F. Burns, who later won two Pulitzer Prizes for the *Times* and who was new to the staff, to look into the treatment of Korry. Burns spent weeks reviewing stories and speaking at great length with Korry, who showed him numerous documents to argue his case. Burns concluded in a long internal report that the issues were "extraordinarily complex" and the "best fix" would be for Korry to be given magazine-length space to argue his case. "Korry had a story to tell," he said. "That story would exonerate him." But Burns did not blame Hersh, who, he said, was "always operating on the edge of the unknown. A lot of things were not entirely clear." Korry never did write his version in the *Times*, settling for a long memoir that never found a publisher. Rosenthal might just have been fed up with the Korry matter by this point. One observer said he was heard to scream, "I never want to see Korry's name in the paper again."27

Hersh—enjoying near celebrity status now—quickly moved to other big stories while Ed Korry suffered mightily. "The family name was besmirched," his son said. "We all suffered." He was only fifty-three, but "it was like living in an isolation chamber," Patricia Korry said. "It was very hard. Everything around you falls to pieces. Hersh absolutely devastated two people's lives with his tactics." Korry recalled that Hersh once said to him, "The American press is shitty. And he operated on that principle." Only one reporter, twenty-eight-year-old Joe Trento of Delaware's *Wilmington News-Journal*, believed Korry. In the winter of 1976 as he investigated the CIA-Chile connection as a freelance, he listened to Korry and scrutinized Hersh's reporting. Hersh did not take kindly to being the one under investigation. He called Trento and yelled: "You have no business reporting on this story. You should turn your sources over to me . . . I work for the *New York Times*, this is our story . . . no one will believe you. You will be laughed out of journalism." Trento persevered and wrote his stories, but no one did listen; his newspaper was too small to matter. The contempt charges pending in Congress against Korry were dropped. Yet the Korrys, feeling like exiles, moved to Switzerland.28

Fast forward to 1981, six years later. Hersh left the *Times* to pursue his obsession—a book on Kissinger. He was researching chapters on Chile, when, he claims, he found "new evidence" that vindicated Korry. He told

Rosenthal, with whom he had maintained good relations despite leaving the paper. "My God, if we were wrong in any way I would want to correct it," Rosenthal said. On February 9, over a three-column headline on page 1, the *Times* ran what was in essence a 2,300-word correction, "an extraordinary front-page mea culpa," said *Time* magazine, indeed the longest correction in the paper's history. "Evidence has come to light," Hersh maintained, "suggesting that Korry was frozen out" of the White House planning for the Allende coup. Hersh's turnaround came from documents he received from a former intelligence officer, corroboration from CIA officials, and memos unsealed by Korry. They showed that Nixon did not trust Korry and proceeded to bypass him in ousting Allende. Moreover, insiders tried to lay blame for Chile on Korry. The Senate and Hersh simply could not believe the ambassador would not know; but he did not. Hersh noted that Korry's "protestations of what he describes as unfair treatment by Congress and the press have generally been ignored." Hersh failed to note, however, that he was the key person who ignored Korry. Only a "J. Trento" of Wilmington got the facts correct, Hersh wrote.[29]

In an interview with CNN, Hersh conceded he got it wrong. Said Korry: "Hersh was the first reporter to stick it to me hard." Admitted Hersh: "I led the way in trashing him." Critics of the *Times* were gleeful. *Time* magazine covered the correction as if it were news. And they zeroed in on Hersh's motivation, implying he only decided to correct his reporting because he needed Korry's help with his Kissinger book. Hersh maintains that only when he was nearly done with his book research did he realize Korry was innocent. Privately he told Trento that Korry "was the only schmuck dumb enough to tell the truth." But he insisted he did not blackmail him, declaring, "I told him the *Times* would run a story. That's being only fair, to set the record straight. But as a quid pro quo for him helping me on Kissinger—no fucking way, it just didn't happen." When the *Columbia Journalism Review*, the nation's premier watchdog magazine, tried to write about the correction, Hersh was uncooperative. Mitchell Stephens, a young scholar who has written important books about journalism, was the writer who tried to interview Hersh. "He yelled at me, said I was trying to embarrass him," Stephens recalled. "He was very aggressive beyond what I was used to. It was a difficult experience in my life." The story never appeared. Stephens did not know why, but he would not be surprised if pressure was applied to kill it. Korry eventually returned to the States and took a teaching job. "Hurt like all pain fades," said Patricia Korry. "But it is not easy watching a whole career go down the tubes." Edward Korry died in 2003. Joe Trento spoke at his funeral. Seymour Hersh did not.[30]

CHAPTER 17

Skeletons Tumble from the CIA Closet

An Investigator's Dream

Daniel Schorr was one of America's most famous broadcasters back when the television networks—CBS, NBC, ABC—ruled the airwaves. Rumpled, gray-haired Schorr, the recipient of three Emmy awards, was part of CBS's Old Guard who learned at the feet of legendary Edward R. Murrow. His reporting earned him a place on Richard Nixon's enemies list. Schorr knew journalism. And he sensed something big was afoot in the fall of 1974 when he and his wife, Lisbeth, had a dinner party for his Washington DC neighbors, Elizabeth and Sy Hersh. Sy talked excitedly about the Central Intelligence Agency coming under increasing scrutiny since Watergate, particularly because younger employees of "The Company" were beginning to "leak" information about the agency's shadowy activities. Schorr understood what Sy was sensing. "Leaking," he said, "was a cottage industry. The anonymous source acquired a new degree of respectability." Walter Pincus, a veteran *Washington Post* reporter agreed, saying, "The town was just more open than ever."[1]

What irked Schorr and Hersh was that people began to believe that reporters lived on "leaks" in putting together stories, that it was all a world of "Deep Throats." Schorr knew better. As he observed, "A little band of Seymour Hershes and Woodward-Bernsteins knew that the story that read so comprehensively, so smoothly that it seemed to have been copied intact from a bestowed document, often was the product of weeks of painful digging, prying and assembling from many reluctant sources." Hersh agreed. "Sources are funny things, a piece there and a piece here. Nobody comes in and lays things on you," he said. A leaked story, "that's usually a story you put 200 man-hours in on."[2] For Hersh, the story and crusade that came next were actually the result of years of work. In the spring of 1973, while looking into Watergate, a Justice Department official who had worked for the CIA told Hersh that the real truth about the break-in might never come out. But, he said, "Some of the dirtiest things weren't done by the White House but by the CIA." His antenna up, Hersh started digging. Some of his Watergate stories nibbled at the edges. He tried to get top Nixon aide Charles Colson to give him information on the CIA connections of Egil (Bud) Krogh, a lawyer in charge of Nixon's "plumbers," assigned to stop White House "leaks." Hersh knew more than Colson, telling him that Krogh had a history with the CIA back to 1971 when he helped stop drug production in South Vietnam. Colson later asserted that Hersh was going to write the Krogh story, but the White House asked him to hold publication because the drug operation was still in progress.[3]

Hersh never wrote a story about Krogh. One he did write, however, in May 1973 brought him closer to the question the nation would soon ask: could the CIA — in pursuit of spies — do anything it wanted on American soil — from spying on citizens to breaking into homes? When a grand jury looked into who planned the break-in of the office of Daniel Ellsberg's psychiatrist as Nixon sought damaging information on the man who leaked the Pentagon Papers, CIA connections surfaced. Hersh explored how the 1947 law that established the CIA expressly forbid it from having "police, subpoena, law-enforcement powers or internal security functions" unless it was following espionage from abroad. The experts were not sure if the Pentagon Papers, about a war abroad, would exempt the CIA. The issue was not debated.[4] Hersh poked at the spying issue three more times over the next few weeks, but none involved the CIA, just the FBI.

Then, in spring 1974, someone in the CIA — probably one of the younger agents upset by the agency's activities — said he had heard rumors of an "in-house operation," meaning CIA domestic surveillance. "I kept on talking to people," Hersh said until someone gave him "hard facts . . . and pretty much laid out the story." Hersh had yet to give anyone at the *Times* a hint of what he was working on. He did not trust his own colleagues. "There is an awful lot of gossip. I don't go to parties simply because I find that I shoot off my mouth," he said. But Hersh also had bad experiences with some colleagues. When the *Times* established an investigative team shortly after he arrived, they had meetings. Hersh attended one. He mentioned that a source—a member of Nixon's cabinet, whom he named—had given him information. "You often have stuff I do not," the cabinet member said. Soon after the morning meeting, the cabinet member called Hersh, angry. He was asked by the White House why he was talking to reporter Hersh. Hersh believed someone on the team had squealed. After that he kept mum and avoided meetings, which did not endear him to other *Timesmen*.[5]

Pulitzer Prize-winning *Times* correspondent Harrison Salisbury recalled that as Hersh began to earnestly pursue the CIA story his desk was "stuffed with CIA materials [that he had been] collecting for years. Interviews, clippings, yellowing stories from foreign newspapers, notebooks with old scribblings." Salisbury called it "the debris of a reporter always too much on the run to sort out the paper, but there it was, an investigator's dream, the raw materials of a dozen smash stories just waiting to be fleshed out." The notes aside, Salisbury pointed out, "Hersh had something else—phone numbers of the men in the Agency, out of the Agency, favorable to the Agency, critical of the Agency," the most important weapon "of the best investigative reporter in the business."[6]

"I Knew How Important This Story Would Be"

William Colby was fifty-three when he ascended to the seventh floor of CIA headquarters in Langley, Virginia, the seventh director of the agency. He succeeded James Schlesinger, who was not well liked—his firing of personnel and changes in polices had irked the old-timers. He had done something else worrisome. After it emerged that the CIA was involved in Watergate, he ordered a report of current or past CIA actions that may have violated the agency's charter. The result was a 693-page document, known as "The Family Jewels," that chronicled twenty-five years of CIA abuses. It was explosive stuff, called by Henry Kissinger "the horrors book." The report was handed over to Colby, who hoped and prayed its contents stayed secret. Then Sy Hersh came along. Before long "The Year of Intelligence" would engulf America, producing an "intensity of emotion," said Salisbury, like Washington had never seen. "It was a grueling year," remembered Colby, one that would threaten the very existence of the spy agency.[7]

Hersh was piecing together his work on domestic spying by the CIA when he was interrupted by Representative Michael Harrington's letter on Chile that started his two-month, twenty-seven-story takeout. The Chile results were still coming in. Former CIA director Richard Helms had to plea-bargain to stay out of jail. The chairman of a Senate oversight committee ordered the CIA to stop meddling in other countries' politics. Kissinger was under more pressure than ever, but he walked away from the Chile matter untouched, declaring years later, "We were right in our assessment of the perils to our interest." America, he insisted, simply sought to "promote a clear-cut choice between the democratic and the totalitarian forces." Hersh was dubious; he had not given up on getting Kissinger, telling a *Rolling Stone* interviewer, "I guess I'm one of those people who doesn't believe that there's anybody who could have been as close as (Kissinger) was to as much as he was who doesn't have some explaining to do." Hersh added. "I'm looking at him very hard to be perfectly honest."[8]

Salisbury, a longtime observer of the press, said that Hersh was "born for this moment"—the best investigative reporter in America going after the unchallenged "secret government." In 1966 the *Times* assembled twenty reporters who put together a five-day look at the CIA, but the result was tame. The *Times* allowed CIA director John McCone to read the articles before publication. This only confirmed whispers that the *Times* publisher and top brass were too cozy with the spy agency. But this was the era before Watergate. Hersh now had much more freedom, not that the forty-nine-year-old *Times* publisher Arthur Ochs (Punch) Sulzberger had much comfort with Hersh. "He can't have liked the disheveled Sy," Salisbury pointed out. "Punch was a neatness fanatic." Moreover, he was publisher of the "establishment's" most trusted voice. Was this story "fit to print"? Meanwhile, Hersh returned to his early CIA sources, saying, "Once you know more about the subject, you can go back." Finally he began to feel comfortable with what he knew. He called Colby to declare he had a story "bigger than My Lai." Colby "stonewalled" Hersh but said privately in a memo that Hersh was "bluffing." Colby's memo leaked to Hersh; he called Colby the next day, warning he was not bluffing.[9]

Colby paid attention, commenting, "Although Hersh and I could usually be found on the opposite side of any issue involving the CIA, I had every reason to respect his journalistic integrity. I owed him the interview he requested and could trust his responsibility both as an American and as a hard-driving newsman." On Friday, December 20, the two met in Colby's office. Hersh said he knew of a "massive" CIA operation against the antiwar movement that included wiretaps, break-ins, and mail intercepts. Colby did not deny it, but called it an exaggerated, "disjointed and distorted account." He did not ask Hersh for his sources, knowing full well that "a journalist of Hersh's standing would protect his sources as fiercely as would we in intelligence." Colby suspected that the minions who had been fired or retired from the CIA were likely talking to Hersh; he did not know the depth of anger in the younger employees. Colby tried to steer Hersh from the exposé, saying, "You would be wrong if you went ahead with your story in the way you've laid it out. What you have are a few indigents . . . straying from the straight and narrow." Sy was not intimidated by the cold blue eyes of The Spymaster. Recalled Colby, "Hersh didn't see it my way at all." In fact, Hersh took his comments as confirmation. He was ready to write, telling Rosenthal what he had. No one asked, Hersh recalled, "Are you sure about this? No one asked, is this gonna be good for America?" Since it was three days before Christmas, the *Times* news pages were full of advertisements. The New York editors told Hersh to keep the story tight. He balked, and Rosenthal backed him. "Take a full page," he said. Hersh was elated. "I knew how important this story would be." When a story is near completion, he said, "It's a certain jubilation. When I've done the last interview, when I've got the last thing I need, then I do my little version of the Snoopy dance and get happy."[10] But no one in the government would be happy.

"We Don't Want a Gestapo"

On December 22, 1974, Hersh hit the front page once again with a four-thousand-word story in the upper right-hand corner with a three-line headline that read: "Huge CIA Operation Reported in U.S. against Antiwar

Forces, Other Dissidents in Nixon Years." Photos of Colby, Helms, and Schlesinger accompanied the story. Ironically, adjacent was a picture of President Ford and Vice President Rockefeller smiling over a new assignment given the vice president. Neither would be smiling very long, and Rockefeller would soon oversee the president's investigation into Hersh's exposé. Hersh's lead stated: "The Central Intelligence Agency, directly violating its charter, conducted a massive, illegal domestic intelligence operation during the Nixon Administration against the antiwar movement and other dissident groups in the United States, according to well-placed government sources." A straightforward summary—but the word "massive" was controversial, adamantly denied by Colby, and tossed around by critics as proof that Hersh was intent on exaggerating and sabotaging the CIA. He said that at least ten thousand dossiers had been compiled on American citizens, including congressmen, conjuring images of a police state. He was hardly exaggerating, in fact, because eventually the government conceded the number was more like three hundred thousand.[11]

The opening salvo—thirty-four articles by Hersh over the coming months and hundreds of follow-up stories by the *Times*—was vintage Sy Hersh. Critical information all came from unnamed "sources," and all of the key players—the president (who was briefed), three CIA directors, and the Justice Department—refused to comment, at least on the record. Much was vague. "No names could be learned nor could any details on alleged break-ins or wiretapping," he wrote. The disclosure "is the first possible connection to rumors that have been circulating in Washington for some time." Some of his sources gasped at what he was revealing. One high-level Justice Department staffer said, "Oh my God, Oh my God, they're not supposed to have any counterintelligence in this country." A professor contacted by Hersh noted that when the CIA was created, Congress was clear: "We don't want a Gestapo." An FBI official, nameless, chimed in: "We had an agreement with them. They weren't to do anything unless they checked with us. They double crossed me all along."[12]

But another persistent side of Hersh was evident—he worked hard to explain the government point of view. Colby would not talk; he pointed Hersh to a speech in which he conceded "some improprieties" but insisted they had been halted, adding, "I think family skeletons are best left where they are—in the closet." Fat chance. The skeletons and the jewels were about to come tumbling out. Schlesinger was actually praised for trying during his tenure as director to halt to the abuses he inherited from Helms. "He found himself in a cesspool," one associate said. Hersh did not know, however, that Schlesinger had ordered an internal investigation, and he had no clue that the "Family Jewels" list—replete with assassinations—was compiled. His story on the domestic surveillance—called Operation CHAOS—was but a small slice of the pie. Hersh's thrust was to explore whether the CIA domestic surveillance might have been justified. "High ranking American intelligence officials" confirmed the outline of Hersh's story but warned him not to draw "unwarranted conclusions." The domestic surveillance was done to nab foreign spies on American soil. Other sources mocked this contention. "If you're an agent sitting in Paris and you're asked to find out whether Jane Fonda is being manipulated by foreign intelligence services," one official said, "you've got to ask yourself who is the real target, the spies or Fonda?" He called the scenario "very spooky," adding, "every one of these acts was blatantly illegal. . . . the agency did things that would amaze both of us."[13]

And then Hersh came to most bizarre part of his story—a peak into the world of James Jesus Angleton, the mysterious head of the agency's most powerful unit, counterintelligence. Alternately known as "Old Kingfish" or the "Master Spy," Angleton was the man who stopped their spies from infiltrating our spies. Colby had long wanted to ease Angleton out of power; after twenty years his Cold War mentality was an anachronism. Moreover, he was responsible for many of the illegal domestic forays. Colby worried about Angleton's mental health and feared if fired he might kill himself. He tried to ease him into a new position, but Angleton refused. Colby learned that Hersh would allege that Angleton had run illegal spy operations. Hersh called Angleton for a response. And the spy who had lived an invisible existence talked, telling Hersh that his people knew their jurisdiction. Then, confirming Colby's fear, he rambled on about intercepts of information in Korea, about black militants, and about how a source in the Soviet Union, still active, had provided important intelligence. FBI agents were shocked that he was discussing this with a reporter. "That's even a better story than the domestic spying," an indignant congressman (no name) told Hersh. On the day that Hersh's story appeared—unbeknownst to the reporter—Colby called Angleton to his office. "This story is going to be tough to handle," he said. "We've talked about your leaving before. You will now leave, period." Hersh's story had not yet hit the press, and already there was one victim. The Master Spy was out in the cold.[14]

Gerald Ford was on his way to Vail, Colorado, for a skiing holiday, when the story broke. By the time he arrived, the press was buzzing around. Kissinger called him twice; Schlesinger also checked in. He had already heard from Colby, who promised, "Mr. President I want to assure you that nothing comparable to the article's allegations is going on in the Agency at this time." Ford asked Colby for a report—"within a matter of days"—to go to Kissinger, still in charge of national security. Kissinger initially wished Colby had denied it all in talking to Hersh until he learned that the domestic surveillance was the tip of the iceberg. Neither he nor Nixon knew about "the Family Jewels." "Now I see why you couldn't" deny Hersh's disclosures, he told Colby. Laurence Silberman, the acting attorney general, visited Colby the day the article appeared, waving the newspaper. "What else have you boys got tucked up your sleeves?" Did Colby have evidence of criminal activities? Hersh, of course, was looking for follow-up stories.

While the Ford team figured out how to respond, Hersh received a troubling call from Angleton. "Do you know what you've done? You've blown my cover. My wife, in 31 years of marriage, was never aware of my activity until your story. And now she's left me." Hersh said, "I was stunned by the despair in his voice." He mumbled an apology about a newsman's obligation to truth. And then a CIA source, laughing, told him: his wife did leave him three years ago to live in Arizona; she has since returned, and she always knew about his work. The spy was just playing Hersh, but it made him nervous. After his CIA stories appeared, he went to a restaurant where a waiter belligerently approached him, yelling, "What are you doing to my friend Jim Angleton?" The spooks were angry at Hersh for turning their world upside down. Hersh was trying not to look over his shoulder. "I don't think about it," he said. "I don't think about my phones being tapped. I just use them. Otherwise I'm forced into some perverted position. Forced to act like some of the people I don't approve of. Let them tap me." Nonetheless, scrambling began inside the government. "No series of news stories since Watergate has had so quick an impact on government," wrote *New Republic* editor Walter Pincus, a Hersh friend.[15]

The Firestorm

In unmasking CIA involvement in Chile, Hersh put the agency on the run for its foreign endeavors. Chile was its greatest crisis. But now things had gotten worse. Hersh was attacking the tentacles that reached onto domestic soil where its charter forbids activity. Hersh was alleging that snooping had begun in the 1950s and then got worse as Nixon became furious with antiwar protestors and militants. Cold Warriors such as Angleton were sure they were inspired by communists, but Hersh made clear no one else believed that. How close to reality was Hersh? Did he exaggerate? Were his sources to be believed? Couldn't someone go on the record? Wasn't there some document that could prove the spying? The counter-attack on Hersh's work was furious. "The grey *New York Times* has decided to undertake what I consider advocacy journalism in its news columns," wrote Pincus. Even people inside the *Times* were suspicious.[16]

Five days after Hersh's story, John Oakes, editor of the editorial page and nephew of the *Times* founding publisher, Adolph Ochs, wrote a nasty note to Rosenthal, calling Hersh's story the latest example of "tendentious reporting in the *Times*." Oakes complained that the "breathless, prejudicial, pejorative and truly non-objective manner" of the Hersh stories "seem to be a betrayal of the Times' own standards of objective journalism." After the New Year, Rosenthal fired back at Oakes's "embarrassing harangue," adding, "Your emotional, pejorative, denunciatory, and self-serving style brings out the worst in me. Let me leave it at this: Hersh and The Times broke a story that will go down in the annals of American journalism as one that contributed vitally to the understanding of our times and the betterment of our society." Rosenthal could not resist a parting shot: "If indeed you have encouraged investigative reporting on this paper, it certainly has been a well-kept secret." Oakes volleyed back.

"You must be kidding. Your hysterical and personally insulting response to my memo . . . is hardly an example of rational level of discourse." Quietly, however, even Rosenthal was concerned. He told Hersh that "as valuable and fruitful for The Times and yourself as the period . . . has been, the years ahead will be even more so, and that's saying a hell of a lot." But the editor cautioned: limit your anonymous sources. "It's our obligation to be extremely careful, restrained and judicious. Using them puzzles the reader at the best, and raises questions about the credibility of the story at the worst."[17]

Rosenthal backed Hersh because he was keeping the *Times* ahead of all competitors and because he knew who Hersh's sources were; they did exist. But something else made Rosenthal get behind his star reporter. In the fall, when the Chile stories were appearing, Hersh and Rosenthal visited Colby. "How come every time I come across the CIA I find they are on the side of the fingernail pullers?" he asked the director, who replied, calmly, "We are only a function of what the President wants." Rosenthal was shaken and told Hersh to keep probing.[18] Meanwhile, Hersh lurched around for fresh angles—and support. "You don't think," he said, "I'd relish a helluva good story by somebody who found a couple of undercover CIA guys who'd tell what the truth is?" The *Washington Post* called Laurence Stern back from a leave to get on the story, but its editorials attacked the *Times* story as lacking proof. Conservative syndicated newspaper columnist James Kilpatrick asked how Hersh could call the CIA actions illegal. "No one ever named Hersh a federal judge," he said. Another columnist, John Lofton, called the story "over-written, overplayed, underresearched and underproven." Leslie Gelb, the *Times* national security correspondent, found that "the story immediately became suspect, not only in predictable conservative quarters, but in some parts of the liberal establishment in general and the news media in particular." In essence, Hersh and the *Times* were all alone, like Bernstein and Woodward were for a long time on Watergate. It did not stop Hersh's allegations from becoming fodder for Georgetown cocktail parties—Kissinger was the leak in order to get rid of Colby! No, it was Colby who was trying to get back at Richard Helms![19]

Both *Time* and *Newsweek* recognized the import—and controversy—of the exposé, writing stories in the same week in January. *Time,* calling him "an almost unrivaled master of the governmental exposé," found Hersh "talkative, churning, abrupt, zealous, egotistical and abrasively honest . . . like a blast of air rushing in and out of the insulated corridors of Washington's secretive institutions." Being an investigative reporter, Hersh told *Time*, "is like being a freak. You're trying to get information other people don't want you to have. I read, I listen, I squirrel information. It's fun." It could not have been that much fun, however. The attacks intensified. Angleton told the TV networks that Hersh was a "son of a bitch" who was helping the KGB, adding, "You've done them a great favor." Hersh was in "a lonely and difficult position," observed David Wise, a former reporter who wrote one of the first books about the CIA.[20]

On New Year's Day Hersh reported that "well-placed government sources" told him that Colby had confirmed the *Times'* allegations. The *Times* lost no chance to promote its story. In the three weeks after the story appeared, it ran thirty-two follow-up stories and mentioned its own scoop thirty-eight times, prompting publisher Sulzberger to write: "Let's stop blowing our own horn, because it is certainly overly noticeable." Behind the scenes, aides to Ford—in particular, Richard Cheney—were urging the president to aggressively mount his own investigation as a way to forestall worse revelations and to stop Congress from taking over. Kissinger warned Ford that Hersh's stories "are just the tip of the iceberg. If they come out, blood will flow." On January , Ford announced that he had asked Vice President Rockefeller to head an eight-man panel (including Ronald Reagan) to look into the allegations and report back in ninety days. It was the first victory for the *Times*. Then both the Senate and House of Representatives declared they too would investigate. Senator Frank Church, a squeaky-clean South Dakota senator with presidential aspirations, assembled a fifty-three-person staff to start an investigation, while Otis Pike of Long Island, New York, an old Hersh source, chaired the House probe. Before they got organized, a Senate committee on intelligence called Colby to testify. He went behind closed doors, but then he gave the committee permission to release his forty-five-page statement, prompting Kissinger to complain, "Colby must be brought under control." Colby insisted to Congress that the CIA never engaged in "massive" domestic surveillance, but, he conceded, about ten thousand dossiers had been compiled. "Whether we strayed over the edge of our authority on a few occasions over the past 27 years is a question for those authorized to investigate these matters to judge," he observed. The *Times* spread the admission across the top of page one![21]

With Colby's concession in hand, the investigation of the CIA's misdeeds took off. "In Congress and the mainstream media, the boundaries of debate suddenly expanded. Elite opinion leaders were willing to question institutions that had never been challenged before," observed political scientist Kathryn S. Olmsted. While Hersh wrote some stories with new revelations—spying on actress Eartha Kitt; a threat to shred the ten thousand dossiers—mostly the story took on a life of its own, and Hersh backed away—for two reasons. First, it was hard to separate him from the scandal. His story was constantly raised, and it was his allegations that the government was investigating. Hersh had become part of the story. But he said the reason was simpler—his wife, Liz, had been accepted to medical school in New York, and the Hershes were planning to move. Family matters pulled him away, a rarity for the man who worked morning, night, and weekends. Nicholas Horrock, over from *Newsweek*, and John Crewdson, who had worked on Watergate, took over coverage of the three major investigations. The revelations that followed were head spinning and well beyond Hersh's small piece of the puzzle: the CIA plotted with the mob to kill Fidel Castro, Patrice Lumumba of the Congo, and Rafael Trujillo of the Dominican Republic; it experimented with using LSD on unsuspecting Americans; the Post Office helped in opening Americans' mail; a girlfriend of President Kennedy had links to organized crime; and New York congresswoman Bella Abzug's mail had been rifled by the agency. Pandora's box was open, thanks to Sy Hersh, and as one scholar noted, the last major battle of the liberal crusade against executive branch secrecy was underway. "The crusade began with Vietnam, continued through Watergate and ended with an assault on the institutions of secrecy themselves," declared Olmsted. Two questions remained: Would the intelligence investigating committees conclude that a "massive" surveillance of American citizens had taken place? And would it mean anything—could America really be ready to reform or change the CIA?[22]

CHAPTER 18

The Submarine Caper

The "Clark Kent Hero"

As the CIA story splashed across America's front pages, Sy Hersh became the darling of the national media. He had experienced this before after My Lai. Now it happened again as the press corps caught up with him. "I'm sort of cast in the mold of Cracker Jack reporter, the Clark Kent hero," he observed, and the ego-driven Hersh did not shy away. In fact, his high profile made investigative reporting all the fashion. *Times* publisher Arthur Sulzberger actually told his newsroom to stop saying the paper had hired investigative reporters. "All reporters should be 'investigative reporters' for whatever that means," he wrote. But no one paid much heed. Teams of investigative reporters became the norm at large newspapers, and an entire organization, Investigative Reporters and Editors (IRE!) was created. "It's fashionable now to call some of us investigative," Hersh admitted.[1]

Time and *Newsweek*, America's largest-circulation magazines, wrote profiles of Hersh in the same week. The *Washington Post*'s Leonard Downie wrote a long book chapter on him for *The New Muckrakers*. He marveled at Hersh's "defiant, tenacious, often badgering, and sometimes belligerent style of reporting seldom exhibited by any newspaper's Washington correspondent, much less one for the prestigious and proper *New York Times*." One of Hersh's anonymous sources described him as "a man on the run, like Sammy Glick, running all the time. On the phone he is almost breathless, and I mean at two in the morning!" Other sources complained about Hersh's "screaming tantrums" when they wouldn't talk, but conceded he could also be charming. Hersh admitted he was frustrated by the success of the *Post*'s Woodward and Bernstein, saying, "I'm in a situation where I'd like to make more money. It's a very crass materialistic thing to say, but it's a fact. I wouldn't mind making a million dollars on a book, having Robert Redford play me would not bother me at all." The Hersh-Woodward rivalry was in full swing.[2]

No movie was forthcoming, but his fame was enough for *Rolling Stone* magazine to send writer Joe Eszterhas, later a famous Hollywood screenwriter, to conduct a two-part interview. Annie Liebovitz, the famous photographer, was sent to capture Hersh—his feet propped on a desk; at an airport telephone getting in one last call; carrying a typewriter at his Washington house, with a rare glimpse of wife Liz and son Matthew. Hersh, who was drinking, was loose lipped to Eszterhas, who called him "a hurricane of a man who seems to approach life as if it were a battlefield. He walks and talks like a speed freak but the energy is all natural; he doesn't even smoke." Reflecting on his fame, Hersh said, "I don't get any sense that I am an American folk hero at all." In fact, he said, "We should be looked upon maybe as super schlemiels. My God! We're responsible for letting them get away with it." As for his exploits, Hersh said, "I'm doing the same thing I did in 1959 and '60 and '61, just trying to tell as much as I can about something." But the CIA story worried him. "I do not have a piece of paper that says: 'top secret, the following is a summary of CIA domestic operations.' Without that piece of paper, no reporter feels comfortable. No matter how good your sources are, how careful you are, there's always a certain amount of anxiety when you drop a bomb."[3]

And the powers-that-be kept pounding away at Hersh. Colby warned about "serious damage to our country's essential intelligence," insisting Hersh's story was filled with "exaggerations and misrepresentations." *Times* columnist Tom Wicker fired back, pointing out that "the oldest bureaucratic defense known to man is . . . to convince the public that the critics are the problem rather than the thing being criticized."[4] Former *Times* columnist Leslie Gelb, in the *New Republic*, took apart Colby's testimony before Congress and, in essence, confirmed all of Hersh's allegations. His only beef was with the word "massive." But make no mistake about it, Gelb noted, "the city is in motion on the subject of covert activities."[5]

Judgment on Hersh's work—at least partially—finally came on June 2 when the 350-page report of the Rockefeller Commission was released with fanfare. The vice president said there indeed had been violations of law, "but in comparison to the total effort they are not major." They were not "massive," Rockefeller said, adding, "That does not mean there were not things done that were wrong." Hersh's original exposé did not come up, but it was still the talk of the town. Enough so that former Kissinger aide Morton Halperin wrote a long analysis for the *New Republic* and, like Gelb three months earlier, reached the conclusion that Hersh was on the mark. He compared point by point the Hersh story to the commission's findings, concluding, "Every fact save one in *The Times* story is confirmed by the commission. The agency pulled out all the stops in the effort to divert attention from its activities to a discussion on how Sy and *The Times* could have gone so wrong."[6] This *was* a massive operation, Halperin insisted. *Times* columnist Anthony Lewis was angry, proclaiming, "there can be no doubt any longer about the correctness of the Hersh story—or of *The Times'* decision to play it prominently." If anything, Hersh understated the horrors. Hersh should be thanked, not pilloried: "The politicians did nothing until Seymour Hersh forced their hand."[7]

Hersh finally got to comment in the *Times* Sunday "Week in Review." He did not crow nor even review whether the Rockefeller report confirmed his reporting. He asked a bigger question: "Is it possible for an agency as secret and powerful as the CIA to operate at all in a democracy?" He was indignant the report was so "dry and legalistic, as if the issue were a dispute over corporate book keeping." What about "the lack of morality" in the CIA? What is needed now, he said, is a new evaluation of what and who constitute a threat. The CIA's troubles, Hersh lamented, "are far more deeply rooted" than Rockefeller can admit. What was still not clear, however, was if Hersh's work—and two congressional investigations—would make a difference in the way the CIA operated or was controlled. Eventually the Church Commission issued a 214-volume report, thorough and exhaustive. And for a while at least it appeared the beast had been corralled.[8]

The consensus of historians and political scientists who have studied the Hersh-CIA episode is not a surprise—the immediate reaction was profound, dramatic, "a truly major event." The impact initially caused a shift in public opinion that exerted great pressure for reform. And Congress did begin much closer oversight. But in the long run, the agency not only survived but got past the crisis to resume its power, albeit not on American soil. The public moved on as the story faded and the various investigations dragged on. There continued to be "some unease," commented scholar Cynthia Nolan, but "no outcry." Historian Kathryn S. Olmsted concluded that "by the end of the 1970s, Americans knew more about their government's secrets and misdeeds than any people in history. And the more they learned, the more they suspected that the government was still hiding bigger, more explosive secrets." But they also grew nervous about wrecking the agency. Writer William Greider declared: "There is a strong wish all over town, a palpable feeling that it would be nice if somehow this genie could be put back in the bottle." By the time the investigations were over, Olmsted maintained, the press, the Congress, and the public "preferred to maintain their basic deference to the secret government." Would the Scoop Artist bow and scrape before the badly wounded CIA or keep going for the kill? The answer was mixed as the great *Glomar Explorer* submarine caper soon proved.[9]

The "Family Jewels" started out as the CIA's deepest dark secret, to be protected at all costs. Sy Hersh's exposé of the government's illegal domestic surveillance opened the door for the jewels to come spilling out. But in its day the article was rebuked. Hersh thought it deserved a Pulitzer Prize. In April 1975, when the winners are announced, he called one Pulitzer judge. "Did I win?" he asked repeatedly. "Sy, you know I can't tell you that." Hersh called the juror the next day to tell him he had learned he did not win. "I am sorry, I know," the juror said. "Ah ha, so I didn't win. You could have told me that yesterday." And then Hersh hung up, his bluffing tactics having worked again.[10] The Pulitzer board rejected his article—the decision was leaked to the press—because, as one judge said, it was "overwritten and under proven." This, despite that its facts were all borne out and it launched three major investigations. The real reason: the jurors wanted to avoid the controversy that had dogged its choices in previous years. In a condolence note to three *Times* reporters who lost, editor Rosenthal said: "If the work each of you did this year had been recognized, not one journalist in the country would have been surprised. The fact that none of you did tells a lot about the selection problem. But the hell with that." Hersh's right-wing critics were gleeful. John

Lofton, still smarting from Hersh's My Lai award, gloated that a Pulitzer juror had told him "they did not care for Hersh's reporting at all, not at all." When Rosenthal was contacted by Lofton, he cursed and screamed and said the reporting would be proven "totally accurate." Which it was. Hersh brushed it off and turned to another direct confrontation with the Ford administration.[11]

The CIA's Deep, Dark Underwater Secret

Seymour Hersh is always open for business. His home and office phone numbers are publicly listed. He answers his own phone, usually in an impatient tone: "Hersh." He works the phones night and day. "I'm the clearinghouse for every tipster in the country," Hersh says. "I talk to anybody." After the CIA story the calls increased. He chased one story for weeks. "When I got all done I realized I didn't like it. It didn't smell right. I killed it," he recalled. Some panned out. For example, a man who worked for the CIA in the mid-1960s came forward after Hersh's big exposé and described how he was one of twenty-five agents assigned to monitor radical activities in New York City, sometimes undercover.[12] The detail the ex-agent supplied satisfied Hersh. "You fly by the seat of your pants to a point," Hersh said. "You use your instincts and common sense." He spent a week interviewing the CIA agent. Not all sources got such a welcome, especially reporters prying into his work. After the CIA exposé a reporter called, asking if he had been on the phone with CIA director Colby in the last six months and trying to discern Hersh's sources. What do you want? he asked. Just answer the question, she said. "I told her to go to hell," Hersh recalled.

The constant trolling of sources coupled with people who inevitably sought out the great investigative reporter paid dividends. In late fall 1973, as Hersh worked on Watergate and Chile stories, a source gave him a tip about "this crazy scheme" being worked on by the CIA. The government was planning a top-secret maneuver to lift Russian missiles from the Pacific Ocean floor. The missiles, he was told, had been fired from Central Asia on a test course and settled sixteen thousand feet below the surface. The project needed a huge barge to lift the missiles. The name Project Jennifer kept coming. Hersh called all over town to check the tip, which alerted the CIA. What alarmed them was the real story of what was about to take place beneath the ocean floor and the risk posed to the nation's security.[13]

What resembled something out of a Tom Clancy novel began in 1969 when a Soviet submarine, with three nuclear missiles, sunk in the Pacific for reasons that were not clear. All ninety-seven seamen died. The Russians, of course, knew the sub was missing but had no idea where it had gone down. Recovery efforts failed. American intelligence also knew the sub was lost, and advanced American detection equipment located it 750 miles northwest of Hawaii. After the United States took nearly twenty thousand photos, the navy and the CIA came up with a plan—build a trawler with a mammoth undercarriage, hook up claws longer than any ever used, retrieve the sub, missiles intact, and tow it back to California. The missiles could reveal enemy codes, a potentially huge intelligence find, even if they were outdated. Early in the Nixon administration, it was approved. The big question: could a ship be built big enough to hold the 328-foot sub and to lift this two-thousand-ton vessel. To some it was a folly; no one had ever gone this deep for a salvage. The government's top two admirals were opposed. To others, including Kissinger and Defense secretary Melvin Laird, it was worth the try.[14]

The estimated cost of the project was $300 million, although the figure rose to $800 million. Ideally, in a democracy, a risky venture with such a price tag would be vigorously debated by Congress and public. But the project had to proceed in absolute secrecy. The government was convinced if the Russians knew—and they did not—they would force a military confrontation. The Russians would not easily give up missiles or secret codes. Nor did they want a vessel with dead Russian soldiers disturbed. Keeping such a huge venture—with hundreds involved from the military, the CIA, and a private shipbuilding company—under wraps would be a challenge. So when Hersh began his inquiry, CIA director William Colby knew he faced a serious hurdle. "I realized," said Colby, "there was no chance that any number of hard-nosed investigative reporters would overlook the tantalizing references to the CIA." And, he knew, "they would surely be led by Seymour Hersh."[15]

Could he convince Hersh to drop the story? On January 9 and 21, 1974, he talked with science adviser Carl Duckett, who was involved in the CIA's most sophisticated intelligence-gathering endeavors, to discuss their "problem with newsman," namely, Hersh. They both believed he was working on a book on the submarine, which was not true. On January 22 in a conference call, possibly with Henry Kissinger, the speaker (the name is deleted from the CIA transcript) told Colby that "you should proceed to see the one gentleman [Hersh] and do the best you can." If "forced to," the speaker said, "go ahead and yield and say . . . we will give them the 'best story.'" The CIA was willing to make a deal—have Hersh hold the story, and when the time was right, they would give him the most information. Colby replied: "The only trouble about this is that I just had lunch with (name deleted) and some others and they were horrified at the name of the first gentleman." They were afraid of dealing with Sy Hersh. And, in fact, Kissinger told Colby he was "crazy" to be talking at all to Hersh. "I think they are wrong," Colby said. Most of all, Colby added, if he did not get Hersh on board, "it is hopeless"—the story will come out. Later in the afternoon, the morning caller spoke again with Colby and said not to speak directly with Hersh, but to try "either of his two bosses." No names are mentioned, but one is surely Clifton Daniel, Washington bureau chief, and the other Arthur Sulzberger, the *Times* publisher, who later received phone calls directly from Colby and Kissinger. They avoided A. M. Rosenthal, who had fought them on the Pentagon Papers. "Most of the guys up there in New York—a naked appeal will do you no good," the caller told Colby.[16]

On January 30 Colby called someone in the *Times* DC bureau, probably Daniel, who, after all, was President Truman's son-in-law. Colby explained that Hersh had been talking about "a particular subject, which I would rather not discuss on the phone, which gives me a great deal of concern, and I would like to talk to him about them." Colby, politely, asked if the *Times* would object. "I obviously have no authority over him . . . but I thought I might appeal to him," he said. The *Times* editor said he had "no objection" to anyone on the staff talking to Hersh, but he was out ill that day.[17] Later in the afternoon, however, the editor called Colby back to say that Hersh "has risen from his bed and is in the office right this minute. He is a little puzzled about what it is you are talking about."

Told many years later that someone in the *Times* office was reporting to the CIA on his activities, Hersh said, "Pretty pathetic, isn't it? Actually surprises me that someone would be such a patsy . . . at that time . . . for the Agency." Colby wasted little time when he learned that Hersh was in the office, calling to discuss "a subject which I would rather not talk about over the phone . . . but it does give me a great deal of concern."[18]

"I can guess what you are talking about, and I think you should recognize I have not published," Hersh pointed out as both men avoided mentioning Project Jennifer. He complained about CIA "game-playing," but added, "For all the trouble we give you, look at the story we do not write." Colby then said what was really on his mind: he wanted Hersh to not even mention the submarine story, to not even talk about it to sources. "It is terribly important to me—to all of us," Colby said. He wanted to come in that afternoon but instead made an appointment for Friday, February 1, at the *Times* office.

Bob Phelps was Sy Hersh's main editor in Washington, working closely with him on Watergate. Sy ran to Phelps's desk and said he needed help. The director of the CIA was coming to the eighth-floor offices; Sy wanted a witness. Colby pulled up in a stretch limousine; the office was in a twitter. Hersh brought Colby to Phelps's office. He sat in a straight-back chair and Sy in a rocker. Phelps was in the dark about the subject. "I had never heard of the sunken Soviet submarine until that meeting," he said. "That was normal in our bureau. Reporters often worked on stories without telling the editors." Colby appealed to Hersh to withhold the story. "Sy danced around the question," Phelps said, "trying to convince Colby he knew everything and fishing for more information."[19] Actually Hersh did not know very much, but he bluffed, telling Colby that the flawed technology would not work. He insisted his job was to get the story, and then his editors would decide whether to print. Phelps said it would be sent to New York for a final decision. "If it was a national security question, the publisher would decide," Phelps told Colby. When Colby left, the New York editors were told of the visit. Colby left feeling that, at the least, as he told a colleague, "I have a firm commitment from him to show me anything before he prints." Hersh actually had no plans to tackle this story for at least six months. "There is too much going on with Watergate," he said. But he warned Colby that his main source was "blabbing" the story around town. "I said I could not help that," Colby said, stressing to Hersh's superiors, "I was as interested in their keeping their mouths shut and pens quiet."[20]

Colby called a number of officials after the meeting, exultant to have convinced Hersh not to even talk about the story. Now he wanted to get others at the *Times* on board. On February 20 Colby went to a New York luncheon with Sulzberger and top *Times* editors. This was commonplace. In fact, during Hersh's CIA spying stories, a White House luncheon with President Ford caused a flap. In discussing the Rockefeller Commission investigation, Ford said the investigators were to stay away from foreign operations of the CIA, which he labeled a "cesspool." Asked for clarification, he revealed that assassinations of foreign leaders would be uncovered. *Times* editors were shocked. But the meeting was off the record, and they were sworn to secrecy. Hersh got wind of something, but Rosenthal simply told him, "Keep on working." "On what?" Hersh asked. Rosenthal could not say. Eventually, Hersh's friend Daniel Schorr learned of the comments and reported the president's remarks, scooping the *Times*. Nonetheless, the off-the-record luncheons continued. At the end of the February 20 gathering, Colby took Sulzberger aside, briefing him on the submarine story and his conversation with Hersh. "He was great," Colby reported. "He was delighted to be trusted." So much for the adversarial press-government relationship. With Hersh busy and Sulzberger urging his staff to avoid the story, the submarine venture was not going to soon see the light of day—until an unexpected burglary occurred in February 1975, nearly a year later.[21]

First Silence, Then a Roar

While Hersh chased Watergate and Chile, the CIA moved ahead with its daring attempt to lift the Soviet submarine. It was one of the most complex, expensive, and secretive intelligence operations of the Cold War, "unquestionably the most ambitious and the most audacious ocean engineering effort ever attempted," wrote two scholars. And it all had to be done without media attention or, more importantly, the Soviet Union learning of the venture. That was why Colby felt so strongly that national security was at stake. "It would mean war," said a Soviet naval officer. The Howard Hughes Company was enlisted as cover, insisting the *Glomar Explorer* was being built to mine minerals, which was believable given the reclusive billionaire's penchant for deep-sea ventures.[22]

On June 5 the secret 40 Committee, headed by Henry Kissinger, approved the plan. But on that very day the Hollywood headquarters of the Summa Corp., the Hughes Company's California headquarters, was broken into. Burglars stole documents including one in which Hughes outlined its connection to "Project Jennifer," the top-secret sub caper. The burglars asked for a million dollars for return of the documents; Summa refused and informed the CIA. On July 4 the *Glomar Explorer* arrived at the submarine site in the Pacific to begin work. Twice Soviet vessels came close, sending helicopters overhead, but they were told it was a mining operation and left, wishing the crew good luck. By August 3 *Glomar* had hooked the Soviet sub and raised it three thousand feet. Then, suddenly, the claws failed; the submarine broke off and fell. Only thirty-eight feet of the ship was captured along with bodies of six sailors; the missiles and secret codes were lost. The mission, for now, was over—a failure. *Glomar* headed back to California for repairs. The disappointment at CIA headquarters was palpable, but the government quickly began to discuss a second mission for the following summer.[23]

And then on February 6, 1975, as Hersh's CIA surveillance story was causing ripples, the *Los Angeles Times* learned that two *New York Times* reporters were preparing a story on the break-in at Hughes' office. How dare the New Yorkers poach their California turf? The *LA Times,* moving aggressively, put the story on page one of its early-bird Saturday edition on February 7, reporting that the submarine mission had taken place in the Atlantic, one of many factual errors. Worried, Colby declared, "Better call downtown to Kissinger." Colby sprang into action, calling *LA Times* editor William Thomas to plead national security. Thomas concurred, bumped the story to page eighteen for later editions, and then told his staff to do no follow-ups. The *NY Times* story appeared the next day, but it had little about the *Glomar Explorer* mission. Colby was temporarily satisfied, saying that both stories "were garbled and error-ridden enough to throw anyone off the scent."[24]

"The Los Angeles publication sent Hersh into frenzy," reported *Timesman* Harrison Salisbury. The Scoop Artist had been scooped, at least in part because he had gone along with the government's request for cooperation. He returned to the story with a vengeance. Hersh flew to Los Angeles. He told Colby he was back on the story, and Colby tried to butter him up, saying, "You've been first-class about this thing a long time." "It is not a question of being good," Hersh replied. "I am a citizen, too." He was later embarrassed by the remark. "He didn't like anything that undercut his image as a tough, 'bad ass' reporter," pointed out Salisbury. He also may have been playing Colby, whom he would now need. In fact, some speculated that Colby had helped Hersh with the CIA surveillance story because he was holding the submarine story. Colby, privately referring to his "Seymour Hersh problem," now feared that his year-long agreement with Hersh was over. Taking no chances, he called Sulzberger three times right after the burglary story. "I hate to bug you on this," Colby said. "You do not bug me ever," Sulzberger, the former marine, answered in a February 8 conversation. Two days later, Sulzberger told Colby, "I very gently passed on the word and I think everyone understands." In other words, sit on the story.[25]

Hersh was furiously trying Defense Department contacts and Hughes officials. And many of them were immediately informing the CIA. Hersh could hardly burp without the CIA knowing. When he stayed with *Parade* magazine editor Lloyd Shearer in Los Angeles, a source immediately called the CIA. They knew that Hersh's mantra in phone conversations with sources was that the CIA should be proud of what it had done, but that it also was a waste of money and no longer secret. He told one source he did not believe the CIA's national security "mumble-jumble." Deputy attorney general Laurence Silberman, a Hersh Watergate source, had a long conversation with Hersh, who in his "inimitable, fast talking, long discussion, monologue" cursed out Colby but wanted to know whether he really should hold the story. "I cannot sit on it much longer," he said. Silberman called Colby to report the discussion.[26] And Hersh knew this was happening. He told one source: make sure you report all this back to Colby. Colby wondered if it was time to call Hersh for another talk, especially since around February 20 the reporter was telling sources he would publish in two or three days. But, Colby said, "I do not know what the hell to tell" him. Kissinger aide General Brent Scowcroft called for a progress report, saying, "I hear Sy Hersh is on the move again." "I cannot believe his boss would let him run a story," Colby replied. Scowcroft asked, "Is that still a live assurance?" Yes, Colby said, "I have made his life a little unpleasant with the *New York Times* in the last day or so." It is unclear what he meant. Nonetheless, Hersh had them worried. As Hersh got close to publication, bureau chief Clifton Daniel set up a meeting for February 27 at CIA headquarters with Colby. The CIA bosses rehearsed their pitch to the *Timesmen* in their last-ditch effort to contain the story. "One argument on this one," Colby said, "is that you (*The Times*) can torpedo this if you want." Duckett said he heard that Hersh would try to get approval for publication but promise to kill three paragraphs of his story in return. Before the meeting Colby also warned Scowcroft that "we have a little problem coming up. I think Henry should know about this." Hersh has written his story and they are coming to discuss it, Colby reported. "They have been very good about this; even Seymour has been good." But, he added, "The story could hurt us now."[27]

Colby was not the only one nervous. Daniel, Hersh, and top editor Bill Kovach went to meet Colby. Daniel, who long ago bought Hersh new office clothes, called him a "demon reporter, nemesis of evildoers," but he was also a "tense, fidgety fellow." Hersh worried: Would they be interrogated? Body-searched? "Stop fretting," Daniel said. "We will be waived right in like VIPs." And they were. On the elevator, however, a burly CIA aide stood behind Hersh. "If looks had been a laser beam," Daniel said, "Sy would have been incinerated—a little pile of ashes on the elevator floor." He was, after all, the man whose stories threatened the agency's existence. But the meeting went smoothly. Duckett tried to ingratiate himself with Daniel and Kovach, both southerners, by noting he was born halfway between them. Neither man appreciated what Salisbury called "this cornball con." They were not "old boys." Duckett told Hersh things he did not know, and he promised more if they held the story. No one made any promises, but, frankly, the story was out of Hersh's hands. The publisher decided national security issues. "They are scared someone will scoop them," Colby reported. Kissinger called Daniel soon after the meeting to reiterate the importance of censoring the story, and calls were made to Sulzberger and A. M. Rosenthal, the top *Times* editor. Meanwhile, Hersh was working day and night to pull together a story before someone else did. Hersh "was not happy," Daniel recalled. "He felt the *Times* was suppressing news and risking a scoop, forgetting that he himself has been sitting on the story at Colby's request."[28]

Finally, in early March, even though the *Los Angeles Times*, *Washington Post*, *Time* and *Newsweek* magazines, National Public Radio, and columnist Jack Anderson all were close to having the story, the *Times* decided to withhold publication, as did everyone else. "Everyone is sitting on it," Colby gloated. Sy was not involved in this decision, learning of it when Rosenthal told him Daniel had drafted a letter of agreement with the CIA not to publish unless the CIA completed another attempt or gave up on lifting the submarine, or someone else broke the embargo. Colby promised that the moment a competitor readied the story for publication, he would call the *Times*, vowing to carry everyone's telephone numbers with him day and night. Hersh was angry; he fired off a three-page memo to Rosenthal, conceding it was an ongoing military operation—but so was the Vietnam War when the *Times* published the Pentagon Papers. Rosenthal responded that he had a "feeling in his stomach"—this was different. The difference was his publisher breathing down his neck and his newspaper already being charged with sabotaging the CIA with its exposés. Hersh retreated.[29]

And then, on March 18, Jack Anderson called Colby to say he was not sure he could hold the story much longer. "We have not made up our minds," Anderson said. "I have never turned you—or Helms—down." But Anderson said he was sure others were going to write it. Colby reeled off the names of all the news organizations withholding publication. "Everyone else is sitting on it," he said. Anderson said he feared "one guy in particular who knows all about it will not sit on it. " It was Hersh, who might even have been feeding details to Anderson. If he went public, Hersh could write his story. Colby said, yes, he knew his "severest critic," Hersh, was on it, but "he has been absolutely splendid." Anderson concluded, "We are going to agonize a little more." Colby quickly called the *Times*, probably Daniel, who seemed to be his contact. "It sounds to me that we are left with our conscience on this matter," Daniel said. "That is the case all along," Colby countered.[30] Anderson, feeling jittery about the story, called Hersh and announced he was broadcasting the story that night. "Jesus," he said to Hersh, "is this story all right?" "I'll stake my reputation on it," replied Hersh, who then alerted the *Times*, which decided to put Hersh's story—already written—into its first edition. Anderson hit the airwaves at 9:00, and the *Times* was on the street by midnight with Hersh's story blaring across page one: "CIA Salvage Ship Brought Up Part of Soviet Sub in 1968, Failed to Raise Atom Missiles." Hersh could not resist a jab at Rosenthal. "Why should we run it now? It still involves national security . . . why should we do it now just because Anderson does it?" Rosenthal was in no mood for bantering. "Aw. Shut up, Sy," he said. Little did he know—that would be the government's response also. The Ford administration wanted to find a way to make Sy Hersh shut up.[31]

CHAPTER 19

Going after "The Godfather"

Did Hersh Roll Over?

How did the director of Central Intelligence get the entire press corps to cooperate? William Colby called it "the weirdest conspiracy in town . . . an American conspiracy." He viewed the silence of the press as "a great tribute to our journalists." But for others it was a mockery of the adversarial role envisioned by the First Amendment. In 1977 *Times* columnist Anthony Lewis revisited the *Glomar* self-censorship question. A journalist from *Rolling Stone* had sued the CIA, forcing it to turn over transcripts of Colby's conversations with publishers and editors as he sought to "fight like hell" to suppress publication. "The whole press has been just splendid," he said. That appalled Lewis. "After these papers, it will be harder for journalists to believe in their self-image as a tough, skeptical lot, immune to government cajolery," he wrote. Lewis noted one exception. "Not everyone in the press was so uncritical," he said. Hersh "kept relentlessly after the story, and Mr. Colby and others worried a lot about him." History professor Kathryn S. Olmsted agreed, writing, "Seymour Hersh was one reporter who refused to roll over for the agency."[1]

And that is worth pondering. Hersh did hold the story a year, making no promises to Colby. But there was something implicit that he would back off. More pressing stories—Chile and the CIA—intervened. Hersh just did not get to *Glomar*, but one wonders how big a priority it was, and whether also the cooperation from Colby made him less than his usual aggressive self. And, moreover, one wonders if he sensed there was just no support from the *Times* top brass. He did not know that Henry Kissinger had called Punch Sulzberger and Clifton Daniel. Given his dislike for the secretary of state, that fact might have pushed him into more aggressive action. Nonetheless, Hersh liked very much the platform the *Times* offered. In fact, he reveled in it. He might not have wanted to upset that apple-cart—just yet. He may have consequently been oblivious to certain tips that would have jump-started the story. James Phelan, a freelance writer, was researching a biography of Howard Hughes in 1974 when he met Hersh in Washington. Phelan mentioned a possible CIA-*Glomar* connection; it went over Hersh's head. After the story broke, he told Phelan, "Nobody seems to have known about Glomar." "I did," Phelan answered. "Did you tell anyone?" Sy asked. "I told you," he said. It took the LA *Times* to finally move him into action. When he saw their story, he recalled, "I hit my head and said, 'dumbell.'" And then, the competitive urge kicked in.[2]

Working with *Times* editor Bill Kovach, Hersh the relentless combatant reappeared. "Every place we went," said columnist Jack Anderson, "Hersh had been there." Anderson called Daniel the night the story broke, offer-ing it to the *Times*. Daniel declined, which must have made Hersh wince. Kovach had already given the outline of the story to John Siegenthaler, publisher of the *Nashville Tennessean,* and to Charles Morgan, a promi-nent attorney. Kovach thinks Morgan leaked it to Anderson. And clearly Anderson called Hersh to discuss the story; the journalism fraternity at the working-class level was more likely than publishers to want to publish. Hersh's story had been sitting in New York for a while, awaiting a go-ahead. "I pushed and pushed to get the story in the paper," Kovach said. "I did everything I could."[3] It took a competitor to finally push the *Times* from behind the bogus national security rock. "So is it a game?" asked Hersh. "No, it's more than a game. But there's a dance that has always gone on between us and them. We push it as hard as we can.... There's always this tension, and sometimes it's ratcheted up."[4]

And what did all of it get Hersh? Despite his soft-pedaling the story, Hersh's conservative critics saw his CIA stories as more proof that he was the leader of the left-wing press cabal trying to wreck American intel-ligence. "Hersh had as much as any American to do with the turning of the American mind against the CIA," charged Edward Korry, the former ambassador to Chile who had scrapped with Hersh in 1974. *Commen-tary* magazine's Arthur Herman, detailing a thirty-five-year war on the CIA, observed that "the real sea change in the public perception of the

CIA" came the day Hersh wrote his *Times* story on domestic surveillance. "Suddenly all the strands of the past half decade came together."[5] Those criticisms of Hersh were, in essence, the backlash against Woodward and Bernstein and against Sy Hersh. By the mid-1970s historian James Boylan found a "flow of comment" that "pictured modern journalism as a usurper. Journalists, it was alleged, were out of control and out of line with dominant social values; they had come to constitute a separate and subversive class." Hersh was the leader of the pack. *New York Daily News* editor Michael O'Neill declared, "We should make peace with the government, not be its enemy. . . . We are supposed to be the observers, not the participants—not the permanent political opposition." The new mind-set did not bode well for Seymour Hersh.

Cheney Takes Aim at Hersh

After three months in office, Gerald Ford, like every president, got angry at leaks of information to the press. At a February 7 meeting of the National Security Council he complained that secrets were routinely getting out. "I read the whole story in the newspapers," he said about a treaty negotiation with the Soviet Union. "I was upset, to put it mildly." CIA director William Colby then tepidly brought up the *Glomar Explorer*. "I hate to raise this but the *Los Angeles Times* just asked whether we raised a piece of a Soviet submarine," he said, adding that the CIA asked the publisher to kill the story. "I really don't know what to do about this," Ford said. "I just want you all to know I am disturbed. I want you all to do whatever you can about it." He might have been taken literally. Sy Hersh's exposé of the CIA's domestic surveillance in December kicked off a firestorm about its accuracy, but there was little suggestion he had done anything illegal. Ford aide Dick Cheney wondered if the government should ask the Justice Department "to determine whether or not actions should be taken to initiate an investigation of possible criminal violations." This suggestion went nowhere until Hersh began to probe the top-secret *Glomar* project. Colby regularly referred to Hersh as his "harshest critic," and Kissinger, of course, knew that Hersh was probing his every move.[6] They never had any grounds to move against him, however, until a *Glomar* follow-up presented an opportunity.

With the *Glomar* story, he essentially wrote all he knew in one big story. "It's hard for him to come in under 5,000 words, he has so much good stuff," commented his editor, Abe Rosenthal. But a critic of Hersh's dense style of writing, demurred, saying, "When Sy starts on a story, he just goes and goes and goes."[7] Hersh did not return to *Glomar* per se for nearly nineteen months. In the meantime he moved the story in a different direction, writing on May 25, 1975, that the United States had at least four submarines that were secretly entering the three-mile protected coastal zone of the Soviet Union to collect intelligence. Sources told him the intelligence could be gathered with much less risk. The critics came to Hersh saying they wanted to change the American policy, known as Holystone, on use of the subs. A similar story, with the same information, was written sixteen months earlier by Hersh's rival, the *Washington Post's* Laurence Stern. When it appeared in the *Times*, however, it caused the Ford Administration to fret. Was Hersh breaking the law by publishing classified information?[8]

Cheney, who became George W. Bush's vice president, took the lead in pursuing options against Hersh. Maybe, Cheney mused after a meeting with Attorney General Edward Levi, the government should "go after papers" in Hersh's apartment (he lived in a house!). Or maybe the FBI should investigate Hersh's sources. A third alternative: seek "immediate" grand jury indictments of both Hersh and *Times* executives. Of course, Cheney added, the government could simply "discuss informally" their concerns with *Times* executives, as Colby did with Sulzberger. While prosecutors studied the legality of the options, someone in the Justice Department, where he had good sources, warned Hersh. "Duh. Big deal," he said. "What do I care? I'm still doing my business. It's still America. I'm not afraid." Hersh felt the White House would never prosecute because "if they do, I'm gonna scream and moan and—be a hero, and give more trouble than they would if they'd just left me alone. The political cost of moving against me . . . is too high." In fact, Cheney did worry about "the Pentagon papers syndrome," when the government prosecution against the *Times* and *Post* became a cause célèbre. "Will we get hit with violating the 1st amendment to the Constitution?" Cheney worried. Justice Department lawyers were concerned whether they could even make a case. After all, part of the classified secret had already been published by Stern. Also, to pursue the case would mean having to confirm the United States was going into Soviet waters. Even an attempt to simply find out who leaked to Hersh, the lawyers concluded, would fail and turn into a "feeble effort" that would cause embarrassment. Levi concluded that "the most promising course of action, for the moment," would be to quietly discuss the problem with publishers. Many years later Hersh was cocky. "You can't trample the Constitution," he said. "When Cheney and Rumsfeld were looking at me, the attorney general said, 'Get outta here. I decide what to do. You guys in the White House can't decide whether to open a case.'"[9]

While the plotting to get Hersh took place, he was packing his bags. His wife Elizabeth had been accepted to New York University Medical School in New York City. So she could be with her family, they would have to relocate to Manhattan, and Hersh would have to leave the source-rich confines of Washington. "Sy didn't want to go to NY," observed his editor, Bob Phelps.[10]

"Stick to Murders and Blood"

The feuding between the New York and Washington offices of the *Times* was legendary. Fighting over who would get on page one, over which bureau was most important, the jockeying over which editor from which bureau might become the paper's top overseer—all led to fierce bureaucratic infighting. Would the financial capital or the political capital rule? The "Old Gray Lady" was in a constant cat fight. When forty-eight-year-old Abe Rosenthal took over as managing editor in 1970, he moved carefully to get the DC bureau under his control and to push the *Times* into the era of investigative reporting. "Abe was bound and determined to get more aggressive reporting in the bureaus," observed Bill Kovach, who was brought in to oversee an investigative team. But Kovach knew that Hersh had, in essence, "a private contract" to report directly to Rosenthal. "He was not a team player. He was his own person, had his own style and his own stories," said Kovach, who, despite trying, could not alter the "Abe-Sy axis" thing that no other reporter had. When Hersh announced he was leaving Washington for New York, no tears were shed in DC. "To one extent or another, just about every reporter resented" Hersh, Kovach recalled, although he added about his reporting: "Sy was so good, was so important." Rosenthal, on the other hand, welcomed him to New York with open arms. "It will be a pleasure for all of us having you in New York, and I am convinced you will enjoy the hell out of it," he wrote Hersh in January 1975.[11]

Elizabeth Hersh's start date at NYU Medical School was delayed a year; the family did not arrive until August 1976. With two children in tow, Matthew, seven, and Melissa, five, they faced the inevitable problem of child care in a new town. Hersh moved the family north because it was something Liz wanted; now it was his turn to sacrifice. More of the child rearing would fall to the thirty-nine-year-old who grew up in a household where his mother was out cleaning houses and his father worked long hours at the dry cleaner. On his first workday in New York, Hersh did not have a babysitter. But he had his own office (something usually only columnists were given) at the *Times* eighteen-story, 43rd Street Times Square building. He brought his children to work. Reporter John Darnton, both of whose parents worked for years in the *Times* newsroom, noted that the office was "a cathedral, a sanctuary. *No one* brought children or wives," he said. But Hersh did, and it quickly brought Abe Rosenthal into the reporter's office. Mockingly, he asked, "What if Plato brought his kids to work? What if Aristotle brought his kids to work? There would be no work." Abe was joking, but others could not get away with it. Rosenthal's patience with Hersh would soon enough grow thin, but all those Polk Awards, all those magazine profiles on the rock star—America's best investigative reporter deserved a bit of space. Of course, Hersh, as was his wont, quickly tested the limits. As he searched around for stories, he had time on his hands. He used some of it to play tennis. An editor, looking to please the star, assigned a copyboy to play tennis with Hersh in the middle of the workday. Rosenthal assistant Peter Millones was angry. "We all like to maintain our sense of humor and our perspective around here," he wrote Hersh, "but it becomes damn hard when we have to run a playground for some editors and reporters." He called it a "sad commentary" and an "embarrassing situation."[12]

What exactly Hersh would do in New York—aside from play tennis—was unclear. Kiddingly he told one interviewer after the bruising CIA battle that he might just like to cover meetings. Fat chance. The *Times* top brass were looking for big topics for him. Thus far Hersh's reporting had been incremental—an exposé with follow-up stories as investigators pounced on his leads. Now Hersh was to become more of a projects reporter, to investigate for months and then write multiple articles. Even Hersh wanted to broaden his reporting, commenting that he might like to write "the Sy Hersh continuing saga of how the world really works." And this would take him away from Henry Kissinger and government.[13] Managing editor Seymour Topping sent a memo to editors in January 1977 that sounded like an advertisement. "Sy Hersh is now available for new assignments," he wrote. "I would like your private advice if there are any prime investigative stories pending in your coverage area." Foreign editor James Greenfield suggested he look at the Lockheed Corp. City editor Sydney Schanberg said Hersh should investigate Medicaid. Surely he would find "the deep corruption that pervades the entire system." Or, Schanberg said, let him probe Nelson Rockefeller's paltry tax payments. Did anyone ask Hersh if he wanted suggestions? After all, this was the reporter who juggled a dozen stories and was unlikely to take much guidance. In fact, he was eying another biggie, one way more dangerous than the snarky world of Washington.[14]

The man's parents were from Eastern Europe, Jews who left the old country to come to America. They settled on the South Side of Chicago. Their son was a bright, aggressive youngster. He played sports. And then went off to law school. People remembered him as a tough guy; he didn't take shit from anyone. The description sounds amazingly like Seymour Hersh, but it was not. For Hersh's next target was "The Fixer," a power broker lawyer who had ties to mobsters from the Capone Era, Jimmy Hoffa and the nation's biggest unions, casino owners in Las Vegas, and the biggest stars and producers in Hollywood. His name was Sidney Korshak. "He was the godfather," Hersh declared. But no one had ever heard of the sixty-nine-year-old behind-the-scenes power broker who worked in a shadowy world of mobsters, racketeers, and legitimate business. "He's undoubtedly the best contact organized crime has in the United States today," one FBI agent told Hersh, who had never taken on a gangster.

Government officials might threaten to cut you off, get an injunction to halt publication, or ponder breaking into your house. Korshak was different. "There's no question, he ordered people hit," Hersh said.[15]

The idea for the story came from Rosenthal, who—after it was revealed that John Kennedy had a girlfriend who was also the lover of a Chicago mobster—wondered how far the reach of organized crime really went. Hersh first heard about Korshak from Adam Walinsky, a speechwriter for Bobby Kennedy. "If you want the great story of all time, I'll give it to you," Walinsky said. "Two words: Sidney Korshak." Hersh then spoke with a federal investigator who briefed him on Korshak's connection to powerful unions, especially Hoffa's Teamsters. Hersh was told the real expert on Korshak was Jeff Gerth, a thirty-four-year-old Berkeley freelance journalist who had probed Korshak for five years and was then embroiled in a multimillion-dollar defamation lawsuit for a *Penthouse* magazine article on organized crime. Gerth and Hersh hit it off. "I just liked him right away," Hersh said, possibly because Gerth, like Hersh, was a golf nut—more likely because he was a tough-minded investigative reporter. The *Times* hired Gerth as a consultant. For the next six months the two traveled coast to coast to unravel the Korshak mystery as Gerth became the only reporter to ever work closely with the loner Sy Hersh. The *Times* gave the duo $30,000 to undertake what Hersh called "a massive undertaking."[16]

The biggest problem in tackling Korshak was that his activities were cloaked in secrecy; records would not be found in public documents. "You have to do an incredible amount of work," Hersh said. "I'm learning about being a kid reporter again, going into courthouses and looking into . . . who has what trust." He added, "It is fun, [but] you can't live off what the cops give you, or the feds. You gotta go out there and do it."[17] Journalists call it spade work, which is what Hersh and Gerth needed as they literally had to dig up their first break. They met a retired FBI agent in Reno, Nevada. Korshak had helped organized crime legally penetrate Las Vegas casinos, remarkably like what was depicted in *The Godfather* movies. The federal government had prepared a 250-word dossier on casinos and Korshak. The FBI agent had the report. "That was incredible," Hersh said. "We leaned on it a lot." But to get it the agent led the two reporters to a deserted spot where it was buried. Hersh and Gerth dug it up. Their next break came when a Los Angeles Police Department detective—a Gerth contact—turned over many of his inside sources on Korshak, who moved his law practice from Chicago to LA in the 1960s as he took on A-List Hollywood clients to shed his connections to gangsters from Chicago where he made his name.[18]

Knowing that disgruntled employees were always good whistle-blowing sources, Hersh and Gerth sought someone who was angry at Korshak—and willing to risk talking. Joel Goldblatt, a Chicago department store owner, fit the bill. He was Korshak's first client in 1946 as he entered private practice. When a labor dispute threatened to ruin Goldblatt's business, Korshak, mysteriously, made the labor trouble go away. "The fixer" did his magic. But many years later Korshak sided with Goldblatt's ex-wife in a divorce proceeding. "We figured Goldblatt might be mad," said Hersh. Korshak, aware that Hersh was meeting Goldblatt, warned his old ally not to talk—but he did, with the promise of anonymity, giving the reporters one of their best anecdotes. In 1950 Democratic senator Estes Kefauver of Tennessee, a candidate for the presidency, was probing racketeering and making headlines. He brought his investigating committee to Chicago, but Korshak got showgirls to lure him to a hotel where they took compromising photos of the well-known womanizer. Goldblatt saw the photos, which when shown to Kefauver immediately ended his Chicago probe. The story was old but startling.[19]

Hersh and Gerth split their time between Chicago, Las Vegas, and Los Angeles, but little did they know that Korshak was tracking their every move. One day, while making hamburgers for his children in his Manhattan home, Hersh received a phone call from the LA district attorney John Van de Kamp, who told Hersh to go to a pay phone. "What do you mean?" Hersh asked. "Just get to a pay phone," he said. Hersh went to the corner candy story and called collect to Van de Kamp, who said, "Korshak has all of your phone records and all of your expense accounts from inside the *Times*." A former *Times* employee had tipped off the DA.[20]

"We were worried about the safety of our sources," Gerth said. The reporters began to submit phony travel receipts. But their own safety became questionable. Hersh wanted very much to talk with Korshak. He came close once by chance while having lunch in a New York restaurant at the same time as the mobster. The historian Arthur Schlesinger, who knew Korshak, was in the restaurant and tried to broker a meeting. Korshak's aides refused. When their first story on Korshak appeared on June 27, 1976, Hersh simply wrote that when reached by telephone, Korshak declined to talk, accusing Hersh of "having slandered me . . . from one end of the country to the other." As Hersh told Korshak's biographer, the truth was more chilling. Hersh was in LA and simply phoned Korshak. He took the call. "Mr. Korshak, I am here," Hersh said. "I won't see you," Korshak said, adding, "Mr. Hersh, let me ask you a question?" Hersh recalled, "I'll never forget it as long as I live." Korshak said to him: "What are you doing? You're an expert in mass murder, you write about crimes where people are dead and there are bodies all over. Why are you writing about me? You write about murder. Blood running in the ditches, and murders. Why are you interested in me? I'm just a businessman. Go back to your mass murders. Go back to the blood and the killings and gore that you write about. Not about me." Hersh remembered vividly that Korshak "just kept talking about murders and blood. He never said a word that was threatening, but the whole context was 'murder, murder, blood, murder.' It set me on edge. It was pretty chilling." Gerth recalled one similar threatening incident, but he would not discuss it.[21]

After conducting three interviews, Hersh submitted his four-part, twenty-five-thousand-word series on Korshak, but it took weeks to be edited. Lawyers perused it for libel, editors wanted the reporters to beef it up, and two editors wanted to kill the series. Publisher Arthur Sulzberger, who was friendly with Korshak as a movie-going pal, could hardly have been thrilled (especially when the night before publication the *Times'* unions struck the paper), but no one ever pressured Hersh to pull punches. However, the articles needed a lot of work. One critic called them "long winded, repetitious cops-and-robbers-style exposé" that should have been condensed to two parts, not four. Rosenthal, tartly, wrote Hersh that "at this moment a good part of the *New York Times* has come to a standstill because [so many editors] are tied up as they have been all day, for days past, in trying to get your series into printable form. If I were a reporter whose work needed that much attention, I would be slightly embarrassed and hugely grateful."[22]

"The Contrasting Lives of Sidney R. Korshak" hit the *Times* first page on Sunday, June 27. The articles were unlike anything Hersh had done before. He did not lead with a particular element that charged some major abuse. Instead, Hersh reached back to his feature-writing AP days and drew a picture of a powerful mobster whose hands were in legal and illegal pies but whom the federal government could never touch, even though his name figured in twenty investigations. Each article was broken into mini-chapters in book-like style. But this was no human-interest feature—it was a profile of a man who, Hersh alleged, was "the most important link between organized crime and legitimate business, [a] behind-the-scene 'fixer' who has been instrumental in helping criminal elements gain power in union affairs and infiltrate the leisure and entertainment industries." Although largely unnoticed, Korshak was long involved in bribery, kickbacks, extortion, fraud, and labor racketeering, Hersh and Gerth pointed out. Over the next three days they laid out the case against Korshak in a way no one had ever done before—his union connections, complex schemes to defraud, shady work for major corporations, outright bribery of local and state officials. Korshak's biographer, Gus Russo, called the articles "seminal," using them as building blocks in his 2006 book, *Supermob*. But critics were not as kind. They expected Hersh to expose Korshak's illegal activities in a way that would lead to an indictment.[23]

When writer Frank Lalli read the series he said his "cereal turned soggy—a few firecrackers, perhaps, but no dynamite." Hersh "kept insisting Korshak is a bad man," but it is never proven, he argued. And Nat Hentoff, a noted civil libertarian, wrote in his *Village Voice* column that Hersh "set out to get Sidney Korshak," but forgot that there was a Bill of Rights. Two senior staffers from the Kefauver crime committee had their attack on Hersh inserted in the *Congressional Record*. "Disparage, distort, denigrate, and defame"—that is all Hersh had in mind.[24]

It all sounded remarkably like the attacks on his My Lai and CIA exposés. For sure, some of the Korshak anecdotes and quotes do seem gratuitous and gossipy. For example, part of Korshak's popularity in Chicago stemmed from throwing parties with pretty showgirls. "Not your $50 girl, "Hersh wrote, "but girls costing $250 or more." Or, Korshak was a frequent diner at a swanky Beverly Hills bistro where he showed off wads of cash, sitting at a corner table with two telephones where "all the beautiful women come over and give him a kiss. It's almost like a movie scene watching him," Hersh wrote. Once, the reporters found, Korshak came to a fancy Las Vegas hotel for a conference. The presidential suite, the hotel's best, was taken by Teamsters boss Hoffa. When Korshak arrived, management moved Hoffa out and gave the suite to Korshak. Nothing illegal in that—as in many of the anecdotes Hersh retold—but the overall picture that emerged was surely of a man who, mysteriously, always came out on top, an unchecked and hidden power broker.[25] Many years later, Gerth scoffed at the criticism. The federal government, he pointed out, spent years investigating Korshak and could never lay a glove on him. Nonetheless, Gerth insisted, the series was a first-ever look into Korshak's secret powers and his startling penetration of legitimate business. The problem for Hersh was that he had set the bar too high. Surely someone must go to jail. The Los Angeles Examiner managing editor Donald Goodenow said Hersh "failed to get Korshak. But he wrote the series anyway." Korshak, in fact, was never charged with a crime. The feds simply did not have the resources—or the ability. "Maybe if we committed the whole federal Strike Force to it, we might be able to nail the guy," one prosecutor said.[26]

After the series Korshak supposedly told friends that the Times "solved my advertising problems." The truth was that he may not have been so jocular, ending up in the hospital as the story was published. Nerves? A breakdown? The hospital said it was a colon problem. Some Korshak friends found him dismissive and unconcerned about the attack, saying, "I put that up on my bulletin board. He ain't got nothing on me." "He didn't get depressed then or ever," one friend recalled, "but he was unhappy to be attacked by this guy." Hilton Hotels president Barron Hilton said, however, that the articles did trouble Korshak. He "was quite depressed with the adverse publicity."[27]

Lalli called the series Hersh's "first major disappointment" that "will have little effect." Gerth fired back, saying "journalism wannabes" did not know what they were talking about, that the series holds up—a clear picture of how hidden power brokers run much of the country with methods and tactics that should land them behind bars. The government had failed to nail Korshak, not the reporters. The Times, seeming defensive, wrote an editorial that explained the articles' purpose: "The basic responsibility of the press is to lay out evidence when it points to a serious threat to the public interest." Hersh and Gerth, the *Times* declared, revealed a long list of indictable offenses—and a government failure to pursue them. "Major reforms are needed in the administration of criminal justice and of corporate law," the editorial insisted.[28]

An appraisal of the Hersh-Gerth work depends on which view of journalism you take. If the reporter is supposed to be prosecutor, judge and jury, sending the bad guys to jail, then Hersh failed. But if, as in the tradition of the early twentieth-century muckrakers, the journalist is supposed to dig below the surface and show where power resides and how the people are denied the true ability to understand their affairs, then Hersh nailed it. "Who better than Korshak symbolized how organized crime moved effortlessly at the highest reaches of society," said Gerth—including with the *Times* publisher. If Rosenthal started the project by wondering about the reach of organized crime, Hersh finished it by showing that the mob's tentacles were complicated, long—and untouchable.[29]

CHAPTER 20

The Big Apple Turns Sour

"They're Going to Go after Us"

Sy Hersh never aspired to be an editor. He was too restless to be desk
bound or the comma police, but he had ideas how a newspaper should
be run. He told Rosenthal, "The paper must always have a least one or
two special projects in the works, some story or series of stories that make
us different, that provide an edge that helps make the paper what it is.
The biggest story in America in the next ten years is going to be corporations," he said in 1975. "If your local butcher pulled some of the acts these
corporations pulled, he'd be in jail."[1] And he and Jeff Gerth knew which
corporation they had in mind: Gulf and Western Industries, a fast-growing
$3.4-billion New York–based company—the nation's nineteenth largest
employer—that owned Paramount Pictures, Simon and Schuster, Madison
Square Garden (including the New York Knicks and Rangers), the world's
largest sugar mill, and millions of acres of real estate. Its president was
Charles G. Bludhorn, a hot-tempered, hard-driving workaholic, once
dubbed "The Mad Austrian of Wall Street," who took a small auto-parts
company and turned it into a Fortune 500 behemoth. Bludhorn had ties
to none other than Sidney Korshak, which is how Hersh first encountered
him.[2] Following the path from Korshak, Hersh proposed an "extensive
takeout" on G&W, "one of the most investigated conglomerates in modern
times; almost an archetype of what is wrong, or suspected to be wrong,
about modern big-time conglomerates." This company, he said, "grows
bigger not by building better products, but by playing the stock market."
Hersh felt the Gulf story could "help explain how things work in this
nation." He told Rosenthal, "I've been trying to get into big business
stories since coming to NY, and this one is the ultimate." Hersh again

enlisted Gerth. The duo had taken on a mobster, but what was in store for them now was even more hostile.[3]

Investigating business has always been tricky. A primary function of the press is to check on government. Policymakers never like it, but they accept it. Disagreement begins, however, when it comes to its role vis-à-vis the private sector. Of course, the press is a business, beholden to advertisers, which might tamp down its enthusiasm for going after business wrongdoing. Consequently the function of checking on business has always been spotty. Certainly Ida Tarbell had no qualms when she tackled John D. Rockefeller and Standard Oil Company in 1902. Nor did Upton Sinclair hold back in his condemnation of business values in *The Jungle* in 1906. Nonetheless, the great investigative reporting surge that emerged in America in the late 1960s was more an attack against government malfeasance than business. Enter Hersh, the business school dropout who had written nothing about the corporate sector in his seventeen-year career.[4]

Hersh and Gerth began to prowl around—in public records, of course, but also looking closely at the fourteen investigations involving Bludhorn and Gulf and Western, many of which had been kicked off by the Internal Revenue Service and the Securities and Exchange Commission, which were looking at complex schemes that entangled the company. It led the reporters to conclude that company executives had lied to the government, destroyed damning documents, and duped shareholders and banks. Bludhorn, they felt, was using the company as his personal candy store, as backing for private loans and lavish personal purchases that he hid from shareholders. Over four months, the reporters spoke to seventy-five former company officials. Gulf and Western insisted that no one in the company but a spokesperson talk to them. About five weeks after Hersh wrote his initial memo scoping out his story, G&W fired back. Charles Davis, a vice president who was the front man in dealing with the *Times*, asked assistant managing editor Seymour Topping for a meeting.

Your reporter, he said, is "spreading lies, although he bluntly asserts them as facts—lies of the most vicious kind. We are being investigated by a man whose repeated statements must lead us to believe that he is, in his own words, 'out to get' us." He then cited some of the things Hersh was saying: "I am going to make trouble for G+W. . . . They tried to bribe IRS agents . . . I am repulsed by their lack of morals. . . . Bludhorn is friendly with Mafia members." Declared Davis: "There are boundaries which no newspaper man working for a great newspaper should overstep. We believe Mr. Hersh has exceeded those boundaries." Told of the complaints, Hersh was unbowed. "It is now, in my opinion, as good a story as I've worked on since joining the paper." He had "hard evidence" of stock and tax irregularities.[5] When Topping declined a meeting, Davis insisted to *Times* counsel James Goodale that a reporter with an "open mind" cover this story. Goodale refused. "Mr. Hersh has made no personal threats against your company," he wrote, and has the *Times*' "full confidence." Hersh, increasingly agitated, reported to Topping that Davis would not meet because he felt Sy was "prejudiced." If they won't talk, Hersh said, then he and Gerth would have to "call up high officials of the company at their homes (and, in some cases, begin evening visits). I see no other recourse but to continue to be aggressive as possible." Evening visits to sources' homes is not normal journalistic practice.[6]

Davis kept up his verbal assault on Hersh's "sick, twisted, malicious, hateful tactics," saying, "We are clearly a legitimate area of inquiry," but citing again the awful things Hersh was "spewing out across the country . . . under the guise of making an investigation." Davis claimed Hersh said such things as, "You better see me, otherwise you are going to jail with the others. . . . G+W is a piece of shit. . . . Why is G+W like the mafia where no one wants to talk. . . . Bludhorn lied to me. . . . A lot of blood is going to flow. . . . Davis is a son of a bitch." Gulf was taping Hersh's phone calls. Hersh denied to Topping that he made any "threats or accusations." As for the rest? "Many of the other comments have an element of truth," he said. And, yes, he did call Davis a son of a bitch. "Often," Hersh said, "I will state something as categorical fact in order to provoke a truthful response."[7]

None of this was a surprise to anyone who had watched Hersh work—or to his previous targets. "Overhearing Sy on the phone angrily pushing his victim on the other end to come across with information . . . was a special newsroom treat for all passersby, from copyboy to executive editor," recalled Rosenthal aide Arthur Gelb. Pulitzer Prize-winning reporter Sydney Schanberg recalled that once, in New York, he overheard Hersh try to get a U.S. senator to come to the phone on a crucial story. The senator, through an aide, declined to talk. Hersh told the aide, "You tell the senator if he doesn't talk to me I'll have to talk to someone about that affair he is having." The senator then came to the phone. "He will say anything to get people to say something," Schanberg said, adding, however, that "he is the best investigator in America." Hersh "could make people cower on the phone," Gelb said. Bill Kovach, Hersh's editor in Washington, said "what worried me most [was when] I would listen to him make a phone call. It scared me." One reporter told Kovach about a call he overheard Hersh make to the Pentagon. "This is Sy Hersh at the New York Times. Can you ask the general to call me?" He gave his name again and phone number, then: 'It's about the fellatio story.' Long pause. "Fellatio, f-e-l-l-a-t-i-o!" Sy said and slammed down the phone. The return call came about thirty seconds later.[8]

Another Hersh editor in Washington, Bob Phelps, remarked that Hersh "scared the shit out of secretaries: 'You tell that sunuvabitch I'm gonna print this if he doesn't talk to me. He's hanging himself.'" Usually the source would speak with Hersh. Tom Goldstein, who was writing about the press for the *Times*, remembers Hersh screaming at some high official, "Do you know who I am?" But, he added, "He would do it publicly, not privately," as if his extortion tactics were an accepted part of journalistic newsgathering. Bob Woodard, his Watergate rival, said he heard tales of Hersh's methods. Since he had no direct knowledge, he would not comment, but he observed, "It would not be acceptable at the Post."[9] Even top editor Rosenthal overheard Hersh's tantrums and taunts. When he walked through the newsroom and got near Hersh's desk, he put his hands over his ears. He did not want to hear—but he could not avoid hearing the complaints from Gulf and Western about a story that had yet to appear. Davis wrote Rosenthal and publisher Arthur Sulzberger to complain bitterly.

Meanwhile, as Hersh was pushing Davis to meet him, he sent, in prosecutorial fashion, five pages of questions—an audacious list that he could never have expected to be answered: in-house legal opinions; responses to IRS questions; itemization of assets; lists of company cars and planes. Does Mrs. Bludhorn take frequent air trips paid for by G&W, he asked.

If nothing else, G&W knew what they would be asked when Gerth and Hersh finally met for three hours on May 9 with Davis and a company attorney. The meeting was bruising. "It was the most distressing interview I've had in more than 17 years in the business," Hersh told Topping. "These two men repeatedly insulted us and directly threatened us with legal action." The lawyer called the Korshak series a "rathole," saying *Times* editors had told him it was below the paper's standards. "All of this was done in the most pugnacious, personal way," Hersh said. "I've never felt such personal animosity in all of my career, and that includes all of the reporting I've done" on the CIA and FBI. A week later, Hersh scheduled another meeting with Davis, who told Hersh they were investigating Gerth and had developed damning evidence about his father. "My father died when I was 16, so I guess they're not going to bring him up," Hersh quipped. Years later Gerth said that in his four decades of investigative reporting he never encountered such intimidation. About their next meeting, Hersh said, "if they start pulling their gutter tactics and attempt to be abusive, we may just walk out."[10]

Hersh only made things worse, however. Looking for information on Davis, he decided to talk to his ex-wife, who he believed was living at their house in Westport, Connecticut. He thought Davis had moved out. He called the house and left a long voice mail explaining what he was seeking. But it turned out the ex-wife had moved; Davis was still there. He got the message and called Hersh, furious. "You have no ethics. You are in the gutter," he said. You make me "want to throw up." He then hung up. Nonetheless, a week later, Davis agreed to meet. This meeting was calmer. And once they started to write their articles, Hersh told Topping, "We have uncovered 30 to 40 questionable and seemingly illegal transactions involving the company." But, he added, "These guys (at G&W) are the toughest I've ever encountered. They're going to go after us . . . with everything."[11] To check Hersh's work, veteran business editor John M. Lee was enlisted. He called a first draft "excessive, diffuse and poorly organized," observing that it was "to say the least . . . an unusual story for the *Times*." Yet he also saw it as a "unique opportunity" since "corporate misbehavior is too important a news topic for us to ignore." Lee feared, however, the story was libelous. The *Times* needs "to demonstrate that we did not publish recklessly." The U.S. Supreme Court had made clear that public officials would have to prove knowledge of falsity or wanton disregard for journalistic canons to win. Of course, Hersh's crude attacks in conversation must have worried the lawyers. "Quite possibly" the *Times* will be sued, but Lee insisted that Gulf "is on shaky ground."[12] Nonetheless, Gulf did threaten. The fact that Hersh had not given Gulf a chance to respond to every point in his articles indicated a "reckless disregard for what the truth may actually be," complained Davis to Sulzberger. More than "waving the First Amendment like a flag" is needed, he warned. Goodale shot back: "I urge you to call the reporters without delay and provide them with details which you believe they are lacking." One unexpected major conversation loomed as the reporters readied the story.[13]

When Sy Hersh worked on a story, everyone in town knew about it. What will Sy do next? Who will he go after now? Word was out that Gulf and Western was in his crosshairs, so much so that the company and the government worried the stories would cause the company's stock prices to tumble. Davis complained to Sulzberger that Hersh was a "spy" for the Securities and Exchange Commission, the federal agency that oversees Wall Street. Moreover, he claimed, Hersh's "pipeline" of leaks from the SEC was illegal. The *Times* "would want to think long and hard before it aided and abetted" the commission of crimes, Davis wrote Goodale.[14] Then, on June 30, Stanley Sporkin, the director of the SEC's Division of Enforcement, called Hersh in a person-to-person phone call for a "formal conversation" on the record. Gulf's Arthur Liman, a well-known lawyer, was with Sporkin, who said the pending articles were so well known that he feared it was affecting Gulf stocks. Recounting the call, Hersh said Sporkin explained there was a "strong possibility . . . that if your series did not come out in a reasonable time he would be forced to take some steps." He mentioned "suspension of trading." Sporkin was not seeking to stop publication; on the contrary, he wanted the series in print! His hope was to "end some of the speculation about Gulf and Western."[15] Sy Hersh had not even printed a word; yet already results were coming in, and G&W was quite nervous.

The best part about Hersh's Gulf and Western articles, which all ran on page one on July 24 to 26, was the feuding and fussing that came before publication. This is not to say the stories weren't significant, but stories devoted to questionable tax practices, shady corporate shenanigans, and preferential treatment by large banks—these were of little surprise or interest to general readers. Moreover, the accusations that Hersh made, based on the government probes that were under way, were dense, complicated, tedious, and difficult to follow.[16] Probably the very tight editing by a wary band of editors and lawyers neutered some of the better material. Lee made the reporters kill anonymous quotes, which Hersh always used to brighten up his stories (and irk Rosenthal.) They did find interesting anecdotal material—such as a group of G&W employees carting boxes of company records from New York to Connecticut because IRS auditors in New York were too rigorous. And an ex-employee told how company president Bludhorn made him arrange for personal loans from banks. When he balked, Bludhorn fired him. The angry back and forth between Hersh and Davis is mentioned only in passing, even though Hersh felt it was important. Hersh simply noted that G&W complained about one of the *Times* reporters, accusing him of making malicious statements. Topping said he investigated the complaints and found Hersh's behavior appropriate.

"Sy is essentially a very nice guy," Topping observed years later. "He found out that adopting that manner in phone calls produced results. People became intimidated and said things they would not otherwise say." It was just a "reportorial technique," although one, he conceded, that certainly "was not the norm." Hersh agreed: "I have no ethical, moral or other problems with such actions; to me, such steps are a part of the good reporting process." G&W, however, told Reuters on day two of publication that the articles were "riddled with falsehoods" that would be dealt with at an appropriate time and in an appropriate forum." It was bluster; they never went after the *Times*.[17]

Despite all the prepublication hubbub, *New York* magazine concluded that "the general reaction [to the series] has been a big yawn." A friend of Rosenthal's applauded the series in a note to Abe, but pointed out that 70 to 90 percent of corporations do these things. Nonetheless, he said, "The piece was a threshold story . . . of ethical problems which face men torn between profit and morality."[18] The articles do offer a window into corporate behavior in ways that the public did not usually see. Topping, who was responsible for starting the *Times* daily business section, felt, in retrospect, the paper may have overplayed the articles. Nonetheless, he said, "It is one of the first times a major investigation had taken place of a big American company." Nonetheless, nothing calamitous resulted. The day after the first article appeared, Gulf and Western was the most actively traded stock on the New York Stock Exchange, with the stock dropping about 10 percent, less than many had feared. But a Gulf official told an Abe Rosenthal biographer, "These articles had devastating impact on everyone in the company. *The Times* was calling us criminals and thieves and shyster businessmen on the front page."[19]

G&W never sued, however, because the articles were careful and because in a defamation lawsuit the company's books would open in ways it might not like. And no one—from Bludhorn to Gaston—was ever charged with committing a crime. However, the SEC did pursue two civil lawsuits, getting Gulf and Western to make a $39-million settlement over its Dominican Republic investments in 1980. More significantly, they backed up much of what Hersh and Gerth had written about Bludhorn, charging him with wide-ranging fraud, including using company employees and resources for his personal gain. It was an absolute affirmation of Hersh's stories. Oddly, the SEC settled the case after a three-and-a-half-year investigation without penalty against Bludhorn. The company simply agreed to make serious internal reforms. "It's the not the first time the government didn't do what it should," Hersh said. Critics saw it as proof, however, that alleged wrongdoing by Bludhorn simply could not be proven. Steven Brill wrote a long magazine piece that faulted the SEC for having an informer whose allegations could not be verified. Hersh said, quite simply, that he and Gerth were following the outlines of the SEC investigation. "Journalistically it is very easy to write about an investigation," Hersh said. "It's always an easy way out. That should not be a shocker. Newspapers usually don't like to initiate investigations into corporations." But, he told Brill, with or without the SEC probe, "I'd be willing to stand behind all that we said about Gulf & Western." Brill did not dispute Hersh's view, writing, "The articles were good reporting."[20] His criticism was more with the *Times* for not making clear years later that the SEC investigation that it splashed on page one for three days basically fell flat on its face. Not that it helped the company very much.

Gulf and Western went into a slow decline after the articles appeared. Wall Street was now suspicious of Bludhorn and his tactics, and the company's value declined. Bludhorn died in a plane crash in 1983. In 1985 the large G&W sign that adorned the company's offices at Columbus Circle in Manhattan was removed as the company name was changed to Paramount. Sy Hersh may have had bad journalistic manners, and no one went to jail, but G&W was no more.

The End of the Times

After the G&W series, Hersh may have been a bit lost. He never wrote another investigative piece for the *Times* as a full-time staffer. He returned to his favorite hunting grounds, the CIA, writing about sagging morale and cuts to personnel. He gave his old source, William Colby, a chance to sound off by quoting excerpts from his memoir as he fired back at Ford and Kissinger for trying to muffle the truth. It was only fair; Hersh's revelations had gotten him fired. When a photo appeared of Hersh talking to Colby, Washington bureau chief Clifton Daniel could not resist gibing, "Has he gone soft since he got to New York? The Sy we knew would have his . . . dukes up."[21] Hersh did a long magazine piece on the mysterious super-spy James Angleton, and he followed up with a few minor new revelations about *Glomar Explorer*.[22] But, for the most part, he was a man without a country. Overall, observed colleague Tom Goldstein, "These were frustrating years for him."

Hersh and Rosenthal began to scream at each other—in Hersh's office, in Rosenthal's office, in the middle of the newsroom. "They fought all the time," Gelb said.[23] Some fights were good-natured; some not, as Hersh would turn red-faced. He regularly called Rosenthal "motherfucker," but also said he was "the smartest cocksucker who ever walked into a newsroom." Hersh called the relationship "complicated" and said he did not really understand it, except to say, "any investigative reporter must eventually end up in total conflict with his editor—or he's not doing his job."[24] Rosenthal and Hersh were both similar oversized personalities. They could be crude and blunt, as well as charming. Both had big egos and huge ambitions; both came from immigrant Jewish families with modest backgrounds, and both held Pulitzer Prizes. Hersh came aboard the *Times* because Rosenthal needed a star investigative reporter to match up with Woodward and Bernstein. Hersh gave him that. But he also gave him a headache, all the time. Publisher Sulzberger was not enamored of Hersh's style, nor did he like the *Times* to be so activist. It was the paper of record, but it did not seek to create or make that record. Rosenthal both loved and hated Hersh's progressive and activist bent. Reporter John Darnton remembers a meeting in New York during which Rosenthal asked his editors: who in the newsroom was trying to make the paper an advocate? Darnton described it as chilling; Rosenthal was trying to root out the liberals. But Darnton said Hersh was immune from such pressures. Abe would walk through the newsroom and, approvingly, pat Hersh on the head, saying, "Well, well, how is my little commie today?"[25]

After six years of the *Times* tolerating Hersh, however, his time was coming to a close. "The *Times* wasn't nearly as happy when we went after business wrongdoing as when we were kicking around some slob in government," Hersh said. Rosenthal once compared Hersh to "a puppy who isn't quite house broken, but as long as he's pissing on Ben Bradlee's carpet, let him go." Now it was Sulzberger's carpet that was sometimes being soiled.[26] Pulitzer winner Denny Walsh, whom Rosenthal fired in 1974, said, "Abe didn't see him as a loyal employee." He was much too outspoken and impatient with the *Times'* often arcane rules. Pulitzer Prize–winning columnist Russell Baker added, "I never thought of him as a *Times* guy. He was a loner."[27]

CHAPTER 21

Scoop Artist versus Dr. Kissinger

"Love to Get That Son-of-a-Bitch"

Sy Hersh was at the pinnacle of success at the *New York Times*. But just as he had worn out his welcome at the City News Bureau, at the Associated Press, and with Eugene McCarthy, by 1979 he was finished at the *Times*. His abrasive personality, feuds with editor Abe Rosenthal, publisher Sulzberger's increasing unease—all led to the inevitable. Rosenthal admitted that by the late 1970s he had reservations about some of Hersh's work. Approaches applauded five years earlier no longer looked so attractive. "We were all learning how to do things," he said, defensively. But Hersh's departure was compelled by a project that was too controversial for the *Times*: he wanted to take on Henry Kissinger, the man who might have been "the most powerful and celebrated public servant in modern American history." There was no middle ground on this Harvard professor who rose to secretary of state. He "aroused controversy of a distinctly personal sort—hatred and veneration, animosity and awe," observed biographer Walter Isaacson.[1] He was the darling of the political right, untouched by the seamy Watergate scandal. To the left, he was a soulless Dr. Strangelove, mastermind of bombing and war.

James Silberman, editor of Simon & Schuster's Summit Books, first came to Hersh with the idea in 1977; Hersh declined. "It wasn't something I was lying in wait to do," he said. Then he approached Hersh again in 1979 with a $250,000 advance. "I didn't want to do the book particularly until someone threw a lot of money at me," he said.[2] One must wonder how true that was; Hersh had been eyeing Kissinger from the day he joined the *Times*. "I have been a Kissinger watcher for 11 years," he wrote in a 1983 letter. At the *Times* he did more than watch Kissinger, but his attempts to implicate him always fell short—Lavelle, Cambodia, Allende. No doubt the reporter known as "Henry's nemesis" roughed up Kissinger and tarnished his image, but he needed the time a book would give to locate Kissinger's fingerprints on questionable White House activities. "I am not going to tell you I am writing a friendly book about Kissinger," he wrote, a warning on which his critics would pounce. His intention was spelled out a decade earlier, when he told colleague Harrison Salisbury: "I'd really love to get that son-of-a-bitch."[3]

Hersh asked for a leave of absence; Rosenthal said no. Generally, the *Times* did not grant book leaves. Roger Kahn, the best-selling author of *The Boys of Summer,* recalled that Rosenthal once offered him a sports column; Kahn said he wanted to write books. Rosenthal countered, "Roger, we write our books in the morning, before work." Kahn declined the offer. Editor Seymour Topping said two of his books were written at night, after work was done. Top Rosenthal aide Arthur Gelb said his 1956 Eugene O'Neill biography was written while he worked full-time. "Your loyalty was to *The Times* only; go ahead and figure out how to work full time and write a major book." Sometimes, however, book leaves were given. "If the person was invaluable you tended to give the leave," observed Al Siegal, a retired editor who was expert on *Times* policies. But as invaluable as Hersh had been, Rosenthal let him go.[4]

Hersh and Rosenthal made an arrangement, which was unusual, that he could freelance for the paper. Hersh immediately embarked on a ten-day trip to Communist Vietnam, filing seven articles. He found a black market flourishing in Saigon, now called Ho Chi Minh City. The nightclubs and girlie shows were all shuttered, and the people were unhappy. In Hanoi top officials gave him hours of interviews and took pot shots at the Carter administration. But as he wandered the city where he started his *Times* career in 1972, he found that Western culture had penetrated—blue jeans, rock music, teens holding hands. His critics saw his visit as evidence that the left-leaning Hersh was at it again. "It is with breathless interest that one reads the series of dispatches," commented Richard Grenier of the conservative *American Spectator.* "One is astonished to find Hersh . . . sitting at the feet" of Vietnam's acting foreign minister "without the faintest hint of skepticism." Hersh, as Grenier saw it, was a dupe of the

Commies, the man who aided the enemy going back to My Lai. Grenier did not seem to care, as one official told Hersh, that the United States "dropped 50 million tons of bombs on our heads."[5]

What Grenier did not know, however, was that Hersh was really in Southeast Asia to convince Nguyen Co Thach, a top North Vietnamese foreign policy aide, to leak documents that showed how Kissinger and Richard Nixon had conducted the war—and muffed chances to end it sooner and save lives. As Hersh searched for evidence, the *Times* was quickly in his rearview mirror. He had begun his pursuit of his next book, *The Price of Power: Kissinger in the Nixon White House,* published in 1983.[6]

Hersh Makes the Gadaffi Connection

Before Google searches and email changed the nature of reporting, Sy Hersh relied on the tried- and-true methods of telephone and in-person interviews and seeking documents, even if the document was classified. An important way to find documents was through the Freedom of Information Act (FOIA), which applies to all federal agencies. Even if a document is public, however, government agencies often turn down requests and force reporters to appeal or resort to the courts. It is meant to discourage release. At times, even when released, a document is so heavily censored it is nonsensical.[7]

Hersh was not adept at using the FOIA. So he reached out to someone who was—Jay Peterzell, a researcher at the Center for National Security Studies in Washington DC, an advocacy group. Peterzell was trying to make FOIA work at a difficult time. The Reagan administration was gutting the 1966 law. The CIA wanted to be exempt. Most of Peterzell's requests, however, went to the State Department to elicit information on how it dealt with elections in Vietnam. The documents, of course, only told part of the story. Daniel Ellsberg, who leaked the Pentagon Papers and became an antiwar hero, talked to Hersh about his first meeting with Nixon. It is one of the dozens of fascinating anecdotes that make their way into the book. Ellsberg was one of a group discussing with the president how to promote democratic elections in Vietnam. Major General Edward G. Lansdale of the air force told the president, "We want to make this the most honest election that's ever been held in Vietnam." Nixon replied, "Oh sure, honest, yes, honest, that's right. *So long as you win.*" Nixon winked, driving his elbow into Lansdale's arm. "My teammates turned to stone," Ellsberg said.[8]

More of Peterzell's time was spent at the Library of Congress, assembling books, magazine articles, and newspaper accounts of the White House from 1968 to 1972. He assembled, for example, a fifty-page chronology of the Vietnam War and long analytical documents on disarmament with the Soviet Union. The library material was voluminous, and Peterzell pointed to it as a key to understanding Hersh's method. Many people think he works only by badgering sources. But, Peterzell said, Hersh's approach was to "read, read, read" with an "incredible intensity of purpose." Hersh was like his mentor, I. F. Stone, a prodigious reader of books and government reports.[9]

Sitting alongside Hersh for many hours in his small National Press Club office in Washington, Peterzell got a bird's-eye view of the telephone terrorist as Hersh did more than a thousand interviews for his Kissinger book. Peterzell recalled Hersh's incredibly fast-pasted style with sources. "He overwhelms you with his verbal barrage," Peterzell said, but he was less about asking questions than baiting sources into conversation. "He would usually begin with a nugget," Peterzell said, a piece of information the source did not have. And before you knew it, he and the source were competing. "You are on the journey with him," Peterzell said. He heard Hersh talk to "some fairly big cheese and he got them talking in a matter of minutes." They would get "caught up in the enthusiasm, the importance, his energy." As he did with My Lai, Hersh crisscrossed the country for interviews. John Erlichman was in Santa Fe; Robert Finch in Los Angeles; Anthony Lake in Amherst, Massachusetts; Egil Krogh in San Francisco. He visited professors at Harvard and Stanford. And he tapped a huge number of people in and out of government in Washington and nearby Virginia. He went to see Patrick Buchanan, in McLean, Virginia, where the former Nixon speechwriter recalled how he was swimming in the Florida pool of Richard Nixon when he first met Kissinger. He pulled a document from a briefing book and told Buchanan how much he agreed with writer James Burnham of the conservative *National Review*. Burnham was Buchanan's intellectual hero, and Kissinger knew it. Kissinger knew how to cuddle.[10]

As Hersh and Peterzell assembled material, Hersh could not resist taking a detour. "Hard to do only one thing at a time," he said. *The Price of Power* would not come out until June 1983; that would mean three years without a scoop or a byline. He needed a fix. And it came to him in the person of Kevin Mulcahy, a thirty-eight-year-old employee of the Central Intelligence Agency. Mulcahy's father had been in the CIA for thirty-seven years; it was the family business. Then two former CIA agents—the mysterious and shady Edwin Wilson and Frank Terpil—offered him lots of money to join their company, and he went along. They were involved in various weapons deals in the Middle East. It seemed legitimate. But when Mulcahy came across documents he was not supposed to see, he changed his tune. The two agents were in direct contact with Muammar Gadaffi of Libya, exporting explosives and training his troops for terrorism. Mulcahy went to the CIA to reveal what he knew, convinced that Wilson and Terpil must be still working for the CIA; they were not. When Wilson and Terpil found out he was talking, Mulcahy was a marked man. He went into hiding, sure they were trying to kill him as he met with the FBI and prosecutors. Mulcahy wanted to tell his story to the press, in hopes of reclaiming his life, and he turned to—no surprise here—Sy Hersh, the man who had written so many CIA stories. Hersh, explained Morton Halperin, a longtime confidante and source of Hersh's, is "more capable of getting people to talk than anybody I know. He is reliable and careful. He persuades people that the public has a right to know and he will protect them." Of course, Wilson later insisted that Hersh was duped by Mulcahy, whom he called "a pathetic figure, an alcoholic with mental problems. He fed Seymour Hersh of the *New York Times* the most unbelievable lies, fabrications and untruths." The government's aggressive pursuit for many years of Wilson and Terpil, however, belied Wilson and suggested that both Hersh and Mulcahy had it right. The CIA was not policing its rogue agents, and existing federal law was little help.[11]

As if play-acting in a spy novel, Hersh and Mulcahy huddled all over Washington, with Mulcahy driving to construction sites, parking for free, and posing as laborer. Although he was a CIA computer expert, Mulcahy also had learned about the disguise part of the "spook" business. Hersh concluded that Mulcahy was "tired of waiting for this segment of his life to end. He wants . . . to stop living as if he—and not Wilson and Terpil—had been indicted for wrongdoing. He feels forced now, in effect, to give his testimony in the pages of the *New York Times*." And his testimony, verified by Hersh with documents and interviews, told a sordid tale of an old-boy network of CIA agents meeting secretly in bars to sell weapons. The man who paid them handsomely was Colonel Qadaffi, who was supporting terrorism long before al-Qaeda. The same man whom Ronald Reagan labeled "the mad dog of the Middle East" and whom the president tried to secretly assassinate in 1987 by dropping bombs over Tripoli, a story revealed by another long Hersh article in the *Times* five years later.[12]

But in the 1981 "Qaddafi Connection" piece in the *Times* magazine, Hersh—identified as a former *Times* correspondent at work on a book on Henry Kissinger—laid out a world of shadowy figures who relied on tacit CIA approval to oversee the sale of American technology to terrorist nations. Few American laws prevented it. Hersh was purposeful in telling this "disturbing" story. "The notion that there is no control over an American intelligence official taking his know-how and selling it to the highest bidder seems to be insane," Phillip Heymann, an assistant attorney general, told Hersh.

Over two issues in the *Times* normally drab magazine, Hersh laid out a powerful, complex, and fascinating story of how Mulcahy worked with the federal government as it pursued Wilson and Terpil over four years, finally indicting them in 1980. But both men fled the country, becoming fugitives. Mulcahy knew they would run; Terpil had six passports. They had accumulated $4 million in real estate and millions in profits from arms dealing, often shielded by CIA comrades. Had Hersh still been working at the *Times* he would have had a field day in mounting one of his crusades. The task of follow-up fell to old buddy Jeff Gerth, who pursued the story until 1982, by which time the CIA had passed reforms to stop ex-agents from duplicating the Terpil-Wilson escapades. Hersh's articles, Gerth noted, "were important."[13] Fueled by Hersh's work, Congress began hearings on the control of American technology. The *Times* weighed in, demanding reforms and pointing to the irony that the CIA aggressively went after ex-agent Frank Snepp for daring to write about agency screw-ups in Vietnam but did little to stop rogues from peddling bombs. How can the government "tolerate activities that directly aid despised regimes?"[14] It was the right question, and Hersh would ask it soon enough in his book on Nixon's foreign policy. On December 21, 1982, Wilson, finally apprehended, was sentenced to fifteen years in prison. Terpil eluded the government well into the 1990s, hiding in Cuba. As for Mulcahy, he met a mysterious death on October 24, 1982, before he ever testified. His body was found outside a motel in rural Virginia. Wrote *Time* magazine: he "died as Company men sometimes do in spy fiction: in the cold and dark, of causes unknown." The coroner said he was drunk and had pneumonia. Hersh's little diversion had caused a big ripple, and as much as he might have wanted to follow the Libyan trail, he turned back to Kissinger, leaving Congress, the courts, and Gerth to pursue the Gadaffi connection.[15]

The First Blast Goes Off

Henry Kissinger was nearing his sixtieth birthday and smarting from being out of power. He was a minister without portfolio. He wrote his first memoir—for $5 million—in 1977, and since he refused to ever talk to Seymour Hersh, the journalist would use it as a reference point as he did his research. The book put Kissinger back in the spotlight, but he was often heckled at speaking appearances.[16] During Jimmy Carter's presidency, his successor as secretary of state, Zbigniew Brzezinski, a Harvard rival and soon-to-be Hersh source, held Kissinger at arm's length—and in disdain. Kissinger toyed with making a run for the U.S. Senate from New York in 1980, but no one could envision the jet-setting super-diplomat milking cows in upstate New York. He briefly made headlines as a key go-between when Reagan toyed with making ex-president Gerald Ford, whom Kissinger had served, his vice president. But Ford declined. Reagan's first secretary of State, Alexander Haig, although a key aide to Kissinger, had actually become somewhat of an enemy—as Hersh was to document—and a rival to his former mentor. Kissinger was left to start up a consulting business that made him millions, even though commercial ventures were not his forte. He signed a five-year contract with NBC News to be an expert source and produce one documentary a year. In early 1982, after suffering sharp pains, Kissinger needed emergency bypass surgery for three clogged arteries. He recovered nicely, but more pain was on the way—this time in the form of the first glimpse of Hersh's work, a 15,900-word article that dribbled out in the May issue of the *Atlantic* magazine. Simply called "The Wiretaps," it previewed what was to come—Hersh carefully documenting a Henry Kissinger abuse; a glimpse at the sordid business of the Nixon-Kissinger White House; and a display of the methodology he would use to make his case.[17]

First, foremost, and to the end, Sy Hersh is a reporter and journalist. So even when he writes long book chapters, becoming historian and analyst, his journalism techniques and style dominate—for better and worse. "The Wiretaps" began like a feature story he could have written for the AP. Roger Morris, a Harvard PhD who served on the National Security Council under Lyndon Johnson and who stayed under Henry Kissinger, was on duty in the NSC office one weekend in 1969. An envelope marked "very urgent" arrived from FBI director J. Edgar Hoover. Morris found a memo detailing the extramarital sex life of civil rights leader Martin Luther King. Shocked, he showed it to Lawrence Eagleburger, a top Kissinger aide, who shrugged, saying Hoover sends those all the time. Then he went to a file cabinet and took out folders that indicated spying dossiers had been created on numerous NSC staff members. Their phones were bugged because of leaks to the press and the fear that Kissinger's staff was untrustworthy. Before Nixon ever assembled a unit of "plumbers" to stem the tide of "leaks" from the White House, Hersh alleged that Henry Kissinger was taking the lead in wiretapping his closest colleagues. "Morris was not reassured," Hersh wrote, "but kept his peace." Not for long. In 1977—when Kissinger had become secretary of state—Morris wrote a scathing book attack on the Nixon-Kissinger foreign policy, which offset the fawning biography three years earlier by Marvin and Bernard Kalb.[18]

By the time Hersh went to work on his big book, Morris was one of his best sources, which was no surprise since he had admired the "remarkable investigative journalism" of Hersh. But he was typical of the kind of source that irked the Hersh haters—and Kissinger. "The fundamental problem of 'The Price of Power' is that of Mr. Hersh's informants," wrote Stanley Hoffman, a Harvard colleague of Kissinger, who, in general, lauded Hersh's book as a needed dose of "Kissinger antimemoirs." But his concern was that disgruntled Kissinger enemies—who were either sent packing from the White House or who left unhappily—skewed a reader's view. Hoffman wrote, "The credibility of the witnesses varies greatly, and the reader has no way of separating what is undoubtedly true from what is dubious, exaggerated or false."[19] And yet, right after the disgruntled Morris served up an anecdote, Hersh turns to John Erlichman, one of the powerful Nixon lieutenants who served nineteen months in prison for Watergate misdeeds. Hersh visited him in his Santa Fe home. Nixon, Erlichman remembered, would lambaste liberal Jews—Jewish traitors, the Eastern Jewish establishment, Jews at Harvard—in front of the Jewish Kissinger. "Well, Mr. President—there are Jews and Jews," Kissinger would respond. No moral indignation. Keeping his job secure was more important. Surely Erlichman, who Hersh always trusted, was a reliable source, and he spoke on the record. Similarly, Hersh used Charles Colson, another top White House official who also served time in prison, as he recalled a key moment when Nixon blew up at Chief of Staff H. R. Haldeman for not retrieving sensitive documents he believed were stored at the private Brookings Institute. "God dammit, Bob, haven't we got that capability in place? How many times am I going to have to tell you? Get the documents." Haldeman then took Colson aside and told him, "Take care of it." The result soon after was the creation of the "plumbers" unit to carry out illegal break-ins, including into the offices of the psychiatrist of Daniel Ellsberg. Surely Colson was a good source, with no ax to grind. In fact, Hersh did not selectively pick his sources. Early in his research he came across a complete list—with addresses and phone numbers—of all members of the NSC during the Kissinger years. He called or visited everyone who would talk.

Hersh brushed off the criticism of his sourcing, defending the people he relied on to unfold his story. "With somebody like Henry Kissinger there are always losers," he said. "I've been in this town for 25 years. I know a loser from a winner. And I understand that losers because they are losers often know a great deal and are more willing to talk. It is my function to verify what they say." Many of the "losers" were fired or outcast Kissinger aides. "Kissinger has left in his wake an amazing number of disaffected former associates who still have their tongues," wrote historian Walter LaFeber. "Hersh has apparently found them all."[20]

Many times, however, they would not speak on the record and were granted anonymity by Hersh. When the North Koreans mistakenly shot down an unarmed American plane in 1969, killing thirty-one airmen, the White House faced its first international crisis. As the crisis unfolded, Hersh alleged that Nixon got drunk. "Here's the President of the United States, ranting and raving—drunk in the middle of the crisis," commented a shaken Eagleburger. The source for this quote is a "luncheon friend" of Eagleburger's. At another point, as Hersh tries to show that Kissinger was cutting Secretary of Defense Melvin Laird out of policymaking, he quotes a "senior NSC aide" as saying, "For a long time, I thought Laird's last name was crook. 'Mel Laird's a crook,' Henry would always say." Great damning quotes. But who is talking? In showing how Alexander Haig ingratiated himself with Kissinger, Hersh tells how the general helped Henry get dressed for his first-ever white tie dinner. The source: one former NSC staffer. Bemoaning that Watergate prosecutors never closely scrutinized Kissinger's activities, Hersh finds a prosecutor who listened to Kissinger's meetings with Nixon. "He was like one of the boys, talking tough. One says, 'Let's bring knives.' Another says, 'Let's bring bats.' And Henry pipes up, 'Let's bring zip-guns.'" The prosecutor was surprised: "I thought he might have been classier." But the prosecutor is never identified. These were the kind of compelling quotes Hersh tried to use at the *Times* that were often spiked by Rosenthal. Privately, Kissinger was furious at Hersh's method: "inference piled on assumption, third-hand hearsay accepted as fact, the self-serving accounts of disgruntled adversaries elevated to gospel, the 'impressions' of people several times removed from the scene." His identified sources were "unreliable," Kissinger decried, "but how about his unidentified ones? Indeed, do we really know they exist?" It was a criticism that haunted Hersh's work for fifteen years. Bob Woodward conceded, "There has always been doubt about unnamed sources, and there should be," but, he added, "you're not going to sit down with people who are in sensitive positions and say 'I'd like to talk on the record.' They'll say, 'Were you born yesterday?' It just is not going to happen. That puts pressure on the reporter or author to make sure [the information] is right and validate it and be very careful." And Hersh was adamant: he had it right. His sources were good. Prove he was wrong, he dared his critics.[21]

So, did Sy Hersh finally nail Henry Kissinger in this opening wedge that so signaled what his book would be like? Frankly the chapter seems much like his *New York Times* attempts. He gets oh so close, seems right on the edge, but the "smoking gun" is not to be found, nor is the document or the unimpeachable source who could put Kissinger as the absolute instigator of the wiretaps or as having a key role in starting up the White House plumbers unit. In fact, the chapter probably is more damning of Alexander Haig, then Reagan's secretary of state, as the man who likely destroyed evidence so the wiretaps would not be revealed.[22]

Kissinger later argued that Hersh was selective in what he chose to use, that he had a "rigidly predetermined and relentlessly pursued thesis." Of course, this is what authors do—especially authors of muckraking books, which even Kissinger conceded have a place, but Hersh's work, he insisted, was a "hatchet job." That is an unfair charge. Hersh uses many named sources—Colson, Erlichman, and Egil Krogh, who headed up the plumbers unit. He did use other named sources who need to be taken with some skepticism—like Halperin, who waged a long court battle against Kissinger; and Roger Morris, a bitter foe who simply disagreed with Kissinger's policy choices, and others who were wiretapped, such as Anthony Lake. But these were men of integrity who were in the open, and the reader could judge their trustworthiness. Hersh also uses Kissinger's two memoirs and his public testimony before the Senate on Watergate as a way to measure what Hersh's evidence seemed to say—that Kissinger knew much more about the wiretapping and the "plumbers" than he was ever willing to admit.[23]

Where Hersh is on shakier grounds, and where a more conventional historical account would differ, is in his use of unnamed NSC aides, for example, to provide key evidence at telling moments. "One prosecution official . . . one Watergate attorney." The unnamed people become bothersome. Additionally, his reliance on documents that were not public and to which no one else had access and whose origin he could not name—this presents problems for the reader also. For example, Nixon was obsessed with the Brookings Institute, a liberal think-tank where he believed Halperin and former *Times* reporter Leslie Gelb had stored classified documents that could come back to haunt him. "They've got the stuff over there," Nixon said. Kissinger responded: "Can't we send someone over there to get it back?" The inference is that Kissinger was setting in motion, with Nixon, a scenario that would lead to the creation of the illegal burglar team. But the source of this damning conversation is a Watergate "prosecution file" that only Hersh was allowed to read. Similarly Hersh writes early in his research that "a key Kissinger aide" gave him access to a private journal he kept that recorded conversations between Kissinger and Nixon. Hersh promised anonymity for its author. Once again, however, it leaves the reader wondering, who is this person and why would he betray Kissinger? Kissinger, for his part, says that Hersh bases most of his damning account on people who were his enemies. But Kissinger refused to set the record straight and never talked to Hersh, nor did any of his top aides, at least not on the record.

"If Hersh were an honest reporter, he would have disclosed to the reader the bias of his sources," Kissinger said privately. Still, if Kissinger wanted to rebut Hersh, he might have given an interview—or even told some top aides to respond. Perhaps he felt it was a hopeless cause with Hersh, even though Kissinger had been able to curry favor with the nation's most influential columnists, editors, and reporters. Even Hersh said Kissinger had played him when he was a *Times* reporter. In 1992, when Walter Isaacson wrote the first full-scale biography of Kissinger, he sat down, reluctantly, for twelve long interviews. Granted, Isaacson was not "Henry's nemesis." Could Hersh have gone back to the intermediary whom both Hersh and Kissinger used during Hersh's *New York Times* days, a person who could relay messages, even though the two adversaries never talked directly? That person apparently was Alexander Haig, who would listen to Hersh's explanation of what his stories would imply the next day about Kissinger. Haig would then try to get some perspective for Hersh from conversations with Kissinger. But by the time *The Price of Power* was well under way, Haig had become secretary of state. General Haig was no longer Kissinger's "gofer." Moreover, he and Kissinger were now adversaries. Consequently, Hersh had no contact with his "nemesis." As a reviewer observed, Kissinger's reluctance to talk to Hersh "is difficult to fathom."[24]

As for Kissinger, he never took responsibility for either "the plumbers" or the seventeen wiretaps that continued for three years. However, nineteen years after Halperin's phone was tapped, Kissinger settled one of the longest-running feuds in Washington by apologizing in a federal court. He did not admit he was responsible for the wiretap on Halperin, but accepted "moral responsibility and conceded his office should not have acquiesced in the tapping." After reading Hersh's magazine piece, the liberal *Times* columnist Anthony Lewis said there could be little doubt about Kissinger's culpability: he selected the wiretap targets and hid his role. And why, he asked, would this "intelligent man" so "humiliate himself? To acquire and keep power—and to exercise it in secret," Lewis concluded. Nonetheless, Halperin bemoaned, Kissinger "remained standing." Hersh would try again in December to knock him down.[25]

CHAPTER 22

The Summer's Literary Furor

The Bashing Begins

As 1982 ended, Henry Kissinger's consulting business was snaring big-name, big-paying clients. Appearing regularly on ABC's late-evening talk show *Nightline*, Kissinger was, as James Reston noted in the *New York Times*, "a one-man university . . . on the tube explaining in his amiable growl" how foreign policy and the world should work. But a time bomb was ticking. In the *Atlantic's* December issue Hersh dropped explosion number two, revisiting another of his *Times* topics—the overthrow and death of Chile's president Salvador Allende in 1973. He went back to old sources, especially Edward Korry, the former ambassador to Chile, and with new documents in hand and a more thorough look at the work of the National Security Council and the secret "40 Committee," Hersh saw it more clearly. Kissinger and Nixon tried to block the election of the socialist Allende, and when that failed, they helped put in motion forces that led to his overthrow and death. Maybe Allende was even assassinated. Behind it all was the need to protect American investments in Chile. They are assertions historians continue to debate.[1] Hersh leaned on at least ten books on Chile, but he relied primarily on the two-volume report on Allende's death by a Senate committee, which had, in part, been spurred by his work. Hersh "marshals mind-boggling detail," commented *Washington Post* reviewer Walter LaFeber. As usual, Hersh was able to find sources who fed him inside and gossipy tales. A former Chilean ambassador told Hersh he had met with Kissinger, before the overthrow, and insulted him: "You are a German Wagnerian. You are a very arrogant man." Yeoman Charles E. Radford, a twenty-seven-year-old navy liaison between the White House and the Joint Chiefs of Staff, said he saw shocking documents.

The Nixon administration was weighing options to prevent Allende from taking office in 1969, including assassination. "I realized that my government actively was involved in planning to kill people," he told Hersh. Of course, Radford was also the man who surreptitiously copied and leaked National Security Agency documents to the military brass so they could spy on White House activities—originally also revealed by Hersh. It made him a suspect source, albeit one who had the inside poop.[2]

Some of Hersh's critics yawned. "I am left with this vacuous feeling," wrote Victor Gold, "of having been subjected to 'Rocky XVI' or 'Superman XII'; that I've been in this theater before and heard it all." Kissinger did not respond. Privately he set the tone for a response to Hersh's Chile allegations. "The thrust of his Chilean critique is purely Marxist: that our policy was to defend rapacious American enterprise," he wrote. "This was *not* its thrust." The old Sy-is-an-untrustworthy lefty was the best Kissinger could do. Hersh's trademark, Kissinger added, "is the viciousness and ruthlessness with which he goes after his victims and the tendency to extend the assault to the institutions which they serve."[3] Chimed in William Safire, the former Nixon speechwriter who had become a Pulitzer Prize–winning *New York Times* columnist, "The Hersh attack is a work of vengeance and self-justification." None of this made Kissinger any more comfortable as his sixtieth birthday approached a month before *The Price of Power* was published. The two *Atlantic* installments had come out; everyone knew what was forthcoming. "Everybody talks about it except in front of Mr. Kissinger," wrote Charlotte Curtis in the *Times*. Safire attended a gala sixtieth fete for Kissinger, sitting near Lady Bird Johnson and the Empress of Iran, along with Kissinger journalist pals Joseph Kraft and Marvin Kalb. Why, oh why, Safire wondered, is Sy "obsessed with getting The Man Who Got Away? What is it about Henry Kissinger that turns him into a white whale and transforms an investigative reporter into a monomaniacal Ahab?"[4] The book was not out, but the bashing of Sy Hersh had begun.

Juicy Journalism and Slimy Lies

On June 13, 1983, *The Price of Power* hit bookstores—698 pages, 460,000 words. The front cover showed an illuminated White House in front of a darkened sky. The back cover had a black and white photo of Hersh, wryly smiling, pen in hand, arm on typewriter, more kempt than usual in jacket and tie, with dark large horn-rimmed glasses dominating his face. Summit Books called it "an extraordinary joining of author and subject." One of America's foremost investigative journalists taking on "the most brilliant diplomat of our age." Safire simply dubbed it "Henry and Sy." The book had forty-one chapters, with thirteen devoted to Vietnam and Southeast Asia. In fact, wrote *Washington Post* foreign policy expert Stephen Rosenfeld, this is a book largely *about* Vietnam. Hersh "is still fighting the war. Hating the war—or, rather, hating the American part in it." Hersh did not disagree, saying, "My take on Kissinger is that when the rest of us can't sleep we count sheep, and this guy has to count burned and maimed Cambodian and Vietnamese babies until the end of his life. So he's got his own hell somewhere." "Hitched to [Hersh's] formidable investigative talents," this rage makes the book "juicy as journalism, farcical as history," Rosenfeld wrote.[5]

Hersh covers a five-year period of American foreign policy, ranging from the détente with China to a Strategic Arms Limitations Treaty (SALT) with the Soviet Union, from a crisis with North Korea to the illegal bombing of Cambodia, mixed with domestic intrigue—"the plumbers," wiretapping, the ostracizing of the secretaries of state and defense. Eight chapters and parts of several others were topics that Hersh had reported at the *Times*. Observed *Times* reviewer Stanley Hoffman, Hersh "gives us a picture of an Administration whose mode of operation was somewhere between the Borgias and the Mafia." Everything in this book, he said, "is deeply disturbing: both the story Mr. Hersh tells and the way he tells it." Added the *London Review of Books*, the book is "a bit like watching an old horror film on late-night TV." Most of all, though, it is a scathing portrait of Kissinger as a man consumed with gaining and holding power, even at the cost of foreign policy initiatives that could have saved American lives. "To read these pages," wrote *Times* columnist Anthony Lewis, "is to understand that Mr. Kissinger's methods threatened the deepest American values."[6]

The Price of Power is not a biography; no time is spent on Kissinger growing up in Germany, his formative years, or his time at Harvard. It starts in the days leading up to Nixon's 1968 election and traces Kissinger's rise to unprecedented influence as national security adviser and secretary of state, as virtual co-president when the Watergate scandal overwhelmed Nixon. It is a dense, heavily documented, muckraking book, with a narrow focus, devastating anecdotes—and lots of "scoops." As *Newsweek*'s reviewer observed, "Books are too often called bombshells, yet surely this is one."[7] And the bombshells began right away, in chapter 1, which received the most media attention.

As Richard Nixon and Hubert Humphrey angled for the presidency in 1968, Kissinger wanted it all ways, according to Hersh. He was initially an adviser to New York governor Nelson Rockefeller, who sought the presidency. But when Rockefeller faded, Kissinger went to Humphrey and, according to Hersh, offered to provide "shit files" on Nixon from Rockefeller archives. In September, Hersh reported, Kissinger then cuddled up to the Nixon camp, even at some point allegedly offering information that he had gathered on the highly secret Paris peace talks, a serious breach of security. Nixon's memoirs conceded that Kissinger did give him information, and one aide told Hersh, "I remember Henry as being a both-sides-of-the street kind of guy." Another aide said that twelve hours before Lyndon Johnson announced a halt in bombing, Kissinger called to alert the Nixon campaign. The aide said it earned him a place in the Nixon administration. When the book appeared, the *Times* headlined its long news story: "Book Portrays Kissinger as a Double Dealer." Lost were some of the book's other much more serious bombshells. In a telephone interview with the *Times*, Kissinger denied there were ever any secret files. "These are slimy lies," he said, a phrase that would crop up for weeks in news stories as Kissinger refused to discuss the book. But in a twenty-two-page letter he sent to *Times* editor Abe Rosenthal, marked "not for publication" and never made public, Kissinger devoted the longest section to denying the "double dealing" charges. They are important, he wrote "because it involves my honor."[8]

Kissinger made a compelling case that Hersh "rearranged [the facts] into his typically reckless innuendo." His main source was Zbigniew Brzezinski, a Humphrey aide who became secretary of state under Jimmy Carter. There were no "shit files," simply material on Nixon's policy statements. Anyway, why did Brzezinski wait fifteen years to disclose these "startling details," Kissinger asked. He gives a variety of reasons why Brzezinski's account is "inherently unlikely." As for the "secrets" he allegedly leaked from Paris, Kissinger scoffed. He had no access to secrets, he insisted. What he told the Nixon camp was simply his opinion, similar to what many journalists were writing. A bombing pause was likely. And Nixon should be careful about commenting at a time of delicate peace negotiations. Hardly inside stuff. Hersh said the secret details were originally given to Richard Allen, who told Hersh what occurred. Supposedly Kissinger called Allen from Europe and spoke German to disguise himself. "This all sounds exciting," Kissinger responded. "It is, however, all humbug." If Hersh had "elementary decency," Kissinger insisted, he would have made clear that Allen was an old enemy, angry that Kissinger got the spot in the Nixon administration he coveted. When the *Times* contacted Allen, he confirmed his quotes in the Hersh book, giving credibility to the charges. But, Kissinger said, "I do not doubt that most of Hersh's named sources will confirm his version. The issue is their bias, their credibility, their knowledgeability, the lack of representation of other, usually far more knowledgeable sources."[9]

Hersh's "slimy innuendos," Kissinger repeated, make him guilty of a "modern McCarthyism." On a *Nightline* program, when asked about the book, Kissinger sputtered and repeated his "slimy lies" charge. And then he and a number of his well-known supporters admitted they had not read the book, nor would they. Russell Baker, the *Times* humor columnist and a Hersh pal, could not resist a jibe. A friend, he wrote, had invited him to go to Hersh's house and jeer him because of the unflattering book about Kissinger, who his friend thought was the greatest diplomat since Talleyrand. Baker had not yet read the book. "Is it bad enough to justify hissing Hersh in front of his own house?" Baker asked. "Worse," the friend said. "It is pack of slimy lies." Baker asked, "What are the things Hersh lies slimily about?" "How should I know," the friend said. "I haven't had a chance to read it." But how then do you know it is full of slimy lies, Baker wondered. "Henry says it is," the friend replied. Amazing, out for only three weeks, and Kissinger has read it all. "Are you insane?" the friend says. "You don't think Henry would waste his time reading a book like Hersh's, do you?" Deadpanned *Times* writer Curtis, "The really chic thing in New York, where the Kissingers do most of their entertaining, is to insist you haven't read it."[10] That way you can still get invited to their parties. Even Hersh poked fun at the difficulty one might have plowing through his immense book. "People buy it but it is hard to read," he admitted. Has anyone read it cover to cover, Brian Lamb asked him on C-Span. Chuckling, he said, "Yeah, my wife." Kissinger did assign two researchers to comb the book for errors. (Kissinger did not respond to a written request to be interviewed for this book, and Hersh declined to comment on Kissinger's twenty-two-page letter to Rosenthal, which he had never seen. "Could not care less," he told me in an email message. It is "yesterday's story.")[11]

That readers would have trouble making it through Hersh's book is no surprise. Although he flecks his story with jarring anecdotes and startling quotes, he may be guilty of overwriting. The book is a detailed account of certain policy matters that simply cannot be made into easy reading. The SALT negotiations with the Soviet Union, for example, make it tough to get to Hersh's point—that negotiations for arms limits may have been badly bungled. "It's not that he does not write well, but that he seems to have been unable to leave anything out," said one critic. Another mocked Hersh's "three-inch footnotes and annotations and annotations-to-annotations." Said a British reviewer, "His book is not easy reading. Mr. Hersh's prose creaks under the weight of the information he has collected."[12] But his documentation was actually a strength because, as a reviewer pointed out, his "exhaustive treatment of a difficult subject" makes him "sound like a historian instead of a muckraker," prompting one writer to call his footnotes a "tour de force . . . some of the best documentation on the domestic roots of U.S. foreign policy."[13] Added Stanley Hoffman, a highly regarded scholar, "This is a book that through its factual density avoids the typically hectoring tone of the investigative reporter or the ideologue with an ax to grind." Of course, Kissinger was convinced his "nemesis" did have an ax to grind. Certainly Hersh had opinions about Kissinger and Nixon's policies. Said Hersh: "I thought his Vietnam policies had been immoral and unprincipled."[14]

Blocking Kissinger's Return

Although it seemed that many people were not actually *reading* Hersh's *Price of Power*, lots were buying. Charlotte Curtis called it "this summer's literary furor. Nearly everybody is talking about it." The book hit the *Times* nonfiction best sellers list almost immediately, staying there for weeks. "I guessed there would be interest because Kissinger is an endlessly fascinating figure, whatever you think of his politics," said Hersh's editor, James H. Silberman.[15] Kissinger also had just reemerged. President Reagan appointed him to head up a Latin American advisory committee that might help gain support for military efforts in Central America where Reagan worried about communism. The appointment came in the midst of the book furor as Kissinger eyed a return to power. "He is no doubt disappointed that he is no longer at the State Department or in the White House," observed columnist James Reston. But Hersh was pretty clear: his goal was to prevent that from happening. "You tell the story about this guy. . . . You keep him out of power," Hersh said. "Keep him out of power."[16]

The question, of course, was whether Hersh's telling of the Kissinger story was credible enough to prevent his reemergence. And this depended on whom you listened to. The reviews from the political left—us "Kissinger-haters," said the *Nation's* Alan Wolfe—were almost gleeful. The liberal Colman McCarthy praised Hersh's "moral sensitivity." Lewis declared, "I admire Seymour Hersh as the nation's premier investigative reporter." Added Wolfe, "He is the best of the Washington journalists."[17] And while they worried about Hersh's prosecutorial style, the left reviewers found his evidence totally believable. This was a portrait of an evil man. The political right saw nothing but an obsession- and revenge-oriented journalist (a repeat of Kissinger's private memo to Rosenthal) who used biased sources and who, from the start, never had the remotest thought of being fair. Their biggest complaint was he gave Kissinger no credit for foreign policy victories. "Ah, Seymour my friend," wrote Victor Gold, "your urge to pin all things bad and ugly on the Nixon crowd doesn't always make for the firmest of grasps." Said Safire, stop "slanting history to prove a point." Even friendly reviewers found Hersh "so determined to condemn Kissinger on all fronts that his final balance sheet is well short of a true and fair account."[18]

Actually both sides offered legitimate perspectives. Hersh's sources were often biased, but nonetheless they were individuals with great access to the inner workings of Kissinger's time in power. Hersh had been a great journalist for enough years to know that he had to gauge their believability and that personal bias had to be stifled. "In my Pollyanna way, I am a good old fashioned liberal Democrat," Hersh told an interviewer. "But you know something, forget that business of left and right. It's not whether you're liberal or a Democrat, Republican or conservative . . . it is only your personal integrity that matters." Find something in the book that is wrong, he insisted. "That is all that matters." Part of the issue was perception. Journalists do have political biases, but they don't admit them publicly. And, usually, they don't write letters as their project unfolds making clear that they have reached firm conclusions so quickly. "On balance, I think Hersh proves his case many times over," wrote Peter S. Prescott in *Newsweek,* "but I wish he had taken some trouble about appearances. His book would have been stronger—and no less fascinating—had he appeared to be fair."[19]

Professor Hoffman said the important issue was not Hersh's bias. "It is on the level of substance not of office politics and personal antagonisms that the more serious debate ought to take place," he wrote. Even supporter Wolfe said Hersh "is unable to place the story of Kissinger and Nixon into the larger picture." And on this score it is not Hersh's bias that is predictive; it is his journalistic training. He was schooled to uncover "scoops," to muckrake—and to tell stories. As a journalist he had done little policy analysis. In fact, he eschewed tackling larger questions. He liked to go after bad men doing bad things that might speak to policy. He cared about policy, of course, but he was more concerned—and indignant—about abuse of power. In writing this book, Hersh admitted, "I didn't have any grandiose ideas." He told one interviewer, "I hate it when people ask what I think. Who am I? I mean who cares what I think? Who cares about my thoughts? I just hate that. I report the facts. I'm just a reporter."[20] What he had was a belief that Kissinger had affronted the Constitution. Hersh would hold him accountable. "We do give them an awful lot of power, we do allow them to take our children and fight wars with them," Hersh said. "I see nothing wrong with holding them to some pretty rigid standards of morality, of integrity."

Pulitzer Prize–winner Sydney Schanberg wrote in the *Times* that Kissinger's protectors portray the book as a dispute between "a brilliant statesman" and a "monomaniacal journalist with intent to smear." But, he added, "This discussion is not about personalities. It is about the laws and constitutional rules that are fundamental to our Government and make it different from the other great powers. The alternative is an authoritarian form of government." Hersh might not have been discussing the merits of détente with China, but he was discussing fundamental questions about American values, as seen through the prism of Henry Kissinger's personality and approach.[21]

The other thing to keep in mind about Hersh and *The Price of Power*: he wanted to make money. "You wanna sell books," he said. "That is one thing you want to do. It doesn't mean you change anything." When an Idaho man called Hersh on a TV program, the caller said Hersh should be "shipped out," preferably to Havana. Then he hung up. "I am a very happy capitalist," Hersh said. "This is a happy capitalist venture. It's not the total obsession that people think." And then he fired back: "I am sorry you hung up, but I have as much right to be here as you do, buddy. Even when I was a very sharp critic of the war at (the Associated Press) I always thought it was as much my country as it was the generals. And it is. There is no reason for anyone to back down on any point in this country."[22] Sy Hersh was a feisty capitalist patriot.

Nonetheless, Hersh was on the defensive. Letters from readers over-whelmed him. Many were critical. How dare he criticize the great man? When he appeared on *Nightline*, host Ted Koppel ambushed Hersh. Koppel: "Some of the people with whom I spoke—and here too I'm afraid they want to remain unidentified—said that they received letters from you saying, in effect, 'Give me the dirt on Henry.'" Hersh: "What am I sup-posed to say? 'Some of the people with whom I spoke' . . . I mean, you know . . . Give me a break." Koppel shot back: "It's kind of tough, isn't it? It's tough to respond to unidentified sources." But Hersh did respond, asserting: "It all boils down to Kissinger's version of the truth or mine.

I'm going to stick with mine and pray that critics questioning it will call up the people I asked and make their own effort to find out."[23]

The *Nation* magazine said Hersh's book would "long serve as the official record of the major foreign policy atrocities of the Nixon years." But in reality the final verdict on *The Price of Power* as history would not be settled for some time. "Recriminations, bitter exchanges, and a close checking of Hersh's sources and arguments will follow," noted LaFeber. "Months or years of analysis will be needed before a final verdict can be reached," added the *Christian Science Monitor*.[24] When Hersh's book appeared, Kissinger had published two volumes of memoirs while the Kalb brothers produced a flattering 1974 biography. Roger Morris weighed in with a critical look in 1977, but then Hersh's book came along. Former undersecretary of state George W. Ball concluded, "Kissinger's apologia in the form of two thick volumes and Hersh's massive single volume now so effectively bracket the target that future historians should find it far easier to fix a median trajectory."[25]

History was not Hersh's concern, however. Ruining Kissinger's plans was. More than likely, the book prevented Kissinger from coming back into any high-ranking governmental position under Reagan. "The [Kissinger] cult still breathlessly awaits the 'second coming,'" wrote Ball. But Senate hearings on Kissinger would have opened up the cans of worms Hersh found; hearings would have been ugly. A decade after *The Price of Power*, the first full-scale biography of Kissinger appeared; author Walter Isaacson was more measured but quite critical, even though Kissinger sat with him for numerous interviews.[26] A second savage attack on Kissinger came in 2001 when Christopher Hitchens's *The Trial of Henry Kissinger* accused him of war crimes. It was all ground Hersh had covered. When it was made into a popular documentary film, Hersh appeared on camera, still railing against his old nemesis. Discussing the Allende assassination, the brash Hersh mockingly asked, "Do you think someone wrote a memo on this? That there is a piece of paper for us to read?" Angry at his treatment of Kissinger, some of Hersh's Washington friends took nearly ten years before they would talk to him again.[27]

Alan Wolfe summarized what many in the liberal community were thinking: "Every Kissinger deserves a Hersh. Whatever faults I find with this book are more than balanced by the image I have of Kissinger gnashing his teeth as he reads it and realizes that while he might have charmed everyone else, there was one man he could never reach."[28] Hersh traveled the country lecturing as the book enjoyed success, but a reporter found him in a hotel room missing his family. He wrote: "In the morning he'll head home to his wife and three children in Washington, where, according to reports, no one is allowed to mention the name Kissinger at the dinner table." Little doubt, Nancy and Henry Kissinger were not discussing Sy Hersh either—although sometimes he was unavoidable. Soon after Hersh's book came out, the Kissingers traveled to Turkey with Ahmet Ertegun, the head of Atlantic Records. Ertegun wanted to give out autographed copies of Kissinger's memoir to people they met in Turkey. But he mistakenly ordered copies of *The Price of Power,* so it was Hersh's book that greeted them in Turkey. Kissinger laughed, at least publicly. He could not get away from his "nemesis."[29]

CHAPTER 23

Who Shot Down the Korean Airliner?

A Victory for the Chicago Kid

Henry Kissinger was furious at Seymour Hersh. But as angry as he was, he did not sue. He knew that as a public man, his options were limited. "No public official has a right to demand immunity from criticism, even from a measure of unfair criticism," he wrote. Moreover, he said, "the last thing I desire is a regurgitation of Hersh's charges." He did not get his wish—*The Price of Power* took on more significance when the National Book Critics named it the best nonfiction book of 1983. And then another of Hersh's victims, albeit a minor one, struck back with a defamation lawsuit that forced Kissinger to publicly confront his nemesis.

Hersh was sued for libel by Morarji Desai, India's prime minister from 1977 to 1979 and a minor character in one of the book's most scathing chapters. Desai, eighty-seven when the book came out, was accused by Hersh of being an informant for the Central Intelligence Agency during the Johnson and Nixon administrations. Hersh reported he received $20,000 a year and "was considered one of the Agency's most important 'assets.'"[1] Desai came up only as part of a larger context.

Nixon and Kissinger were secretly attempting in 1971 to arrange for Nixon to visit China, a diplomatic coup if it occurred. Various foreign diplomats helped Kissinger, including President Yaha Khan of West Pakistan. Khan, however, was also the man who unleashed his troops in late March 1971 to quell secessionist forces in East Pakistan. The rampage became genocide with from half a million to three million people killed. Nearly ten million fled to India. Despite protests from the U.S. State Department, America "remained mute," wrote Hersh, adding, America's "conduit to the Chinese would not be challenged." And Khan knew it, Hersh said;

he could get away with slaughtering opponents. To protect the summit meeting, "no price was too great, not even the butchery of hundreds of thousands of civilians." The United States rationalized the policy by saying Khan's opponents were pro-India and pro–Soviet Union. Add to the mix the fact that Nixon did not like Indian Prime Minister Indira Gandhi, whom he called a deceitful "bitch." Nixon and Kissinger said they had "reliable sources" who were telling them Gandhi planned to attack East Pakistan, a blatant attempt to humiliate the Pakistanis that might bring China into the conflict. Hersh said a key informant was reporting to the CIA from India. "Undoubtedly," Hersh wrote, it was Desai, who had been fired by Gandhi as deputy prime minister in 1969, even though he stayed in the cabinet. "I have been able to establish firmly" that Desai worked for the CIA through 1970, he wrote in a footnote. Kissinger "was very impressed with this asset," Hersh asserted. "American intelligence officials," all unnamed, were Hersh's source.[2] The allegations about Desai were contained mainly in one paragraph, 325 words, on page 450. Desai sued Hersh for $50 million.

Since 1964, in order for public officials to win a libel lawsuit they must prove that the writer knew what he or she wrote was false or that the writer was reckless in ascertaining truth. Desai chose a federal court in Chicago (saying he could embarrass Hersh more in his hometown) to prove what is known as "actual malice." Hersh had a team headed by his long-time Washington DC counsel Michael Nussbaum. The case did not get to trial until 1989 (Desai was too ill at age ninety-three to attend) as Desai's attorneys set out to prove that Hersh had uttered "a scandalous and malicious lie." To do so, they sought to force Hersh to name the six sources who told him Desai was an informant. But federal judge Charles R. Norgle ruled that if Hersh turned over his notes from his interviews with the sources, he would not have to reveal their names. He did so.

A six-person jury heard two weeks of testimony, but the highlight came on October 2, when the judge insisted Kissinger appear. It was only the second time he had ever testified (the other time was in a case involving his wife). His lawyers tried to allow a taped deposition to suffice. Coming to court with bodyguards and two attorneys, and dressed in a gray suit, Kissinger declared, "I was not eager to testify." But he did for three and a half hours, appearing calm and collected. Surely to his distress, his testimony actually helped Hersh. He told the jury he never knew any of the names of the CIA's sources, and he had no way of knowing if Desai was an informant. When he was done, Kissinger called a press conference and declared that he, too, seriously considered a lawsuit against Hersh but declined because it would take too much time. Anyway, "The book appeared six years ago," he said. "That's a long time to carry a grudge." Not that he had forgotten. "I'd be just as happy if I never heard of Mr. Hersh again," he said. "Frankly, the quicker he goes out of my life the happier I will be.... I'd rather not rake over all these coals."[3]

In closing arguments Desai's lawyer declared that Hersh had falsified the notes he gave the judge; the sources did not exist. Moreover, he sprinkled lies in his book. "A little curry ... so his book would sell," the lawyer argued. Nussbaum responded that anyone who knew of Hersh's history would scoff at this suggestion. And the jury agreed, taking six hours to return a verdict in Hersh's favor. "This was about whether someone like me can go out, using confidential sources, and write that a former prime minister was a source of the CIA," a jubilant Hersh said. "This court reaffirmed that right."[4] The Chicago kid had a victory on his home court.

Ford's Deal with Nixon

Sy Hersh in public is like Hersh in the newsroom. He is brash, passionate, obsessed, abrasive, outspoken—and controversial. When he came to my university in New Paltz, New York, soon after the publication of his Kissinger book, he was, well, so Sy Hersh. At a workshop he could not stop talking about the substance of his stories, not how he gets them. He marveled at new methods the CIA was using to find secrets, and he expressed anger at what took place in the Nixon-Kissinger White House. Students saw a fire-breathing reporter. At his evening leclture to a packed auditorium of 750 people, he used only two three-by-five-inch cards with scribbled ideas. And off he went, for nearly an hour, stream-of-consciousness commentary, trenchant, lively, coherent. It was clear why he often gets in trouble at speaking engagements. He has no script; he says what is on his mind, not what he can prove or what he would write. That characteristic has gotten him in trouble many times. A few days after he left New Paltz to go to Syracuse, New York, he was asked how his colleagues reacted to his criticism of the press. "What do you think? How would you feel if I told you your wife has been having an affair with Henry Kissinger? Not only that but she's been doing it in the bed next to his." But audiences like his candor. At New Paltz he took forty-five minutes of questions. A standing ovation completed the night. Speeches filled his coffers for a while, but what could he do for an encore? He told the Syracuse audience he was toying with taking the place of Theodore White in writing a book on the 1984 presidential campaign. The best book written recently about politics, he said, was Hunter S. Thompson's satiric and farcical *Fear and Loathing on the Campaign Trail*. But facts, not farce, were his forte.[5]

Unlike a scholar who often pursues a direct line of research, Hersh goes after many stories at once. Toward the end of the Kissinger project, as he awaited publication, he looked back at Gerald Ford's controversial pardon of Richard Nixon. When the president announced his decision on Sunday morning, September 8, 1974, the controversy was enormous. Using the rich sources he had developed in the Nixon administration as a *Times* reporter and information he developed in the writing of the Kissinger book, looking at "the pardon" was a natural. He produced a 17,500-word article for the *Atlantic*, and like much of what he writes, it made headlines and caused controversy.[6] Using government reports, documents unearthed by the Freedom of Information Act, anonymous high-level government sources, and an exclusive sit-down interview with Ford, Hersh concluded that Nixon and Ford had cut a deal, brokered by General Alexander Haig, to make Ford president if he would pardon Nixon. "The transfer of power in August of 1974 was not a triumph for democracy," Hersh concluded. The deal was cut, Hersh wrote, at a meeting between Ford and Haig, who was Nixon's chief of staff. The meeting did not show up on government records because Haig, not wanting anyone to know, falsified the logs in the vice president's office and put in the name of another government official. Haig refused to speak with Hersh, even though he had been Hersh's go-between with Kissinger. According to Hersh's version, Haig laid out various options for Ford, as he awaited the day Nixon would resign in disgrace.

Included was a complete pardon for Nixon, even though Nixon had not been indicted. Hersh said Ford listened, promising only to get back to Haig. The day before the pardon was announced, Nixon called Ford, furious, thinking Ford was going to backtrack. Nixon threatened, according to Hersh's anonymous sources, to tell the public about the promises Ford had made because he was so eager to become president. Ford was angry, saying he had already decided to give the pardon before the call. Hersh's source for this dramatic phone call was "those few White House aides who knew of the private call." As in so much of his work, it is always key anonymous people—"one of the original Watergate prosecutors," "one of Ford's aides"—who deliver the most damning parts of the narrative. And the narrative was explosive: Special Watergate prosecutor Leon Jaworski did not want to indict Nixon because if he stayed in Washington much longer he faced a serious tax liability; the secretary of defense warned military commanders that Nixon might resort to unspecified military means to retain his presidency; Nixon was originally going to pardon all his staff from Watergate crimes but then backed off. NBC News put Hersh on the air to tell the nation his findings. Newspapers across the country picked it up. He was feeling pretty cocky. Why would the former president of the United States talk to Hersh? "It was wise for him to talk to me," Hersh said. "He had an obligation to talk." Not really, but when Sy Hersh knocks even the ex-president had to know it would make headlines. "Hersh has attained a kind of mythic status as a journalist," wrote *People* magazine. Said Hersh: "There's a certain amount of 'Geez, what a great reporter." But, he added, "The story is just there, you know? Go do it, man."[7]

After the Kissinger book Hersh worked on freelance articles for the *Times*, but he also tried his hand at documentary film writing. He connected with award-winning producer Don Obenhaus, who had won Emmy Awards in consecutive years for his two PBS *Frontline* documentaries. Sticking with what he knew—the intelligence community—Hersh spent six months researching *Buying the Bomb*. The story of a Pakistani businessman who tried to smuggle devices that could be used as triggers in nuclear weapons aired on the Public Broadcasting Service on March 5, 1985. But first he let the *Times* have it—a page one story that took the U.S. Justice Department to task for not prosecuting for what Hersh found were direct links to the Pakistani government, which, he alleged, was aggressively trying to become the world's seventh nuclear superpower.[8] They denied this was the case, but Pakistan did develop the weapon in 1998, and Hersh would return to the topic years later for the *New Yorker*, as the world feared that terrorists in the Pakistani military might seize control of the weapons. While researching the documentary, however, his interest was piqued by one of the most mysterious news stories of the 1980s—the shooting down of an unarmed commercial Korean airliner over the Soviet Union.

A Mystery Unraveled

The August 31, 1983, Boeing 747 flight from New York City to Seoul was routine—snacks, meals, movies, and a stop in Alaska for the 269 passengers, including Congressman Larry McDonald, a Georgia Democrat who was also chairman of the ultraconservative John Birch Society. The captain had flown the route many times. But Korean Air Lines Flight 007 went terribly off course, somewhere past Anchorage, and veered toward the coast of the Soviet Union. The crew, either not paying attention or terribly misled by misprogrammmed tracking systems, was unaware it had strayed. The Soviet Union was not. Its radar systems picked up the plane, although, it turned out, no one knew it was a commercial flight. Given that American spy ships routinely cruised the skies in this region, including earlier that day, often baiting the Soviet Union and looking for clues about the communists' intelligence behavior, it is likely KAL 007 was believed to be a spy plane. A Soviet fighter plane was ordered to intercept. No radio contact was made, but a warning shot was fired. KAL 007's crew, not knowing they were being tracked or that they had penetrated Soviet air space, likely did not even see the warning. Moments later, on orders from the ground, the Soviet fighter jet fired at KAL 007. And then the pilot declared, "The target is destroyed." The plane plummeted into the Sea of Japan as nearby fishermen watched, dazzled and horrified. All 246 passengers—including 22 children and 23 crew members—were killed.

As the news spread, claims of horror and angry Russian-bashing came from the United States, especially the Reagan administration, which saw the downing as a convenient way to push the president's "evil empire" claims about the Soviet Union (not to mention his desire for a "Star Wars" defense). Secretary of State George Schultz went on national television to condemn the Russians in some of the harshest language heard in many years. Reagan followed with a vicious verbal attack. The ratcheting up of Cold War language heightened tensions to levels not seen since the U.S.-Soviet Union standoff over Cuba in the early 1960s. A day later, Sy Hersh received a call from a military source who said KAL 007 had been parked at Andrews Air Force Base in Maryland the week before. The implication: the American military had loaded it with spying devices, using a commercial flight to conduct a secret mission. An editor at the *New York Times* also called Hersh to ask him to use his sources to see if the plane had been outfitted with intelligence equipment. "At the time it seemed to be a very logical and prudent request," Hersh noted. In fact, at first he felt "this was going to be a story about something dastardly our government may have done, or acquiesced in."9

Hersh got hooked on the story. Was the plane on a spy mission? Did the Soviet Union know it was shooting down a commercial airliner? Could America have prevented the shooting? Could America's persistent spying have befuddled the Russians? Were the Russians so heartless as to simply shoot down an unarmed passenger plane? The conspiracy theorists had a field day with the answers. Those on the political left—the *Nation* magazine, for example—were convinced the CIA had masterminded the flight. The right saw a Russian plot to hit back at the fire-breathing anticommunist Reagan. A huge literature emerged, and eventually seven books were written and magazines filled with wild speculation. But as one review observed, unlike other authors, Hersh "does not succumb to conspiracy theories."10

Hersh did not know who did what or why when he began. To get answers he had to pierce and master one of the most difficult intelligence communities, the vast American snooping industry with satellites, listening posts, and murky foreign government interactions. "A secret intelligence world whose operations are known to few outside the Pentagon," Hersh wrote. As the unfolding controversy heightened, Hersh's agent, Sterling Lord, who had represented Ken Kesey and Jack Kerouac, peddled a Hersh book on the KAL tragedy. Random House jumped. "Hersh went after the story with typical relentlessness," said one observer. His big break on the story was "total serendipity," he recalled. Late in 1984 a U.S. military officer sent Hersh a penciled note with potential air force intelligence sources. Now he had to find them at the National Security Agency, which ran the ultra-secret eavesdropping on the Soviet Union. Would anyone talk to him? He asked to meet with NSA employees. "I learned a long time ago that one of the interesting things about Washington is that the military . . . and conservatives are a terrific source of information," he said. "Many of them have integrity and do not like what their own government is doing." Not that it came easily. "I didn't just call people up and they said, 'Sure, come on over,'" he explained. "They said, 'Well, let me call you back in two days,' and they'd check me out." One in particular liked what he learned and opened up. "This book began," Hersh wrote in his preface, "because of the courage of a senior military intelligence officer."[11] The source, asking to be anonymous, gave Hersh a key insight: the day after the shooting down of the plane, as the government compiled data from various agencies, many of which did not talk to each other, the air force assembled a briefing book far more detailed than other military divisions. The air force information indicated that the Soviet Union thought KAL 007 was an American spy plane that had been in the vicinity an hour earlier. They then shot down the plane by mistake. The Russians screwed up. This flew counter to all assumptions that top Reagan administration officials had made—that the Russians were simply evil. The air force intelligence was essentially ignored; ideology came first.

That nugget enabled Hersh to convince other insiders, some retired, to speak. Both he and the sources, Hersh insisted, were careful not to either discuss or reveal damaging secrets. "The real secrets," Hersh called them. "I guarantee you," Hersh said, "that we in the press have as good a sense of what's important and what's good for America as the people in the CIA." Next Hersh spoke with fifty-four-year-old Major General James C. Pfautz, the air force officer who headed the unit that uncovered the Russian mistake. Pfautz was brilliant, ambitious, overbearing, and abrasive—like Hersh. "I generally feel that American intelligence officers should not talk to the press," he said, but he reluctantly spoke with Hersh, who had gleaned much of the story already. When Reagan and

Schultz went on television, ignoring the facts and using the tragedy to score political points, many insiders were angry. Hersh did not call Pfautz for an appointment; he just showed up at his Alexandria, Virginia, house one night. He was invited in.[12]

Pfautz's findings were the lynchpin to Hersh's research. He supplemented it, of course, with dozens of interviews, including with officials in Japan, which had been secretly helping the American spying, and with tons of reading, including technical material in magazines such as the *Journal of Electronic Defense.* Lastly he enlisted a Washington advocacy group that worked on nuclear weapons issues to make Freedom of Information requests that produced key documents. As he neared writing, two phone calls jarred him. The first came from the Soviet Union nine months after he had begun work. High-ranking officials of America's arch-enemy were inviting Seymour M. Hersh to come to their country to discuss KAL 007. It was unheard of for military officials, secretive and rarely quoted, to reach out to a journalist, no less an American journalist, to be interviewed. "I thought, 'Wow, whammo! They really have something,'" Hersh recalls. "I just assumed the Russians knew something they didn't want to go public with and maybe they would let me onto it." In May 1984 he met with Marshal Nikolai Ogarkov and Deputy Foreign Minister Georgi Nornienko in an ornate Moscow conference room. Meetings went on for five days. The Soviets produced no documents, pilots, or anyone who knew what took place. Hersh was disappointed. "I really was, frankly, depressed," Hersh recalled. "I was really sort of crushed that they didn't have anything."[13] Yet they made clear their thesis: KAL 007 was meant as a provocation, and American intelligence was behind it. They simply wanted Hersh to uncover the role of the American CIA. Hersh laughed, asking the officials if they supposed they were his editors. They answered in English: "Your assignment is to find that it was an intruder." Hersh was amazed at their faith in a free press. "I'm sure that the day will come when we know the reasons why this mission was arranged."[14] Hersh never found that evidence because, he concluded, there was no spy mission, the Russians had screwed up, and the Americans knew it but wanted to use the dastardly error to fan the anticommunist flames—and the Reagan administration did not want anyone to know.

In June 1986, as publication neared, Hersh received the second call, from seventy-three-year-old William J. Casey, the CIA director. He bluntly told Hersh he faced criminal prosecution if the book contained intelligence secrets. Casey wanted to see Hersh's manuscript. He knew nothing specific about the book's contents; only that Hersh had pierced the veil of the intelligence community, as he had done many times previously. "I'm apprising you that there is this damn law and we have to take it seriously," he declared. Exactly what law the government could pursue was unclear. The Supreme Court has given the press broad protection from prior restraints. Hersh wanted to tell the crusty director that this was an "outrageous and unwarranted interference," but he mumbled only that the book would debunk rumors that KAL 007 was spying. Casey did not back off. The call "shook me up," Hersh said; he recommended Casey call Random House's president. Hersh knew the government was watching closely; many of his sources had been told not to talk. Hersh's attorney, Michael Nussbaum, warned him the FBI could, with a search warrant, rifle through his Washington house or his downtown office. He spent a night going through notes, deleting references to secret sources. "Chilling doesn't begin to describe my feelings," Hersh said. Meanwhile, as Random House wavered, Hersh recalled "tension" with his publisher, nothing new to the man who always ruffled feathers. No classified material had been used in the book, yet the government still insisted that "secrets" could not be published. Their argument was thin, at best. Casey was trying simple hard-ball intimidation. Random House's chief executive, Robert L. Bernstein, finally decided not to submit the manuscript to the CIA, declaring the government only wanted "to stop publication of the book."[15]

The government took no action against Hersh or Random House when *"The Target Is Destroyed": What Really Happened to Flight 007 and What America Knew about It* came out in August. But the book was greeted with the typical reaction to a Hersh publication: the *Times* put the story on page one, magazines and newspapers wrote profiles of "America's foremost investigative journalist," and the reviewers all flocked to comment on what one called "this highly anticipated book."[16] Observed the *Washington Post*, "It took three years and one of the nation's best reporters, but we finally have a carefully researched, reasonable, readable explanation" of how KAL 007 was shot down. The *Times* gave Hersh his best review ever, calling it a "careful, detailed, lucid account with an important theme." Unlike his book on Henry Kissinger, noted Thomas Powers, this one is "fair and temperate," and Hersh's "evenhandedness" makes his thesis all the more believable. His explanation was simple: the crew misprogrammed the plane's tracking devices; the plane flew way off course; the Soviets mistook it for an American spy plane and then shot it down, without ever making radio contact. And then, even though it understood Russia's gross mistake, America used the downing to propagandize while the Russians refused to concede their mistake, insisting it shot down a spy plane. Consequently, the world grew close to the edge of a military showdown. Hersh's narrative is much cleaner than the Kissinger book, and his mastery of complex intelligence systems is impressive. The book, observed one reviewer, "is more rigorous than anything else in print." Good reviews, however, did not help sales. The book did poorly at the cash register.[17]

The bugaboo that was clearly now his stock in trade—the anonymous source—was more evident in this book than anything he had ever written. He admitted: "This is a book whose key allegations hinge on unnamed sources . . . 'mysterious' government officials' and 'intelligence analysts.'" And yet, because the book dealt with sources who obviously needed protection and because it did not attack an individual, the sourcing raised few hackles. "Those familiar with U.S. intelligence operations will recognize the authenticity of his sources," declared one reviewer.[18] Not everyone was happy with Hersh, of course. Edward Luttwak, a military historian and sometimes intelligence operative, had scathing words in the small but influential *New Republic*. Sarcastically, he acknowledged that Hersh was America's super sleuth, looking always for dark secrets and conspiracies, "dedicated to the exposure of secret America's ill deeds." But when he looked into this one, he found nothing; this book "contains no revelations at all" and, in fact, is "boring" and is "made of the leftovers of a failed investigation." What upset Luttwak most, however, was Hersh's moral reasoning: "That whole line of argument in Hersh is based on the assumption the Soviets are allowed to shoot down a U.S. reconnaissance aircraft," Luttwak said. His honesty "is not in doubt, but how could he so easily let the Soviet Union off the hook for the "murder" of civilians, even if the plane strayed? Where is the outrage for that behavior? Of course, one might have asked where Hersh's outrage was for the simple fact that nations spend absurd amounts of time and effort on clandestine forays and military provocations. But Hersh did not criticize intelligence gathering—just how it was being used by the White House. Hersh brushed off Luttwak's criticism. "It was going too well," Hersh joked. "I'm glad I finally got a bad one." The reviews of his books would get much more hostile in the near future. But he was pleased with what he felt he was accomplishing. "I have to believe that my profession can make a difference, that writing books and articles and newspaper stories can make a difference," Hersh said. "My job is to get this story, tell as much as I can and throw it out there, and if people don't want to listen to it, tough." As for what was next, he told *People* magazine," "I'm working on something now that's terrific."[19]

Hersh's sources in intelligence—CIA, FBI, Defense Intelligence Agency, National Security Agency—and his access to officials in the White House made his possibilities endless. And those sources paid off again when he was able to piece together the story of General Manuel Antonio Noriega, "the Panama connection." Because of his control over the Panamanian military, the forty-seven-year-old Noriega was de facto dictator of this Central American country that is smaller than South Carolina but of great strategic importance because of the Panama Canal. Noriega, like many other strongmen, had curried favor with the United States by supplying intelligence and offering a friendly locale for American military activities. But he was also a corrupt thug, as Hersh revealed to the country on June 12, 1986, in a story that ran at the top of page one in the *New York Times*.[20]

The old scoop artist still had a friendly home at the *Times*. And why not? The piece was chock full of shocking revelations: Noriega was a key figure in running guns and narcotics. Stopping him might put a huge dent in international narcotics trafficking. Noriega had rigged a 1984 election in Panama and killed one of his vocal opponents. He was laundering millions of dollars. And while U.S. intelligence was well aware of his activities (the Nixon administration toyed with assassinating him in 1972), he was allowed to remain in power because his friendly posture aided American foreign policy.[21] It was a first-class scandal, an embarrassment to Ronald Reagan, and a prod to public opinion, even though Hersh's exposé did not have one named source, except for the general's spokesman, who denied it all.

Hersh's story was the first full-scale national exposé of Noriega. The Hersh article "accelerated the political landslide" against the dictator, wrote one scholar, and "delivered the most important blow of the early fight against Noriega." The day after his story, Bob Woodward had to play catch-up as the *Washington Post* reported a split inside the CIA about how to deal with Noriega. Unlike Watergate, Hersh was way ahead.[22] Three congressional hearings followed as a furor erupted in Panama. Noriega, in Washington DC to accept an award when Hersh's article appeared, was furious, throwing his breakfast on the floor, canceling engagements, and flying back home. Six days later he gave an exclusive interview to the *Times*, denying all charges and attacking Hersh. "You don't mention any official," he said. "In the presentation you mention sources, unidentified officials. But this isn't presented in the truth of justice or else it would be immediately invalidated." His convoluted defense was to no avail. The Reagan administration turned on him. In fact, it was Admiral John Poindexter of the National Security Council who approved leaking evidence to Hersh.[23]

Three years later, the United States invaded Panama and hunted down the man who had been an employee of the CIA since 1967. He was captured in a manhunt watched by the world and then brought back to the United States to stand trial; he was convicted and sent to an American prison. He remains in prison today, thanks, at least in part, to Seymour Hersh. William Arkin, who worked with Hersh on the KAL book and is a long-time friend, said he always imagined Sy as an AP reporter in Chicago "biting on someone's ankle. Now, he bites on bigger ankles."[24] In fact, Hersh had become one of the world's biggest big game hunters as he helped take down "the Panamanian connection."

Reporting the Worst-Kept
Secret in the World

An Unhappy Stop in Hollywood

On December 20, 1989, the United States launched an invasion of Panama that was promptly and roundly condemned by the United Nations. The goal was to seize Manuel Noriega. Twenty-four American soldiers were killed, but on January 3, 1990, the Bush administration captured the dictator and brought him back to America. Sy Hersh, who always collected more facts than he could fit in his newspaper articles, was Johnny-on-the-spot. His cover piece in *Life* magazine, on "Our Man in Panama," explained in detail how the "thug" had been recruited by the United States. He made the rounds of television talk shows to "pimp" his article. He told CBS that "all the American intelligence agencies were running amok," adding, "From Noriega's point of view, there wasn't much the U.S. could teach him about morality or law." He went on ABC *Nightline* and butted heads with former CIA director Stansfield Turner and an undersecretary of state, Elliott Abrams, about whom he declared: "I hate to agree with Elliott Abrams about anything." When Abrams explained his position, Hersh jumped in, "That's only part of the story, Mr. Abrams." He detailed what Abrams left out: "You backed away on the notion of getting rid of him. Why did you do it then?" Sy Hersh was clearly out from behind the pen—and it drew the attention of famous Hollywood director Oliver Stone, the man who saw conspiracies behind every rock. In fact, his controversial movie, *JFK*, was coming out in 1991, and he was looking for a timely project that would point fingers at American misbehavior.[1]

Hersh's old friend, David Obst, was living in Los Angeles. After Dispatch News Service folded in 1970, he made lots of money as the book agent for Bob Woodward and Carl Bernstein. But he fell out with the reporters after his 1998 memoir alleged that the famous secret source, "Deep Throat," was made up. "Woodward said he thinks I am asshole," Obst said. "If you speak to him, don't mention my name."[2] Obst, like his buddy Hersh, was not very good with money. He was broke in the late 1980s and called Sy for help, saying he could get a $250,000 advance from Stone to write a script for a movie on Noriega. Hersh had applauded Stone's movie *Platoon* as helping change views on the Vietnam War; they seemed a good team. He set out to write the dramatic story of Noriega—the Panamanian teenager recruited by the U.S. Army who rose to command the country, albeit also as a drug merchant protected by three American presidents. But the relationship with Stone did not go smoothly. According to Obst, when Stone came to Washington DC, Hersh invited him to his home for dinner—and Stone brought a female friend, not his wife. Hersh recalled that a woman did show up after dinner. Obst recalled Hersh being miffed by Stone's boorish behavior in front of his family. Hersh is abrasive, but he is not a womanizer and is described as a bit prudish by friends. But Hersh does not recall being put off, saying the woman "was totally his business." Perhaps more offensive to the reporter, Stone wanted to play fast and loose with the facts. He was, after all, a Hollywood filmmaker, not a documentarian. His look at "Wall Street" told a larger truth about finance, but it was fiction. His movie *JFK* was a hit, but its allegiance to facts was suspect. Hersh, brashly, told Stone he would be a "historical war criminal" if he made his fictionalized version of the Kennedy assassination. Hersh also toyed with a screenplay called *The Adviser*, a White House thriller. Who was that about? "You can guess," Hersh said. But none of the movies were ever made. Hersh tried, partly because Obst needed the money, but when Stone made wholesale changes to the Noriega script, Hersh backed out. Obst recalled a meeting where Hersh just quit. He left a lot of money on the table, Obst said without any bitterness, recalling fondly dinners he had with Sy at his mother Dorothy's house in California, where she lived until she died in 1998. The screenplays were fun and paid some bills, but Hersh returned to reporting. "I wouldn't work with Oliver a second time, but I'm sure the feeling was mutual," Hersh said.[3]

One of the biggest scandals of the Reagan administration slipped by Hersh as he worked on his books. And that was the Iran-Contra affair in

1986. Max Frankel, Hersh's first editor in the *Times* Washington bureau, had replaced Abe Rosenthal as executive editor. Hersh and Frankel never hit it off, yet he toyed with bringing Hersh back to tackle Iran-Contra, a scheme to clandestinely sell weapons and use the profits to fund an insurgency in Nicaragua. Eventually, eleven were convicted. Frankel said everyone had warned him that "I risked another Watergate embarrassment if I did not immediately hire Seymour Hersh . . . and fervently devote myself to the pursuit of this one story." But he did not—until the scandal made headlines. Then the *Times* let Hersh write a long magazine article that implied Congress had let President Reagan walk away from impeachment because it feared hurting his chances to reach agreements with the collapsing Soviet Union. His mix of government insiders and intriguing anonymous sources is classic Hersh—a behind-the-scenes indictment of tradeoffs that let the president walk away from what could have been his Watergate.[4]

Hersh, who describes himself as "insanely competitive," might have been spurred to weigh in on Iran-Contra by his ongoing rivalry with Woodward. The forty-seven-year-old *Washington Post* reporter reeled off a string of best-selling books after Watergate, steering away from just public policy as he profiled actor John Belushi. And then in 1987 he poached Hersh's turf in *Veil* when he looked into the Central Intelligence Agency's attempted foreign assassinations and payoffs to foreign leaders, all ground Hersh had covered. Woodward's supposed bedside talk with CIA director William Casey was juicy fodder for critics.[5] CBS's Bob Schieffer called Woodward "the master chronicler of Washington's deepest secrets," and one reviewer wrote, "Woodward has established himself as the best reporter of our time." Hersh must have been boiling mad. "There's a huge rivalry between Woodward and Hersh," observed former CIA agent Robert Baer, an occasional Hersh source.[6] The rivalry perhaps forced Hersh to overreach in his next two big projects.

Sampson, Not Suicide

Seymour Hersh's father, Isador, arrived from Lithuania at the port of Boston on February 12, 1921. His surname, Hershowitz, was changed to Hersh in 1930 when he became a citizen in Chicago. Like many Jewish immigrants before him, Isador shortened his name, in this case to Hersh, in order to sound more American. Isador lived on the South Side of Chicago with his mother, Minnie, a widow, and his sister, Anna, both of whom immigrated in 1923. Hersh's mother, Dorothy Margolis, six years younger than Isador, came to America from Poland. It is not clear why they left Eastern Europe or why they went to Chicago. But between 1881 and 1924 over two and one-half million East European Jews left for America because of persecution and the lack of opportunity and because of the availability of jobs in the United States. By 1930 Chicago had 270,000 Jews (9 percent of the city's population), outnumbered only by New York and Warsaw.[7]

Dorothy gave birth to twin girls, Phyllis and Marcia, in 1932; twin boys, Seymour and Alan, followed in 1937. While the parents spoke Yiddish in the home and the Yiddish-language *Jewish Daily Forward* was a household staple, there was no indication that Judaism played a major role in the family's life. Hersh seemed more influenced by the movies he saw at the Victory Theater across from the family's apartment. He mentions watching Americans shoot down enemy planes in movies more than he does about things Jewish. He calls his view on Judaism "vague," adding, "I like a lot of the historical stuff; I'm agnostic about the religion. But I certainly understand the power of faith." Hersh let his own children decide if they wanted to be bar mitzvahed. "I'm a believer in you do what you want to do," he said. Hersh's biggest connection to being a Jew, he explained, came from reading Saul Bellow and Philip Roth. "But it's so irrelevant that I am Jewish when I write about Jewish issues," he declared. "It's just like it is irrelevant what my personal opinion is on things." The culture of Judaism might have influenced Hersh more than he would admit, however. Dr. Gerald Sorin, an author and professor of Jewish studies, points out that many Eastern European Jewish immigrant families "brought with them to America working-class loyalties as well as a hatred of autocracy." Second-generation Jews—Sy Hersh—were attracted to left-liberal politics. Progressive ideology, Sorin believes, was "attractive to Jews who were moving away from the faith of their more traditional parents." Religious or not, Hersh was a Jew, and he would have to decide if that affiliation also meant a "dual loyalty," to America and to Israel, the homeland of Jews. His next project tested his loyalties.[8]

Sy Hersh's books on Henry Kissinger and the shooting down of the Korean Air Lines flight brought him increasingly into foreign policy and diplomacy. The impetus for his next book might have come from an off-hand remark a Kissinger aide made while Hersh was researching *The Price of Power*. The aide stayed clear of discussing someone accused of diverting enriched uranium to the Israelis—maybe for a nuclear weapon. "You don't mess with the Israelis," he added. Hersh's interest—and competitive juices—were piqued by the comment. He tucked away the question: Did Israel have a nuclear weapon? And he likely thought, "I will mess with anyone I please." When KAL and Noriega were behind him, Hersh dove into one of the world's worst-kept secrets—but a secret nonetheless—that Israel, despite its denials, possessed the "bomb in the basement." "It's another sneak book describing something that not much is known about," Hersh said before publication. "I like telling stories no one else wants to write." And yet, he had to know, as former arms negotiator Paul Warnke pointed out, "The fact that Israel has nuclear weapons comes as no sur-prise." His researcher found five books that nibbled around the fact that Israel had secretly joined the U.S., France, England, and the Soviet Union in the nuclear club. But Hersh had bigger fish to fry than mere exposé, although there was much exposé and controversy in this book.[9]

Hersh followed his now patented pattern—reading everything he could, hiring a researcher, tapping experts to bring him up to speed on nuclear policy and Mideast history, and finding sources, many anonymous, who could get him below the surface. He decided not to go to Israel to fact-find, fearing the Israelis would insist on seeing his work and censor his findings. "I could not submit to Israeli censorship," he declared, even though some critics pooh-poohed this fear. He felt he could get what he needed in Europe and the United States; after all, he never left the States to get My Lai. Max Friedman, who had just graduated from Albion Col-lege and was working for National Public Radio, got the task of going to the Library of Congress to bring Hersh reading matter. He was awestruck working for Sy Hersh. "To me he was a legend," said Friedman, who spoke five languages, earned a PhD, and became a professor. "I felt like I was meeting a force of nature," he said. "He spoke so much faster than any other human being. This rapid-fire elliptical fashion." He also listened to Hersh work his sources, often high-level military and intelligence officials. "The legend is that he is a table-pounder," Friedman said, that he badgers sources. "Can you imagine screaming at a decorated general? It does not work. He wins their respect. He learns so much about a story that he is able to just talk with people easily." And there was a lot to learn in the dark worlds of intelligence and nuclear weapons. And so Hersh began to wonder: "Can the world afford to pretend that Israel is not a nuclear power because to do otherwise would raise difficult issues? Can any international agreement to limit the spread of nuclear weapons be enforced if Israel's bombs are not fully accounted for?" Some Israelis and American Jews would not like Hersh's answers.[10]

In short, Israel, which became a country in 1948, decided to seek a nuclear weapon in the early 1950s, carving out a facility in the Negev Desert while secretly receiving the help of France. The United States was unaware, learning about the construction from U-2 spying missions. The Eisenhower administration talked softly and in private about how to respond. But at Eisenhower's insistence, nothing was put on paper. "There aren't any written records on this one," Hersh said, nothing new to the reporter who had to find sources to expose the CIA. The spooks do not put on paper secret activities. John Kennedy, an advocate of stopping the spread of nuclear weapons, was caught in a bind. Political contributions from Jews and the Jewish vote were key factors in his election. But he tried nonetheless to get Israel to submit to inspections, even though the country insisted—even to France—that it only wanted to develop nuclear power for peaceful purposes. (It was a claim Hersh would vigorously research when Iran insisted to a skeptical world in 2011 that its nuclear prowess was not for bombs.) Israel finally did allow inspections, but, Hersh found, they built a fake control room for inspectors who year after year were fooled. Lyndon Johnson pushed for inspections, but because his administration was bogged down in Vietnam, the issue was always on the backburner. Finally, under Richard Nixon, the United States conceded—privately—that Israel should have a nuclear capacity. Jimmy Carter also pushed for nuclear nonproliferation, but when he tried to convince Pakistan to back off its research, he was told, simply, speak to your Israeli friends.

The story, although difficult for Hersh to flesh out, was fairly clear-cut. Hersh told his story, as his old source Roger Morris wrote, with "a cast of characters few novelists could summon." The crusty old lion, David Ben-Gurion, Israel's founding prime minister, growling at the neophyte President Kennedy. The wheeler-dealer Jewish Democratic fundraiser helping Democrats and Israel, and pressuring America to look the other way. The portly American ambassador to Israel, whose name never appeared in the press and who was a lackey to Israel. Hersh was not gentle with anyone: Ike was portrayed as dumb, Moshe Dayan as a greedy womanizer. And then there were the spymasters—Dino Brugioni, the American who masterminded secret U-2 flights; John McCone, the CIA chief who leaked to the press, trying to get Israel to halt production, but failed; Ari Ben-Menashe, the mysterious Israeli intelligence agent who either exaggerated all he knew or was remarkably knowledgeable and who filled Hersh's notepads before he fled the United States after running afoul of Israel. Hersh knew he had a great story—and he did want to sell books—but he cared more about the larger question: shouldn't Israel be held to the same standard of accountability as the rest of the world? The issue was not whether they should be able to protect themselves, as he allows numerous American and Israeli sources to say. In fact, former defense secretary Robert McNamara, as he looks the other way, told Hersh: "I can understand why Israel wanted a nuclear bomb. The existence of Israel has been a question mark in history, and that's the essential issue."[11] Hersh did not disagree. Israel just needed to 'fess up and allow inspections, like everyone else.

The title for the book, *The Samson Option*, came to Hersh when he understood the Israeli thinking. Nearly two thousand years ago a thousand Jews, greatly outnumbered by Roman legions at Masada, were thought to have committed mass suicide rather than be annihilated. In contrast the biblical figure Samson, chained in a Philistine temple, pushed apart the pillars, and the temple collapsed, killing himself and his enemies. No suicide for Samson. The Israelis, Hersh discovered, had chosen the "Samson Option"—they would fire nuclear weapons to avoid a slaughter even if it meant annihilation. Before anyone knew the book's title, Washington was buzzing again about what Hersh had. His assistant,

Friedman, said the word on the street was that more Hersh bombshells were about to explode.[12]

An Author of "Highest Integrity"

In the summer of 1991, as Random House prepared to publish *The Samson Option: Israel's Nuclear Arsenal and American Foreign Policy*, a major event took shape on the world stage. Spain hosted the Madrid Conference, with the United States and Soviet Union cosponsoring. The aim was to start a peace process involving Israel and the Palestinians as well as Syria, Lebanon, and Jordan. It was an unprecedented stab at peace. And Hersh's book, alleging Israeli duplicity and American connivance, put a harsh glare on the alliance. Coupled with the publication of the Cockburns' *Dangerous Liaison: The Inside Story of the U.S.-Israeli Covert Relationship*, some wondered whether Israel's time as a "special case to which normal standards of morality and international law do not apply" was coming to an end. Was the Jewish kid from Chicago putting the Jewish homeland in jeopardy? "If Hersh and his colleagues have their way," screamed the *Jerusalem Post*, "Israel's fate will resemble Samson's. By destroying Israel's strength, its reputation as a trustworthy democracy, Israel-bashers hope to render it helpless."[13]

Even though Sy Hersh was still working on projects under contract for the *Times*, the newspaper saw Hersh's book as big news, as did most major American newspapers. A long story, "Israeli Nuclear Arsenal Exceeds Earlier Estimates, Book Reports," hit page one on October 20 and summarized the news nuggets the 354-page book produced. Israel had a larger nuclear capacity than anyone suspected, and three times—twice during a 1973 war—the Israelis put their nuclear weapons in place to fire on other Mideast nations or the Soviet Union. In response to Hersh's book, Israel would only say that it "would not be the first to introduce nuclear arms in the Middle East." Some analysts actually thought Israel was glad to get the "secret" out to more effectively deter attacks. The *Times'* Joel Brinkley noted that much of what Hersh wrote "has been told before . . . but many of his specific allegations are new, and no one has published so exhaustive an account."[14] Many of Hersh's allegations, he added, could be corroborated, many could not, and in particular, one of Hersh's main informants, Ben-Menashe, was a controversial and suspect source. Ben-Menashe would become, in fact, Hersh's albatross.

While the reviews were decidedly mixed, some angrily calling Hersh a self-hating Jew, they all agreed that readers would get their $23 worth in a book that revealed sometimes startling information about the four-decade cat-and-mouse game between the United States and Israel. Among the findings: in the late 1970s Israel stole reconnaissance intelligence from American satellites to target the Soviet Union; Israel threatened Nixon with the use of nuclear weapons during the 1973 Yom Kippur War to force the White House to send supplies; in 1979 South Africa and Israel together successfully tested nuclear artillery; a prominent Jewish fund-raiser also raised millions for Israel's nuclear weapons and was repeatedly able to influence American policy; and, fearing the alienation of Jewish voters, four American presidents tiptoed around the issue of Israeli nukes.

The biggest controversies, however, ones that lingered for months after publication, surrounded convicted American spy Jonathon Pollard and British newspaper publisher and magnate Robert Maxwell. Pollard, Hersh alleged, leaked to Israel more significant intelligence material than previously believed, and the material was given, in part, to the Soviet Union by Prime Minister Yitzhak Rabin, who heatedly denied the charge. As for Maxwell, who along with Rupert Murdoch was the most well-known publisher in England, Hersh asserted that in 1986 he and one of his top editors worked with Israeli intelligence, officially or otherwise, to successfully discredit an exposé of Israel's nuclear program about to be published in a rival paper. In essence, many concluded, Maxwell was a spy for Mossad, Israel's CIA. Maxwell filed a defamation lawsuit against Hersh, but then, two weeks after the book was published, he mysteriously died in a drowning accident while cruising in his luxurious yacht off the Canary Islands. Was he a victim of his own spying? Was Hersh complicit? Critics, on both sides of the political aisle, had a field day.[15]

Perhaps because of the headlines or maybe just because it was Sy Hersh, *The Samson Option* sold well in its first few weeks. In Europe it was a best-seller. But something happened in America: American Jews, a big part of the book-buying public, turned against Hersh. "Nobody cared," he said. "In the bookstores on the Upper West Side, (of Manhattan) heavily

trafficked by New York Jews, who are terrific readers, it wasn't moving."
At first, synagogues invited Hersh to speak. Then the invitations were
canceled. "They all thought I was in favor of the bomb," he said. Once
they learned otherwise, they canceled. At one prosperous suburban temple
the questions turned hostile. "What's wrong with us having bombs? Arabs
are crazy." Hersh said: "It was the most bizarre experience of my life, and
I was called a kapo—a self-hating Jew." (In Nazi concentration camps,
kapos assisted the Nazis and were often brutal; some kapos were Jews.)
So hostile was the crowd that Hersh asked the rabbi to give him a few
minutes lead time to get to his car. "It was a pretty amazing experience,"
he recalled.[16]

The reviewers mirrored the public—enthralled, skeptical, and many
extremely hostile. "This is an excellent piece of investigative reporting,"
wrote Geoffrey Stevens in the *Toronto Star*. "A good read" and a "welcome" addition to a topic that has been ignored, offered the *Washington
Post*. The *Boston Globe* said, "nothing has dealt with the explosive topic
as authoritatively" as Hersh. And former Kissinger aide Roger Morris
said the "stunning" book "bristles with authenticity." This "gripping and
detailed account," offered Paul Warnke, should make clear that there
should be "no room for the Samson option."[17]

But it was all downhill after that. Hugh Wilson called Hersh one of the
grittiest investigative journalists in the United States but brought up the
old bugaboo: "We can only take Hersh's word that his unnamed sources
are credible." Peter D. Zimmerman, a nuclear physicist, dismissed the
book as little more than "a retelling of a well-known story." He added,
"Trusting Sy Hersh's reporting skills and his ability to separate the self-
serving puffery . . . from the facts was once a reasonable thing to do."
No longer does his "trust-me" journalism work. The book, he charged,
is "weak journalism and poor scholarship." Award-winning journalist
Steven Emerson's critique was more vicious. Probing the Israelis "is a
perfectly legitimate area for journalistic scrutiny," he wrote, but it does
not translate "into a license for well-known authors to publish outright
inventions." Hersh's mere reputation, Emerson huffed, has given him a
license to publish virtually anything he wants. "If anyone else wrote this
book, it would have never seen the light of day." How does one reconcile

that foreign policy experts found the book authentic while others refused to trust it? By 1991 Hersh was ripe for the picking; his years of anonymous sourcing made him vulnerable. And a key source, Ben-Menashe, known as the "Spinner of Tangled Yarns," really opened a can of worms. Furthermore, Hersh had entered the impossible- to-navigate world of Israeli politics, anti-Semitic slights, disinformation campaigns, and spies who play with the truth.[18]

Ben-Menashe is a character out of a Robert Ludlum novel. A Jew born in Iraq who went to work for Israel's intelligence services, he penetrated Israel's government and then became a turncoat—a source for dozens of journalists and a witness for Congress on Ronald Reagan's "October surprise," an alleged deal with Iran, right before the 1980 presidential election, to stop Iran from releasing American hostages. But how much Ben-Menashe really knew and how much was fabrication was always the issue. "He is a journalist's ultimate nightmare, a professional liar who knows some of the greatest secrets in the intelligence world," wrote Craig Unger. Hersh turned to him for those secrets. "Of course I was aware of the need to carefully confirm any information" from Ben-Menashe, Hersh said after being rebuked. He said they spent weeks together in hotel rooms and restaurants in New York, London, Los Angeles, and Washington. They went to meetings with retired American and Israeli intelligence experts. He insisted he spoke to reliable top-level operatives who swore Ben-Menashe was the real deal—with knowledge of dealings at the highest levels. Hersh's assistant Friedman made long-distance calls to double-check Ben-Menashe's information. And yet the critics lambasted Hersh for using him. Writing in the neo-conservative *Commentary*, Emerson called Ben-Menashe "an abject fraud and impostor." The *Jerusalem Post* labeled him a "notorious, chronic liar." In the most vicious attack, Rael Jean Isaac said his use of Ben-Menashe was simple to understand: Hersh is "under the influence of assorted Marxist and Trotskyite groupings" who see Zionism as the product of Western racism and colonialism. "To attack Israel was to attack what was worst about the United States." It is a charge, frankly, that is preposterous. Hersh may be Progressive, but hardly a Trotskyite. Isaac relied heavily on Emerson's criticism, using, in fact, much of his exact language. And Emerson, although initially viewed as an emerging star journalist, has been largely discredited as an anti-Arab wheeler-dealer who, some believe, was simply parroting the words of Israeli intelligence officials who desperately needed to discredit Ben-Menashe. Hersh calls Ben-Menashe "an enigma . . . who has a need to embellish constantly," but, he insisted, "it would have been derelict not to publish" the allegations he made that Hersh said he verified. His most serious charge was that Yitzhak Shamir had personally given over purloined U.S. secrets to the Soviet Union (in hopes of gaining the release of Jewish prisoners), a charge Hersh confirmed—unfortunately with a source he could not identify. The stubborn reality, said Isaac, is that statements by people guaranteed anonymity allows "angry bureaucrats to take revenge on superiors or rival bureaucracies or to spin their own far-out theories as fact." The charge was old-hat to Hersh, who pointed out he had a dozen or more high-level intelligence sources who were extensively used—and named—throughout the book.[19]

While the critics hurled insults at Hersh, the book made headlines in England because of the scandal Hersh had unearthed—dubbed "Mirrorgate"—surrounding Maxwell and his top editor. The complicated story, in short, was that Maxwell and editor Nick Davies worked closely with Israeli intelligence. In 1986, Hersh alleged, they revealed the whereabouts of one Mordechai Vanunu, a whistleblower who gave out details of Israel's weapons program. The Mossad kidnapped Vanunu in Rome and brought him back to Israel, where he was sentenced to eighteen years in prison. The publisher was furious at Hersh's allegations, at one point trashing his hotel room, and calling the allegations "ludicrous, a total invention." Maxwell then filed a lawsuit against Hersh and his British publisher, dramatically serving the libel writs during a packed Hersh news conference. "The only thing I can say is that what I've written is true and I stand by it and I'm prepared to defend it in any place I have to," declared Hersh, who insisted he checked these facts more than anything he had ever written. The front-page stories made Hersh's book a best seller. And then, two weeks after the lawsuit was initiated, Maxwell died, making international headlines. "I think the real story about Maxwell," Hersh said, "is going to be the stuff of newspapers and thrillers for years." But the libel case proceeded. In July a British court threw out the lawsuit, saying a jury would "laugh it out of court." Davies was fired. Maxwell's lawyers appealed but lost two years later when his company was ordered to pay damages, pay Hersh's legal costs, and apologize. Hersh, the apology said, is an author "of the highest integrity," and the *Mirror's* criticisms of him were "entirely improper."[20]

Hersh's critics cringed. After all, they felt, he was a character assassin, an unreliable journalist, a left wing propagandist—and now an anti-Semite. The first three were nothing new to Hersh, but the last one stung. "My family suffered in the Holocaust as much as any American Jew's family," he said. "My father was from Russia, my mother from Poland, you can imagine what happened to the remnants of our family." But what also stung was that the major point of his book—the prospect of spreading nuclear weapons in the Mideast that could kill millions—was ignored or, as he wrote, "sank without significant mention." The Israeli arsenal, he reminded, "was still in place and no one publicly cared much about that." Reviewing his book, the *Nation* concluded: "An administration serious about peace must start talking openly and honestly about Israel's bomb, and about how to rid the entire region of the threat of nuclear warfare. Otherwise this talk of peace will remain just talk."[21]

CHAPTER 25

Sex, Lies, and Fraud

The Big Money, Finally

Sy Hersh was a twenty-seven-year-old novice in 1963, working the night shift for the Associated Press, earning twelve dollars a week and living in a rented room in Chicago. A roommate woke him early in the afternoon on November 22 to tell him that President Kennedy had been assassinated. "I sat there, glum, like everybody else," Hersh recalled. And then he cried. Like so many young and idealistic Americans, he adored Kennedy. His first vote in a presidential election in 1960 was for the man from Massachusetts. Kennedy, he said, "was beautiful." When he went to work in Washington, Hersh heard rumors about women with whom Kennedy cavorted. But, he said, "We were proud of the fact that we had a President who scored with women . . . a man's man. Don't forget, we were coming off the Eisenhower years. Eisenhower was very boring." Hersh's view on Kennedy evolved, however. When he covered the Pentagon, he grew to hate the Vietnam War. It was Kennedy, he knew, who sent American advisers and introduced napalm. And then, when the Pentagon Papers came out in 1971, he got a clear look at the duplicity of a succession of administrations, starting with Kennedy. He tucked it all away.[1]

When *The Samson Option* was done, Hersh trolled for a new project. "You can't make a living writing about Israeli nuclear weapons," he said, a reference to the book's mediocre sales. He wandered back to the Nixon White House. The disgraced president was waging a furious battle to prevent the release of four thousand hours of recordings made in the Oval Office. By 1987 some 950 reels of recordings had been transcribed by the National Archives Administration, but Nixon's attorney had blocked the release of what Charles Colson told Hersh was "the black side to our natures." The battle for disclosure, Hersh wrote, was not about finding more about Watergate. The tapes, he argued, might "provide firsthand evidence of previously unknown and potentially prosecutable crimes." And thus far, Hersh lamented, Nixon was winning the battle in "keeping what happened in his White House from the public." The government did not get control of the tapes until 2007.[2]

The Nixon article was more essay than exposé, but Hersh returned to his muckraking mode in September 1994 when he questioned whether George H. Bush's family profited from the 1991 Gulf War. Three months after he left the presidency, the ex-president went to Kuwait, the tiny oil-rich country his administration had saved from Saddam Hussein's clutches, to receive the nation's highest medal. The Kuwaiti people deluged him with gifts valued at thousands of dollars. He did not refuse them, nor did two of his sons, Marvin and Neil, who accompanied their father. And while it was not illegal for private citizens to accept such gifts, Hersh pointed out, "certain things" after a war "are beyond the bounds of decency." Hersh wondered why former top-level Bush aide James Baker was meeting with representatives of the oil giant Enron? And what of John Sununu, another top Bush aide, who joined the former president as consultant for Westinghouse, which was seeking a billion-dollar contract? Was it unseemly to seek big-bucks deals so soon after American soldiers risked their lives? Hersh asked. Or was this simply the American way—to the victor goes "the spoils of war"? Neither Marvin nor Neil Bush would answer Hersh's questions. Marvin, the youngest son, had not spoken to a reporter in twelve years. Neil said he had not spoken to the press since federal regulators accused him of a banking conflict in 1990. Hersh had touched a raw nerve. But General Norman Schwarzkopf did talk, confirming he had turned down millions of dollars because, simply put, he represented 541,000 American troops, "not some private companies. Why should I profit from their sacrifice?" When Hersh traveled to Kuwait, he found many Kuwaitis and Americans uncomfortable with the Bush entreaties. "I felt sleazy," one American banker told him.[3]

The word *sleazy*, however, was just about to enter Sy Hersh's journalistic vocabulary in a serious way. James Silberman, who had published *Price of Power*, was lobbying Hersh to tackle the legend of Jack Kennedy. "I resisted it for a few years—I'm sure because it was someone else's idea," Hersh said. But each time he encountered Silberman, the publisher repeated, "Kennedy, Kennedy, Kennedy." Hersh came around. "The original idea was to see if we can figure out how this president died by looking at how he lived," explained Hersh. Although there had been the 1963 Warren Commission and a 1976 congressional committee to investigate the death of the forty-six-year-old, thirty-fifth president, Hersh felt he could find things no one else had. After all, he was the greatest investigative reporter in the world, wasn't he? But this would be a bigger and longer project than anything he had ever tackled. No problem, Silberman said. Little, Brown and Co. was offering a million-dollar advance, putting him, finally, in the Bob Woodward stratosphere. "I'm pathological on the subject of Woodward's money," Hersh commented. "I'm totally envious. . . . I'd love to have some of that." Now he did.[4]

Hersh remembered his Izzy Stone lesson: "You can't write without reading." From Stone "I learned to read everything. It's all there, if you look."[5] And that was indeed true with John Kennedy. A cottage industry of books—nearly a thousand—had developed around the president. They fell into two categories: the paeans that came from historian Arthur M. Schlesinger Jr., speechwriter Ted Sorensen, and personal aide Kenny O'Donnell. Their books soon after his death turned him into a cult-like figure. The legend of a Camelot White House was born—King Jack and Queen Jackie. The vigorous young leader who inspired a generation and led America out of a nuclear showdown; the family man who Americans concluded was one of our greatest presidents. Schlesinger and Sorenson built their careers around the legend. "They were in love with him," Hersh said, dismissively. But he did agree with O'Donnell, that "Johnny we hardly knew ye," except that what we hardly knew was how dark Camelot was.[6] And then the debunking began as the journalist Richard Reeves explored the more tawdry side of Camelot, as did presidential historian Michael R. Beschloss, who looked at the "crisis years" of 1960 to 1963. Nigel Hamilton, a Brit, discovered Kennedy's "reckless" youth, including incessant womanizing. But Hamilton got a dose of what was in store for Hersh: the Kennedys were so furious at his look at Kennedy's private life that he never wrote the second part of his biography.[7] For an entire year Hersh devoured the Kennedy literature. "Sy read voraciously," said research assistant Max Friedman. He felt the Kennedy hagiography "needed a corrective." Observed Hersh: "I had no idea that the Kennedy story would be as bad as it was."[8]

Finding the Mistresses

Friedman got the task, as with *The Samson Option*, of finding scholarship on the major moments of Kennedy's presidency—the failed Bay of Pigs invasion, the Missile Crisis with Khrushchev, the dustups in Berlin, the early steps into Vietnam. The triumphs—space exploration, the Peace Corps, civil rights—were not on Hersh's radar. "I'm looking at the bad side," he said. And since Hersh was not writing a scholarly account of the Kennedy years ("Who wants to write a book for historians," he hissed), he needed to find people—he did more than a thousand interviews—to get underneath the public maneuverings of Kennedy's foreign policy.[9] To understand the president, he had to explain the family. So he started with Kennedy's maternal grandfather, John F. (Honey Fitz) Fitzgerald, a two-time Boston mayor booted out of Congress in 1919 because of voter fraud. All this was known, but the details had been sealed until Hersh's sleuthing unearthed a 1969 file revealing Honey Fitz's never reported manipulations. And that became relevant when Hersh tackled the question of whether the Kennedys fixed the 1960 election, as had been rumored. Hersh went to his hometown, Chicago, where, legend had it, Mayor Richard Daley's Democratic machine put in the fix. But Hersh pursued another avenue, finding evidence that Kennedy's powerful father, Joseph, was the fixer. "Old Joe" partly made his fortune trafficking booze during Prohibition when he made contacts with organized crime figures.

Hersh took the story further, alleging that the elder Kennedy, using a friendly Chicago judge, met directly with Sam Giancana, the reputed boss of organized crime in Chicago, and offered enough money—and the promise of favors—to throw the election in Illinois. "I don't have a videotape of the meeting," he said. Hersh also wanted to show that Joe was his son's role model in other ways. Once, former Florida senator George Smathers told Hersh, he and Lyndon Johnson were lunching with Rose Kennedy at the Kennedy compound in Palm Beach when Joe

Kennedy walked in, with a beautiful eighteen-year-old on his arm, and simply went to an upstairs bedroom. They all then heard noisy sexual intercourse take place. "The lunch went on as if nothing had happened," Hersh wrote. Bobby Baker, a top aide to Lyndon Johnson, repeated the smarmy tale to an eager Hersh.[10]

Election fixing focused Hersh's attention, and West Virginia was the key state that went Kennedy's way in the Democratic primary, again, according to legend, because of voter fraud. Hersh's evidence indicated that Ted Kennedy traveled the state as early as 1959 with satchels full of cash, handing over money to sheriffs who had the power to influence the polls. The family put out between $3 and $5 million to influence the election. But some sources eventually felt used by Hersh, saying he had his mind made up that fraud had occurred before he collected evidence. "He called me a lot, and he both educated me and disturbed me," said Charles Peters, editor of the *Washington Monthly,* who chaired the Kennedy campaign in a West Virginia county and was interviewed five times. Peters said Hersh would just not be convinced that his estimates of Kennedy money were exaggerated. Whenever he disagreed with Hersh, Peters says, Hersh would scream: "Bullshit! Bullshit! Bullshit!" He was not the only source to scrap with—or become disillusioned with—Hersh.[11]

Kenny O'Donnell was one of the so-called Irish mafia around Kennedy at all times. And according to Hersh, he was also a key figure in supplying the president with women, often prostitutes, as he traveled. Along with aide Dave Powers, Hersh alleged, and others have confirmed, O'Donnell made sure the president did not lack for female companions. In fact, as Hersh pictures it, the aides acted as virtual pimps and often joined the president in sexual activities at the White House pool. The picture that emerges is sordid. O'Donnell died in 1977, but Hersh contacted his daughter Helen at 7:00 one morning. Hersh began by "telling me my father was a drunk and a thief and that I should meet with him so that he could tell me the kind of man my father really was," said O'Donnell. "He ended the conversation by saying, 'You need me more than I need you!'" She told Hersh to never call again. Hersh the bully was alive and well. "I probably handled it badly. I probably shouldn't have said that," Hersh said.[12]

But Hersh the charmer—and indefatigable reporter—was also working his magic in the five years he spent on Kennedy. For example, a source told him that Lyndon Johnson only got the nod as vice president because he blackmailed Kennedy, saying he would reveal Kennedy's sexual secrets—and there were many—unless offered the number two slot. Hersh needed corroboration for a story many doubted. To blackmail Kennedy would be political suicide for Johnson. Hersh located in Chicago a campaign strategist, Hyman Raskin, who had been often overlooked. He interviewed Raskin a number of times in 1994-95. Raskin laid out the LBJ blackmail, but Hersh wanted corroboration. When Raskin died in October 1995, Hersh got a surprise: Raskin's widow, Frances, called him. She met Hersh when he visited, and she liked him. "This darling, sweet lady from the south side of Chicago . . . who liked me because I'm a nice Jewish boy taking her to dinner—and she's a lovely lady—calls me," Hersh recalled. "And she said to me: 'Did you know? There's a memoir.' It was unpublished. "Bang, slam, bam! I'm in Kinko's the next week."[13] And then he felt comfortable to accuse LBJ of blackmail.

The picture, as Hersh unfolded it, was getting darker. He understood the foreign policy adventures, the Kennedy family, and the 1960 election; but the other hidden part of Kennedy's life—women who were not his wife, Jackie—he now had to tackle. Up to this point in his career, Hersh steered clear of private matters. "Everybody's entitled to his peccadilloes," he said in 1975. "Where do you draw the line? I feel like a fuddy-duddy on this. . . . we can improve our political coverage without necessarily delving into . . . who's sleeping with whom." In fact, he insisted he had juicy information on both Nixon and Henry Kissinger he did not use. He told a group of journalists he had tangible evidence that Nixon had beaten his wife, dating back to 1962 and continuing in the White House. But, Hersh said, he could not tie the abuse to public policy. Specious logic perhaps, especially in the case of a criminal act, but he withheld it as private behavior. Now he began to collect evidence of Kennedy's sex life—to see if it put the nation and the presidency at risk. The answer, he found, was yes. Of course, he knew also it would sell books.[14]

Early in Kennedy's presidency Bobby Baker, a top aide to Lyndon Johnson when he was a senator, was invited to the White House to meet with Kennedy. The president did not want to talk business, Baker told Hersh.

"You know," Kennedy told Baker, "I get a migraine headache if I don't get a strange piece of ass every day." Hersh set out to find the women who made the headaches disappear and to pierce Kennedy's "dark side." And find them he did—some who were famous and talked off the record. Some were just thrilled to be in bed with the president. One of the women, whom Hersh did not identify (one of the few sources unnamed in this book) was a Radcliff coed who slept with the president at his Georgetown home the night before his inauguration. Kennedy could not remember her name. "I was just another girl," she told Hersh.[15] Hersh was still trying to tie the private dalliances to public policy when he talked to a good source in the CIA. The source said the only way to know how reckless Kennedy might have been was to find Secret Service agents who protected him. Hersh got a list of a hundred retired Secret Service agents and called them all. Many stuck to the agency's code: nothing they learn about the president is *ever* to be repeated. "Many people told me to go to hell," he said. But four agents spoke to the reporter, an unprecedented action. "They have kept their silence, until now," Hersh wrote in melodramatic fashion. Why would they now talk to Hersh? "I kept my mouth shut for 35 years," one explained. Until Hersh called. It was time—and their stories would be shocking.[16]

Hersh went to Colorado to see Larry Newman, who joined the presidential team in 1961. He recalled how sheriffs brought prostitutes to the president. The agents had no way of knowing if the women were security risks. He watched aides O'Donnell and Powers bring well-known Hollywood starlets with scarves around their head for trysts. "Some of the names are pretty staggering," observed Hersh. All agent Newman knew was, "This was the President of the United States, and you felt impotent and you couldn't do your job." Tony Sherman spoke to Hersh in Salt Lake City. "There were women everywhere," he said. They would stay overnight in the private quarters; once at Palm Beach Sherman walked in on the president cavorting nude at poolside with a prominent European socialite. "We didn't know what to think," he said. He left the White House after two years. William McIntyre sat with Hersh in Phoenix and recalled his own pool story, this one in the White House. Mrs. Kennedy wanted to swim, but McIntyre could not let her because the president was there with two women. When the pool was finally cleared, he said, you could see three sets of footprints leading to the Oval Office. "I was disappointed by what I saw," he added, fearing he might be guilty of a crime by not reporting the prostitutes.[17] But still, as shocking as the sexual activities were, they did not meet Hersh's rule—to report it means it effects public policy or illegal activities.

And for that Hersh turned next to the woman who everyone knew had been Kennedy's paramour—Judith Campbell Exner, or "Judy" as Hersh called her. A beautiful dark-haired, twenty-five-year-old, she was introduced to Kennedy in 1959 by Frank Sinatra and became his regular—but secret—lover into his White House years. She too decided to speak with Hersh, perhaps because it was Hersh's 1975 exposé in the *Times* of the CIA's domestic spying that led to her first being identified. The Senate's Church Committee mentioned her, not by name, in a footnote. Reporters quickly found Exner, who became a celebrity mistress, writing her own memoir. (In 1988 Kitty Kelley wrote a long profile of Exner for *People* magazine, headlined "The Dark Side of Camelot.") So identifying her was not new, but Hersh added significant ripples, including what sex positions Kennedy took because of his injured back. More significant: she told Hersh when they met in her Newport, California, home in 1994, the president gave her bags of money to deliver to Giancana, with whom she was later also romantically involved. She was the first known connection between the mob and the government, either to pay off election favors or to pay for assassinating Fidel Castro. She had lied in her government testimony and in her memoir, she told Hersh, but now—suffering from cancer and three years from death—she was telling the truth to a reporter who had captured her fancy.[18] "Hersh is incredible," she said. Hersh seemed almost smitten with Exner. Said Hersh, who had a twelve-year-old daughter: "If you look at her picture, you see what she was. A total innocent. She wasn't dumb; she was naive. I liked her very much. She was really a nice girl, and John F. Kennedy, our president, took complete advantage of her." Like most of the women who Hersh found, she spoke tenderly about Kennedy; all seemed to think he was in love with them. One who got away from Hersh, Mimi Alford, surfaced years later to tell her story, and it was more jarring as she explained that she was a nineteen-year-old intern, and the president took her at the White House in rape-like fashion.[19]

Starlets, coeds, socialites, prostitutes—Hersh found them all, explaining, "The notion that I'm using it in some sort of titillating way amuses me to no end. There's a whole other level I didn't get into; some of the sexual stuff is even worse than I've reported." But the story of Kennedy and his lovers would not be complete without one final pursuit—Marilyn Monroe. And that pursuit plunged Hersh down a path that perhaps overshadowed almost everything else that came out of his look at Kennedy. The controversial Cusack Affair—one of the great American forgeries—was about to begin.[20]

Sy Hersh was having dinner one night in December 1994 at a Japanese restaurant in Washington DC. An acquaintance—everywhere Hersh goes in the capital, people engage him—told him that well-known Atlanta documents dealer Thomas Cloud was peddling newly discovered Kennedy memorabilia for big bucks—private letters and notes. "There's some great stuff out there," he said. Of course, Hersh was interested. "Anybody who says they weren't should be in another business," he declared. "I'm a newspaperman. You go after stories. That's a great story."[21] Exactly who called whom is unclear.

The documents had originated with Lawrence X. Cusack III, a forty-seven-year-old paralegal in New York City whose father was a prominent attorney who died in 1985. He had done significant legal work for the Catholic Church but also, said the son, for the Kennedy family and the estate of Marilyn Monroe. While going through his father's papers, he located a document indicating John Kennedy had set up a trust fund for Monroe's mother, Gladys Baker. The reason: she was threatening to expose Monroe's love affair with the president if he did not help. She was said to also have a photo that showed Kennedy, the mobster Sam Giancana, and Monroe together. In total, Cusack would unearth 350 documents with startling new information in them. This was the mother lode for Hersh, who called the documents "gorgeous." Salivating, the reporter added, "They get you hard." As a tip, he said, "they were incredible. It's like somebody calling me up and saying, 'I know about a mass murder in Vietnam.'"[22]

But Cloud, Cusack, and a third partner, John Reznikoff, a Stamford, Connecticut, antiques dealer who described himself as "the Indiana Jones, of paper and relics," were equally interested in Hersh. Cloud knew that collectors would clamor for the Cusack trove. Since the 1970s the market for handwritten manuscripts from the famous had greatly expanded; Kennedy was particularly in demand. Cusack—making $40,000, in debt, stuck in a stalled career—needed the money. He would get an 80 percent cut of what could amount to millions. They knew, however, that to increase the value of the papers and make their existence known, they needed someone famous to write about the collection in a credible fashion. Reznikoff told a client, Hal Kass, about the documents. Kass's wife already knew that an alleged Monroe-Kennedy trust agreement was going for $450,000. "If you know Kennedy stuff—and I've seen a mess of it—this was better than a lot of the stuff I'd come across," he said. Kass said he could see if Sy Hersh was interested. They needed a big-time writer. Never bashful, Hersh declared: "I'm the biggest. The only one who sells more . . . is Bob Woodward."[23]

Enter Sy Hersh, well along on a Kennedy book that his publisher was trumpeting this way: "This monumental work—five years in the making—will change our view of the Kennedys forever." It was a perfect marriage. Hersh needed to convince Cusack to let him access the documents, and he began to "romance" Cusack, who was sitting on what the archivist at the John F. Kennedy Library called "the Holy Grail."[24]

Hersh put on a full-court press, dining right way with forty-seven-year-old Cusack and his wife at a Manhattan steak house. Cusack recalled his father going to the Kennedy compound in Hyannis Port, Massachusetts, to play golf with "Old Joe" and discussing Rose Kennedy's sweet potato pie. He said his father advised Kennedy on a divorce from Jackie. He mentioned also that he had been in naval intelligence. The two men drank and hit it off, just as Hersh, the chameleon, had with murderer William Calley and superspy Ari Ben-Menashe. "Was I romancing them?" Hersh asked. Of course. "You think I wouldn't sell my mother for My Lai? Gimme a break." Charming letters followed over the next six months. "We got along so well at that dinner Tuesday night because, I like to think, we are all what we seem to be."[25] Of course, in reality, everyone was play-acting.

On April 14, 1995, Hersh wrote again to Cusack. "There is no question the value of the historical documents would increase dramatically if they were shown to be part of a major new interpretation" of Kennedy. "Once we have published . . . I believe your documents will have even greater value and be more in demand—especially in Hollywood." The use of "we" is curious since Cusack was not being offered any role in the forthcoming book. But Hersh might have been referring to Michael Ewing, who in 1995 was Hersh's coauthor. Ewing worked on the staff of Iowa senator Harold Hughes, a key Hersh source, and they had become friends. Ewing was also a key staff member for a House committee that investigated Kennedy's assassination. He was, Hersh said, "the heavyweight of assassination researchers. The single best."[26] He and Hersh would split the million-dollar book advance. Ewing was wary of the Cusack documents, telling Hersh he smelled a rat. Hersh did discover that Cusack was never in intelligence, but he was relieved Cusack was not a spy. Once they got the documents, he felt, they could better check authenticity. "In my business," he declared, "you don't really go around psychoanalyzing people who give you stuff. You grab it. I deal with all sorts of wackos." Still trying to convince Cusack, Hersh sent him a portion of an unpublished memoir by Dr. Max Jacobsen of New York, who had given Kennedy amphetamines. "Dr. Feelgood" became part of a litany of secret health issues that plagued Kennedy—including venereal disease—that ended up in the book. See, he was telling Cusack, the book will be chock full of important documents. "Desperate and seamy things were going on in the White House," Hersh warned Cusack. "The very concept of Democracy is endangered." But Hersh and Cusack would cleanse the Republic. "I am sitting here, frankly, scratching at the door like a Chihuahua trying to get in," Hersh later said.[27]

Finally Cusack relented, agreeing to let Hersh see the documents. He flew to Atlanta three days before Christmas in 1994. Cloud "tells me what he has to tell me, shows me some paper, makes it clear how big it is," Hersh recalled, and then he pulled out the originals from a vault. Among them a secret trust arrangement: "Agreement made this third day of March, 1960, between John F. Kennedy . . . and Marilyn Monroe." Because of her relationship with Kennedy, "MM believes she has suffered irreparable harm. . . . And that such has been the cause of personal hardship and suffering. . . . MM shall never discuss nor reveal . . . the said relationship between her and JFK. Monroe will refrain from discussing her knowledge of any meetings or discussions . . . which may have taken place at which were present JFK and Giancana."[28] Hersh was dazzled. He signed an agreement: he would get sole access to the papers, but pay no money. "We must be holier than the Pope—and that means we cannot, simply cannot, pay for any information," Hersh wrote to Cusack. The reporter was giddy, telling author Gore Vidal he had found a gold mine. "How are you doing sleuthing the Monroe thing?" Vidal asked him. The answer: he was wheeling and dealing to help Cusack market the papers, trying to get a lucrative television deal to coincide with the publication of the book, and aggressively reporting. "Digging and digging and digging," he said, to verify the Cusack documents, which would be part of a chapter on Monroe and JFK.[29]

Hersh understood that Cusack and Cloud were using his credibility to market the documents. They wrote letters to investors, for example, bragging that Hersh and Cusack would sign books together when publication dawned. One eighty-seven-year-old investor, a judge, met Hersh and told him, "Hersh, you will win another Pulitzer Prize because of this work." Hersh was pulled into the marketing scheme. Once, in Atlanta, Cloud introduced him to two investors, and he enthusiastically endorsed the documents. As he left the office, Hersh declared, "If I could buy these documents I would mortgage my house." Defending his participation, Hersh later said, "There wasn't much I wouldn't say to get more paper." And the documents kept appearing. As discrepancies turned up, Cusack and Cloud would produce documents that explained away the problems. At another dinner in New York, when Cusack produced more damning documents, Hersh loudly proclaimed, "Those Kennedys . . . are the worst." So exuberant, he spilled wine on the table.[30]

When Hersh wrote about My Lai and brought a soldier for a national TV interview, he felt that was a turning point, essential to the story's prominence. He felt the same way about the Cusack documents—he needed TV. Mark Obenhaus, with whom he had worked on two documentaries, discussed with Hersh a TV special on JFK's "dangerous world." NBC gave

Hersh and Obenhaus $1 million. The documents and the chance to have Secret Service agents talking on camera had them all excited. But NBC became leery of the Cusack papers. What is remarkable is that Hersh was not more suspicious earlier. Cusack lied about his military record; he turned up at events wearing fake medals; his wedding notice in the *Times*, easily available to Hersh, said he graduated cum laude from Harvard and was studying law. These were lies. Hersh brushed it off and spent the next year trying to verify the documents. And he did; the documents looked better and better. Meanwhile, a number of sources insisted to Hersh that the Cusack documents were fakes. Ted Sorensen said he had seen better forgeries. A Kennedy secretary said a signature on one document was not hers. And yet Hersh knew that Reznikoff had used distinguished handwriting experts to analyze the Kennedy signature; they believed it was the president's. The Kennedy people were not to be believed, Hersh felt.[31]

Increasingly nervous, NBC pulled out, saying, "Serious questions have been raised . . . that we cannot answer." They paid Hersh $400,000 to kill the deal. But ABC News and Peter Jennings now entered, agreeing to produce the documentary and pay $2.5 million. Although the documentary would deal with more than Marilyn Monroe, the documents were the sexiest part and the selling point. They had to be verified. Obenhaus's assistant producer Ed Gray, pouring over the memos, found one with a zip code. The problem was that when it was written the U.S. Postal Service had not yet started using zip codes.[32] Cusack explained that his father often post-dated letters, by which time zip codes had come into use. Gray and others were suspicious. Hersh and ABC hired forensic experts. Hersh's reporting seemed to verify key aspects, but the experts now looked more closely at the originals. What they found was devastating: some of the typefaces were not in existence when the memos were supposedly written, and some of the ink ribbons also were not available. "Oh shit," Hersh said. Hersh whispered to Gore Vidal: "It may prove all to be untrue." ABC concluded that a massive forgery had taken place; hundreds of investors had been swindled. Cusack still insisted the documents were real. Hersh scrambled. He wanted to get out the news that it was all a forgery so that he was not legally liable—and so he could move forward with the Kennedy book. The news of the forgery exploded. When the *Washington Post* called Hersh to get his reaction, he was grumpy. "That's journalism," he said. "I'm sorry if people want to magnify and dramatize. . . . Big deal."[33]

On September 25 Peter Jennings confronted a sweating Cusack on national television. "I'm bound to ask you, Mr. Cusack. Did you forge these documents?" Replied Cusack: "No sir, I did not." He was lying, and he tried to blame Hersh. "I totally relied on Seymour Hersh. He continually reassured me of the veracity and authenticity of documents, and suddenly he totally abandoned it." Actually it was not so sudden. It took him nearly two years. Robert Sam Anson wrote a long and vicious article on Sy Hersh's "Secrets and Lies" for *Vanity Fair*. "One of Sy's great strengths is once he finds he's been going down the wrong path, he turns around on a dime, and that's commendable," said Anson, a friend of Hersh's. "However," Anson added, "it would have been a lot more commendable if he'd had this change of heart two years earlier." The Jennings broadcast let loose a torrent of stories on a forgery being compared to the infamous fraudulent "Hitler diaries." "JFK-Monroe 'Affair' Papers Faked," headlined the LA *Times*. "Incendiary JFK Story Goes Up in Smoke," declared the *Washington Post*. Once again, Seymour Hersh's book had not even hit bookstores, and it was making headlines across America. A federal grand jury indicted Cusack for fraud. One Kennedy lawyer said he spoke to Hersh to tell him he was being duped, but he would not listen. It was "like talking to someone in an asylum. I thought he'd really flipped," he said. Others agreed that Hersh was quite emotional. In interviews with the press—and he gave a lot of them—Hersh seemed calm.[34]

"Any investigative journalist can be totally fucking conned so easy," he explained. "We're the easiest lays in town. You can still sell me bridges. It's what I print that matters." And, he snickered, it will sell a lot of books, even though the Monroe-JFK material would never see the light of day. Hersh got rid of that chapter and moved on. He was in the eye of the hurricane again, but he knew it would get even stormier. "The book will cause trouble," he said.[35] He was right. Publication was scheduled to coincide with the anniversary of Kennedy's death. ABC aired a documentary—minus the Cusack papers—that whetted the public's appetite. Little, Brown readied a first-day run of 350,000 copies of *The Dark Side of Camelot*.[36]

CHAPTER 26

Going after Sy Hersh

"They're Going to Come after Me"

The controversy over the forged John Kennedy–Marilyn Monroe papers was both a nightmare and godsend for Sy Hersh. Everyone now knew he had a big new book on the way. "The bottom line," he declared, is that if it hadn't been for the forgery scandal, "the buzz on the book would have been much less." On the other hand the lambasting of Sy Hersh was also well under way even before *The Dark Side of Camelot* touched a bookstore shelf. Maureen Dowd wondered in the *New York Times* how the "poor schnooks," Peter Jennings and Hersh, did not know the letters were forged. She said she had just unearthed a cache of letters under a floorboard in her Georgetown house where Kennedy once lived. "Dear Jack," one letter began, "Those other letters I wrote to you were fakes. This one is really, really written personally by I and it is really, really valuable." It was signed "Marilyn." Dowd, of course was being tongue-in-cheek; others were more serious. About the Kennedys, Hersh said, "They're going to come after me." And so would just about everyone else.[1]

Little, Brown and Hersh had worked hard to keep what one reviewer called the book's "reeking bag of dirty linen" from the public before publication. But now, in mid-November, they were ready to launch as Hersh, the sixty-year-old author, got set for the biggest book tour of his career. He confided to Robert Sam Anson, "I'm tired of doing books. I'd like to make a score and get out. Retire." But first, the pimping would begin. "Here's how I think it'll work," he said awaiting an interview on *The Today Show*. First the interviewers will try to discredit sources, find someone misquoted or who says he lied. "They won't find anybody," he said. Then everyone will focus on the book's sexual activities. "That's shocking and perfect for TV." Finally the focus will turn to American foreign policy and Kennedy, which, Hersh reminded, "is the reason I wrote the book in the first place." Hersh left out one thing—everyone would wonder if the book could be believed at all after the great reporter had been so duped by Cusack, who was sentenced to ten years in prison. "How believable is his controversial new book?" asked *Time* in a cover story. "Do you think you were blinded by the desire to tell a sordid tale?" asked NBC's Matt Lauer.[2]

"As far as I'm concerned," Hersh shot back, "investigating those papers and doing everything I did is part of the business. . . . I've been criticized for a lot of things I've written . . . but this is the first time I've been criticized for what I thought. The bottom line is that I didn't publish them. I don't understand what's so bad about chasing a story, finding out it's not real and saying so." The forgeries, however, were just part of the controversy that swirled around Camelot. The book, wrote one critic, "has indeed met with an astonishing reception; astonishing in its vitriol."[3]

Camelot caused a furor for a few reasons. First, Hersh was stepping on the toes of a cult hero, the glorious son of America's most beloved political family. "A handsome, charming, witty man who had a fling with Marilyn Monroe is as close to a god as we have," quipped Frank Rich. "I think I touched a nerve," Hersh told TV interviewer Charlie Rose. Second, Hersh's no-holds-barred approach to promoting himself never endeared him to anyone. He had enemies everywhere, and now they had their scalpels out, waiting to pounce. "It is not hard to find a lot of people who don't like me. I have a lot of blood enemies," Hersh admitted. "Hard stories produce a lot of anger."[4] It would now be fun to savage the cocksure and abrasive Hersh.

Third, conservatives had long despised Hersh, but this time it was the liberals, who saw Kennedy as the progressive who inspired a generation. Hersh was turned on by his crowd. "Hell hath no fury like liberals with their icons threatened," observed the *Times of London*.[5] How odd, as even Hersh noted, that arch-conservative icon William F. Buckley Jr. liked Hersh's book. Fourth, Hersh was wading into the uncharted territory of the private lives of public people. The Kennedy-Judith Exner affair had first raised the question of whether private sexuality was ever the public's business, but in Hersh's "diligently distasteful" book "the line of decorum" has been crossed, charged the *Times'* William Safire, a conservative. "What are the limits, if any, to justifiable historical curiosity?" asked Buckley. Whatever the answer, he wrote, "It is gratifying not to be seated in the cockpit of a newsroom when Seymour Hersh's story comes by."[6]

And, finally, although Hersh named virtually all his sources, the historians and critics simply would not accept his thesis or the way he tried to prove it. "Character is the issue in this book," he explained. "It's character more than circumstance that determines foreign policy. My thesis is you can't really separate the private recklessness from the public recklessness." His evidence and allegations instantly became, as one writer noted, "the topic of a national talkfest." The *New York Times* headlined the book on page one: "Book Portrays J.F.K. as Reckless and Immoral." Much of the attention went to the sex and Hersh's own reliability. "It may be one of the most penetrating—or disgusting—revelations ever printed about John F. Kennedy," offered the LA *Times*, but its headline added, "Seymour Hersh's Book on JFK's Faults Raises Questions about His Own." Kennedy *and* Hersh were in the spotlight while *Camelot* got countless reviews *and* generated news stories.[7]

The 498-page book had twenty-five chapters, but only six were devoted to sex, and one of those was about whether Kennedy had a wife, before Jackie, and never divorced. Foreign policy really is the meat of the book, centering on what Hersh saw as Kennedy's obsession with assassinating Fidel Castro, which is why, in part, he needed the mobsters. The Kennedy obsession, Hersh argues, brought the world to the precipice of nuclear war. The reckless private Kennedy was equally reckless in his public policy. Hersh supplemented his thousand interviews with sixteen new tape recordings, various unpublished memoirs, and newly released FBI documents. When he found something exclusive, he was not bashful: "not revealed until this book," "in the most candid interview she ever gave," "in an extraordinary series of interviews," "in a series of unusual on-the-record interviews for this book." Page after page is filled with a self-promotion that became tiresome—and offensive—to many critics. "It is as if he wants to make absolutely sure that the reader doesn't miss what he says are the scoops he has unearthed," complained Jules Witcover. Whether Hersh was just trying to be clear about what was the product of his research or simply stooping to a yellow-journalism self-promotion that would justify the hoopla and his big advance is not clear.[8]

"A Terrible Hit for Journalism"

When the Cusack forgeries surfaced, the Kennedy family decided not to comment, for fear it would give the documents more credibility. But when *Dark Side* was published, the family was not silent. "The book is fiction," Senator Edward Kennedy said in a statement. "We don't intend to comment further on this malicious gossip and innuendo." They did not have to because the acolytes assaulted. "The Seymour Hersh book is a really ridiculous book," said Arthur M. Schlesinger Jr., whose memoir of Kennedy, *A Thousand Days,* won him his second Pulitzer Prize in 1965. Schlesinger, known as the Kennedys' "court historian," added: "When the book was sent to me, I almost fainted, I was so embarrassed. He is the most gullible investigative reporter perhaps in American history. He will believe anything so long as it discredits John Kennedy." Ted Sorensen, a Kennedy adviser and speechwriter, called it "a pathetic collection of wild stories.[9] Jerry Bruno, who worked on Kennedy campaigns, said: "I have to picture this book as nothing more than 'The Dark Side of Seymour Hersh' trying to make cash from garbage. It's mind-boggling." Hersh shot back: the Kennedy crowd are "trapped rodents."[10]

But the response from those who were not in the Kennedy camp was equally vicious. The one that many pointed to as particularly compelling was Gary Wills's essay, "A Second Assassination," in the *New York Review of Books.* Wills was a Pulitzer Prize–winning historian and journalist, a conservative and respected intellectual. His book assault on Richard Nixon was a shock to the conservative choir. What he had to say about Hersh carried weight. In essence, he said the Hersh evidence for his spectacular allegations was flimsy. Exner told Hersh that she carried a bag of money from Kennedy to mobster San Giancana, a story she had never told before. The Kennedy relationship with Giancana was also seconded by Tina Sinatra, who said she heard it from her father (she conveniently told this to Hersh just as she was seeking publicity for a TV special on

Frank Sinatra). "It would be reassuring to think that Hersh's treatment of the Giancana connection were an exception to his book's general trustworthiness," Wills wrote. "Unfortunately, it is entirely typical, and not even the worst case." That criticism was echoed by many others, but he added, "Like many investigative reporters, he is not so good at analysis, or even at writing." Almost gleefully, Wills listed all the glitches in Hersh's writing. "Is there nothing of use in this book?" he asked. "Practically nothing." Concluded Wills: "It is an astonishing spectacle, this book. In his mad zeal to destroy Camelot, to raze it down, dance on the rubble . . . Hersh has with precision and method disassembled and obliterated his own career and reputation."[11] Responded Hersh, "He is entitled," but he added, seemingly taken aback, "Pretty intemperate angry tone of voice. I am very proud of this book. I anticipated the heat."

Even some of his friends, however, lashed out at Hersh in what *Washington Post* media critic Howard Kurtz called "unusually personal terms, as though he were some sort of high-class Kitty Kelley." Journalist Richard Reeves, a respected author of a critically acclaimed Kennedy biography, seemed crestfallen, writing that the book "has shaken me as much as anything I remember in my professional life. This is a terrible hit for journalism. It is shocking that a tribal elder as admired as Mr. Hersh could do a book so shoddy. Some of it is just embarrassing."[12]

The bad reviews poured in: the *Times*' Richard Bernstein called the book "deceitful." Observed the *Washington Post*: "a patchwork of conspiracy theories, third-hand rumors, wild conjecture and anecdotal evidence, couched in tones so relentlessly adversarial and vindictive as to render it utterly without credibility." This book, wrote the noted author Edward Jay Epstein, "turns out to be, alas, more about the deficiencies of investigative journalism than about the deficiencies of John F. Kennedy." *Time* magazine tried to have it both ways, giving historian Alan Brinkley space to observe: "Reading this book is a depressing experience . . . because of its relentless descriptions of the sordid private world of the Kennedy presidency. . . . But what is even more depressing is to see such shoddy and careless arguments and such self-serving credulity coming from a celebrated investigative reporter." Despite that criticism, *Time* offered a special publication for educators to take a fresh look at the Kennedy presidency.[13] And so it went in review after review—a malicious book, lots of rehashed information, weak evidence. Only the testimony of the four Secret Service agents seemed to provide even his critics with some pause. Their information about Kennedy's private sexual escapades certainly offered a new look at the man. Of course, this too created a firestorm. A month after publication, the director of the Secret Service wrote a sternly worded letter to all present and former agents, warning them to maintain the privacy of the people they protect. The comments in the Hersh book, he said, "were very troubling and counterproductive." But one agent who spoke with Hersh responded: "This is a slap at us. I liked JFK. But he was reckless morally."[14]

While the overwhelming majority of commentary on *Dark Side* was critical, Hersh did have defenders, most prominently Thomas Powers, a Pulitzer Prize–winning reporter who wrote a cover page review in the *Times Book Review*. "Hersh does not write history in the usual sense of the term," he observed, "but he makes life difficult for historians by digging up just enough about distressing matters so they can't honestly be ignored." The man, he said, "is a great investigative reporter, no lie, and when he says somebody told him something he makes it easy for doubters to check it out." A scholar in the *Presidential Studies Quarterly* agreed, writing, "The book enhances our understanding of Kennedy's presidency."[15]

Steve Weinberg, who was director of Investigative Reporters and Editors and is a well-known reviewer, noted that Hersh has his own dark side. "At times brash, loud, profane, given to browbeating recalcitrant custodians of information, driven to be the most successful investigative reporter of his era. Hersh is despised by some." But, he stressed, "none of that should obscure this truth: [the book] is a reliable product of a reliable process. It is a convincing work of contemporary history." Reviewer Jacob Weisberg agreed: "Hersh does hyperventilate from time to time, but he still manages to present his case in roughly the way a fair-minded historian or journalist should."[16]

And some historians agreed. Thomas Reeves, who wrote an important book on Kennedy, went on William Buckley's popular TV program, *Firing Line*, to face off with the éminence grise of American history, Arthur Schlesinger. *Dark Side* is "a bad book," Reeves noted, but "it has expanded our knowledge of Kennedy in a way that neither Mr. Schlesinger nor I would have wanted." Moreover, Reeves said, taking aim at Schlesinger, the Kennedy family and their coterie have tried to hide from the public the truth about the Kennedys. The truth, of course, was that John Kennedy was neither all saint nor all sinner. Hersh knew this, but as he did with Henry Kissinger, he could hardly acknowledge anything positive. Theodore Roosevelt once complained that the muckrakers only look at the muck. That was Sy Hersh. "Hey, you know what?" responded Hersh. "It's not called The Bright Side. It's not called The Complete Biography. It's not called The Balanced, Well-Rounded Biography, His Good and His Bad. It's called The Dark Side."[17]

The assault on Hersh's work seemed not to shake him. "This is a good book," he declared. But it is one that brought him the worst criticism of his professional life, and it may not have made him much money for the five years he spent on it. Weinberg said he ran into Hersh at a Washington bookstore soon after publication; he confessed he was broke. Michael Ewing, his former co-author—with whom he had a bitter argument as they parted ways—complained that Hersh borrowed money from him in order to fly his family on fancy vacations. Hersh dismissed Ewing as unstable.[18] Nonetheless, Hersh's dream of producing a big best seller and getting out would not happen. Not that Seymour Hersh would ever really want to get out. There were just too many "scoops" out there. What is interesting to watch in the hundreds of stories written about *Dark Side* is how Sy Hersh saw himself. He is always a journalist, not a historian, not an author. He calls himself a "newspaperman." When two scholars from Harvard University reviewed the book in a long essay for *Diplomatic History* in 1998, they wrote a savage critique, but the journal asked Hersh to respond, which, he said, was "unprecedented in my thirty years of writing books, and too good to pass up." He goes tit for tat with the scholars, not giving an inch—in fact, taking them on in virtually all their critiques. Ed Gray, who worked with Hersh on the ABC documentary, said Hersh has some "mysterious genetic gift of curiosity, comprehension, and intellectual analysis. His intelligence is so sharp and fierce." The scholars dismissed him as just a journalist, but the scoop artist took no guff from the academics. "Their defense of all things Kennedy does them little honor," he wrote.[19] Of course it is possible that Hersh's attack on Kennedy as only a bad guy did not do him that much honor either.

"It is a sorry spectacle when tabloid standards can claim so distinguished a convert," wrote Evan Thomas in *Newsweek*. Jonathan Yardley wrote in the *Washington Post:* "*The Dark Side of Camelot* can and should be read as a case study in how not to do investigative journalism. . . . Hand it to the city editor of the Dogpatch Gazette and it would bounce back so heavily blue-penciled that scarcely a word would remain." No matter. Hersh had lots of words remaining. America had gone to war again. The Middle East was in disarray. He had bills to pay. And Tina Brown and the *New Yorker* were calling. Hersh was moving on—and up—the only thing to do when you have bottomed out. *The Dark Side* chapter was closed.[20]

CHAPTER 27

The *New Yorker* Years

A Little Book with No Bite

Pulitzer Prize–winning war correspondents Seymour Hersh and David Halberstam sat on a panel together soon after the Gulf War in 1991. Halberstam won his award because when he reported from Vietnam for the *New York Times* he often contradicted the Kennedy administration, which wanted him fired. Hersh, on the other hand, never left the country and simply tracked down soldiers when they returned to the States. But they both knew the key to war reporting was access to soldiers. With the lesson of Vietnam fresh in mind, the Bush administration put unprecedented restrictions on the press in the Gulf. Hersh was indignant. "You know, David," he said, "you and I would have walked through the desert if we had to reach the troops."[1] The reality: Hersh had never gone near any battles. He went to Hanoi in 1972 but never got to the prison camps he wanted to see. Nonetheless, while the Gulf War piqued his interest, his books on KAL, Israel, and Kennedy had occupied his attention. He was ready to shift gears.

In June 1998 Hersh published *Gulf War Syndrome: The War between America's Ailing Veterans and Their Government,* an odd little tract that came right after the debacle of his Kennedy book, which was so soundly rebuked that one would think Hersh would retreat. He was hardly finished with his promotional tour, however, when he dove into a topic that swirled around Washington since 1991 when American troops invaded Kuwait to push back Iraqi forces: an unexplained malady from which 90,000 troops suffered. "It was the perfect war," Hersh observed. Bombs fell with precision. A ground assault—led by new American heroes Generals Colin Powell and Norman Schwarzkopf—seemed to go off with nary a casualty, an antidote to the still-bitter aftertaste of Vietnam. The war, Hersh said, "restored the integrity of the American GI." But Hersh, the scoop artist, was not one to write about sweet victories. He had been listening to sources for nearly seven years on the war's "glitches." The vaunted Patriot antimissile system was a failure; America knocked out none of the Iraqi scud missiles; of the 146 Americans killed—admittedly an amazing low count—one-fourth were killed by "friendly fire"; American "smart bombs" were nowhere near as effective as the public had been told. And that was no surprise because the Bush administration—looking at the press coverage that so hounded the living room war in Vietnam—found a press eager to accept the Pentagon mythmaking. "It was a Teflon war," Hersh concluded.[2]

But the conduct of a war was not his target—that would come soon. He set out to see if the thousands of returning American troops—he puts the number at 15 percent—with unexplained illness (chronic flu-like symptoms, memory loss, aching joints) were merely suffering from a war fatigue, as the government insisted, or if they had been victims of a chemical or biological assault not detected. Or, even worse, was the government keeping this possible deadly seepage a deep dark secret?

Gulf War Syndrome should have been Hersh's story from the start. Had he still been at the *Times*, it would have been. Back in 1968, remember, he launched a warning shot when he wrote a book on the threat posed by germ weaponry. The great fear as America entered the first Gulf War was that Saddam Hussein would unleash these weapons, as he had done on his own people. The U.S. government worried intensely about this. And, yet, as Hersh found, most of the masks supplied to American soldiers did not fit properly and were useless. Moreover, systems in place to detect a poisonous attack would not register in time to protect the troops; soldiers would be dead before the system went off. "For all their brave talk about future warfare," Hersh concluded, the men who run America's military have been unwilling—perhaps even unable—to learn the real lessons of the Gulf War."[3] So Hersh set out to find out what those lessons might have been when it came to the mysterious "Gulf War Syndrome."

But this 103-page book lacks the punch of his earlier work and remains an exploration that came up will little new and nothing startling. Readers could have simply watched PBS's *Frontline* broadcast on January 20, 1998, "The Last Battle of the Gulf War," and learned much the same. Hersh gets six soldiers to tell their stories on their maladies and the government's indifference. He comes close to offering an explanation for their mysterious symptoms. American intelligence knew before the Iraqi invasion in 1991 that nerve gas was stored in Khamisiyah, but somehow the attacking forces were not told, and they destroyed the complex. "Upwards of a hundred thousand American soldiers were in the path of the huge clouds of smoke . . . that were generated," he wrote.[4] But Hersh was unable to follow the trail. No evidence surfaced that Washington tried to cover up the miscommunication between the CIA and the troops. "That failure was a criminally negligent mistake, but it was not a cover-up," he found. And did the plumes of chemicals cause the myriad illnesses returning soldiers then reported? Hersh can't conclude—nor could government, congressional, and private investigators. Even the Pentagon's harshest critics on the nerve gas foul-up could only conclude, "The experts are going to be arguing about cause for the next fifty years." In the end, the reader is left wanting to be told, as Hersh usually does, who is to blame. Instead, he wrote, "any conclusive determination will await future research, and may never be possible." To some questions, he added, "there are no answers." Why, frankly, did the book get written at all? "The price of war," he concluded, "is high." But there was little new in that conclusion, and little explanation of what occurred.[5] No headlines and news stories resulted. Hersh was marking time. New exposés and controversies were around the corner.

The "Highway of Death"

In the fall of 1999 Hersh undertook new investigations with old themes. The world of spying still fascinated him. The National Security Agency was falling behind in new technology, he uncovered, and its ability to track terrorists was in jeopardy. Typically he found no fault with massive new budgets for spying; he was simply upset the NSA was not modernizing. He looked back to provide more detail about convicted American spy Jonathon Pollard and clarify his finding that files Pollard stole in 1984 ended up in the Soviet Union, a charge that kept him squarely on the

Pollard defenders' hate list. He explored in great detail how the CIA used UN arms monitors in Iran to overhear telephone messages that showed a renewed friendship between Saddam Hussein and Russia. The CIA, Hersh found, was less interested in finding Saddam's hidden weapons than with assassinating him. Saddam survived, but the UN inspectors were thrown out of Iran.[6]

But Hersh turned his attention away from spying when he decided to look into America's latest foray in Latin America, a $1.6 billion "war" on Colombia that was aimed at stopping export of the country's ample cocoa crop. The effort to interdict was led by retired army general Barry McCaffrey, who headed President Clinton's cabinet-level drug policy office. He was Clinton's "drug czar." Who better to lead a military-style assault on drug traffickers than a decorated Vietnam veteran who earned three Purple Hearts? "He radiated command presence," Hersh wrote.[7]

McCaffrey was a forty-eight-year-old, chiseled jaw West Point graduate with, as Hersh admitted, "the best resume of any retired combat general in the United States Army," the nation's youngest, most decorated four-star general when he joined the White House in 1996. He belonged on the cover of an army recruiting manual, and his name was whispered for high political office. But as Hersh looked into McCaffrey's plan to go after drugs in Colombia, he discovered that generals who served with him in the first Gulf War did not like or trust the man. McCaffrey, said retired lieutenant general James H. Johnson Jr. of Sarasota, Florida, "does whatever he wants to do." The hostility toward McCaffrey was not surprising. Generals often competed, and McCaffrey was General Schwarzkopf's favorite. Hersh did find one general, Terry Scott, working at Harvard University, who endorsed his "high character and high standards," testimony that later allowed Hersh's new editor, David Remnick, to insist that "Overwhelming Force," Hersh's 25,000-word opus on McCaffrey in May 2000, was a "balanced" story.[8]

What was most surprising, however, was how many generals talked—on the record—about how McCaffrey conducted his part of the war. They all steered Hersh toward the Battle of Rumaila, also known as the "Battle of the Junkyard" because when it was over, American forces under McCaffrey had trapped a five-mile convoy and then launched a four-hour tank, artillery, and helicopter rocket barrage that destroyed more than seven hundred vehicles—rocket launchers, tanks, trucks. Perhaps four hundred Iraqis died while American troops and vehicles went virtually untouched. The "Highway of Death" became one of the war's most recognizable images. McCaffrey described it as "one of the most astounding scenes of destruction I have ever participated in." Normally, destruction of the enemy (which had, after all, invaded Kuwait and was being chased out by 956,600 coalition troops) would be applauded. But a Gulf War ceasefire was already in place. "There was no need to be shooting at anybody," said Johnson. "They couldn't surrender fast enough." Lieutenant General Ronald Griffith noted, angrily, "He made it a battle when it was never one. It was just a bunch of tanks in a train." To Lieutenant General John J. Yeosock, McCaffrey was "looking for a battle."[9]

Hersh dove into researching the Battle of Rumaila. For six months he flew around the country—on the *New Yorker's* dime—interviewing three hundred people and stirring the pot as only Sy Hersh could do. By the time he was finished, the sixty-three-year-old reporter was in the eye of another national storm that forced Barry McCaffrey to frantically mount a counter-offensive. Hersh's typical tactics, strong-arming some sources and bullying others, led to speculation on what he found about the highway massacre and two other incidents, all of which had already been investigated and dismissed by the U.S. Army. McCaffrey was not Henry Kissinger in stature, but the pursuit was similar—Hersh was convinced he had found a dark character, who, at the very least, had overstepped his authority, walking away unscathed. And he was also convinced he had found another instance, similar to My Lai, in which the army investigated what amounted to an atrocity and yet tried its best to make it go away. "You had an investigation that simply didn't do the job," he told an interviewer. "I do believe that they weren't worth the paper they were written on."[10] McCaffrey was adamant and very public in firing back. "Hersh does not in any way substantiate his allegations," he wrote. "The story was from the start nonsense."

Smelling a great story, Hersh dug into hundreds of pages of transcripts of the army's official investigations and pried loose new documents. Most importantly, he found witnesses, soldiers at low levels, who filled in the blanks of what they believed was the killing of retreating or surrendering Iraqis. The story, as Hersh pieced it together, was simply that McCaffrey and his troops were itching to get a piece of the war that ended too quickly. Hersh portrayed McCaffrey and his troops as ruthless and then regretful. On the third day of the war, for example, Hersh reported that an Iraqi truck was hit by an American shell. As it burst into flames, twenty or thirty soldiers came out. "We opened fire," a private told Hersh. "The soldiers we fought never had a chance [and were part of] the biggest firing squad in history." In another incident, on the fourth day of the war, a stream of Iraqi soldiers came out of the desert, "scared and crying," according to Specialist James Manchester, all looking to surrender. The Americans, following the rules of war, rounded them up, seized weapons, and provided food and water. The ragtag bunch was desperate to surrender. When told he was now a prisoner, one replied, "Thank Allah."[11] But later, as the prisoners sat in a circle, tanks from a distant location fired at the prisoners. A tape recording that a GI supplied to Hersh revealed someone saying, "It's murder." Another said, "We shot the guys we had gathered up." Six soldiers recounted the incident to Hersh, but when the army investigated they could find no evidence of bodies. "There was not any accidental shooting of prisoners," McCaffrey insisted. A spokesperson for McCaffrey, Bob Weiner, later declared, "The incidences simply did not occur." Just as Judith Exner never gave Sam Giancana a bag of money—so Hersh's skeptics said—American soldiers never slaughtered Iraqis.[12]

The battle near Rumaila was Hersh's main focus. He argued that McCaffrey, along with many Americans, wished President Bush had allowed troops to seize Baghdad before signing any cease-fire. "Personally, I think it would have been militarily an easy option," McCaffrey explained to investigators.[13] But he was ordered to stop advancing unless facing "imminent attack." And here the story gets very murky. Hersh's reporting indicated that McCaffrey moved his troops into a position to attack the retreating convoy of Iraqi vehicles without informing his superiors, twenty-five miles from where he was thought to be. McCaffrey insisted "it is simply not credible" that with satellites tracking troop movements he could have falsified his position. But some commanding officers insisted to Hersh it took place. McCaffrey claimed Hersh did not talk to the one officer who would say otherwise. Next, according to McCaffrey, Iraqi tanks fired on his troops although most tanks had their turrets turned backward to indicate retreat. "My troops on the ground were under attack," McCaffrey wrote to the *New Yorker*. "My sole focus was the safety of my soldiers." McCaffrey refused, however, to talk to Hersh; he submitted a thirty-two-page letter to Remnick answering questions. Hersh, by the way, now had an editor who was actively involved in his reporting, as well as a battery of fact-checkers, which Hersh called "both marvelous and daunting." Not since Abe Rosenthal at the *Times* did Hersh have someone so closely watching his work, insisting on knowing each anonymous source. Given accusations that Hersh was prone to making errors and exaggerating, the *New Yorker* team could only help the veteran.[14]

In essence, Hersh wrote that McCaffrey deceived his superiors, disobeyed cease-fire orders, and then killed the Iraqis. Even if there was some gunfire aimed at his troops, McCaffrey's response was out of proportion. The general was furious at the charge. "Do you understand that when you actually apply power, you don't want a fair fight?" he told *Newsweek* magazine when it jumped on Hersh's accusations. The Battle of Rumaila, he insisted, was "one of the happiest days of my life."[15] But Hersh sculpted out a view that went beyond this one battle. Colonel John Le Moyne, a top McCaffrey aide who investigated the eventual allegations, told an army historian that victory at Rumaila was a statement about the professionalism of U.S. troops, asserting: "This war has had no Lieutenant Calleys in it. . . . It's just a very professional army." Given that the press was denied access to the battlefield and soldiers, Le Moyne's view was impossible to check, at least in 1991. But when Hersh revisited the assault ten years later, he re-created an alternate view. Major James P. Kump, an officer in the field during the attack, told Hersh: "I knew of no justification for the counterattack. I always felt it was a violation of the ceasefire." Sergeant Stuart Hirstein, who rushed to the scene when he was told they were under attack, said of the retreating Iraqis, "They were not firing. It pissed me off." Another soldier, James Manchester, who was never called to testify, witnessed the events and called it "fucking murder." McCaffrey insisted Hersh's witnesses were not close enough to the action to make such charges, and some said they were misquoted.[16]

Weeks before Hersh's article appeared, McCaffrey launched a counter-attack, preparing his staff in the drug office to respond. He sent letters to news organizations, rebutting charges not yet made. In a May 8 letter to Remnick, McCaffrey said of Hersh: "I have no trust in his objectivity. He has poisoned the well in his interviews with sources by his openly expressed animosity and contempt." Seeking endorsement letters, he wrote to human rights groups that knew his work in Colombia. "Would ask for your help to discredit the Hersh article," one McCaffrey memo said.[17] They declined. And he readied a line of attack that built on the criticism that had dogged Hersh, blasting his techniques, as had targets for three decades. "I've gotten calls from dozens of friends over the last three months reporting a series of accusations by Mr. Hersh, ranging from bike theft at age 11 to atrocities in the Gulf War," he told a reporter. "They are defamatory and sort of frightening to my friends and family." McCaffrey also hired a well-known Washington law firm that promptly wrote a threatening letter to Remnick warning that "potential for damage to [McCaffrey's] reputation and future opportunities . . . is . . . immense." This was hardball. McCaffrey insisted Hersh was writing "revisionist history," ten years after the fact, using reckless sourcing.[18]

The doubters insisted Hersh was an unreliable relic. Remnick scoffed: "These are not ballplayers, all right? They're not going to dry up and go away when they're 34." McCaffrey's aides "were trashing Sy," recalled CBS's Pentagon correspondent David Martin. "Seymour Hersh has a storied career," explained McCaffrey spokesman Weiner. "He has done some wonderful things. But . . . he's been trying to reinvent My Lai." This story, he declared, "is fiction!"[19] As one publication rightly concluded, "A Gulf War shootout has resurfaced in a new firefight between a retired general and a famed investigative journalist." Observed another, "The great American reporter Seymour Hersh is at war with the American military." Hersh was once again in the middle of what one wag called "a major food fight that will be waged in political, military, and media circles across the country."[20]

Whereas Hersh's book on "Gulf War Syndrome" fell on deaf ears, this article—at thirty-four pages, the longest in the magazine since 1993—shot round the world. A Sydney, Australia, newspaper blared: "Besieged general fights for reputation." The London *Guardian* said McCaffrey "attacked defeated Iraqi army."[21] And the *New York Times* treated the article as news with a long story over six columns. The Hersh article "pits a tenacious investigative reporter against one of the nation's most aggressive military men," wrote Michael R. Gordon. He talked to McCaffrey, who complained bitterly about Hersh's tactics. "I have been dealing with the press for years, but nothing prepared me for this," he said.[22]

On Monday, May 25, the day after the *New Yorker* hit the newsstands, Hersh and McCaffrey appeared on NBC's *Today* show, speaking from separate locations. "I'm not a cop," Hersh proclaimed. "I'm just simply telling what happened. It's there. Everybody's named. I think the only fair word to use would be that it was covered up inside the Army." McCaffrey replied: "This is old history. The wrongdoing was absolutely refuted. We stand on the record, and we're proud of what these soldiers did. I think Hersh and his article lack any journalistic integrity."[23] The dispute spilled over to the editorial pages of the *Wall Street Journal*, where McCaffrey wrote a 1,325-word attack on Hersh, whose article, he said, was "unfair and untrue." Hersh, the general argued, "has the safe luxury of judging battlefield decisions 10 years after the fact. We didn't have that luxury." Editor Remnick jumped in forcefully, calling Hersh "one of the great journalists of his generation." Rebuking McCaffrey, he wrote, Hersh's "work of 'revisionist history' is essential to understanding" a war that "remains strangely unexamined." After all, he argued, "history and journalism are all about questioning the record and the assumptions that we take for granted." Two scholars who had written a history of the war five years earlier also were skeptical of McCaffrey's defense.[24]

Hersh had another key supporter: his old employer, the *New York Times,* which, in an editorial, demanded "an unflinching examination of the facts," adding the army's internal inquiries "are not an adequate answer."[25] McCaffrey welcomed a debate about tactics, insisting that using overwhelming force against an enemy—unlike Vietnam—was reasonable. But he said the facts of what occurred in Iraq did not need an investigation because four separate inquires had cleared him. Hersh mocked this answer, saying McCaffrey "was never asked any of the questions I posed. The notion that this was a serious investigation," insisted Hersh, is "ludicrous." The real issue, Remnick and Hersh argued, was "proportionality." McCaffrey ordered the massacre of surrendering and retreating troops. Was the response proportional? One scholar believed Remnick asked the wrong question. Former marine-turned-professor Gary D. Solis wrote that the issue of proportional response was never meant for battlefield commanders, only for officers who run a war. The Battle of Rumaila "did not constitute a violation of proportionality," he said. If the enemy fired, then commanders are not obligated to "finely tune" their responses, unless there were civilians involved. Moreover, he said, in modern warfare fleeing soldiers might regroup tomorrow as viable military units. Hersh was unapologetic, however. McCaffrey made an immoral choice for the wrong reasons; the army should investigate.[26]

McCaffrey's criticism of Hersh, however, generated other support. Georgie Anne Geyer, whose foreign affairs column appeared in 120 newspapers, wrote that this "seemingly endless piece . . . overwhelms you with facts" but offers no real proof, a charge that, frankly, is difficult to swallow. Hersh offered eyewitnesses and hundreds of pages of summarized documents. Geyer, it seems, like a legion of Hersh haters, just did not like Hersh's style of journalism. "In his writings about Vietnam, the Kennedys and many others, [Hersh] has come to personify the anti-authority 'get them' school of journalism. This time, he didn't get anybody." Joe Lockhart, President Clinton's spokesman, agreed. After expressing Clinton's full support for McCaffrey, he added that Hersh was just "a journalist who thinks if you throw enough stuff up against the wall, maybe something will stick." Remnick called the response "unsettling" and "amazing."[27]

But CBS's Martin better explained the government's response: "They don't want to tarnish the army's finest hour." And they didn't. The Pentagon and Congress declined to re-open an investigation. McCaffrey opened a private consulting business and became NBC News's national security analyst, although talk of McCaffrey as a candidate for higher office faded. Some of the generals said they were quoted out of context, but as Remnick pointed out, their quotes were not only checked but cleared; their complaints did not wash. Martin, tongue in cheek, said perhaps the reason for their confusion was when you are interviewed by Sy Hersh, "he is coming at you from 10 different directions. When you're finished, you have no idea what you said." McCaffrey was not laughing, however. Hersh suddenly did not seem so washed-up. But both men were standing when this battle was over. McCaffrey might have been more bloodied. "It caused intense pain to my wife," he told me. But "it did me no career damage then or since."[28]

Hersh ended his *New Yorker* article on McCaffrey with an interview with James Manchester, a soldier who hoped to become a marine. He had watched what took place at Rumaila and was still troubled, many years later. There have to be limits, even in war, he said. "Otherwise the whole system breaks down." Hersh tucked that comment away. He would soon enough have time to test it out. A new war was beckoning.

CHAPTER 28

An Alternative View of the Mideast

The Old Sources Pay Off

The Barry McCaffrey episode both energized and demoralized Sy Hersh. He won no awards. General McCaffrey observed, "Hersh was and still is outraged that there was no career fatality." And he was disappointed that no publisher asked for a book.[1] Hersh was probably still too hot to handle, or, possibly, even publishers did not want to diminish the glorious Gulf War. Hersh holed up in his nondescript two-room office on Connecticut Avenue in the nation's capital, mounds of reports and legal pads surrounding him. "It is the office equivalent of a freshman dorm room, minus the pizza boxes," observed his editor, David Remnick, who, although twenty-nine years younger, became mentor to the combustible Hersh. Sy was never one to look back or worry about bumps in the road. "A lot of people hate me," he once told me. After the Kennedy-Camelot book, he admitted, "I was beaten up. You can get the hell kicked out of you, and we survive."[2] Hersh just moved on. He was his old self—relentless and energetic at the age of sixty-four. Quipped Remnick: Hersh has "the reporting energy of 16 hummingbirds in a cage." At a journalism conference, a questioner told Hersh how he admired his work. "Rock on," he yelled. "I'm so old I can't rock," Hersh replied. True, he was gimpy from a knee injury that limited his tennis, but his nose for news still twitched. And he was as cantankerous as ever. When a journalist compared his reporting zeal and his fierce tennis, he snarled: "Blah, blah, blah. Why am I commenting on your questions?" He insisted *he* was not the story.[3]

And then he went back to working the phones with his legendary sources. "I have friends I have had for years," he said. "But I make new ones all the time. Sometimes it takes two years. Not do too much when you first talk to people. Nothing happens. Call again in three weeks." The *New Yorker* gave him months to work on stories. Eventually the sources would pay off. He still trolled lists of recently retired CIA agents and top-level military officers. And the new Internet search engines made it easier than ever to find people. Sometimes he had to be careful, calling people from phone booths and stuffing notes into mailboxes. At a conference on sources Hersh scoffed when well-known writer James Bamford said he went out to lunch with sources. Hersh sarcastically noted, no one wants to be seen in public with the scoop artist.[4] Then there were the constant calls from sources who wanted Hersh to write certain stories. A reporter interviewing Hersh heard him tell a source: "Let someone else write that shit. It's just not my cup of tea." Before abruptly ending the conversation, he added: "My free advice: it's garbage." Who was that, the reporter wondered? "Somebody I've known for thirty years who used to work in the CIA, giving me a tip." Moments later, Hersh switched from brusque to seductive, leaving a message: "Hi, it's Sy Hersh, I'm just checking in. Call me. Let's talk." Hersh has "an extraordinary stable of knowledgeable, well-placed sources who trust him," Remnick notes."[5] The breadth of those sources and four decades of digging into layers of government was about to pay off in ways neither he nor Remnick could ever have expected.

"It's an Incredible Moment"

After the McCaffrey story, Hersh gravitated to the Middle East, but he was still in a Cold War, multinational-corporations-are-evil mood, tackling a murky story of how, during the Clinton years, Mobil Oil engaged in a multibillion-dollar oil swap involving Iran. Under federal law Mobil was forbidden from dealing with Iran. How could so much money float around with so little oversight? The answer, he concluded, was the oil companies felt they were immune. After all, they believed, "we make it warm, and we make it light." Hersh was following a logical trail. "I think there are great stories to be written," he observed about Bill Clinton's "pretend government," adding, "We're going to pay a price for all this corporate power-taking."[6] Worries about big money, however, disappeared on the morning of September 11, 2001, when nineteen men with connections to the Islamist terrorist group al-Qaeda hijacked four passenger jets. Two of the planes—as the world quickly found out—flew into the World Trade Center, incredibly, killing 2,700 people. A third hit the Pentagon, the symbol of America's military might. The fourth, headed to the Capitol, was downed in Pennsylvania. The 9/11 attacks—the first-ever assault on America—shocked the nation. And many lives were unalterably changed. George Bush became a war president and Sy Hersh a war correspondent. Hersh learned of the attacks when he was backing out of his driveway. "Like anybody else, I was really mad," Hersh said. "It was really senseless what had happened." Within an hour, Hersh in Washington and Remnick in New York talked on the telephone. "We know what we're doing for the next year, don't we," Remnick said, adding: "We agreed that he would have to follow this story no matter where it went and that he would publish more frequently, digging into foreign and domestic intelligence, the military, the State Department, and the White House."[7] Over the next three years, on the road to Abu Ghraib, Seymour Hersh produced twenty stories and nearly 110,000 words. A nation's nightmare became a reporter's dream. "We're in a new war, a strategic war against a group of fundamental terrorists who want to destroy America," he said. "It's an incredible moment. A great story."[8] For Sy Hersh, all the world was one great story, to be reported more than analyzed. Others could ponder and comment; Hersh would report. Hersh got to answer questions everyone was asking: What went wrong with American intelligence? Could we have known the hijackers were coming? Did rules promulgated because of Hersh's 1970s exposures tie the hands of the CIA? Could America's slow-footed military fight terrorism? Were American troops up to the task of fighting a messy guerrilla war? And, while we chased terrorists, would a new Mideast country develop a nuclear weapon? Was George Bush really in charge, or had a small band of unelected neoconservatives taken over?

Hersh began simply enough, asking, "what went wrong?" What he found was an American intelligence community "confused, divided, and unsure about how the terrorists operated, how many there were, and what they might do next." Some sources felt the terrorists were "a cohesive group," while others saw them "like a pickup basketball team." Either way, Hersh concluded, "the intelligence community was in no way prepared to stop them." His sources, all unidentified, worried about a second attack. "Do they go chem/bio in one, two, or three years?" one senior general asked. "We must now make a difficult transition from reliance on law enforcement to the preemptive." Hersh was foreshadowing what was to come next—attacks on what President Bush called the "evildoers." And how to get it done? Hersh's sources—in the FBI, CIA, and the military—all suggested that bending rules and breaking laws would be required. "We need to do this—knock them down one by one," a source said. "Are we serious about getting rid of the problem—instead of sitting around making diversity quilts?" Hersh offered no one to rebut the suggestion that law breaking was needed. But, surprisingly, he said, flat out, "Today's CIA is not up to the job." He rarely entered his stories in such an obvious way. But this was the CIA that he knew as well as any writer in America. And his pessimism—a month after 9/11—was evident. Intelligence agencies don't talk to each other; spies were being forced out of retirement; no one speaks the language of the attackers. "These people," one source said of the enemy, "are so damned good."[9]

Hersh's intelligence sources, whom he had been tapping for years, paid off. He took a look at America's most important Arab ally—the Saudis. And his sources revealed secret satellite intercepts showing a corrupt royal family supporting bin Laden. The Saudis had "gone to the dark side," a source said. As if he was a daily reporter, Hersh also was able to more closely follow events as they unfolded, a kind of reporting he had not done for two decades. He produced immediately, learning that on the second day of the war in Afghanistan an unmanned American reconnaissance aircraft had zeroed in on a convoy carrying Mullah Omar, the Taliban leader. But neither the CIA nor the nearest U.S. military authorities in Bahrain had the authority to fire; only officers in Florida could give the order. When approval came through, Mullah Omar was gone. Defense secretary Donald Rumsfeld is "kicking a lot of glass and breaking doors," a source grumbled. "If it was a fuckup," one official said, "I could live with it. But it's not a fuckup—it's an outrage." A senior Bush administration official blamed political correctness: "Kill the guy, but not the guy next to him." A Mideast oil executive (an odd source, indeed) observed, "This fabulous military machine you have is completely useless."[10] And while Hersh was not explicit, who he chose to quote implied his growing impatience with how the United States was fighting this new war against terrorism.

Was the enfant terrible of the political left making a hard turn to the right? Some observers worried. "No journalist has made more of a splash since September 11 than Seymour Hersh," commented Michael Massing in the liberal *Nation* magazine. But "it's odd to find someone with Hersh's background embracing the views of [Israel], Big Oil and proponents of a more aggressive CIA." Was the man whose exposé led to a ban on assassination of foreign leaders rethinking? No, no, he insisted; he opposed covert action but otherwise was unapologetic: "It's a tough world. You have to rely on unsavory people. It's real easy to say 'forget about it' until you start thinking about your own kid being a hostage."[11]

Hersh's political view became murkier—and perhaps irrelevant—when he latched on to another "scoop." On October 20 more than a hundred Army Rangers parachuted into a Taliban airbase. Cameras beamed the scene to audiences as an example of American troops on the move in Afghanistan. "It was sexy stuff," one general told Hersh, but "it was a television show." What audiences were not told was that the elite Delta Force had been sent into a compound looking for Mullah Omar, who was not there. When they exited into the night, the Taliban was waiting. "The shit hit the fan," one senior officer said. "The chaos was terrifying," Hersh wrote. Twelve soldiers were injured, three seriously, he reported, a statistic the Pentagon disputed before Hersh's article on the "escape and evasion" of the soldiers hit newsstands. The Sunday news talk shows all discussed what one observer called Hersh's "stunning new information." Hersh is wrong, insisted General Richard Myers. "The Taliban were in complete disarray."[12]

But by the year 2001, Hersh had a new weapon when the government attacked him. He was in demand on the greatly enlarged TV and radio talk show circuit to argue his case. Charlie Rose, Amy Goodman, Wolf Blitzer, Bill O'Reilly—they all wanted the controversial reporter. Hersh, no shrinking violet, felt he owed it to the *New Yorker* to promote ("pimping," he called it) his work. He wanted it known the Delta Force soldiers came to him, unhappy how the Pentagon was using them. "Delta Force doesn't deal with reporters very often," Hersh said. "They're throwing a message . . . to the leadership, really, through me." And part of the message was that America needs to fight the war more effectively. "It was General Motors comes to Afghanistan. And it doesn't work," he said. "They don't want to operate in a suicide mission that doesn't get it done anyway." Sy Hersh had become the defender of the troops.[13]

Hersh's comments—as usual—ruffled feathers. The conservative *National Review* took the military's point of view, wondering if "Sly Sy" hadn't gotten it all wrong—again. *Slate* magazine looked in detail if "King Sy" had misjudged what happened. "It's important to remember that General Hersh wasn't there," one critic sneered. Hersh shot back: "Terrible things always happen in war, and the responsibility of the press is publish the truth." But he was not holding his breath about getting the truth from George Bush. "This is a dream war for the Pentagon spokesmen," said Hersh. "They can say what they want." Not, of course, if Hersh had his way.[14]

In essence Sy Hersh was becoming the gadfly opposition voice as people turned to his *New Yorker* reporting to get an "alternative view" of the Mideast war—and the approaching invasion of Iraq. "The audience is really tuned to him now, and that's a big thing," said Pulitzer Prizewinner David Halberstam. Remnick knew it also; he watched *New Yorker* circulation figures soar to one million as Hersh's stories came fast and furious. The ability to report more frequently had his adrenaline flowing. "He's just boiling with energy." Remnick said.[15]

Hersh's second big scoop about another war foul-up came in January 2002 when he learned that American troops had inadvertently aided top Taliban and al-Qaeda leaders escape Afghanistan, another embarrassment for Bush. Hersh flew to Delhi, where Indian intelligence sources gave him the story how American troops had surrounded a small hill town but, at the request of Pakistan's president, airlifted Pakistani military out of the country. Included in the five thousand people who left were top al-Qaeda leaders, maybe even bin Laden's family. Rumsfeld declined to speak to Hersh but told a TV interviewer, "I do not believe it happened." Calling Rumsfeld "an honorable man," Hersh said, nonetheless, "If he doesn't know, he doesn't want to know," adding, "Dirt got through the screen." Hersh worried about the press's dilemma. "We really don't know what's happening. We don't have an ability to get in, and they do have an ability just to simply stonewall us."[16] Upset about a Hersh report that the United States was ready to seize his country's nuclear weapons, Pakistani president Pervez Musharraf flew to America to query the president. Hersh "is a liar," Bush told him. The war between Hersh and Bush was in full swing. As one newspaper headlined, Hersh was the "reporter whose scoops give the Bush administration nightmares."[17]

As the wars in Afghanistan and Iran deepened, Hersh pounded away—at an inept prosecution of the man thought to be the twentieth hijacker; at the lack of cooperation between intelligence agencies, months after 9/11; and at the Bush administration's increasingly aggressive assassination efforts. "There are five hundred guys out there you have to kill," a former CIA official told Hersh. "You just have to kill them. And you can't always be sure of the intelligence." And American intelligence, Hersh warned, was indeed often faulty.[18]

Hersh tore apart arguments that weapons of mass destruction justified the invasion of Iraq and argued—with evidence and anonymous sources—that top Bush administration officials avoided facts that did not fit their belief that Saddam was connected to terrorism. The intelligence community had ignored the sacrosanct "stove piping" rule—that only carefully vetted information should go up the chain of command. "It's a very strange world at the top of this government," Hersh told an interviewer. "It's a cocoon. And no bad information [is] invited. I'm talking about in the leadership."[19]

Hersh versus Perle

Over time, however, as Hersh understood more and more about the White House, he concluded that George Bush had ceded key policymaking to a small cabal of neoconservatives who had finally reached the zenith of power—and were determined to use it. These advisers, he wrote, "have produced a skein of intelligence reviews that have helped to shape public opinion and American policy." He included Rumsfeld, deputy secretary of defense Paul Wolfowitz, defense policy aide Douglas Feith, Vice-President Cheney's chief of staff I. Lewis Libby, editor of the *Weekly Standard* William Kristol, and longtime Republican insider Richard Perle. "I'd love to be the historian who writes the story of how this small group . . . made the case and won," said W. Patrick Lang, a former high-ranking intelligence official. He did not know it was a history that Hersh would tackle in the near future about neocons under the sway of University of Chicago philosophy professor Leo Strauss, who, in short, led them to believe that preemptive and unilateral action against perceived enemies was justified. But Max Boot, a former editor for the *Wall Street Journal*, pooh-poohed Hersh's concern, calling him "the journalistic equivalent of Oliver Stone: a hard-left zealot who subscribes to the old counterculture conceit that a deep, dark conspiracy is running the U.S. government." By telling such tall tales, Hersh, he stated, has "twisted the neocons' identities and thinking on U.S. foreign policy into an unrecognizable caricature." Hersh's sources—and presumably Hersh—thought otherwise about this dangerous cabal. "They have convinced themselves that they're on the side of angels, and everybody else in the government is a fool," one source said.[20]

Of course, the fact that so many of Hersh's sources in his attacks on the neocons—and in all his Mideast reporting—were again anonymous led to the old chorus of complaints. How can readers trust these unidentified people, if they even exist? "What can I tell you? The story is either true or not," Hersh replied. "I've been hearing about anonymous sources forever. And the only way you measure my stories in any reasonable way is to say that I've been writing an alternative history of the war. And the question is: Is it basically right? And I think overwhelmingly it's right." And it was. Remnick vigorously defended Hersh, explaining that in covering intelligence "it is usually impossible to get officials to provide revelatory . . . information . . . they risk their jobs and at times prosecution." Remnick added that he knew every unidentified source and that the *New Yorker*'s fact checkers speak with them before publication. Still, "given Hersh's track record," charged one of Hersh's most severe conservative critics, Rael Jean Isaac, "the highest order of skepticism is warranted."[21]

The neocons—real or imaginary—were now forced out of the closet, thanks to Sy Hersh. Could he stop them or take them down? At least one of them was about to find out. When he worked for the *Times*, Hersh bumped into Richard Perle, a Princeton graduate who was a senior staff member on the Senate Armed Services Committee; later he was a source for Hersh's Kissinger book. "Almost no one understands arms control the way Perle did," Hersh explained, adding, "He's smart, tough and competent. He has always been open and honest with me." Perle became a top official in the Defense Department under Ronald Reagan but declined a spot in the Bush administration, opting to become chairman of the Defense Policy Board, an advisory group made up of respected former government officials. The group meets a few times a year to assess defense policy—and is important. "Under Perle's leadership," Hersh wrote in the *New Yorker*, "the board has become increasingly influential." Perle was effective. In fact, some saw him as the architect of the Iraq invasion. "It's an impressive achievement that an outsider can have so much influence," a source told Hersh.[22]

Policy Board members can keep their private jobs but must adhere to regulations on conflicts of interest. "You don't take advantage of your federal position to help yourself financially," a former government attorney said. Which brought Hersh to the "lunch with the chairman." Hersh learned that on January 3, 2003, Perle, a partner in a venture capital company, had a private lunch in the south of France (where he owns a home) with Harb Saleh al-Zuhair, a wealthy Saudi. The lunch was brokered by Adnan Khashoggi, a controversial deal maker who was involved in the Iran contra weapons-for-hostages controversy. Perle, sixty-three, was seeking money for Trireme Partners, a homeland security company. The company, Hersh implied, stood to profit if America went to war against Iraq. Hersh sought out the director of Washington's nonprofit Center for Responsive Politics, who said, "It's not illegal, but ... it's enough to raise questions about the advice he's giving to the Pentagon and why people in business are dealing with him." A fellow Policy Board member, not identified, was more definitive. "He's the chairman! Seems to me this is at the edge of or off the ethical charts. I think it would stink to high heaven." Hersh spoke with Kashoggi at his penthouse apartment overlooking the Mediterranean. He confirmed the lunch and conceded that Perle, with his political connections, was "the hook"—the person who could close a deal. Hersh waited until the end of his 4,100-word piece to make clear his feelings: "in crisscrossing between the public and the private sectors," he wrote, Perle "has put himself in a difficult position. He is credited with being the intellectual force behind a war that ... many suspect, however unfairly, of being driven by American business interests. . . . He has set up a company that may gain from a war."[23]

In several conversations with Hersh, Perle denied he was cutting any deal that would line his pockets or that conflicted with his role as a government adviser. Anyone who saw such a conflict, he warned, was thinking "maliciously."

The article, predictably, caused an immediate flap. Four days later the *New York Times* offered a story on another alleged Perle conflict. A congressman requested an investigation. At a time when he should have been exultant at the American invasion of Iraq, Perle was under fire. He used the *Wall Street Journal* to defend himself, writing, "The incoherence of the piece reflects Mr. Hersh's Houdini-like twists and turns, intended to question my integrity. [It] is a masterpiece—of falsehood and innuendo." And he threatened to sue for defamation (he never did). Hersh had two reactions. "I'm not sure that he will sue me," Hersh said. "But he has every right to. He has every right to call me names." And, of course, he did, commenting on a TV program that "Sy Hersh is the closest thing American journalism has to a terrorist, frankly." The comment has been repeated endlessly. Hersh's other reaction: anger at himself for not digging deeper. "I immediately knew that I had hit something big," Hersh recalled. "I mean, he's calling me a terrorist. Perle is a tough guy, he can take a little of this sort of thing. I thought to myself, whatever you did, you didn't get it all." The *Times* agreed with Hersh, writing in an editorial that Perle would "have to choose between the gain and the office."[24]

On March 28, less than two weeks after Hersh's exposé, Richard Perle—dubbed the "Prince of Darkness"—resigned as chairman of the Policy Board, telling defense secretary Rumsfeld that the controversy will "distract from the urgent challenge in which you are now engaged," even though the charges are "based on errors of fact." Responded Hersh: "The funny thing is, I liked him. He's very smart and informative—a spin master, but, so what?" Eventually a government inquiry cleared Perle of any technical violations, conceding that he "arguably represented" two companies with matters pending before the government while he was also an adviser. But to violate existing rules, the inquiry found, an employee must work at least sixty days a year. Officially Perle had only worked eight days. He was off the hook, and his lawyer insisted he won because, "whether you like or hate his politics . . . it wasn't hard to prove he was an honest guy because he is an honest guy." But he was off the Policy Board, a Hersh victim. "Too bad for Perle," observed the *Nation's* Eric Alterman, that "Rabbi Sy Hersh decided to take a look" at him. Hersh was not done. He now turned his attention to the man running the war in Iraq, Donald Rumsfeld.[25]

CHAPTER 29

Back on Top

"Pictures like That, You Could Die For"

Sy Hersh, sixty-seven years old, and Secretary of Defense Donald Rumsfeld, seventy-two, had been dealing with each other for thirty years. Hersh called him "funny and attractive and witty, seriously good company. You call him, he calls you back. You have a lot of fun. You laugh. He laughs." And that was despite the fact that in 1975 Rumsfeld, President Ford's chief of staff, had gone along with suggestions that the FBI consider breaking into Hersh's house to see if he had copies of stolen secret documents. But no one at the Pentagon cared much about that anymore, Rumsfeld's spokesman said in 2004. "That's not the way people are around here," explained Lawrence Di Rita. "They're much too busy." As was Hersh, who was zeroing in on his old enemy. "He doesn't talk to me any more because I am not on the reservation," Hersh said. "Everything I do, I have to sneak. I have become a professional sneak."[1] And the sneaking was paying off. In the spring of 2004 someone leaked to Hersh a devastating critique of the war in Afghanistan prepared by a retired colonel. He talked, reluctantly, only because he knew Hersh had independently obtained the report, which, Hersh wrote in the *New Yorker,* "describes a wide gap between how Donald Rumsfeld represented the war and what was actually taking place." The Bush administration "has consistently invoked Afghanistan as a success story—an example of the President's determination." But the country is still a haven for thousands of al-Qaeda loyalists; Osama bin Laden and Mullah Omar are still on the loose; Afghan's president has little control outside Kabul; and heroin production is soaring. The victory in Afghanistan was not, in the long run, a victory at all. The situation, Hersh asserted, "is deteriorating rapidly." Quipped Jon Stewart to Hersh about

his gloomy portraits: "It is a pleasure to talk to Sister Mary Sunshine."[2] Much of the gloom was directed at Rumsfeld. And it soon got worse.

Always trawling, Hersh was in Damascus, Syria, in spring 2003 soon after Baghdad fell to U.S. forces. For four days he met with an Iraqi—"a two-star guy from the old regime." They talked about many things, including prisons, and he told Hersh that some of the women in prisons under U.S. control had asked relatives to come kill them because they had been molested. "I didn't know whether it was GIs playing grab ass or what, but it was clear that the women had been shamed," he said. And then Hersh heard about photographs—of other activities.

Hersh was a prolific daily reader: *Washington Post, New York Times, Wall Street Journal, Al-Jazeera, Der Spiegel*, all the London papers. But this information surprised him. Perhaps it should not have. The American press had nibbled at this story for some time. In March 2003, right before the U.S. invasion of Iraq, the *Times*' Carlotta Gall wrote about the homicide of an Afghani prisoner; it was buried on page fourteen. Then, on December 26, 2003, Dana Priest and Barton Gellman of the *Washington Post* revealed how al-Qaeda and Taliban suspects were often severely beaten to make them talk. Some officials bragged about the treatment. Some suspects were whisked out of the country to secret locations to be tortured. Outside of a few human rights organizations, however, the stories did not cause a stir, as everyone fretted about threats to domestic security. Hersh seemed not to have seen these stories. He kept coming back to the photographs. He knew that when My Lai was revealed, the country was in denial—until photographs surfaced, and no one could deny the massacre.[3]

And in 2004 a new digital world had dawned. Many soldiers in the Mideast had laptop computers, mostly to watch movies. But it also enabled them to compile and share photographs. At some point a mother in the Northeast contacted Hersh about her married daughter, who returned from the Mideast severely depressed. Hersh met the mother, who said her daughter had left her husband and was covering her body with tattoos, as if to blot out her past. He helped her get counseling, actually the kind of work his wife, Elizabeth, did in Washington. The woman also told Hersh that when using her daughter's computer she looked in a file labeled "Iraq." She found dozens of shocking photos. "The photographs tell it all," said Hersh, who later described some of them to his international audience:

In one, Private [U.S. soldier Lynndie] England, a cigarette dangling from her mouth, is giving a jaunty thumbs-up sign and pointing at the genitals of a young Iraqi, who is naked except for a sandbag over his head, as he masturbates. Three other hooded and naked Iraqi prisoners are shown, hands reflexively crossed over their genitals. . . . . In another, England stands arm in arm with Specialist Graner; both are grinning and giving the thumbs-up behind a cluster of perhaps seven naked Iraqis, knees bent, piled clumsily on top of each other in a pyramid . . . . Yet another photograph shows a kneeling, naked, unhooded male prisoner . . . posed to make it appear that he is performing oral sex on another male prisoner, who is naked and hooded.

As Hersh explained, "such dehumanization is unacceptable in any culture, but it is especially so in the Arab world," where homosexuality is against Islamic law. "It's all a form of torture," a professor of Mideast studies told Hersh. And now he faced the question, what to do with photographs that were sure to enrage the Muslim world?[4]

"Let me tell you something," Hersh said. "Pictures like that, you could die for." But still, he did not write every story he uncovered. One soldier, for example, called him to talk about a massacre of friendly Iraqis by American soldiers. Hersh said he told the soldier: "Just shut up. You're going to get a bullet in the back. If I had a million years to report this story, I wouldn't do it. When he comes back, that's another story. He's over in Iraq, for Chrissakes—he's in combat." But the torture story was different. "It's nothing like we had in My Lai," he observed. "These kids didn't murder people. But we have convinced the Arab world that we are a bunch of perverts." He knew the consequences of the story: the damage to America's reputation—particularly in the Middle East—would be "every bit as devastating" as My Lai.[5]

Torture at Abu Ghraib

Hersh has long insisted—despite what his critics say—that ideology and political partisanship do not drive his reporting, although often they determine what stories he pursues. On this one, however, it is worth pondering whether his venom for the Bush administration in the spring of 2004, with a presidential election looming, might have swayed his decisions. "Real reporting plays it straight and gets it right, and the reader simply can't trust him to do either," barked one conservative critic. "Hersh is a hard-left ideologue who disdains facts that collide with his dark theories. His purpose is a pre-election mauling of the sitting president."[6]

When I called Hersh in August of 2004 to say I was working on his biography, he told me, unabashedly: "I just don't have the time to sit down for long interviews. Until this sunuvabitch is out of the White House, I just can't do interviews about myself." No pretension there about how he felt. And, in fact, he was unrestrained in speech after speech during the pre-election period. "I think history's going to judge Bush as one of the worst presidents we've had," he declared. This administration, he asserted, "has brought . . . the art of lying not only to the world . . . but lying to the American press, systematic misrepresenting and lying. They brought it to a new art form." In a radio interview, he stated, "They're really a bunch of little mice." To another audience, he added. "It's not the Manson clan—but we really have been taken over, and we have to do something to stop it, and let's hope we can do it electorally."[7]

As the prison pictures unfolded before him, Hersh knew he had his chance to effect the election—and step back on the national stage as he had not done for three decades. But partisanship aside, Hersh was also just reacting in his instinctive way as a journalist: "I could give you some platitude about how it's all about the truth and stuff, but the bottom line is I'm just a reporter. I see a story and I write it." He knew prison torture was awful—and huge. He learned that the CBS News magazine *60 Minutes II* had photos from Abu Ghraib, a prison twenty miles west of Baghdad, infamous because of torture and murder there under Saddam Hussein. "CBS had the pictures and I knew because I'm sort of tuned in," Hersh explained. But the chairman of the Joint Chiefs of Staff had asked Dan Rather to withhold the story, fearing American soldiers might also be tortured. CBS agreed. Hersh then acted. "When they didn't run the story the first week, even before the second week I said, 'The hell with it.' I knew where to get the stuff, so I got it." He called Remnick at 4:00 o'clock on a Saturday morning—which the editor had become used to—to say he had nailed down the story on Abu Ghraib. The abuse, he declared, is "ten times worse than you can possibly imagine." The *New Yorker*, ponderous and slow-moving, with long turnover times, went into overdrive to get Hersh's 4,030-word piece ready.[8]

CBS then learned that Hersh was readying an exposé, and on April 28 Rather ran a short piece with a few of the photos, somewhat censored, and an interview with General Mark Kimmitt in Iraq, who said the photos did not represent how America treated Iraqis. Two days later, on the *New Yorker* website, the first of three Hersh articles on Abu Ghraib appeared, headlined, simply, "Torture at Abu Ghraib." He asked, "How far up does responsibility go?" Two photos accompanied the story—one the now iconic photo of an Iraqi in black, wearing a pointed hood, his hands spread out with electrodes attached to his body, including his covered penis. The other was of a smirking Private Lynndie England with naked detainees. Remnick refused to run more photos, fearing sensationalizing an already sensational story.

And although CBS had beaten Hersh to the story, he had a scoop—a leaked copy of a secret fifty-three-page report of an investigation that Major General Antonio M. Taguba had conducted, which had been turned over to authorities on March 3. Taguba spared no one. He detailed a litany of horrors: pouring phosphoric liquid on naked detainees; beating detainees with a chair; threatening males with rape; sodomizing a detainee with a broom stick, and using military dogs to intimidate prisoners. The report, Hersh wrote, is "an unsparing study of collective wrongdoing and the failure of Army leadership at the highest level." Hersh promptly waded into the key philosophical question at stake: would harsh interrogation of prisoners—even if legal—really produce reliable intelligence? It was a question that hovered over interrogation techniques at Cuba's Guantánamo and is still being argued today. An army criminal investigator with thirty-six years' experience answered the question: "They'll tell you what you want to hear, truth or no truth. You don't get righteous information." It was a position Hersh argued repeatedly over the following weeks. Abu Ghraib, he wrote, "had become another Guantánamo. These detentions have had enormous consequences: for the imprisoned civilian Iraqis, many of whom had nothing to do with the growing insurgency; for the integrity of the Army; and for the United States' reputation in the world."[9] It was "King Sy" versus the government, once again.

Hersh's years at the *Times* made him one of the best in the business at finding new angles and mounting a crusade. A week after his first story appeared he began to put pieces together: the civilians in the White House, who knew of the abuses, worked hard to keep it from military officials. "Knowledge of the nature of the abuses—and especially the politically toxic photographs—had been severely, and unusually, restricted," he wrote. The reason: "They foresaw major diplomatic problems," an unnamed Pentagon official said. No surprise, Hersh wrote, since "secrecy and wishful thinking . . . are defining characteristics of Rumsfeld's Pentagon." No one wants to hear bad news, which, of course, quickly made Taguba a bad guy who eventually left the military because of his damning report. Hersh hinted where he was headed with his reporting. Rumsfeld admitted, "It's going to get still more terrible," conceding, "I failed to recognize how important it was." But it was not enough to satisfy Hersh who wrote: "No amount of apologetic testimony or political spin could mask the fact that, since the attacks of September 11, President Bush and his top aides have seen themselves as engaged in a war against terrorism in which the old rules did not apply." Hersh unearthed memos with Rumsfeld's underlings bemoaning that it took much too long to act on intelligence about terrorists. "We must accept that we may have to take action before every question can be answered," one memo said. And would that include ignoring Geneva Convention rules on the rights of prisoners?[10]

Abu Ghraib events moved quickly. On May 7 and 11 Rumsfeld testified before Congress, saying that international rules had not been violated. But he conceded that "sadistic, blatant, and wanton criminal abuses" occurred. May 19: a low-level soldier was sentenced to a year in prison. May 21: 454 prisoners were released from Abu Ghraib. May 23: Brigadier General Janis L. Karpinski, who was in charge, was suspended. The press pack was in full swing now as headlines all over the world blared the news, and the photos appeared everywhere. The coverage was endless on the Arab networks, as Hersh predicted.

Hersh had one more wallop. He took full aim at Rumsfeld, writing on

May 24 in his opening paragraph, "The roots of the Abu Ghraib prison scandal lie not in the criminal inclinations of a few Army reservists," but in Rumsfeld's decision last year to expand "a highly secret operation" that initiated interrogations of Iraqi prisoners. The decision, Hersh asserted, "embittered the American intelligence community, damaged the effectiveness of elite combat units, and hurt America's prospects in the war on terror." It was, for a magazine story, a surprisingly hard news lead paragraph, the kind he usually put late in his stories. But in this 5,500-word article he was blunt: the abuse at Abu Ghraib stemmed from Rumsfeld's gloves-off approach and his order for secret interrogations. Round up Iraqi men, torture and humiliate them, then put them back on the street—fearing they will be outed with the photos—and make them deliver information on the insurgency that was making the Iraq War so difficult to win. "So here are fundamentally good soldiers ... being told that no rules apply," one former official said. "We've changed the rules ... and created conditions where the ends justify the means." The disgraced Karpinski gave Hersh an interview and admitted, shockingly, even she did not know who was in her prison interrogating detainees. Rumsfeld has "lowered the bar" for the treatment of prisoners, said the top official of Human Rights Watch. The last of what the *Columbia Journalism Review* called "three historic articles" by Hersh made Rumsfeld and the Pentagon furious.[11]

In a news release responding directly to Hersh's story (a rarity), the Pentagon called his allegations "outlandish, conspiratorial, and filled with error and anonymous conjecture," reflecting "the fevered insights of those with little, if any, connection to the activities in the Department of Defense." Moreover, it claimed, "With these false claims, the Magazine and the reporter have made themselves part of the story." Rumsfeld spokesman Lawrence Di Rita defended his boss: "This is the most hysterical piece of journalist malpractice I have ever observed." Hersh is "one of history's great conspiracy theorists." Hersh scoffed: "Ignore all those bombastic words from that guy at the Pentagon, he's paid to do that." As the scandal grew, calls for Rumsfeld to resign mounted, and, privately, he offered to resign; Bush declined his offer. But Sy Hersh was back where he always seemed to be—in the middle of a major public policy fight and in the eye of the storm once again. *Newsweek* magazine summed it up: "Thirty-two years after breaking My Lai, he's still scooping everyone. If there's a journalistic equivalent to Viagra, he's on it." Laughing, Hersh said, "I'm not sure that's as much of a compliment as you might think." But then he turned deadly serious: "We're picking a fight with 1.3 billion people." In Hersh's view, the blame for the torture at Abu Ghraib came from the top in policies that stemmed from the president and Rumsfeld. As Nixon did with My Lai, Hersh insisted top officials would try to pin it all on a few low-level soldiers. And although Hersh acknowledged that there was no specific order from Bush, when the president did learn of the torture, he did "nada." Later reporting by others showed that the Justice Department had written memos that seemingly encouraged the torture of detainees.[12]

"A True American Hero"

Sy Hersh's exposé of the scandal at Abu Ghraib—deeds not as dastardly as My Lai—put him once more in the spotlight. "This is a good time, no doubt about it," he said about the fame and adulation that suddenly surrounded him again. "There were a lot of years when nothing much was happening." Everyone wanted to write about Sy Hersh, "a true American hero," one reporter wrote. Seymour Hersh, another said, "may not be the last angry man of U.S. political journalism, but he's arguably the angriest."[13] Finally, the brutal attacks on his Kennedy book seemed far away. HarperCollins agreed to publish a compilation of his *New Yorker* reporting called *Chain of Command: The Road from 9/11 to Abu Ghraib*. Hersh, the TV and talk-show veteran, knew the drill on how to promote a book. Even though Hersh complained, "I am tired, bone tired. I can't do any more," he plowed into a book tour and gave a lot of speeches. In San Francisco, he did a noontime talk at the Commonwealth Club, taped an interview for local news, spoke with a reporter from the *Chronicle,* and then appeared at an evening fund-raiser for *Mother Jones* magazine. The next day he flew to Santa Barbara for a talk, then to New York to receive a $50,000 LennonOno Peace Prize at the United Nations. The day after he was back to give a keynote address at UC Berkeley.[14]

Hersh knew how to get applause: "1,181 days in the Bush Presidency.

That is the bad news. The good news is tomorrow morning when we wake up there will be one less day." And he was a bit like a politician with a standard stump speech. When you have a family, he said over and over, the one thing you expect is trust. "We don't even have *any* expectation that they're going to have the same trust and integrity in conducting their affairs as we do in our own personal life." Bush, he said, sends "our children in the name of democracy to go kill people and be killed and torture and perhaps be tortured in return." And so, "there's nothing wrong with holding these people to the highest possible standards." What troubled him most: "Is our democracy so fragile that it can be taken over by zealots, ideologues?"[15]

When he returned to Washington—to start reporting again—Hersh found himself more famous than ever. "I can't pick my nose in public anymore, and that's a downer," he mused. But he did not mind so much. He left his office one day, tailed by a reporter. "You're out saving the world," one man yelled to him. A woman on the street ran up and kissed him. "I don't want to distract you from the great work you're doing," another said. "Oh fuck you. Goodbye," Hersh replied, laughing. He was clearly enjoying it, showing a reporter a photo of a child at an antiwar demonstration in Belgium holding a placard reading: "Protect Seymour Hersh, the last independent journalist in the usa."[16]

Of course, in typical Hersh fashion not everyone was so happy with him—or his new book. "This once-distinguished journalist is working awfully hard to become the Kitty Kelley of Abu Ghraib," charged Andrew McCarthy in the conservative *National Review*. Added an Iranian journalist, "Hersh uses the method of medieval scholastics: first choose your belief, then seek proofs." The new book, opined another reviewer, "is less than satisfactory, a mishmash and excessive repetition of facts and arguments." The Hersh-as-bad-writer refrain was sounded again: "Hersh's skills at dogged, balanced reporting exceed his literary ones. The book undeniably drags." And his use of anonymous sources once again irked some who called it "a book without a spine."[17]

The critics were correct, at least about the structure of *Chain of Command*. It began with Abu Ghraib, and then doubled back to his post-9/11 reporting. Most of it was simply his *New Yorker* reporting (he said forty thousand words were old, thirty thousand new) republished. Nonetheless, more critics than not liked it very much. The *New York Times* said it "is the best book we are likely to have" that explains how the United States went from leading a cartel against terrorism to the abuse at Abu Ghraib. It is, wrote another, the "brave work of a dedicated journalist doing his duty for the American public." But in the end *Chain of Command* was largely retreaded material, albeit from Hersh's spectacular *New Yorker* reportage. A reader could find some of the same material in other books, including one by Bob Woodward.[18]

Ironically, the publication of *Chain of Command* coincided with Woodward's twelfth book, *Plan of Attack*, his second on the Mideast War. The two longtime stars were both on the best-seller list, although Woodward had been there—and remained—for many weeks. Even with his rediscovered top-of-the-heap status, Hersh could not shed Woodward, although their books say much about their styles, thirty-five years after their great Watergate rivalry. Woodward was as smooth as ever, novelistic in telling the White House's story of how and why it fought a war in Iraq. But it was a top-down version of events. President Bush, who called him "Woody," gave three and a half hours of interviews and told White House insiders (who would not give Sy Hersh the time of day) to talk to Woodward. Said Hersh: "I disagree with his point of view. He starts at the top and goes down." It was a criticism he made in conversation with Woodward. "I don't go to the top because I think it's sorta useless. I see people at six o'clock in the morning somewhere, unofficially."[19]

New Yorker writer Mark Danner, author of a book on Abu Ghraib, explains that while Woodward says his work gives a deeper version of events, it is in the end still an official version. Hersh, Danner says, "much more frequently gives you a version that the government does not want public—which is to say, a version that contradicts the official story of what went on." This was not to say, Hersh points out, that Woodward's reporting was not important; his first Mideast book, *Bush at War*, told Americans much about Bush's thinking. But the sixty-one-year-old Woodward was the consummate Washington insider, "smooth, well-mannered, seemingly on a first-name basis with every power broker in the capital," pointed out David Shaw, the respected *LA Times* media critic. Hersh, on the other hand "screams, bellows, snarls, curses." It is unthinkable that a President would invite him into the Oval Office.[20]

Former CIA agent Robert Baer, an occasional Hersh source, observed that Sy "is an unguided missile, sort of a lone-wolf guy. He can get almost anywhere in Washington without having to kiss the ass of the White House." Bill Kovach, who was Hersh's *New York Times* editor in Washington, adds: "Bob has become the diarist of sitting administrations, and Sy has continued to be the muckraker. Sy continues his outrage." Mr. Inside, Mr. Outside, but nonetheless the two most respected investigative reporters in America, four decades and counting.[21]

Sy Hersh insists he is not jealous of Woodward's fame or wealth. "It's not like I'm not celebrated," Hersh says. "There's no secret about it. I've been rewarded for it. There's nothing heroic about it. I've had a great life. I don't have to go to office meetings. I can be the most difficult (expletive) in the world, and I can get away with it. I can be the prince of all time and just do what I want. I can be so prissy. . . . and everybody cuts me slack. 'Oh, he's so important. So busy.'"

Of course, Hersh *is* important and feared and despised—all at the same time. Woodward stayed on the best-seller list as the awards for Hersh's work poured in. Three of his 2003 *New Yorker* articles won a National Magazine Award for Public Interest. In 2004 his Abu Ghraib articles earned him his fifth George Polk Award, and in 2005 he won another National Magazine Award, an Overseas Press Club award, and the National Press Foundation's Distinguished Contributions to Journalism award. "I never let this stuff go to my head," he insists. "There's always tomorrow." And tomorrow, probably at 6:00 a.m., he would be on the phone to another source for another story. "Sy is America's safety valve," says David Obst, his old friend who helped him market the My Lai story. "People in authority and power . . . they know they can get a fair hearing for their beef if they bring it to Sy." And other people in power know that Sy Hersh, the scoop artist, is looking to nail them.[22]

Epilogue

A Muckraker's Unfinished Business

Sy Hersh was buried in research and writing. Hersh's housekeeper-babysitter was at his Washington DC home when the phone rang. Hersh's number had always been listed publicly. In a thick accent the anonymous caller told the housekeeper exactly where her three children were at that moment. And then he told her where Hersh's three children were. Sy and Elizabeth Hersh took the threat seriously. "For the next six months," he said, "I started my wife's car every morning." He told the story to a conference of investigative reporters in answer to a question about his personal safety. It is one reason Hersh has always treated his family life as private. But threats, veiled and otherwise, have never stopped him from pursuing one very tough story after another—scores over the past forty years on tough national security issues. After his exposé on conditions at the Abu Ghraib prison in Iraq, some of the old anger against Hersh, leftovers from revelations of domestic spying to attacks on Henry Kissinger, flared anew. "I find Mr. Hersh a despicable character," wrote one reader of the *New Yorker.* "If I could get away with it I would render him useless with my bare hands." Hersh was asked if the Abu Ghraib criticism rattled him. He snorted; it did not compare to My Lai in 1969, he said. Soldiers, after too many beers, would call him at 3:00 a.m. and tell him what they were going to do to his private parts. After one call, he said, "I shook for half the night. I was scared to death."[1] He had been there before.

Seymour Hersh says he is not a courageous journalist. He calls himself a "smart ass" reporter, which he is. And he mocks the question of the danger risked by American journalists, saying that he and others win awards for their daring while journalists in foreign countries get killed for the kind of courage they exhibit. The pressures aside—from lawsuits to irate presidents and secretaries of state to personal threats—Hersh has long thrown himself into stories that others avoid. "He is a bomb thrower, the one who runs into the machine guns first," said author Bob Woodward, his longtime friend and sometimes rival. "We don't have enough Sy Hershes out there charging out of the safety and comfort of the trenches to run at the sources of power and secrecy. We need more of that."[2]

So what kind of journalist has Seymour Hersh been in a career spanning four decades, from wars in Vietnam to wars in Iraq and Afghanistan, with a trove of scandals, revelations, and spy stories in between?

For one, Hersh has never followed the pack. Scholar Robert Entman, assessing press coverage after 9/11, notes that "even when government is promoting 'war' against terrorism, media are not entirely passive receptacles for government propaganda," which is, after all, their job. Among the reporters who deviated, he cited Seymour Hersh. Indeed, Hersh was among a tiny media elite after 9/11 that did not genuflect to patriotism and the flag at the expense of truth; in 1969 he was the lone reporter who aggressively pursued a story of American atrocities in war. Before Hersh, no one had even questioned such things. This is not to say that he is not patriotic. "There's a kind of fearlessness, a love of justice and a strain of American Puritanism there," explained the Pulitzer Prize–winning author and journalist David Halberstam in interpreting Hersh. "He takes songs like America the Beautiful seriously."[3]

Hersh's relentless pursuit of stories is legendary, the stuff of journalistic myth and metaphor. Author Thomas Powers, capturing the essential Hersh, said he had a "professional style notoriously similar to the single-minded ferocity of the wolverine . . . known among fur trappers of yesteryear for its ability to tear its way through the log wall of a cabin for a strip of bacon." In the same vein, wrote *Time* magazine's defense correspondent Mark Thompson, "A lot of Washington journalists act like hedge-trimmers or pruning shears. Sy is a noisy, smoke-spewing chain saw—and a relentless stump-grinder, to boot."[4] And then there is David Wise, an author who has an office next to Hersh's. "No one can dig up a story like Sy. He's fiercely independent. And once he's on a story, he's like a bulldog."

David Remnick, the *New Yorker* editor, watched the bulldog at work for a decade starting in 2004 and engaged in the shouting matches, hang-ups, arguments, and threats to resign that came with the turf for anyone who had edited Sy Hersh. He observed: "Is he volcanic? Yes. Is he lovely? Yes." He also knew that Hersh had helped transform the lumbering *New Yorker* into a publication that could break big national defense stories and influence the course of wars. "We weren't built for this," he observed after Hersh began to throttle the Bush administration in his Iraq war stories. "Imagine you're in a car that starts to shake at 80 miles an hour. Then you look at the speedometer and you see you're doing 120. Well, Sy's doing 120." Ben Bradlee, the legendary editor of the *Washington Post*, who watched Hersh work in the Watergate era, observed that part of the reason for his success is how hard he works. "You have to get up very early in the morning to beat Sy Hersh," he said.[5]

Aw shucks, says Hersh, self-deprecatingly. Don't over-intellectualize it all. "I just follow stories." Describing how he works, Hersh once com-mented: "Boy get story. Boy write story. Boy fight editors. Boy wrestle. Boy throw typewriter. Boy scream. Boy have tantrum." And, of course, that might explain why just about everywhere he has ever worked he has worn out his welcome or left in a snit. The City News Bureau in Chicago would not take him back when he returned from the army. He left the AP fighting with the top brass over the editing of his stories. He resigned as press secretary to Eugene McCarthy because he disagreed with the senator over policy. Publisher Arthur Ochs Sulzberger and editor Abe Rosenthal were ultimately relieved when he left the *New York Times* in 1979, despite all the plaudits he brought for the newspaper. "He is unique, and driven, and his own worst enemy," observed Bill Arkin, who worked with Hersh in the 1990s. He called Hersh a friend, but one of the most "annoying" people you will meet. After working with Hersh, he said, "I needed a valium or a shower."[6] It was a refrain repeated many times by people who have worked with Hersh—he is driven, abrasive, and obsessive.

It would have been easy for Hersh, at age sixty-seven, to slow down after Abu Ghraib. But he wrote twenty-two more articles afterward for the *New Yorker* and even kept up a regular blog. Some of his work has caused great controversy, of course. He insisted in 2005—in print and in speeches—that the Bush administration was going to invade Iran, and he repeated this allegation five more times in articles. Each time he went on the talk-show circuit to explain what sources in the military were telling him. Commented one critic: "If there is one thing that Hersh—known to every aspiring journalist as the greatest investigative reporter of his generation—has been consistent on, it's his uncanny ability to be utterly wrong."[7]

Nonetheless, to the legion of Hersh's critics and enemies, errors of fact and judgment are a hallmark of his work. One wrote an entire article on "King Sy's mistakes" while another wrote in great detail about "the deceits of Seymour Hersh." One critic observed, not without merit, that Hersh often makes outlandish claims in public speeches, but he will not write those same things.[8] General Barry McCaffrey, who Hersh so excoriated in 2000 and who went on to become an NBC commentator, told me that in his "long history" dealing with the media he found reporters were "extremely keen on getting the facts right. Mr. Hersh was an exception." What should be noted, however, is that Hersh's harshest critics have usually been his targets or have written for conservative journals, often repeating the same anecdotes as if working from the "we-hate-Sy-Hersh playbook." "Has he made mistakes?" asked Steve Weinberg, a long-time observer and admirer of Hersh. "Any journalist who does that many high-stakes stories and has to depend on so many sources, whose truthfulness cannot always be determined, may be misled some of the time." Added author John Weisman: "Sy's a long ball hitter. He's gonna strike out a lot."[9]

Added Arkin, "He can get every fact wrong but get the story correct." And he has been right on so many big stories—from My Lai to illegal Cambodia bombing to the CIA's domestic surveillance to the bumbling early efforts in the Mideast war. Of course, he may have been very wrong on Iran, but it is very possible that his reporting—based on inside sources—actually prevented George Bush from pursuing another Mideast invasion. In fact, Hersh says that one of the reasons he has not contemplated retirement is that sources inside the U.S. government need him. "I am a mouthpiece for people in the inside," he says. "You get a sense I am vehicle for a certain form of dissent." And the dissenters inside government who go to

Hersh have made him the enemy of six presidents, from Lyndon Johnson to Barack Obama. In 2009 he insisted that Iran did not have a nuclear weapons capability, and that Israel and the United States should stand down. It was Hersh's first public encounter with Obama. "The Obama White House can't abide me," he says. "Within a month, they were going behind my back to my editor: 'What's your man Hersh doing?'"[10]

Hersh was doing what he has been doing for forty years—raking the muck, looking for "scoops," taking down big men. Sy Hersh's career in journalism has left a long line of victims—from General John Lavelle to former Chilean ambassador Ed Korry to Henry Kissinger to Manuel Noriega, to mention just a few. Hersh is a big-game hunter. And each time he shoots, his critics howl that he shot the wrong man. Dick Cheney is next, by the way. As this book goes to print, Hersh was writing, rewriting, and still finding new material on the former vice president, with whom he has tangled since 1975. "The best is yet to come," Hersh told me in one email. "It is just amazing how many secrets the government can keep," he said in another email about a book that he claims will be, in essence, "the covert history of our times." That after four decades of reporting Hersh could still be amazed—and indignant—explains why he is still reporting. When the book comes out, it will no doubt make headlines. And the pundits and the bloggers will bring out the old labels: Sly Sy, King Sy, Rabbi Sy, Fucking Sy, Terrorist Sy, Spooky Sy. There is a grain of truth to each label.[11]

Pulitzer Prize–winning *New York Times* columnist William Safire once called Hersh the American Javert, the fanatic police inspector from Victor Hugo's novel *Les Miserables* who relentlessly pursues his opponents. Indeed, Hersh is the great American detective, who never lets up on what he perceives as the evils of modern government. Some consider Hersh—and Javert—misguided, inflexible, and cruel. I think not. This kid from Chicago who used to bring laundry from his father's dry cleaners to houses of prostitution in Chicago has sat with world leaders who have invited him into their offices. And he talks to them on a par with a secretary of state, a representative of the American people. His countless sources in the middle of the American government tell him of the abuses or fumbles by those at the top. And then he comes back to his scrubby office in Washington and tells the world how things really are, not how the White House would like us to believe they are. He tears down all the institutions that he wishes could be trusted but cannot. "He is an iconoclast about everything and everyone, including himself," says Woodward. "I do think I wear the white hat," admits Hersh. "I think I'm fighting the good fight as a journalist and trying to do what I can, and I feel virtuous." Of course, not everyone will agree. Animosity from those who think he represents a 1960s left-wing culture goes back forty years.[12]

What has angered him most over those forty years, as he has leapt from one scandal to another, is the lack of morality he has found in decision making. Yes, he likes to make money. Yes, he can be threatening to targets as he researches. Yes, he uses way too many anonymous sources. And, yes, he loves the spotlight. But anger is what fuels Hersh. He is as, one author suggests, "a man on fire." "The word morality or immorality is never part of the debate," he complains. Too often, "It's not even on the pages." Hersh is unabashed in describing what he thinks is the job of the reporter, a description that, if you follow the arc of career in this book, mirrors his work. "I've been at it for 40 years," he says, "but I still consider myself a newspaper man. That's my soul. It's such an important business. You have to hold the people at the top to the highest possible standards. Those people who have the right to send our sons and our daughters to die in the name of democracy. You have to say to them . . . that the same things that are so valuable in our personal lives and our family lives—we don't want to lie, we want trust in that relationship. It's this business that gives us a chance, the average person, anybody—gives us a chance to hold the highest people to the highest standards, to put your finger in their eye. It's a great way to spend your life."[13]

Selected Works of Seymour Hersh

A complete bibliography of Seymour Hersh's work would take dozens of pages. He wrote hundreds of articles for the Associated Press alone from 1963 to 1967; then, from 1972 to 1979, hundreds more for the *New York Times*. From 1999 to the present he has written dozens of articles for the *New Yorker*. The bibliography that follows represents a small sliver of his most important articles and ends, in essence, where this book ends, soon after Abu Ghraib in 2005. A complete bibliography through 2011 can be found at http://faculty.newpaltz .edu/robmiraldi/index.php/scoop-artist-bibliography.

1967

"Just a Drop Can Kill," *New Republic*, May 6, 11–15.
"But Don't Tell Anyone I Told You," *New Republic*, December 9, 13–14.
"Gas and Germ Warfare," *New Republic*, July 1, 12–14.

1968

"The Secret Arsenal," *New York Times*, August 25, SM26.
Chemical and Biological Warfare: America's Hidden Arsenal (Indianapolis: Bobbs-Merrill).

1969

"Dare We Develop Biological Weapons?" *New York Times*, September 28, SM28.
"Germ Warfare: For Alma Mater, God and Country," *Ramparts*, December, 20–28.
"The Story Everyone Ignored," *Columbia Journalism Review*, Winter 1969– 1970, 55–58.
"Officer Charged with Murdering 109 in Viet," *Chicago Sun Times*, November 13, 1, 19.
"GI's Story of Pinkville: 'Point-Blank Murder,'" *Sun Times*, November 20, 1, 4.

"Hoosier's Story 'I Killed Dozens in Pinkville,'" *Sun Times,* November 25, 1, 6.
"'Like Wild Animals' prior to Pinkville: Story of GI in Unit," *Sun Times,* December 2, 57.
"Germs and Gas as Weapons," *New Republic,* June 7, 13–16.
"On Uncovering the Great Nerve Gas Coverup," *Ramparts,* June, 12–18.

1970

"How I Broke the My Lai Story," *Saturday Review,* July 11, 46–49.
My Lai 4: A Report on the Massacre and Its Aftermath (New York, Random House).

1971

"The Reprimand," *New Yorker,* October 9, 101–2.

1972

(Unless otherwise noted, all articles from 1972 to 1981 are from *New York Times.*)
"Coverup," *New Yorker,* January 22, 29, 34–40, 40–48.
Cover-up: The Army's Secret Investigation of the Massacre at My Lai 4 (New York: Vintage Books).
"General Bombed in North before President's Order," June 11, 1.
"General Testified He Made 20 Raids without Orders," June 13, 1.
"Airman Says Raid Reports Were Falsified on Orders," June 14, 3.
"Sargeant Says 200 Men Helped Falsify Bomb Data," September 7, 1972, 1.
"Ex-Airmen Tell of 20 Planned Raids a Month in '70–71," June 16, 3.
"You Might Call It 'Protective Aggression,'" June 18, E1.
"Somebody Higher Up Must Have Known,'" September 17, E1.
"How We Ran the Secret Air War in Laos," October 29, SM18.
"Decline and Near Fall of the U.S. Army," *Saturday Review,* November 18, 58–65.

1973

"4 Watergate Defendants Reported Still Being Paid," January 14, 1.
"Pressures to Plead Guilty Alleged in Watergate Case," January 15, 1.
Hersh, "McCord Reported Linking Payoffs," April 9, 1.
"Watergate Jury Believed Seeking a Haldeman Link," April 22, 1.
"CIA Memos Show Political Fears over Watergate," June 4, 1.
"New Dean Charge on Nixon Awaited," June 24, 1.
"Colson Is Accused of Improper Use of His Influence," July 1, 1.

"Cambodian Raids Reported Hidden before '70 Foray," July 15, 1.
"U.S. Confirms Pre-1970 Raids," July 17, 1.
"Secret Raids on Cambodia before '70 Totaled 3,500," July 18, 1.
"Falsifying Military Records . . . ," July 22, 153.
"Cambodian War: Cover-up Keeps On Unraveling," July 29, E2.
"Secret Air Raids Extended to Laos, Senators Believe," July 29, 1.

1974

"Spying in the White House Said to Have Begun in '70," February 3, 1.
"President Warned Justice Department against Inquiry on His Watergate Role" May 2, 1.
"Senate to Query Justice Officials on Cover-up Case," May 9, 1.
"Nixon Use of Ethnic Epithets Is Reported," May 12, 1.
"Huge CIA Operation Reported in U.S. against Antiwar Forces, Other Dissidents in Nixon Years," December 22, 1.

1975

"Colby Said to Confirm CIA Role in U.S.," January 1, 37.
"CIA Admits Domestic Acts, Denies 'Massive' Illegality," January 16, 1.
"CIA Salvage Ship Brought Up Part of Soviet Sub Lost in 1968, Failed to Raise Atom Missiles," March 19, 1.
"Submarines of U.S. Stage Spy Missions inside Soviet Waters," May 25, 1.
"Report on CIA Is Praised, but Recommendations Are Called Weak," June 12, 23.
"Great Power and Secrecy: A Formula for Abuse," June 15, E1.
"Kissinger and CIA Said to Conflict in Testimony on Chile Plot," November 21, 53.

1976

"The Contrasting Lives of Sidney R. Korshak," June 27, 1.
"Korshak's Power Rooted in Ties to Labor Leaders," June 28, 53.
"Major Corporations Eager to Seek Korshak's Advice," June 29, 63.
"Korshak Again the Target of a Federal Investigation," June 30, 77.

1977

"SEC Presses Wide Investigation of Gulf and Western Conglomerate," July 24, 1.
"Gulf and Western's Relationship with Banks Is Issue in SEC Study," July 25, 45.
"Gulf and Western Tax Practices Coming under Wide Examination," July 26, 61.

1978

"The Angleton Story," June 25, SM13-15.

1980

"The Iran Operation: Hard Questions That Need Answers Now," May 1, A31.

1981

"New Evidence Backs Ex-Envoy on His Role in Chile," February 9, A1.
"The Qaddafi Connection," June 14, SM32-34.
"Exposing the Libyan," June 21, SM8.

1982

"Kissinger and Nixon in the White House," *Atlantic*, May, 35-53.
"The Price of Power," *Atlantic*, December, 31-48.

1983

The Price of Power: Kissinger in the Nixon White House (New York: Summit Books).
"The Pardon," *Atlantic*, August, 55-62.

1985

"Pakistani in U.S. Sought to Ship A-Bomb Trigger," *New York Times*, February 25, 1985, 1.

1986

"Panama Strongman Said to Trade in Drugs," *New York Times*, June 12, 1986, 1.
"007's Last Minutes," *New York Times*, August 31, E15.
"The Target Is Destroyed," *Atlantic*, September, 46-53.
The Target Is Destroyed: What Really Happened to Flight 007 and What America Knew about It (New York: Random House).

1987

"Target Qaddafi," *New York Times*, February 22, 1987, SM16.
"Who's in Charge Here?," *New York Times*, November 22, 1987, SM34.

1990

"The Iran Contra Committees: Did They Protect Reagan?," *New York Times*, April 29, 46-47.
"Our Man in Panama: The Creation of a Thug," *Life*, March, 81-85.

1991

The Samson Option: Israel's Nuclear Arsenal and American Foreign Policy (New York: Random House).

1992

(Unless otherwise noted, all articles below are from the *New Yorker*.)
"Nixon's Last Cover-up: The Tapes He Wants the Archives to Suppress," December 14, 76.

1993

"The Spoils of the Gulf War," September 6, 70.

1994

"Spy vs. Spy: The Central Intelligence Agency Needs More Than an Overhaul," August 4, 4.

1997

The Dark Side of Camelot (Boston: Little, Brown).

1998

Against All Enemies: Gulf War Syndrome, the War between America's Ailing Veterans and Their Government (New York: Ballantine).

1999

"The Traitor: The Case against Jonathan Pollard," January 18, 26.
"The Intelligence Gap: How the Digital Age Left Our Spies out in the Cold," December 6, 58.

2000

"Overwhelming Force: What Happened in the Final Days of the Gulf War?," May 22, 48.

2001

"What Went Wrong: The CIA and the Failure of American Intelligence," October 8, 34.
"King's Ransom," October 22, 35.
"Escape and Evasion," November 1, 50.
"The Iraq Hawks," December 24, 58.

2002

"The Getaway," January 28, 36.
"The Debate Within," March 11, 34.
"Missed Messages," June 3, 40.
"The Twentieth Man," September 30, 56.
"Manhunt," December 23, 66.

2003

"The Cold Test," January 27, 42.
"Lunch with the Chairman," 6.
"Who Lied to Whom?" March 31, 41.
"Offense and Defense," *April* 7, 43.
"Selective intelligence," May 12, 44.
"The Stovepipe," October 27, 77.

2004

"Torture at Abu Ghraib," May 10, 42.
"Chain of Command," May 17, 38.
"The Gray Zone," May 24, 38.
Chain of Command: From 9/11 to Abu Ghraib (New York: HarperCollins*)*.

2005

"The Coming Wars," January 24, 40.
"The Iran Plans," April 17, 30.
"Last Stand," July 10, 42.

Seymour Hersh Timeline

1937   Born April 8, 1937, in Chicago to Isador and Dorothy.

1954   Graduates Hyde Park High School.

1958   Receives a degree in history from the University of Chicago.

1959   Begins University of Chicago Law School but flunks out.

1959–60   Works for the City News Bureau in Chicago.

1960   Serves in the U.S. Army in Kansas.

1961   Publishes a weekly newspaper in Evergreen, Illinois, a Chicago suburb.

1962–63   UPI correspondent in Pierre, South Dakota, the state capital.

1964   In May he marries Elizabeth Sarah Klein; they will have three children—Matthew, Melissa, Joshua.

1964–65   Works as general assignment reporter for the Associated Press in Chicago.

1965–67   Works for the AP in Washington DC and becomes part of its first investigative team.

1968   Working as a freelance reporter, he writes about chemical and biological weapons; his first book on this topic leads the Nixon administration to ban biological weapons.

1968–69   Works as press secretary for Eugene McCarthy's fabled presidential campaign.

1969   Uncovers and reports the My Lai massacre story, leading to an international scandal.

1970   My Lai story earns him the Pulitzer Prize for international reporting.

1972   Hired as an investigative reporter in the Washington bureau of the *New York Times*.

1973   Begins to cover the Watergate story, allowing the *Times* to catch and surpass rival *Washington Post*.

1973	Uncovers the Nixon administration's illegal bombing of Cambodia.
1974	His December story on the illegal domestic spying of the CIA leads to sweeping reforms.
1975	His *Times* stories on American involvement in the overthrow of Chile's president leads to various investigations and more reforms.
1976–77	Works in the *Times* New York offices while his wife goes to medical school in New York; writes long series of articles on a mob lawyer compared to *The Godfather* and stories about a large American corporation that causes a furor.
1979	Leaves the *Times* to begin work on a book on Henry Kissinger.
1983	*The Price of Power: Kissinger in the Nixon White House* is published, causes great controversy and wins the National Book Critics Award.
1984	Works on and narrates documentary films.
1986	His articles in the *Times* and *Life* magazine lead the U.S. to invade Panama, apprehend the dictator, Manuel Noriega, and bring him to the U.S. for trial.
1991	His book *The Sampson Option*, on Israeli nuclear weapons, causes great controversy and leads to a libel lawsuit from publisher Robert Maxwell, who soon after dies in a mysterious drowning accident.
1993	Becomes a regular correspondent for the *New Yorker* magazine.
1997	Publishes *The Dark Side of Camelot* about John Kennedy's presidency; it is viciously attacked for its prying look into Kennedy's sex life, perhaps the nadir of his career.
2001	His articles for the *New Yorker* after the 9/11 attacks bring great critical acclaim as he provides exposés on war foul-ups and intelligence problems and offers an alternative view of the wars in Afghanistan and Iraq.
2002–3	His steady stream of *New Yorker* articles reestablishes him as one of America's premier investigative reporters, but President Bush labels him a "liar," and another critic calls him "the terrorist of American journalism."
2004	Hersh exposes the torture and abuses at Abu Ghraib prison in Iraq; his three *New Yorker* articles win him numerous awards and great celebrity.
2004	Publishes his eighth book, *Chain of Command: From 9/11 to Abu Ghraib.*

Notes

Prologue

1. Seymour M. Hersh, *The Price of Power: Kissinger in the Nixon White House* (New York: Summit Books, 1983).

2. "Author Contends Deceit Is Common in Foreign Policy," *Poughkeepsie Journal*, October 18, 1983, 1. "Hersh Slams U.S. Secrecy, Enthralls Crowd," *Kingston Freeman*, October 18, 1983, 1. See www.alanchartock.com.

3. Bob Thompson, "The Hersh Alternative," *Washington Post*, January 28, 2001, w9.

4. I exchanged emails with Hersh and his brother and spoke with his sister and brother on the telephone.

5. Seymour M. Hersh, telephone interview by author, July 12, 2010. Thompson, "Hersh Alternative."

6. David Jackson, "The Muckraker," *Chicago Tribune*, June 25, 2004, 1. Deborah Hastings, "Journalist Hersh Shuns Fame for Stories," Associated Press online," May 21, 2004. Scott Sherman, "The Avenger," *Columbia Journalism Review*, July/August 2003. Joe Eszterhas, "The Reporter Who Broke the My Lai Massacre, the Secret Bombing of Cambodia and the CIA Domestic Spying Stories" (part 1), *Rolling Stone*, April 10, and "The Toughest Reporter in America" (part 2), *Rolling Stone*, April 24, 1975.

7. Leonard Downie, *The New Muckrakers* (New York: Signet, 1976). Marianne Szegedy-Maszak, "The Many Secrets of Sy Hersh," *Esquire*, November 1991, 142–47. Robert Sam Anson, "Secrets and Lies," *Vanity Fair*, November 1997.

8. Wajahat Ali, "Going 15 Rounds with Seymour Hersh," *Counterpunch*, January 15, 2008, http://www.counterpunch.org/2008/01/15/going-15-rounds-with-seymour-hersh/.

9. Joe Nocera, "The Biographer's Dilemma," *New York Times*, October 25, 2011, A31.

10. Mehdi Hasan, "The Obama White House Can't Abide Me," *New Statesman*, November 26, 2009.

1. *The Story No One Wanted*

1. Geoffrey Cowan, telephone interview by author, August 8, 2007. Cowan was dean of the University of Southern California's Annenberg School for Communication from 1996 to 2007 and director of the "Voice of America" in the Clinton administration.

2. Cowan, interview. Seymour M. Hersh, *Chemical and Biological Warfare: America's Hidden Arsenal* (Indianapolis: Bobbs-Merrill, 1968). "Miscue on the Massacre," *Time*, December 5, 1969, http://www.time.com/time/magazine/article/0,9171,901621,00 .html.

3. Seymour M. Hersh, interview, *San Francisco Chronicle*, September 7, 1989, A7.

4. Cowan has never revealed his source. He was miffed that Hersh later identified him as his source. Cowan, interview. Initially Hersh simply called Cowan "a young man." Seymour M. Hersh, "How I Broke the My Lai Story," *Saturday Review*, July 11, 1970, 46. He later called Cowan "a source with Pentagon connections." Hersh, "The Story Everyone Ignored," *Columbia Journalism Review* 8, no. 4 (Winter 1969–70): 55. But in an interview with Joe Eszterhas in *Rolling Stone* magazine, he referred to "one of the Cowan brothers, Geoff Cowan." Eszterhas, "Reporter Who Broke," 52. Hersh, radio interview by Steve Bookshester, "How the My Lai Story Broke," 1969, Pacifica Tape Library, Berkeley Library.

5. David Obst, *Too Good to Be Forgotten: Changing America in the '60s and '70s* (New York: John Wiley, 1998), 136. John Schultz, *Motion Will Be Denied; A New Report on the Chicago Conspiracy Trial* (New York: Morrow, 1972). Jason Epstein, *The Great Conspiracy Trial: An Essay on Law, Liberty, and the Constitution* (New York: Random House, 1970). Elliot Landy, *Woodstock Vision: The Spirit of a Generation* (New York: Continuum, 1994). Rob Kirkpatrick, *1969: The Year Everything Changed* (New York: Skyhorse, 2009).

6. Walter LaFeber, *The Deadly Bet: LBJ, Vietnam, and the 1968 Election* (Lanham MD: Rowman & Littlefield, 2005). Jeffrey P. Kimball, *Nixon's Vietnam War* (Lawrence: University Press of Kansas, 1998). A. J. Langguth, *Our Vietnam: The War, 1954–1975* (New York: Simon & Schuster, 2000). George C. Herring, *America's Longest War: The United States and Vietnam, 1950–1975* (New York: McGraw-Hill, 1996). Rich Perlstein, *Nixonland: The Rise of a President and the Fracturing of America* (New York: Scribner, 2008).

7. Eszterhas, "Reporter Who Broke," 83.

8. Associated Press, "Army Accuses Lieutenant in Vietnam Deaths in 1968," *New York Times*, September 7, 1969. Also, Hersh, "How I Broke the Story," 46. Winant Sidle, "Massacre at My Lai," in *Crisis Response: Inside Stories on Managing Image under Siege*, ed. Jack Gottschalk (Detroit: Gale Research, 1993), 334–35.

9. Hersh, "How I Broke the Story," 46. Eszterhas, "Reporter Who Broke," 74. Morton Mintz, "Financing Our Best Work," *IRE Journal: Investigative Reporters and*

Editors 21, no. 2 (March/April 1998). John Hyde, "When a Few Dollars Make a Big Difference," *Nieman Reports*, Spring 2008, 32.

10. Thompson, "Hersh Alternative,"w9.

11. Hersh, "How I Broke the Story," 46. On Latimer, see, "George Latimer," The My Lai Courts-Martial, 1970, http://www.law.umkc.edu/faculty/projects/ftrials/mylai/myl_blati.htm; and "George S. Latimer Is Dead," *New York Times*, May 5, 1990. Wayne Greenshaw, *The Making of a Hero: The Story of Lt. William Calley Jr.* (Louisville KY: Touchstone, 1971), 175–76. Eszterhas, "Reporter Who Broke," 74.

12. Downie, *New Muckrakers,* 82. Hersh, "How I Broke the Story," 47. Eszterhas, "Reporter Who Broke," 74, 77. I am using Hersh's version of how he chased down the story. I believe it is reliable. He repeats the story in three magazine articles and then partly in his book about the incident (*My Lai 4: A Report on the Massacre and Its Aftermath* [New York: Random House, 1970]), and finally again in a radio interview. All versions are the same. Hersh's interpretations of events throughout his reporting career are often disputed, but his version of the facts is rarely challenged.

13. Hersh, "How I Broke the Story," 47–48. Hersh refers to Lewellen in *My Lai 4,* 120. Eszterhas, "Reporter Who Broke," 78.

14. Joseph Goldstein, Burke Marshall, and Jack Schwartz, eds., *The My Lai Massacre and Its Cover-Up: Beyond the Reach of Law? The Peers Commission Report* (New York: Free Press, 1976), vol. 4, exhibit M-58, 245.

15. Hersh, "How I Broke the Story," 48–49. Eszterhas, "Reporter Who Broke," 78, 80. On Calley, Arthur Everett, Kathryn Johnson, and Harry F. Rosenthal, *Calley: The Full, Compelling Story of a Case as Bitterly Controversial as the Vietnam War Itself* (New York: Dell, 1971). William Calley, *Lieutenant Calley: His Own Story, as Told to John Sack* (New York: Viking Press, 1971). Tom Tiede, *Calley: Soldier or Killer?* (New York: Pinnacle Books, 1971). Greenshaw, *Making of a Hero,* 42n9.

2. The Scoop Heard 'Round the World

1. Hersh, *My Lai 4,* 3.

2. Eszterhas, "Reporter Who Broke," 80. I wrote numerous letters to Calley, but he would not grant an interview. He has consistently refused to speak to the press. On August 21, 2009, Calley, then sixty-nine, made his first public comments, apologizing for his actions. "Calley Apologizes for Role in My Lai Massacre," Associated Press, NBC News, August 21, 2009, http://www.msnbc.msn.com/id/32514139/ns/us_news-military/.

3. Michael Bilton and Kevin Sims, *Four Hours in My Lai* (New York: Penguin), 98. They do not contradict Hersh's basic account.

4. Hersh, "Story Everyone Ignored," 56.

5. "Lieutenant Accused of Murdering 109 Civilians," *St. Louis Post-Dispatch*, November 13, 1969, 19. Seymour M. Hersh, "The My Lai Massacre," *Reporting*

Vietnam, part 2: *American Journalism, 1969–1975,* comp. Milton J. Bates, Lawrence Lichty, Paul Miles, Ronald H. Spector, and Marilyn Young (New York: Library of America, 1998), 13–22.

6. Kendrick Oliver, *The My Lai Massacre in American History and Memory* (Manchester UK: Manchester University Press, 1984), 24.

7. Hersh, "Story Everyone Ignored," 56.

8. Obst, *Too Good,* 124.

9. Obst, *Too Good,* 160–61.

10. Obst, *Too Good,* 124, 166–67. Richard Dudman, telephone interview by author, July 30, 2007. Eszterhas, "Reporter Who Broke," 80.

11. Oliver, *My Lai Massacre,* 44. William E. Porter, *Assault on the Media: The Nixon Years* (Ann Arbor: University of Michigan Press, 1976). Agnew's speech in *Time* magazine: "Naysayer to the Nattering Nabobs," September 30, 1996, http://www.time.com/time/magazine/article/0,9171,985217,00.html. John Coyne, *The Impudent Snobs: Agnew vs. the Intellectual Establishment* (New Rochelle NY: Arlington House, 1972).

12. Peter Braestrup, "U.S. Officer Is Accused of Mass Viet 'Murders,'" *Washington Post,* November 13, 1969. Braestrup, *Big Story: How the American Press Reported and Interpreted the Crisis of Tet* (Boulder CO: Westview Press, 1977).

13. Hersh, "Story Everyone Ignored," 58. Obst, *Too Good,* 167.

14. Ron Ridenhour's letter, March 29, 1969, http://www.law.umkc.edu/faculty/projects/ftrials/mylai/ridenhour_ltr.html. He tells his story at http://www.law.umkc.edu/faculty/projects/ftrials/mylai/myl_hero.html#RON. On Ridenhour, see Bilton and Sim, *Four Hours in My Lai,* 214–21.

15. From 1960 to 1970, Sheinbaum worked at the Center for the Study of Democratic Institutions. See Stanley K. Sheinbaum, NPQ, http://www.digitalnpq.org/about/sheinbaum.html. Obst, *Too Good,* 168.

16. Richard Boyle, *The Flower of the Dragon: The Breakdown of the U.S. Army in Vietnam* (San Francisco: Ramparts Press, 1972), 135. Alexander Cockburn, "The Legacy of My Lai," *Nation,* March 26, 1988, reprinted in *Selections from the Nation Magazine, 1865–1990,* ed. Katrina vanden Heuvel (New York: Thunder's Mouth Press, 1990), at http://www.thirdworldtraveler.com/Independent_Media/My_Lai_SNM.html.

17. The number of dead at My Lai has always been problematic. The U.S. Army estimated 374 dead. The official memorial in the village of My Lai lists 504 killed. See Henry Kamm, "Vietnamese Say G.I.'s Slew 567 in Town," *New York Times,* November 17, 1969, 1.

18. Eszterhas, "Reporter Who Broke," 81.

19. Editorial, *New York Times,* November 22, 1969, 36.

20. Obst, *Too Good,* 169. Thomas Blanton and Dr. William Burr, eds., "The

Kissinger Telcons," National Security Archive Electronic Briefing Book no. 123, May 26, 2004, http://www.gwu.edu/~nsarchiv/NSAEBB/NSAEBB123/#docs.

21. "Nation: My Lai: An American Tragedy" *Time*, December 5, 1969. http://www.time.com/time/magazine/article/0,9171,901621,00.html.

22. Obst, *Too Good*, 169. Oliver, *My Lai Massacre*, 49.

23. Daniel C. Hallin, *The "Uncensored War": The Media and Vietnam* (New York: Oxford University Press, 1986). Todd Gitlin, *The Whole World Is Watching: Mass Media in the Making and Unmaking of the New Left* (Berkeley: University of California Press, 1980.) Oliver, *My Lai Massacre*,121n38. David Packard to Richard Nixon, "The My Lai Atrocity," September 4, 1969, folder: "Possible My Lai commission," Alexander Haig special file, Box 1004, National Security Council files.

24. Sidle, "Massacre at My Lai," 334.

25. See Robert Dallek, *Nixon and Kissinger: Partners in Power* (New York: Harper-Collins, 2007), 185. Oliver, *My Lai Massacre*, 77. "Into the Dark: The My Lai Massacre," Crime Library: Criminal Minds & Madness, n.d., http://www.trutv.com/library/crime/notorious_murders/mass/lai/invest_9.html.

26. Seymour M. Hersh, interview by Amy Goodman, Democracy Now, "1968, Forty Years Later: My Lai Massacre Remembered by Survivors, Victims' Families and U.S. War Vets," March 17, 2008, http://www.democracynow.org/2008/3/17/1968_forty_years_later_my_lai.

27. Hersh, interview by Goodman.

28. Obst, *Too Good*, 170.

29. "Ex-G.I. Tells of Killing Civilians at Pinkville," *St. Louis Post-Dispatch*, November 25, 1969. Seymour M. Hersh, "The My Lai Massacre," reprinted from *Reporting Vietnam*, FlaglerLive.com, http://www.pierretristam.com/Bobst/library/wf-200.htm.

30. David Blum, *Tick—tick—tick—: The Long Life and Turbulent Times of 60 Minutes* (New York: Harper, 2005). Richard Campbell, *60 Minutes and the News* (Urbana: University of Illinois Press, 1991). Don Hewitt, *Tell Me a Story: Fifty Years and 60 Minutes in Television* (New York: Public Affairs, 2001).

31. Downie, *New Muckrakers*, 76. Obst, *Too Good*, 70.

32. Transcript of Paul Meadlo's statement on *60 Minutes*, *New York Times*, November 25, 1969, 16. Thompson, "Hersh Alternative," w09.

33. Stephen E. Ambrose, "Atrocities in Historical Perspective," *Facing My Lai: Moving beyond the Massacre*, ed., David L. Anderson (Lawrence: University of Kansas Press, 1998), 114–15.

34. Obst, *Too Good*, 170. Seymour Hersh, in Warren Bell, David Halberstam, Seymour Hersh, Ron Ridenhour, Kevin Sim, and Kathleen Turner, "Reporting the Darkness: The Role of the Press in the Vietnam War," in Anderson, Facing My Lai, 55. Downie, *New Muckrakers*, 77.

3. Hersh Becomes a Target

1. Downie, *New Muckrakers,* 77. Obst, *Too Good,* 136. John Schultz, *Motion Will Be Denied: A New Report on the Chicago Conspiracy Trial* (New York: Morrow, 1972), 171.

2. William M. Hammond, *The Military and the Media, 1968-1973* (Washington DC: Center of Military History, U.S. Army, 1996), n. 35. William E. Porter, *Assault on the Media: The Nixon Years* (Ann Arbor: University of Michigan Press, 1976).

3. Oliver, *My Lai Massacre,* 76.

4. Kissinger and Melvin Laird, November 21, 1969, Nixon Presidential Materials Project, Box 3, file 3, 083-084, http://www.gwu.edu/~nsarchiv/NSAEBB/NSAEBB123/. John Chamberlain, "$30,000 in Blood Money," *Lebanon Daily News,* December 6, 1969, 10.

5. Jim Lucas, "CBS Admits Paying for Meadlo Interview," *Washington Daily News,* in *Congressional Record,* December 4, 1969, 37176. "War Veteran Says He Killed 35 to 40 in Song My Sweep," *New York Times,* November 25, 1969, 1.

6. James Reston, "The Massacre at Songmy: Who Is to Blame?" *New York Times,* November 26, 1969, 44. *Congressional Record,* December 3, 1969, 37176-77.

7. Editorial, *Congressional Record,* December 9, 1969, 38049.

8. David L. Anderson, ed., *Facing My Lai* (Lawrence: University of Kansas Press, 1998), 76.

9. Jules Witcover, *Very Strange Bedfellows: The Short and Unhappy Marriage of Richard Nixon and Spiro Agnew* (New York: Public Affairs, 2007); Witcover, *White Knight: The Rise of Spiro Agnew* (New York: Random House, 1972).

10. Peter Osnos, "My Lai Story Almost Went Unnoticed," *Washington Post,* December 1, 1969, 10. Institute for Policy Studies, http://www.ips-dc.org/aboutips.php. Richard Strout, "Tragic Human Costs," *Washington Post,* November 24, 1969, 1.

11. John Lofton, "Hersh Reputation Is Far from One of Impartiality," *Yuma Daily Sun,* January 24, 1975, 4.

12. Hersh, "Uncovered," *New Yorker,* November 10, 2003, 41. McGrory's column, *Congressional Record,* December 13, 1969, 6127-28. Lucas, "CBS Admits Paying." Hersh quoted in Bell et al., "Reporting the Darkness," 70.

13. Downie, *New Muckrakers,* 78. Hersh, interview by Goodman.

14. Seymour M. Hersh, "Violence before My Lai," *St. Louis Post-Dispatch,* December 2, 1969, 1.

15. Oliver, *My Lai Massacre,* 54, 134-35.

16. Dallek, *Nixon and Kissinger,* 185.

17. Gloria Emerson, *Winners and Losers: Battles, Retreats, Gains, Losses and Ruins from a Long War* (New York: Random House, 1976). Eszterhas, "Reporter Who Broke," 51.

18. Richard M. Nixon, *RN: The Memoirs of Richard Nixon* (New York: Warner Books, 1978), 499.

19. Eszterhas "Toughest Reporter in America," 49-50.

20. Seymour M. Hersh, "Coverup," *New Yorker,* January 29, 1972, 46.

21. Sanford Ungar, *The Papers and the Papers* (New York: Dutton, 1972). Seymour M. Hersh, *Cover-up: The Army's Secret Investigation of the Massacre at My Lai 4* (New York: Vintage Books), 233.

22. Douglas Robinson, "Journalist Who Disclosed the My Lai Story Now Charges U.S. Officers Destroyed Papers," *New York Times,* January 26, 1972, 9.

23. Richard Hammer, "Under the Rug with My Lai Went Truth, Duty, Honor, Morality," *New York Times*, March 26, 1972, BR3.

24. "My Lai and Its Omens," *New York Times*, March 16, 1998, A25. Hersh, *Cover-up*, 233.

25. Ed Murphy and Zoeann Murphy, *Vietnam: Our Father-Daughter Journey* (New York: Philmark Press, 2006). Dale Andradé, *Ashes to Ashes: The Phoenix Program and the Vietnam War* (Lexington MA: Lexington Books, 1990). Douglas Valentine, *The Phoenix Program,* (New York: William Morrow, 1990).

26. Ed Murphy, email to author, May 28, 2008.

27. Carol Becker, "Pilgrimage to My Lai: Social Memory and the Making of Art," *Art Journal* 62, no. 4 (Winter 2003): 54. Boyle, *Flower of the Dragon*, 143.

28. "The Clamor over Calley: Who Shares the Guilt?" *Time,* April 12, 1971, 19. Oliver, *My Lai Massacre*, 3.

29. Osnos, "My Lai Story," 10.

30. Hallin, *"Uncensored War,"* 162. Hewit, *Tell Me a Story*, 124.

31. Eszterhas, "Reporter Who Broke," 49.

32. John Kifner, "Report on Brutal Vietnam Campaign Stirs Memories," *New York Times,* December 28, 2003, N24. More atrocities emerged. See "Beyond My Lai: New Revelations of Vietnam Atrocities," *Nation*, August 7, 2006, http://www.thenation.com/blog/beyond-my-lai-new-revelations-vietnam-atrocities.

33. Kendrick Oliver, email message to author, July 16, 2007. Charles J Hanley, *The Bridge at No Gun Ri: A Hidden Nightmare from the Korean War* (New York: Henry Holt, 2001).

34. Oliver, *My Lai Massacre*, 41. Seymour M. Hersh, Andrew Burgin, and Matthew Cookson, "Seymour M. Hersh—From My Lai to Abu Ghraib," *Socialist Worker*, June 1, 2005, http://www.countercurrents.org/us-hersh010605.htm.

35. Obst, *Too Good*, 176. The award went to Hersh of Dispatch News Service "for his exclusive disclosure of the Vietnam War tragedy at the hamlet of My Lai."

4. *"Front Page" Lessons in Chicago*

1. David Jackson, "The Muckraker," *Chicago Tribune*, June 25, 2004. Navy Pier, http://www.aviewoncities.com/chicago/navypier.htm; Office of the UIC

Historian, University of Illinois at Chicago, http://www.uic.edu/depts/uichistory/navypier2.html.

2. David Jackson, "Bernard Kogan, 80, UIC teacher," *Chicago Tribune*, February 26, 2001, http://articles.chicagotribune.com/2001-02-26/news/0102260176_1_navy-pier-mr-kogan-model-teacher. Seymour M. Hersh, telephone interview by author, October 12, 2010.

3. Thomas W. Goodspeed, *A History of the University of Chicago* (Chicago: University of Chicago Press, 1916). Eszterhas, "Toughest Reporter in America," 46.

4. Hersh, interview by author, October 12, 2010. On Currie, see "Brainerd Currie" at Wikipedia; Elvin R. Latty, Philip B. Kurland, Roger J. Traynor, Leavenworth Colby, and Robert C. Sink, "Brainerd Currie—Five Tributes," *Duke Law Journal* 1966, no. 1 (Winter 1966): 2–18, http://www.jstor.org/pss/1371392. Downie, *New Muckrakers*, 62.

5. Eszterhas, "Toughest Reporter in America," 46. "New Luster for a Saarinen Gem: Once-Threatened U. of C. Law School Building Is Expertly Recycled by OWP/P," July 1, 2008, http://featuresblogs.chicagotribune.com/theskyline/2008/07/polishing-a-saa.html. Hersh, interview by author, October 12, 2010.

6. A. A. Dornfeld, *Behind the Front Page: The Story of the City News Bureau of Chicago* (Chicago: Academy Chicago, 1983).

7. Hersh, interview by author, October 12, 2010.

8. Casey Bukro, telephone interview by author, email correspondence to author, August 4, 2010.

9. Bukro, interview. Dornfeld, *Behind the Front Page*, 262. Paul Zimbrakos, telephone interview by author, October 12, 2010. Richard F. Ciccone, *Royko: A Life in Print* (New York: Public Affairs, 2003), 64.

10. Zimbrakos, telephone interview by author, August 25, 2010. City News went out of business in 2005 as Chicago's newspapers consolidated.

11. Ciccone, *Royko*, 65. Bukro, interview. Ezterhas, "Toughest Reporter in America," 46.

12. Seymour M. Hersh, interview by Art Levine, *Straight Talk*, at http://www.youtube.com/watch?v=STYVTkVMlvs&feature=related, uploaded August 3, 2009. Zimbrakos, interview, August 25, 2010.

13. Bukro, interview. Dornfeld, *Behind the Front Page*, ix.

14. On Billings see "Robert Billings, 66, Veteran City Reporter," *Chicago Tribune*, August 28, 1998, http://articles.chicagotribune.com/1998-08-28/news/9808280188_1_paul-zimbrakos-city-news-bureau-mr-billings. Zimbrakos, interview, October 12, 2010.

15. Hersh, interview by author, October 12, 2010. Douglas Martin, "Frank Pape, Celebrated Chicago Police Detective, Dies at 91," March 12, 2000, http://www.nytimes.com/2000/03/12/us/frank-pape-celebrated-chicago-police-detective

-dies-at-91.html. "'Most Feared Lawman' Capt. Frank Pape Dies," ISPN, March 7, 2000, http://www.ipsn.org/pape.php. James Janega, "Police Capt. Frank Pape, 91, Called 'Chicago Toughest Cop,'" *Chicago Tribune*, March 7, 2000, http://articles .chicagotribune.com/2000-03-07/news/0003070168_1_evasion-criminals -chicago-police-department.

16. Ciccone, *Royko*, 96.

17. Dornfeld, *Behind the Front Page*, 250.

18. Telephone, email exchanges with Bukro and Zimbrakos, October 15, 2010. Hersh also told the story to *Chicago Tribune* reporter David Jackson. Downie, *New Muckrakers*, 63.

19. Hersh, interview by author, October 12, 2010.

5. Selling, Publishing, Failing

1. Hersh interview by author, October 12, 2010. Downie, *New Muckrakers*, 63. "About CAC," *United States Army Combined Arms Center*, http://usacac.army.mil/ cac2/overview.asp.

2. McKale and Young. *Fort Riley: Citadel of the Frontier West* (Topeka: Kansas State Historical Society, 2000). Fort Riley, Kansas, http://www.riley.army.mil/ NewsViewer.aspx?id=3160.

3. Hersh, interview by author, October 12, 2010. Lee Quarnstrom, telephone interview by author, October 25, 2010. No issues of the *Evergreen Dispatch* seem to have survived.

4. Hersh interview, October 12, 2010. Quarnstrom, interview. Zimbrakos, inter-view, October 12, 2010.

5. Jackson, "Muckraker." Hersh, interview by author, October 12, 2010. Downie, *New Muckrakers*, 63-64. Quarnstrom, interview. Julius Karpen, telephone interview by author, September 12, 2010.

6. Kurt Vonnegut, "City News Bureau," http://members.fortunecity.com/ltaford/ liamtafordspage/id2.html. Gregory Gordon, *Down to the Wire: UPI's Fight for Survival* (New York: McGraw-Hill, 1990). Richard M. Harnett and Billy G. Ferguson, *Unipress: United Press International, Covering the 20th Century* (Golden CO: Fulcrum, 2003).

7. Downie, *New Muckrakers*, 63-64.

8. Downie, *New Muckrakers*, 64.

9. Hersh, interview by author, October 12, 2010. Copies of some Hersh UPI stories were retrieved from newspaperarchive.com.

10. Downie, *New Muckrakers*, 64.

6. From the "Front Page" to the Pentagon

1. Kent Cooper, *Kent Cooper and the Associated Press: An Autobiography* (New York: Random House: 1959). Oliver Gramling, *AP: The Story of News* (Port Washington, NY: Kennikat Press, 1969).

2. Dana Kennedy, "Extra! Secrets to Being an AP Reporter for 49 Consecutive Years!" (interview by Richard Pyle), July 27, 2009, *Huffington Post*, http://www .huffingtonpost.com/dana-kennedy/extra-secrets- to-being-an_b_245329.html. Michael Robertson, *Stephen Crane, Journalism, and the Making of Modern American Literature* (New York: Columbia University Press 1997), 207.

3. Kennedy, "Extra!" No comprehensive archive of Hersh's AP stories exists. More than three hundred are located at newspaperarchive.com. Seymour M. Hersh, "About 60 Persons Injured as Train Jumps Track," *Gazette Telegraph*, May 3, 1964, 1; Hersh, "Mahalia Jackson Has Heart Trouble," *Evening Telegram*, September 24, 1964 , 1; Hersh, "Mahalia Jackson Wages Biggest Fight," *Daily Reporter*, October 12, 1964, 3.; Hersh, "Cops, Negroes Exchange Shots in Riot-Torn Chicago Suburb," *Oneonta Star*, September 18, 1964, 1.

4. Seymour M. Hersh, "Great Lakes Water Levels at Record Low," *Hope Star*, August 22, 1964, 2; Hersh, "Gorilla's Dash for Freedom Halted by Narcotic Pellet," *Daily Reporter,* August 4, 1964, 12; Hersh, "Hoffa, Others Guilty in Fraud Case," *Daily Reporter*, July 27, 1964. Walter Mears, telephone interview by author, June 30, 2009.

5. Seymour M. Hersh, "She's a Popular Northwestern Coed," *Alton Telegraph*, February 5, 1964, A12.Jackie Mayer website, www.jackiemayer.com.

6. Seymour M. Hersh, "Thousands Swarm into Aragon on Sunday for 'Last Dance,'" *Freeport Journal*, February 10, 1964, 1; Hersh, "Youth 'Likes Other Things Too,'" *Freeport Journal*, June 24, 1964, 16; Hersh, "Pistol Packin' Miss Declares War on Crime," *Gazette Telegraph*, November 17, 1964, 1.

7. Seymour M. Hersh, "First Grade Pupils' Book Is Published," *Wellsville Daily Reporter*, June 10, 1964, 4; Hersh, "Music Love Brings Tax Sentence," *Cedar Rapids Gazette*, March 31, 1964, 1.

8. Seymour M. Hersh, "No Football, but at Least He's Alive," *Freeport Journal-Standard*, May 25, 1965, 13, Hersh, "Heart Attack Convinces Gospel Singer She Must Slow Down," *Freeport Journal*, February 9, 1965, 7.

9. Seymour M. Hersh, "Family Planning Vote in Chicago," *Indiana Evening Gazette*, February 16, 1965, 1; "Chicago Baby Boom Slows to Crawl," *Stars and Stripes*, January 20, 1965, 7.

10. Seymour M. Hersh, "Chicago Aims to Whisk Away Smog," *Freeport Journal*, March 8, 1965, 10; Hersh, "Barry Tests Appeal in Illinois Vote," *Cedar Rapids Gazette*, April 14, 1964, 1; Hersh, "Picket Scranton in Chicago," *Manhattan Mercury*, June 30, 1964, 8; Hersh, "Chicago Housewife Fights Party Machine," *Freeport Journal*, January 21, 1964, 10.

11. Seymour M. Hersh, "Missing Joliet Woman Still a Mystery," *Freeport Journal*, September 30, 1964, 20. John Conroy, "Where in the World Is Molly Zelko?," March 11, 1993, http://www.chicagoreader.com/chicago/where-in-the-world-is-molly-zelko/ Content?oid=881563.

12. Seymour M. Hersh, "Mayor Daley Has 10th Anniversary," *Phoenix Gazette*, April 5, 1965, 12; "Great Lakes Water Levels at Record Low, *Hope Star,* August 22, 1964, 2, "Dip in Water Level Plagues Great Lakes Area," *New York Times*, August 9, 1964, XXII.

13. Hersh, interview by author, October 12, 2010. Downie, *New Muckrakers*, 64–65.

7. At War with the Pentagon

1. Various AP staffers helped me understand the AP. In particular Barry Schweid, telephone interview by author, November 24, 2010.

2. Gaylord Shaw, telephone interview by author, November 24, 2010. Carl Leubsdorf telephone interview by author, August 6, 2010.

3. Or see page 1 of the October 5, 1966, *Wellsville (NY) Daily Reporter,* which published thirteen AP stories on page 1 out of a total of fourteen stories, including one by Hersh: "Posthumous Award of Navy Cross for 'Mr. Viet Nam." Many Hersh stories are difficult to trace because many newspapers publish AP stories with bylines removed.

4. Seymour M. Hersh, "Shy Hero Gets Medal of Honor from President," *Ironwood Daily Globe*, June 23, 1966, 1. Kenneth Freed, telephone interview by author, July 10, 2009. Schweid, interview. Hersh, telephone interviews by author, December 20, 22, 2009.

5. Seymour M. Hersh, "900,000 Voters Set as Goal," *Wellsville Reporter,* August 6, 1965, 1; Hersh, "Congress Called Battleground for Rights Movement," *Progress,* September 15, 1965, 1.

6. Schweid, interview. Mears, interview.

7. Seymour M. Hersh, "Astronauts Honored as Sons Clown," *Cedar Rapids Gazette*, 1.

8. Seymour M. Hersh, "LBJ's Surgery Hardly as Serious as Ike's," *Lawton Constitution*, October 6, 1965, 12; Hersh, "Country Has Long Wrestled with Civil Rights Problem," *Mexia Daily News*, October 17, 1965, 8; Hersh, "Peanut Butter Feud Reopens in Washington," *Daily Telegram*, February 7, 1966, 5A; Hersh, "Says Husbands Usually Win," *Daily Sun*, October 21, 1965, 7; Hersh, "LBJ Attention on Great Society," *Indiana Gazette*, December 3, 1965, 27; Hersh, "LBJ to List Guidelines for Dollar Outflow," *Progress*, December 3, 1965, 10.

9. Seymour M. Hersh, "White House Area Campers Urge Funds," *Gazette Telegraph*, April 4, 1966, 4; Hersh, "Living in Tents in Washington 'Is No Picnic,'" *Gazette Telegraph*, April 6, 1966, 4A.

10. Seymour M. Hersh, "Christmas 'Cease-Fire' Hailed as Peace Step," *Commonwealth Reporter,* December 23, 1965, 1; Hersh, "Mansfield Wants U.S. to Extend Truce Offer," *Abilene Reporter-News,* December 23, 1965, 3; Hersh, "Humphrey and Other Leaders Hail 30-Hour Cease Fire," *Gettysburg Times,* December 24, 1965, 9.

Ivan R. Dee, "The Pause That Failed," in Lloyd C. Gardner, *Pay Any Price: Lyndon Johnson and the Wars for Vietnam* (Chicago: I. R. Dee, 1995), 169-293.

11. Kathleen J. Turner, *Lyndon Johnson's Dual War: Vietnam and the Press* (Chicago: University of Chicago Press, 1985), 172. Robert Miraldi, *Muckraking and Objectivity: Journalism's Colliding Traditions* (Westport CT: Greenwood Press, 1991). William Prochnau, *Once upon a Distant War* (New York: Vintage Books, 1996).

12. Zimbrakos, interview, October 12, 2010. Freed, interview.

13. Seymour M. Hersh, "Draft Calls Eased for Next 4 Months," *Daily Reporter,* November 3, 1964, 9; Hersh, "Draft Chance Depends on Local Board," *Daily Plainsman,* September 21, 1965, 5; Hersh, "Men above 26 Labeled Draft-Free," *Cedar Rapids Gazette,* October 27, 1965, 1; Hersh, "U.S. Draft Call Cut May End Problems," *Alton Evening Telegraph.* November 8, 1966, 2; Hersh, "Reclassification Plan May Boost Draft Group," *Commonwealth Reporter,* December 23, 1965, 1; Hersh, "Conference in Chicago Eyes Draft System," *Daily Republic,* December 5, 1966, 1; Hersh, "Draft Liability Period Would End at Age 19," *Abilene Reporter-News,* December 6, 1966, 30; Hersh, "Congress to Tackle Job of Revising Draft Laws," *Daily Telegram,* January 10, 1966, 3A; Hersh, "Congress Expected to Act Changes Loom for U.S. Draft Law," *Port Angeles Evening News,* January 17, 1966, 5; Hersh, "State Draft Boards Divided over System," *Lake Charles American Press,* January 19, 1966, 18; Hersh, "Major Revamping of Draft Predicted," *Freeport Journal-Standard,* February 8, 1966, 1; Hersh, "Reclassification Plan May Boost Draft Group," *Commonwealth Reporter,* December 23, 1965, 1.

14. Seymour M. Hersh, "Unique School for Dropouts," *Port Arthur News,* March 23, 1966, 11; Hersh, "Bolster Youth Corps," *Jonseville Daily Gazette*, April 20, 1966, 7; Hersh, "'Self-Help' for Rural Areas Is Proposed," *Gazette Telegraph*, February 15, 1966, 6; Hersh, "Rockefeller, Sorensen Win," *Daily Times-News,* May 11, 1966, 1.

8. Fighting His Editors

1. Mordecai Lee, "When Congress Tried to Cut Pentagon Public Relations: A Lesson from History," *Public Relations Review* 26, no. 2 (Summer 2000): 131-54. Fred Hoffman, telephone interview by author, November 3, 2010; Freed, interview, July 9, 2009.

2. Seymour M. Hersh, "War Turning Point Near—McNamara," *Wellsville Daily Reporter*, January 26, 1967, 1; Hersh, "U.S. to Test Explosions despite Soviet Protest," *Gazette Telegraph*, September 9, 1966, 1; Hersh, "Posthumous Award of Navy Cross for 'Mr. Viet Nam,'" *Wellsville Daily Reporter,* October 5, 1966, 1. Downie, *New Muckrakers,* 66.

3. Downie, *New Muckrakers,* 67. Sydney Schanberg, "'The Saigon Follies,'" *New York Times,* November 12, 1972, SM38.

4. Seymour M. Hersh, "Navy Reports Shortage of Experienced Officers," *Wellsville Daily Reporter*, September 29, 1966, 1; Hersh, "Corps Extends Duty of Flying Officers," *Brownwood Bulletin*. October 18, 1966, 12; Hersh, "Death of 24 Pilots in Carrier Fire Adds Urgency," *Lawton Constitution-Morning Press*, October 30, 1966, 4.

5. Seymour M. Hersh, "Sharp Boost in Pilot Training Given Approval," *Daily Republic*, December 1966, 11; Hersh, "Senators Will Probe Pilot Shortages," *Ironwood Daily Globe*, December 29, 1966, 1.

6. Shaw, interview.

7. Seymour M. Hersh, "Detailed Denial Offered by U.S. on Hanoi Raids," *Daily Reporter*, December 16, 1966, 1; Hersh, "U.S. Pays $34 for Each Death in Attack Error," *Daily Republic*, September 30, 1966, 1.

8. Seymour M. Hersh, "SAMs Filled Hanoi Skies during Raids," *Brownwood Bulletin*, December 18, 1966, 1.

9. Seymour M. Hersh, "Christmas Lull Opposed," *Brownwood Bulletin*, November 17, 1966, 1. Harrison E. Salisbury, *Behind the Lines: Hanoi* (New York: Harper & Row, 1967). Salisbury, *A Journey for Our Times: A Memoir* (New York: Harper & Row, 1983).

10. Walter Mears, telephone interview, June 30, 2009. Shaw, interview. Seymour M. Hersh, "U.S. to Test Explosions despite Soviet Protest," *Gazette Telegraph*, September 22, 1966, 1.

11. Seymour M. Hersh, interview by author, December 20, 2011. Jean Heller, telephone interview by author, July 19, 2010.

12. Hersh, interview, December 20, 2011.

13. Hersh, interview, December 20, 2011. Annessa Stagner, "From behind Enemy Lines: Salisbury and Wartime Reporting," master's thesis, Ohio University, 2008. Seymour M. Hersh, "Hanoi Area Off Limits," *Port Angeles News*, January 26, 1967, 1.

14. Downie, *New Muckrakers*, 69. Salisbury, Behind the Lines, 433–37, 167–68.

15. Salisbury, Behind the Lines, 168–69.

16. Fred Hoffman, "All in a Day's Work!," *Daily Reporter*, November 8, 1964, 4. Seymour M. Hersh, "Draft Calls Eased for Next 4 Months," *Daily Reporter*, November 8, 1964. 4.

17. Hoffman, telephone interview, November 2, 2010. Seymour M. Hersh, "But Don't Tell Anyone I Told You," *New Republic*, December 9, 1967, 13.

18. Hersh, interview, December 20, 2010.

19. Seymour M. Hersh, "U.S. Could Deliver Deadly Gases, Germs," Associated Press, *Stars and Stripes*, April. 14, 1967, 4. Shaw, interview. Mears, interview. Heller, interview. Downie, *New Muckrakers*, 70.

20. Hersh interview with Art Levine. "Seymour M. Hersh," *Current Biography Yearbook* (New York: H. W. Wilson, 1984, 159.

9. Finding America's Hidden Arsenal

1. Seymour M. Hersh, "U.S. Could Deliver Deadly Gases, Germs," *Stars and Stripes*, April 14, 1967, 4. Hersh's AP stories are located at newspaperarchive.org.

2. Seymour M. Hersh, "Just a Drop Can Kill," *New Republic,* May 6, 1967, 11. Hersh, *Chemical and Biological Warfare: America's Hidden Arsenal* (Indianapolis: Bobbs-Merrill, 1968), 23.

3. Heller, interview. Heller's late husband, Ray Stephens, was an early editor of the unit.

4. Hersh, "Just a Drop," 12.

5. Hersh, "Just a Drop," 11-12. Downie, *New Muckrakers*, 70.

6. Hersh, *Chemical and Biological Warfare*, 1.

7. Hersh, *Chemical and Biological Warfare*, 26.

8. Hersh, *Chemical and Biological Warfare*, 34.

9. Seymour M. Hersh, "Germ Warfare: For Alma Mater, God and Country," *Ramparts*, December 1969, 20-28.

10. "Seymour M. Hersh, "On Uncovering the Great Nerve Gas Coverup," *Ramparts*, June 1969, 13.

11. Hersh, "Uncovering," 14.

12. Hersh, "Uncovering," 6, 15-16.

13. Eszterhas, "Reporter Who Broke," 56.

14. Hersh, *Chemical and Biological Warfare*, 268. Daniel Greenberg, "Certain Styles of Killing," *New York Times,* June 9, 1968, BR6.

15. Charles J. Thoman, Review of *Chemical and Biological Warfare* by Seymour M. Hersh, *Best Sellers Review*, July 15, 1968.

16. Seymour M. Hersh, "The Secret Arsenal," *New York Times Magazine,* August 25, 1968, 26.

17. Jonathan B. Tucker, "A Farewell to Germs: The U.S. Renunciation of Biological and Toxin Warfare, 1969-70," *International Security* 27, no. 1 (Summer 2002): 107-48.

10. Speaking for Gene McCarthy

1. Al Eisele, "New Hampshire 1968: A Primary That Really Mattered," *Huffington Post*, March 3, 2008, http://www.huffingtonpost.com/al-eisele/new-hampshire-1968-a-prim_b_89707.html.

2. Theodore White, *The Making of the President* (New York: Athenaeum, 1969), 79.

3. Curtis Gans, email to author, January 13, 2011; telephone interview by author, January 12, 2011.

4. Walter LaFeber, *The Deadly Bet: LBJ, Vietnam, and the 1968 Election* (New York: Rowan & Littlefield, 2005), 37. Richard T. Stout, *People: The Story of the Grass Roots Movement That Found Eugene McCarthy* (New York: Harper & Row, 1970), 135.

5. David Rubien, "Seymour Hersh," *Salon*, January 18, 2000, http://dir.salon
.com/people/bc/2000/01/18/Hersh/print.html.

6. Seymour M. Hersh, interview, McCarthy Oral History Project, September 9,
1969, tapes 384–85, University of Minnesota.

7. Albert Eisele, *Almost to the Presidency* (Blue Earth MN: Piper, 1972).

8. Doris Kearns Goodwin, interview, January 10, 1970, tapes 646–47, McCarthy
Oral History Project. Richard N. Goodwin, *Remembering America: A Voice from the
Sixties* (Boston: Little, Brown, 1988), 487.

9. R. Goodwin, *Remembering America*, 488–89.

10. Hersh, interview, Oral History.

11. Hersh, interview, Oral History. Ned Kenworthy, "The McCarthy Manner,"
New York Times, December 18, 1967, 33.

12. Hersh, interview, Oral History.

13. Hersh, interview, Oral History. See also Arthur Herzog, *McCarthy for President* (New York: Viking Press, 1969).

14. Hersh interview, Oral History.

15. R. Goodwin, *Remembering America*, 493. Eisele, *Almost to the Presidency*,
79–80, 292. White, *Making of the President*, 80.

16. Eisele, "New Hampshire 1968."

17. Eisele, "New Hampshire 1968." Steven Lomazow, "The Truth about Lyndon
Johnson's Gall Bladder Scar," March 19, 2011, *FDR's Deadly Secret*, http://fdrsdeadly
secret.blogspot.com/2011/03/truth-about-lyndon-johnsons-gall.html.

18. White, *Making of the President*, 99. R, Goodwin, *Remembering America*, 495.
Hersh, interview, Oral History.

19. R. Goodwin, *Remembering America*, 512.

20. Stout, *People*, 175, 181. R. Goodwin, *Remembering America*, 513, 520.

21. White, *Making of the President*, 90, R. Goodwin, *Remembering America*, 300.

22. Murray Kempton, quoted in "United States Presidential Election, 1968,"
Wikipedia, http://en.wikipedia.org/wiki/United_States_presidential_election_1968.

23. Hersh, interview, Oral History.

24. Eugene J. McCarthy, *Up 'til Now: A Memoir* (New York: Harcourt Brace Jovanovich, 1986), 186.

25. R, Goodwin, interview. Mary Louise Oates declined to be interviewed.

26. Hersh, interview, Oral History.

27. Dominic Sandbrook, *Eugene McCarthy: The Rise and Fall of Postwar American
Liberalism* (New York: Knopf, 2004), 142.

28. Seymour M. Hersh, "Unrelated Riots over Nation, Worst in Dixmoor, Illinois,"
Hope Star, August 17, 1964, 1; Hersh, "Cops, Negroes Exchange Shots," *Oneonta
Star*, August 17, 1964, 1; Hersh, "Dixmoor Has Remnants of Recent Racial Rioting,"
Freeport Journal-Standard, August 25, 1964, 11.

29. Hersh, interview, Oral History.

30. Hersh, interview, Oral History. Gans, interview.

31. E. W. Kenworthy, "McCarthy's Staff Split on Campaign," *New York Times*, March 27, 1968, 1.

32. Stout, *People*, 198. Hersh, interview, Oral History.

33. E. W. Kenworthy, "McCarthy's Staff Split." Eisele, *Almost to the Presidency*, 300–307. Hersh, interview, Oral History.

34. Stout, *People*, 199. Seymour M. Hersh, "McCarthy Plays Down Staffer Resignations," *Stevens Point Journal*, March 27, 1968, 3. Russell Baker, "The Pied Piper of Minnesota," *New York Times*, March 21, 1968, 46.

35. Gans, interview. Hersh, interview, Oral History.

11. *Stunning Triumph over Germs*

1. Hersh, interview, Oral History.

2. Donald Janson, "McCarthy to Tour Milwaukee's Slum," *New York Times*, March 30, 1968, 18. E. W. Kenworthy, "McCarthy Shifts to Issues of Race," *New York Times*, April 14, 1968, E3. Harry Kelly, "McCarthy Sees War Controls Adoption," *Charleston Gazette*, March 2, 1968, 43.

3. Hersh, interview, Oral History. Hersh, *Chemical and Biological Warfare*.

4. See Jeanne McDermott, *The Killings Winds: The Menace of Biological Warfare* (New York: Arbor House, 1987). Mark Wheelis, Lajos Rózsa, and Malcolm Dando, eds., *Deadly Cultures: Biological Weapons since 1945* (Cambridge MA: Harvard University Press, 2006). Albert J. Mauroni, *America's Struggle with Chemical-Biological Weapons* (Westport CT: Greenwood, 2000).

5. Tom Mangold, *Plague Wars: The Terrifying Reality of Biological Warfare* (New York: Macmillan, 1999), 54–57. "Nixon Ends Biological Weapons Program," *American Experience*, PBS, http://www.pbs.org/wgbh/americanexperience/features/general-article/weapon-nixon-ends/. Dale Van Atta, *With Honor: Melvin Laird in War, Peace, and Politics* (Madison: University of Wisconsin Press, 2008).

6. Richard D. McCarthy, *The Ultimate Folly: War by Pestilence, Asphyxiation, and Defoliation* (New York: Vintage, 1969). Hersh oral history.

7. Seymour M. Hersh, "Germs and Gas as Weapons," *New Republic*, June 7, 1969, 3–16. Hersh, "On Uncovering the Great Nerve Gas Coverup," *Ramparts*, June, 1969, 17.

8. Seymour M. Hersh, "Dare We Develop Biological Weapons?" *New York Times Magazine*, September 28, 1969, SM28.

9. Van Atta, *With Honor*, 295. Memo, Henry Kissinger to Melvin Laird, "CBW Study," May 9, 1969. Memo, Kissinger to various recipients, "U.S. Policy Chemical/Biological Warfare," May 28, 1969. Memo, "U.S. Policy on Chemical/Biological Research," Kissinger to Spiro Agnew et al., November 25, 1969. These various

memos are at Documents Related to Chemical and Biological Warfare, https://www.mtholyoke.edu/acad/intrel/chemical.htm.

10. Hersh, "Dare We Develop," 28. Philip M. Boffey, "CBW: Pressures for Control Build in Congress," *Science*, June 20, 1969, 1376–1378.

11. Jonathan B. Tucker, *War of Nerves: Chemical Warfare from World War I to al-Qaeda* (New York: Pantheon Books, 2006).

12. For a detailed description of the evolution of policy, see John Ellis van Courtland Moon, "The U.S. Biological Weapons Program," 9–46, in Wheelis, Rózsa, and Dando, *Deadly Cultures*. Moon, telephone interview, June 22, 2010.

13. James Naughton, "Nixon Renounces Germ Warfare," *New York Times*, November 26, 1969, 1. Richard Lyons, "Nixon's Order Covers a Wide Range," *New York Times*, November 26, 1969, 16.

14. Moon, interview.

15. Barry Kissin, interview by Sherwood Ross, "Inside America's Biological Warfare Center," *Smirking Chimp*, February 18, 2009, http://www.smirkingchimp.com/thread/20332.

12. *Scoop Artist Meets the Viet Cong*

1. "Eyes on the Prize: What the Pulitzer Means," *Herald-News*, http://heraldnews.suntimes.com/photos/galleries/4902595-417/eyes-on-the-prize-what-the-pulitzer-means.html. Downie, *New Muckrakers*, 84–85.

2. Robert Katz, telephone interview by author, October 15, 2010. David Jackson, telephone interview by author, October 22, 2010. Gerald Sorin, telephone interview by author, July 20, 2010.

3. Sorin, interview. Hersh has given a basic variation on this speech for many years. Seymour M. Hersh, "Vietnam War My Lai Massacre," Tulane University, December 2, 1994, http://www.c-spanvideo.org/program/MyL. Hersh, "Seymour Hersh and the Hunt for Lt. William Calley," http://www.youtube.com/watch?v=sR3-tc54VPU.

4. Seymour M. Hersh, "Decline and Near Fall of the U.S. Army," *Saturday Review*, November 18, 1972, 58–65.

5. Downie, *New Muckrakers*, 85.

6. Hersh, *Cover-up*, 233.

7. Seymour M. Hersh, "Coverup I," *New Yorker*, January 22, 1972, 34–40, and "Coverup II," *New Yorker*, January 29, 1972, 40–48. Robinson, "Journalist Who Disclosed," 9.

8. Downie, *New Muckrakers*, 86–87.

9. Eszterhas, "Toughest Reporter in America," 65, 67.

10. Seymour M. Hersh, "Hanoi Exhibit Depicts '71 Victory," *New York Times*, March 12, 1972, 2; Hersh, "Hanoi Makes Use of Downed Jets," *New York Times*, March 15, 1972, 8.

11. Max Frankel, *Times of My Life and My Life with the Times* (New York: Random House, 1999), 149.

12. Everett Alvarez, *Chained Eagle* (Washington DC: Potomac Books, 2005).

13. Seymour M. Hersh, "Bridge, Now Symbol to North Vietnam," *New York Times,* March 25, 1972, 3; Hersh, "Haiphong Took a Beating," *New York Times,* March 27, 1972, 14; Hersh, "Hanoi Says It Won't Press South," *New York Times* March 29, 1972, 10.

14. Seymour M. Hersh, "POWs Secondary, Hanoi Says," *New York Times,* March 24, 1972, 1; Hersh, "3 Freed POWs Return," *New York Times,* September 29, 1972, 1; Hersh, "Freed Pilots Begin Tests," *New York Times,* September 30, 1972, 10. Eszterhas, "Toughest Reporter in America," 65.

15. Seymour M. Hersh, email message to author, April 21, 2011.

13. The Times *Calls*

1. Gay Talese, *The Kingdom and the Power* (New York: New American Library, 1966), 6. Seymour M. Hersh, telephone interview by author, April 7, 2011. John Darnton, interview by author, May 17, 2011.

2. A. M. Rosenthal Papers, New York Public Library, February 22, 1972. Rachel Cooke, "The Man Who Knows Too Much," *Guardian,* October 19, 2008, http://www.guardian.co.uk/media/2008/oct/19/seymour-hersh-new-yorker-reporter/print. *Times* editor Seymour Topping said he was responsible for bringing Hersh to the *Times.* Topping, interview by author, May 11, 2012.

3. John L. Hess, *My Times: A Memoir of Dissent* (New York: Seven Stories Press), 159. Eszterhas, "Reporter Who Broke," 67.

4. Seymour M. Hersh, "Hanoi Again Asks End of Bombing," *New York Times,* May 9, 21. Hersh, "Paris Crux: Who'll Rule Saigon?," *New York Times,* May 13, 8. Hersh, "View in Paris Is That Deadlock Still Centers on Thieu's Status," *New York Times,* May 10, 1972.

5. Seymour M. Hersh, "Army's Secret Inquiry Charges 43 Mylai Failures to Top Officers," *New York Times,* June 4, 1. Hersh, "Coverup I" and "Coverup II," *New Yorker,* January 22, 1972, 34–40, and January 29, 1972, 40–48.

6. Reuters dispatch, "Air Force Relieved Its Vietnam Chief for 'Irregularities,'" *New York Times,* May 17, 1972, 17. John David Lavelle, U.S. Air Force Oral History Interview, April 17–24, 1978, 669. "Statement of Senators Levin and McCain on Major General Lavelle's Restoration of Rank," August 5, 2010, http://www.levin.senate.gov/newsroom/press/release/?id=824df79f-56b7-4619-b087-7e933110f0a2.

7. Seymour M. Hersh, "General Bombed in North before President's Order," *New York Times,* June 11, 1972, 1.

8. Seymour M. Hersh, "Pike Charges a Cover-up over General's Dismissal," *New York Times,* June 12, 1972, 4. Hersh, "General Testified He Made 20 Raids without

Orders," *New York Times,* June 13, 1972, 1. Hersh, "Airman Says Raid Reports Were Falsified on Orders," *New York Times,* June 14, 1972, 3.

9. Seymour M. Hersh, "'Reaction' Strikes Called Cover-up," *New York Times,* June 15, 1972, 1. Hersh, "Ex-airmen Tell of 20 Planned Raids a Month," *New York Times,* June 16, 1972, .3.

10. The transcripts of the White House conversations are available at the web site of the Lavelle family attorney, Myers, Brier & Kelly, http://www.mbklaw.com/events/lavelle/.

11. Hersh, interview, April 7, 2011. James Reston, "The Double Standard," *New York Times,* June 14, 1972, 47. Hersh, "'Reaction Strike' Called Cover-up," *New York Times,* June 15, 1972, 1.

12. Tom Wicker, "Protective Reaction," *New York Times,* June 18, 1972, E15. Seymour M. Hersh, "Ex-Airmen Tell of 20 Planned Raids a Month in '70-71," *New York Times,* June 16, 1972, 1.

13. Seymour M. Hersh, "You Might Call It 'Protective Aggression,'" *New York Times,* June 18, 1972, E1.

14. Seymour M. Hersh, "Unauthorized Raids Attributed to Eased White House Control," *New York Times,* June 19, 1972, 2. Hersh, "The Lavelle Case," *New York Times,* June 23, 1972, 36.

15. Richard Moss and Luke A. Nichter, prod., nixontapes.org, http://nixontapes .org/lavelle.html. See also Myers, Brier & Kelly, http://www.mbklaw.com/events/lavelle/.

16. Robert B. Semple, "Nixon Discloses Vietnam Parley Resumes," *New York Times,* June 30, 1972, 1.

17. Seymour M. Hersh, "Pentagon Knew of Unauthorized Lavelle Raid in '71," *New York Times,* September 8, 1972, 3. Hersh, "Air Force Accused of Raid Cover-up," *New York Times,* September 9, 1972, 1.

18. Lonnie Franks, telephone interview by author, April 7, 2011. Seymour M. Hersh, "Sargeant Says 200 Men Helped Falsify Bomb Data," *New York Times,* September 7, 1972, 1. Carl Jensen, "When One Honest Man Made a Difference," Monitor, October 10, 2002. http://www.albionmonitor.com/0210a/jensenpaths ofglory.html. John T. Correll, "Lavelle," *Air Force Magazine,* November 2006, http://www.airforce-magazine.com/MagazineArchive/Pages/2006/November%20 2006/1106lavelle.aspx.

19. Seymour M. Hersh, "Gen. Lavelle Now Asserts He 'Committed No Wrong,'" *New York Times,* September 12, 1972, 1. Hersh, "Raids Approved, Lavelle Asserts," *New York Times,* September 13, 1972, 1. Hersh, "Senators Report Abrams Disputes Lavelle on Raids," *New York Times,* September 14, 1972, 1. Hersh, "Raids Approved, Lavelle Insists," *New York Times,* September 16, 1972, 61.

20. Seymour M. Hersh, "Somebody Higher Up Must Have Known,'" *New York*

Times, September 17, 1972, E1. Editorial, "The Lavelle Case," *New York Times,* October 9, 1972, 30. Nixon's comments made on October 23, 1972 and available on http://www.mbklaw.com/events/lavelle.

21. John T. Smith, *The Linebacker Raids: The Bombing of North Vietnam, 1972* (London: Arms and Armour, 1998). Aloysius Casey and Patrick Casey, "Lavelle, Nixon, and the White House Tapes," *Air Force Magazine,* February 2007, http://www.airforce-magazine.com/MagazineArchive/Pages/2007/February%202007/0207tapes.aspx.

22. Seymour M. Hersh, "Authorizations," *New Yorker,* March 26, 2007, http://www.newyorker.com/talk/comment/2007/03/26/070326taco_talk_hersh.

23. Editorial, "Correction: The Lavelle Case," *New York Times,* August 7, 2010, http://www.nytimes.com/2010/08/08/opinion/08sun3.html. Seth Lipsky, "A General, His Judgment and the Fog of War," *Wall Street Journal,* http://online.wsj.com/article/SB10001424052748704388504575419652907636486.html. Tom Bowman, "General Exonerated for Vietnam-Era Bombings," NPR, http://www.npr.org/templates/story/story.php?storyId=129013259.

14. Digging into Watergate

1. Richard Perez-Pena, "Ex-Timesmen Say They Had a Tip on Watergate First," *New York Times,* May 24, 2009, B4. Robert M. Smith, "Before Deep Throat," *American Journalism Review,* June/July 2009, http://ajr.org/article.asp?id=4754.

2. Robert H. Phelps, *God and the Editor: My Search for Meaning at the* New York Times (Syracuse: Syracuse University Press, 2009). I exchanged numerous emails with Phelps in May and June 2011.

3. Phelps, "Watergate One: How the *Post* Beat the *Times,*" in *God and the Editor,* 166–81. Robert M. Smith, telephone interview by author, June 30, 2011. Seymour M. Hersh, telephone interview by author, June 29, 2011.

4. Smith, "Before Deep Throat." Phelps, *God and the Editor.*

5. Phelps, "Watergate One," 174. Frankel, *Times of My Life,* 546.

6. Phelps, email to author, June 30 and July 1, 2011.

7. Ben Bradlee, *A Good Life: Newspapering and Other Adventures* (New York: Simon and Schuster, 1995), 545, 324.

8. Hersh, interview, June 29, 2011. Memo, Max Frankel to Abe Rosenthal, December 9, 1970, A. M. Rosenthal Papers, New York Public Library.

9. Seymour M. Hersh, interview by Lowell Bergman, *Frontline,* January 8, 2007, http://www.pbs.org/wgbh/pages/frontline/newswar/interviews/hersh.html. Phelps, email, June 30, 2011.

10. Seymour M. Hersh, "Watergate Days," *New Yorker,* June 13 and 20, 2005, 64.

11. Downie, *New Muckrakers,* 1–53. Frankel, *Times of My Life,* 546. Alicia C. Shepard, *Woodward and Bernstein: Life in the Shadow of Watergate* (New York: Wiley, 2007).

12. Downie, *New Muckrakers,* 89. Hersh, interview by author, June 29, 2011. Phelps, interviews.

13. Stanley Kutler, *The Wars of Watergate: The Last Crisis of Richard Nixon* (New York: Knopf, 1990). Keith W. Olsen, *Watergate: The Presidential Scandal That Shook America* (Lawrence: University of Kansas Press), 2003.

14. Bradlee, *Good Life.* Jim Naughton, email to author, June 2, 2011.

15. Ungar, *Papers and the Papers.* Frankel, *Times of My Life,* 344. Eszterhas, "Reporter Who Broke," 52.

16. Clifton Daniel, *Lords, Ladies and Gentlemen* (New York: Arbor House, 1984), 220. Downie, *New Muckrakers,* 89. Bob Woodward and Carl Bernstein, *All the President's Men* (New York: Simon & Schuster, 1974).

17. Profile of Seymour M. Hersh, Hersh folder, Rosenthal papers.

18. Arthur Gelb, telephone interview by author, September 30, 2011. Seymour M. Hersh to Abe Rosenthal, February 22, 1972, Rosenthal Papers.

19. Seymour M. Hersh, "Watergate Defendants Reported Still Being Paid," *New York Times,* January 14, 1973, 1. Downie, *New Muckrakers,* 90-91.

20. Bob Woodward, interview by author, February 8, 2012. Downie, *New Muckrakers,* 90.

21. Phelps, "Watergate One," 187. Mark Feldstein, "Watergate Revisited," *American Journalism Review,* August/September 2004, http://www.ajr.org/article.asp?id=3735.

22. Seymour M. Hersh, "Strachan Said to Have Given Telephone Number," *New York Times,* February 7, 1973, 1. Hersh, "Chapin Said to Have Told Nixon Aide to Pay Segretti," *New York Times,* February 8, 1973, 1. Downie, *New Muckrakers,* 91.

23. Seymour M. Hersh, "Nixon Is Reported to Have Phoned Dean," *New York Times,* April 24, 1973, 85. Hersh, "2 Groups Divided," *New York Times,* May 10, 1973, 1. Hersh, "Dean Tied to Plan for Ring to Spy on Protests," *New York Times,* May 14, 1973, 63. Downie, *New Muckrakers,* 94.

24. Seymour M. Hersh, "Blackmail Laid to Official in Pentagon 'Spy' Inquiry," *New York Times,* January 13, 1974, 1. Hersh, "Pentagon Spy Case," *New York Times,* February 10, 1974, 184. Hersh, "Nixon and Snooping," *New York Times,* February 12, 1974, 23. James M. Perry, "Watergate Case Study," in *Thinking Clearly: Cases in Journalistic Decision-Making,* ed. Tom Rosenstiel and Amy S. Mitchell (New York: Columbia University Press, 2003). Lowell Ponte, "A Life in Investigative Journalism," *Asia Society,* May 14, 2004.

25. Walter Rugaber, email to author, June 13, 2011. Denny Walsh, telephone interview by author, June 15, 2011.

26. "The Watergate Story," pt. 4, "Deep Throat Revealed," June 2012, *Washington Post,* http://www.washingtonpost.com/wp-srv/politics/special/watergate/part4.html. Bob Woodward, *The Secret Man: The Story of Watergate's Deep Throat*

(New York: Simon and Schuster, 2005). A. M. Rosenthal to David Jones, February 8, 1973, Rosenthal Papers.

27. Rosenthal to Jones, February 8, 1973.

28. Arthur Gelb, *City Room* (New York: Putnam, 2003). Gelb, interview by author, June 16, 2010. Downie, *New Muckrakers,* 91. Seymour M. Hersh, "Watergate Jury Believed Seeking a Haldeman Link," *New York Times,* April 22, 1973, 1.

29. Hersh, interview by Bergman, January 8, 2007.

30. Howard Simons, interview, quoted in Phelps, "Watergate One," 188. The interview can be found in the Woodward and Bernstein Watergate Papers, Ransom Center, University of Texas. Woodward, interview.

31. Woodward and Bernstein, *All the President's Men,* 311–12. Tim Madigan, "Mr. Hersh Goes to War," July 22, 2004, Truthout, http://archive.truthout.org/article/tim-madigan-mr-hersh-goes-war. Obst, interview, May 25, 2011.

32. Seymour M. Hersh, "McCord Reported Linking Payoffs," *New York Times,* April 9, 1973, 1.

33. Seymour M. Hersh, "Charges Likely," *New York Times,* April 19, 1973, 1. A. M. Rosenthal to Hersh, April 25, 1973; Hersh to Rosenthal, May 9, 1973; Clifton Daniel to Rosenthal, May 9, 1973, all in Rosenthal Papers.

15. Cambodia, Bombs, and Impeachment

1. Stanley Kutler, *Abuse of Power: The New Nixon Tapes* (New York: Free Press, 1997), 352.

2. Kutler, *Abuse of Power,* 442. Mark Avrom Feldstein, telephone interview by author, July 15, 2011. Feldstein, *Poisoning the Press: Richard Nixon, Jack Anderson, and the Rise of Washington's Scandal Culture* (New York: Farrar, Straus and Giroux, 2010).

3. Seymour M. Hersh, "Dean Tied to Plan for Ring to Spy on Protests," *New York Times,* May 14, 1973, 63. Hersh, "Offers to Talk," *New York Times,* June 3, 1973, 1. Hersh, "New Dean Charge on Nixon Awaited," *New York Times,* June 24, 1973, 1.

4. Kutler, *Abuse of Power,* 580.

5. Downie, *New Muckrakers,* 94, 92. Woodward and Bernstein, *All the President's Men,* 311.

6. Downie, *New Muckrakers,* 92–93. Hersh, "Watergate Days," *New Yorker,* June 13 and 20, 2005, 66.

7. Eszterhas, "Reporter Who Broke," 52. Bob Woodward, interview by author, February 8, 2012.

8. "Who Needs Enemies?" *TWA Ambassador,* 1976. Copy found in Rosenthal Papers, New York Public Library.

9. Kutler, *Abuse of Power,* 616–17. Hersh, "Dean Said to Keep $14,000 Fund," *New York Times,* June 19, 1973, 81.

10. Seymour M. Hersh, "Dean Said to Tell of Krogh Report Impugning Nixon," *New York Times*, June 17, 1973, 1. Hersh, "Watergate," *New York Times*, July 1, 1973, 143.

11. Seymour M. Hersh, "Secret Raids on Cambodia before '70 Totaled 3,500," *New York Times*, July 18, 1973, 1.

12. Seymour M. Hersh, "President Linked to Taps on Aides," *New York Times*, May 16, 1973. Hersh, "The Secret Bombing," in *Price of Power*, 1. William Shawcross, *Sideshow: Kissinger, Nixon and the Destruction of Cambodia* (New York: Simon and Schuster, 1979), 54–63.

13. Bill Kovach, email to author, July 28, 2011. Hersh, "Watergate Days."

14. Seymour M. Hersh, "Broad Role Cited," *New York Times*, May 17, 1973, 35.

15. Seymour M. Hersh, "Cambodian Raids Reported Hidden," *New York Times*, July 15, 1973, 1.

16. Seymour M. Hersh, "Inquiry Press in Secret Raids," *New York Times*, July 16, 1973, 5. Hersh, "U.S. Confirms Pre-1970 Raids," *New York Times*, July 17, 1973, 1. Hersh, "Secret Raids on Cambodia," *New York Times*, July 18, 1973, 1.

17. Hersh, *Price of Power*, 61. Sydney Schanberg, telephone interview by author, July 26, 2005. Schanberg, *Beyond the Killing Fields: War Writings*, ed. Robert Miraldi (Washington DC: Potomac Books, 2010).

18. Seymour M. Hersh, "Military Dispute," *New York Times*, July 19, 1973, 1. Hersh, "Kissinger Denies White House Role," *New York Times*, July 20, 1. Gene Roberts, telephone interview by author, March 8, 2012.

19. Seymour M. Hersh, "Pentagon Admits It Gave Senate False Raid Report," *New York Times*, July 21, 1973, 1. Jerry Friedheim, telephone interview by author, August 15, 2011.

20. Seymour M. Hersh, "Hospital Bombing 1969," *New York Times*, July 22, 1973, 1. Hersh, "Ex-Green Beret Says U.S. Still Hides Actions," *New York Times*, July 27, 1973, 3. Hersh, "Secret Air Raids Extended to Laos," *New York Times*, July 29, 1973, 1.

21. Seymour M. Hersh, "Cover-up Keeps On Unraveling," *New York Times*, July 29, 1973, E2. Hersh, "Asserts Bombing Secrecy Was Nixon's Wish," *New York Times*, July 31, 1973, 1. Tom Wicker, "The Big Lie Requires Big Liars," *New York Times*, July 24, 1973, 35.

22. Richard Madden, "Curbing Military Adventures," *New York Times*, July 22, 1973, 153. Seymour M. Hersh, "The Secret Air War: Some Senators Sense Another Watergate," *New York Times*, July 24, 1973, 4.

23. Seymour M. Hersh, "Wheeler Asserts Bombing Secrecy Was Nixon's Wish," *New York Times*, July 31, 1973, 1. Anthony Lewis, "Without Shame," *New York Times* July 30, 1973, 27.

24. John Herbers, "Nixon Says Raids Were 'Necessary,'" *New York Times*, August 21, 1973, 1. Henry Kamm, "Confusion in Cambodia." *New York Times*, August 15, 1973, 77.

25. Seymour M. Hersh, "Unanswered Questions on Raids," *New York Times,* September 21, 1973, 10.

26. U.S. Senate, *Bombing in Cambodia: Hearings before the Committee on Armed Services,* 93rd Cong., 1st sess. (Washington DC: Government Printing Office, 1973).

27. John Conyers, "Why Nixon Should Have Been Impeached," *Black Scholar,* October 1974. Fred Emery, *The Corruption of American Politics and the Fall of Richard Nixon* (New York: Random House, 1994). The resolution lost 26–12.

28. "2 Times Reporters Win Polk Journalism Awards," *New York Times,* March 21, 1974, 54.

29. Richard Madden, "Curbing Military Adventures," *New York Times,* July 22, 1973, 153.

16. Hunting the Coup Plotters

1. Hersh discussed this in a speech, *The Reporter's Obligation: An Address,* John Peter and Anna Catherine Zenger Award acceptance speech (Tucson: University of Arizona Press, 1975), 7–8.

2. Darnton, interview.

3. Hersh profile included in his original application to *New York Times,* found in Hersh Folder, A. M. Rosenthal Papers, 1959–2004, New York Public Library.

4. Hersh profile. Joseph Lelyveld, "Rep. Harrington a Frustrated Bystander," *New York Times,* September 30, 1975, 23.

5. Seymour M. Hersh, "CIA Chief Tells House of $8-Million Campaign against Allende," *New York Times,* September 8, 1974, 1. Laurence Stern, "CIA Role in Chile Revealed," *Washington Post,* September 8, 1974, 1, 20. Nathaniel Davis, *The Last Two Years of Salvador Allende* (Ithaca NY: Cornell University Press, 1985), 317.

6. Tom Wicker, "Secret War on Chile," *New York Times,* September 13, 1974, 37. Davis, *Last Two Years,* x. On Chile and Allende: Jonathan Haslam, *The Nixon Administration and the Death of Allende's Chile* (New York: Verso, 2005); Paul E. Sigmund, *The Overthrow of Allende and the Politics of Chile, 1964–1976* (Pittsburgh: University of Pittsburgh Press, 1977); and Lubna Z. Qureshi, *Nixon, Kissinger, and Allende: U.S. Involvement in the 1973 Coup in Chile* (Lanham MD: Lexington Books, 2009).

7. Tom Wicker, "Was Ford Conned on Chile?" *New York Times,* September 20, 1974, 39. Martin Houseman qtd. in Robert Schakne, "Chile: Why We Missed the Story," *Columbia Journalism Review,* March/April 1976, 60–62. Laurence R. Birns, "Allende's Fall, Washington's Push," *New York Times,* September 15, 1974, 215.

8. Seymour M. Hersh, "Hearings Urged on CIA's Role in Chile," *New York Times,* September 9, 1974, 3. Michael Harrington, "The CIA in Chile: A Question of Responsibility," *New York Times,* January 2, 1976, 25.

9. Seymour M. Hersh, "Censored Matter in Book about CIA," *New York Times,* September 11, 1974, 14.

10. Seymour M. Hersh, "Senator Church to Press CIA Issue," *New York Times,* September 12, 1974, 5. Hersh, "Concern by India on CIA Related," *New York Times,* September 13, 1974, 11.

11. Seymour M. Hersh, *Price of Power: Kissinger in the Nixon White House* (New York: Summit, 1983), 264, 278. Hersh devotes chapters 21and 22 to Chile.

12. Mark Feldstein, *Poisoning the Press: Richard Nixon, Jack Anderson, and the Rise of Washington's Scandal Culture* (New York: Farrar, Straus and Giroux, 2010), 268-78. Jack Anderson, "ITT and the Allende Government," *Washington Post,* September 26, 1974, 74. Edward M. Korry (son of the ambassador), telephone interview by author, January 30, 2012. Patricia Korry, telephone interviews by author, February 2 and 20, 2012.

13. Wicker, "Secret War on Chile," 37. Birns, "Allende's Fall, Washington's Push," 215. Anthony Lewis, "It's Up to Congress," *New York Times,* September 19, 1974, 43. Editorial, "The CIA in Chile," *New York Times,* September 16, 1974, 16.

14. Tom Wicker, "Kissinger Called Chile Strategist," *New York Times,* September 15, 1974, 1.

15. Seymour M. Hersh, "Ford to Brief Five on CIA Activities," *New York Times,* September 19, 13. Hersh, "Senators Order Inquiry on Chile," *New York Times,* September 18, 1974, 5.

16. J. William Fulbright, "Fulbright on the Press," *Columbia Journalism Review,* November/December 1975, 41-45. John E. Semonche, "Theodore Roosevelt's 'Muckrake Speech': A Reassessment," *Mid-America,* April 1964, 114-25.

17. Peter Kornbluh, *The Pinochet File: A Declassified Dossier on Atrocity and Accountability* (New York: New Press, 2003). Hersh, *Price of Power,* 287n. Alan Wolfe, "Henry's Nemesis," *Nation,* July 1983, 23-30. Anthony Lewis, "Kissinger on Balance," *New York Times,* September 26, 1974. Wicker, "Was Ford Conned?"

18. Richard A. Falk, "Editorial Comments: President Gerald Ford, CIA Covert Operations, and the Status of International Law," *American Journal of International Law* 69, no. 2 (1975): 354-58. Clifton Daniel, "CIA's Covert Role," *New York Times,* September 18, 1974, 4. Seymour M. Hersh, "Should the CIA Abandon Dirty Tricks? "*New York Times,* September 22, 1974, 201. Wicker, "Secret War on Chile."

19. Seymour M. Hersh, "Doubt on U.S. Role in Chile Recalled," *New York Times,* October 17, 1974, 9. Hersh, "CIA Said to Have Asked Funds for Chile Rightists in '73," *New York Times,* October 21, 1974, 2. Hersh, "House Unit Meets on Chilean Leaks," *New York Times,* September 26, 1974, 13. Ray S. Cline correction, *New York Times,* October 22, 1974, 43. Michael Harrington, "The CIA in Chile: A Question of Responsibility," *New York Times,* January 2, 1976, 25; Ray S. Cline, "The Value of the CIA," *New York Times,* November 1, 1974, 39. Morton H. Halperin, "On Behalf of the Public's Right to Know," *New York Times,* July 9, 1975, 31. Daniel Schorr, *Clearing the Air* (Boston: Houghton Mifflin, 1977), 130-34, as does Davis, *Last Two Years,* 356-58.

20. Edward M. Korry, "One of Our Very Best . . . ," unpublished memoir. Bart Barnes, "Edward M. Korry Dies; Diplomat and Journalist," *Washington Post*, January 30, 2003, B6.

21. "Edward M. Korry—U.S. Ambassador during Coup in Chile," *New York Times*, February 1, 2003. Korry was backed fully by Kissinger. Henry Kissinger, *The White House Years* (New York: Little, Brown, 1979), 673.

22. Anderson, "ITT and the Allende Government." Seymour M. Hersh, "State Department Upholds Stand U.S. Did Not Interfere in Chile," *New York Times*, September 10, 1974, 3. Hersh, *Price of Power*, 272. Patricia Korry, interview, February 12, 2012.

23. Edward M. Korry to A. M. Rosenthal, September 13, 1974. His first letter to Rosenthal, summarizing what he saw as the *Times'* inaccuracies, came September 8, Rosenthal Papers. The entire Chile matter, including Korry's role, is summarized in a U.S. Senate committee report, *Church Report: Covert Action in Chile, 1963–1973* (Washington DC: Government Printing Office, 1975), at http://foia.state.gov/Reports/ChurchReport.asp.

24. Patricia Korry, telephone interview, February 20, 2012. Korry also asked for help from another friend, Elie Abel, the dean of the Columbia Journalism School.

25. E. Korry to Rosenthal. Patricia Korry, interview, February 20, 2012. Peter Kihss, "U.S. Took 'Extraordinarily Soft Line' in Allende's First Year, Envoy Says," *New York Times*, September 16, 1974, 8. Edward Korry is quoted in the Church Report.

26. E. Korry to A. M. Rosenthal, September 17 and 21, 1974. Kihss, "U.S. Took 'Extraordinarily Soft Line.'" Wicker, "Was Ford Conned?" Patricia Korry also kept tape recordings of the Hersh conversations.

27. John F. Burns, telephone interview by author, February 22, 2012. Two authors assert that Burns wrote a story for the *Times* about Hersh and Chile, but that it was killed. Burns says his summary was for internal use only. Joseph C. Goulden, *Fit to Print: A.M. Rosenthal and His Times* (Secaucus NJ: Lyle Stuart), 190. Joseph Trento, *The Secret History of the CIA* (New York: Forum, 2001).

28. Edward M. Korry (son), telephone interview by author, February 13, 2012. Patricia Korry, interview, February 20, 2012. E. Korry letter in Goulden, *Fit to Print*, 193. Joe Trento, emails to author, February 13. 15, 18, and 20, 2012. Trento, *Secret History*, 507.

29. "The 2,300-Word *Times* Correction," *Time*, February 23, 1981, 84. Hersh, "New Evidence Backs Ex-envoy on His Role in Chile," *New York Times*, February 9, 1981, 1.

30. Hersh interview, CNN, "The Ambassador vs. *The New York Times*," February 25, 1981. Trento, email to author, February 13, 2012. Goulden, *Fit to Print*, 191. Mitchell Stephens, telephone interview by author, January 30, 2012. Stephens, *The History of News: From the Drum to the Satellite* (New York: Viking, 1988), and *The Rise of the Image, the Fall of the Word* (New York: Oxford University Press, 1998).

17. *Skeletons Tumble from the* CIA *Closet*

1. Daniel Schorr, *Clearing the Air* (Boston: Houghton Mifflin, 1977), 180. Walter Pincus, interview by author, February 18, 2012.

2. Schorr, *Clearing the Air*. Eszterhas, "Reporter Who Broke," 50.

3. Hersh, *Reporter's Obligation*, 8. Charles Colson, White house memo, April 1, 1972, supplied by William C. Gaines, University of Illinois, from Colson Papers, Billy Graham Archives, Wheaton IL. Hersh, email to author, February 12, 2012. Hersh found the memo puzzling and did not recollect this incident.

4. Seymour M. Hersh, "Prosecutors Act," *New York Times*, May 6, 1973, 1. Tom Wells, *Wild Man: The Life and Times of Daniel Ellsberg* (New York: Palgrave, 2001).

5. Seymour M. Hersh, "Dean Tied to Plan for Ring to Spy on 1972 Protests," *New York Times*, May 14, 1973, 63. Hersh, "White House Unit Reportedly Spied on Radicals," *New York Times*, May 21, 1973, 1. Hersh, "A Broad Program," *New York Times*, May 24, 1973, 1. Hersh, *Reporter's Obligation*, 9.

6. Harrison E. Salisbury, *Without Fear or Favor: The New York Times and Its Times* (New York: Times Books, 1980), 529. Salisbury interviewed Hersh.

7. The report is at "The CIA's Family Jewels," National Security Archive, posted June 21, 2007, http://www.gwu.edu/~nsarchiv/NSAEBB/NSAEBB222/index.htm. On the entry page to the site appears a copy of Hersh's *New York Times* exposé of December 24, 1974. Salisbury, *Without Fear or Favor*, 533. William Colby and Peter Forbath, *Honorable Men: My Life in the* CIA (New York: Simon and Schuster), 13.

8. Henry Kissinger, *The White House Years* (New York: Little, Brown, 1979), 677. Seymour M. Hersh, "CIA Told to Curb Activities Abroad," *New York Times*, January 7, 1975, 69. Hersh, "Sparkman Plans Inquiry on CIA Activities Abroad," *New York Times*, January 9, 1975, 20. Eszterhas, "Reporter Who Broke," 68.

9. Seymour M. Hersh, "CIA: Maker of Policy or Tool?" *New York Times*, April 25–29, 1966. Salisbury, *Without Fear or Favor*, 182. Kathryn Olmsted, *Challenging the Secret Government: The Post-Watergate Investigations of the* CIA *and* FBI (Chapel Hill : University of North Carolina Press, 1996) , 32. Hersh, *Reporter's Obligation*, 9. Colby and Forbath, *Honorable Men*, 13.

10. Colby and Forbath, *Honorable Men*, 392, 389. Hersh, *Reporter's Obligation*, 11.

11. Seymour M. Hersh, "Huge CIA Operation Reported in U.S. against Antiwar Forces, Other Dissidents in Nixon Years," *New York Times*, December 22, 1974, 1, 26.

12. Hersh, "Huge CIA Operation Reported."

13. Hersh, "Huge CIA Operation Reported."

14. Hersh, "Huge CIA Operation Reported." Tom Mangold, *Cold Warrior: James Jesus Angleton* (New York: Simon and Schuster, 1991), 316–17.

15. Colby and Forbath, *Honorable Men* 393, 395. Seymour M. Hersh, "The Angleton Story," *New York Times*, June 25, 1978, SM4. Hersh, "3 More Aides Quit in CIA Shakeup," *New York Times*, December 30, 1975, 1. It is not known if the CIA and

FBI launched probes of Hersh. He has declined to request a copy of his dossier. "No interest in any file on me at all," he said. Hersh, email to author, September 13, 2011. Eszterhas, "Reporter Who Broke," 51. Walter Pincus, "Covering Intelligence," *New Republic*, February 1, 1975, 11. John Greene, *The Presidency of Gerald Ford* (Lawrence: University Press of Kansas, 1995), 101–16.

16. Olmsted, *Challenging the Secret Government*, 30. Seymour M. Hersh, "Ex-aides Say They Knew of No Johnson Order for Domestic Office of CIA," *New York Times*, January 18, 1975, 12. Pincus, "Covering Intelligence," 11.

17. John Oakes to A. M. Rosenthal, December 27, 1974; Rosenthal to Oakes, January 3, 1975; Oakes to Rosenthal, January 7, 1975, Rosenthal to Hersh, January 2, 1975, Rosenthal Papers, New York Public Library.

18. Salisbury, *Without Fear or Favor*, 533. Hersh agreed; Rosenthal was alarmed by Colby, email to author February 21, 2012.

19. Eszterhas, "Reporter Who Broke," 51. James Kilpatrick, "Cool Off the CIA Stew," *Idaho Times News*, January 13, 1975. Leslie Gelb, "Bearing Out Seymour Hersh," *New Republic*, March 22, 1975, 15. John Lofton, "Hersh Reputation Is Far from One of Impartiality," *Yuma Daily Sun*, January 24, 1975, 4.

20. "A New CIA Furor," *Newsweek*, January 6, 1975, 65. "Supersnoop," *Time*, January 6, 1975, 10. Ronald Kessler, "Accused CIA Aide Disclaims Spy Role," *Washington Post*, December 25, 1974, 1. David Wise, *The American Police State* (New York: Random House, 1976). See also David Wise and Thomas B. Ross, *The Invisible Government* (New York: Bantam Books, 1965), 193.

21. Seymour M. Hersh, "Colby Said to Confirm CIA Role in U.S.," *New York Times*, January 1, 1975, 37. "Congratulations," *Time*, January 1975. Arthur Sulzberger to A. M. Rosenthal, January 20, 1975, Rosenthal Papers. Hersh, "Ford Names Rockefeller to Head Inquiry into CIA," *New York Times*, January 6, 1975, 1. Olmsted, *Challenging the Secret Government*, 399n5. Hersh, "CIA Admits Domestic Acts, Denies 'Massive' Illegality," *New York Times*, January 16, 1975, 1. Hersh, "Democrats Vote Wide CIA Study by Senate Panel," *New York Times*, January 21, 1975, 1.

22. Olmsted, *Challenging the Secret Government*, 12. Seymour M. Hersh, "CIA in '68 Gave Secret Service a Report Containing Gossip about Eartha Kitt," *New York Times*, January 3, 1975, 25. Hersh, "Ex-Army Agent Says He Briefed CIA in 1967," *New York Times*, January 11, 1975, L11. Hersh, "Bid to Kill Files Laid to CIA Aide," *New York Times*, January 10, 1975, 1. Olmsted, *Challenging the Secret Government*, 44, 46.

18. The Submarine Caper

1. Eszterhas, "Reporter Who Broke," 49. Arthur Sulzberger to A. M. Rosenthal, January 20, 1975, Rosenthal Papers, New York Public Library. James L. Aucoin, *The Evolution of American Investigative Journalism* (Columbia: University of Missouri Press, 2005).

2. "A New CIA Furor," *Newsweek,* January 6, 1975, 10. "Supersnoop," *Time,* January 6, 1975, 65. Downie, "Scoop Artist," in *New Muckrakers,* 54, 59. Eszterhas, "Reporter Who Broke," 98.

3. Eszterhas, "Reporter Who Broke," 51. *Rolling Stone* published five Annie Liebovitz photos, April 10 and April 24, 1975.

4. James Naughton, "CIA Chief Says Charges Imperil Intelligence Work," *New York Times,* February 21, 1975, 65. Tom Wicker, "The CIA and Its Critics," *New York Times,* February 23, 1975, E13. Edward Jay Epstein, "The War within the CIA," August 1978, http://www.edwardjayepstein.com/Colby.htm.

5. Leslie Gelb, "The CIA and the Press," *New Republic,* March 22, 1975, 15–16.

6. Nicholas M. Horrock, "Rockefeller Inquiry Clears CIA of Major Violations," *New York Times,* June 3, 1975, .1. Leslie Gelb, "Led Astray by the CIA," *New Republic,* June 28, 1975, 8–16.

7. Anthony Lewis, "The Teller of Truth," *New York Times,* July 10, 1975, 29.

8. Seymour M. Hersh, "Great Power and Secrecy: A Formula for Abuse," *New York Times,* June 15, 1975, E1. Hersh, "Report on CIA Is Praised but Recommendations Are Called Weak," *New York Times,* June 12, 1975, 23. *Final Report of the Select Committee to Study Governmental Operations with Respect to Intelligence Activities* (Church report) (Washington DC: Government Printing Office, 1976), http://archive .org/details/finalreportofselo1unit.

9. Cynthia M. Nolan, "Seymour Hersh's Impact on the CIA," *International Journal of Intelligence and Counterintelligence* 12, no. 1 (Spring 1999): 19. Kathryn S. Olmsted, *Real Enemies: Conspiracy Theories and American Democracy, World War I to 9/11* (New York: Oxford University Press, 2009), 50. Greider quoted in Olmsted, 202.

10. "CIA's Family Jewels." Darnton, interview.

11. "The Quiet Pulitzers," *Time,* May 19, 1975, 68. A. M. Rosenthal to Hersh, May 15, 1975, Rosenthal Papers. Lofton, "Hersh Reputation." John Lofton, "Pulitzer Prize Jury Finds Hersh Guilty," *Times Record,* May 26, 1975, 4.

12. Eszterhas, "Reporter Who Broke," 52. Seymour M. Hersh, "Underground for the CIA in New York," *New York Times,* December 29, 1974, 1.

13. Eszterhas, "Reporter Who Broke," 52, 51. Salisbury, *Without Fear or Favor,* 540.

14. Norman Polmar and Michael White, *Project Azorian: The CIA and the Raising of the K-129* (Annapolis MD: Naval Institute Press, 2010). Clyde W Burleson, *The Jennifer Project.* (College Station: Texas A&M University Press, 1997). Roger C. Dunham, *Spy Sub: Top Secret Mission to the Bottom of the Pacific* (New York: Penguin Books, 1996). Roy Varner and Wayne Collier, *A Matter of Risk: The Incredible Inside Story of the CIA's Hughes Glomar Explorer Mission* (New York: Random House, 1978).

15. Colby and Forbath, *Honorable Men,* 416.

16. Transcripts of Colby's conversations were released in 1977. See Seymour M. Hersh, "CIA Plan Disclosed in Glomar Incident," *New York Times,* October 26,

1977, 23. The transcripts were supplied to me by University of California Professor Kathryn Olmsted. Two telephone conversations, William Colby and unnamed callers, CIA Files, January 22, 1974.

17. Telephone conversations, Colby and *New York Times*, CIA files, January 30, 1974.

18. Bob Phelps, email to author, March 24, 2012. Telephone conversation, Colby and Hersh, CIA Files, January 30, 1974.

19. Bob Phelps, email to author, March 17, 2012.

20. Colby memos summarizing his conversations with Hersh, February 2 and 4, 1974.

21. The Ford incident: Wise, *American Police State*, 194–95; Salisbury, *Without Fear or Favor*, 536–39. Telephone conversation, Colby and Brent Scowcroft, CIA Files, February 20, 1975.

22. Polmar and White, *Project Azorian,* xi. Matthew Aid, William Burr, and Thomas Blanton, "Project Azorian: The CIA's Declassified History of the *Glomar Explorer*," National Security Archive posted February 12, 2010, http://www.gwu.edu/~nsarchiv/nukevault/ebb305/index.htm. Jeffrey T. Richelson, *The Wizards of Langley: Inside the CIA's Directorate of Science and Technology* (Boulder CO: Westview Press, 2001).

23. Polmar and White, *Project Azorian,* 97–98.

24. The *Los Angeles Times* story went out over the newspaper's syndicated wire and was picked up by United Press International. CIA Files, conversation, Colby and Carl Duckett, February 7, 1975. William Farr and Jerry Cohen, "CIA Reportedly Contracted with Hughes," *Los Angeles Times,* February 8, 1975, 1. Colby and Forbath, *Honorable Men*, 415. James Phelan, "An Easy Burglary Led to the Disclosure of Hughes-CIA Plan to Salvage Soviet Sub," *New York Times,* March 27, 1975, 18.

25. Salisbury, *Without Fear or Favor*, 45. Telephone conversations, Colby and Sulzberger, CIA Files, February 8 and 10, 1975.

26. Memo on Hersh, CIA files, February 20, 1975. Three memos, "Telephone call from Mr. Seymour M. Hersh," all February 20, 1975.

27. Meeting, William Colby, Carl Duckett, and Laurence Silberman, CIA Files, February 14, 1975. Telephone conversations, Scowcroft and Colby, CIA Files, February 21 and 25, 1975.

28. Clifton Daniel, *Lords, Ladies and Gentlemen* (New York: Arbor House, 1984), 220, 221. Bill Kovach, telephone interview by author, July 27, 2011.

29. Telephone conversation, CIA Files, March 18, 1975. No copy of the Hersh memo was in the Rosenthal papers. Hersh believes he still has a copy, but he never found it.

30. Telephone conversations, William Colby and Jack Anderson, Colby and Clifton Daniel, CIA Files, March 19, 1975.

31. Seymour M. Hersh, "CIA Salvage Ship Brought Up Part of Soviet Sub in 1968, Failed to Raise Atom Missiles," *New York Times,* March 19, 1975, 1. Salisbury, *Without Fear or Favor,* 548n.

19. *Going after "The Godfather"*

1. Anthony Lewis, "The Secrecy Disease," *New York Times,* October 31, 1977, 31. Olmsted, *Challenging the Secret Government,* 74.

2. Salisbury, *Without Fear or Favor.* James Phelan, *Howard Hughes: The Hidden Years* (New York: Random House, 1976), 540.

3. Bill Kovach, telephone interview by author, July 27, 2011.

4. Hersh, interview with "Frontline," January 8, 2007.

5. Korry, "One of Our Very Best. . . ." Arthur Herman, "The 35-Year War on the CIA," *Commentary,* December 2009, 11.

6. NSC, Memorandum of conversation, February 7, 1975. Cheney memo, "CIA—Colby Report," December 27, 1974, Richard Cheney Files, Box 5. Both in Ford Papers, Ann Arbor MI.

7. Elizabeth Peer, "Salvaging the Sub Story," *Newsweek,* March 31, 1975, 66.

8. Seymour M. Hersh, "Submarines of U.S. Stage Spy Missions inside Soviet Waters," *New York Times,* May 25, 1975, 1. Laurence Stern, "U.S. Subs Spying in Soviet Waters," *Washington Post,* January 4, 1974, 1.

9. Cheney memo, "Unauthorized disclosure," May 29, 1975. Edward Levi, Memorandum for the President, May 29, 1975. Cheney Files, Box 6, "Intelligence—New York Times articles by Seymour Hersh," Ford Papers. Hersh, interview, January 8, 2007. Lowell Bergman and Marlena Telvick, "Dick Cheney's Memos from 30 Years Ago," *Frontline* documentary, posted February 13, 2007, http://www.pbs.org/wgbh/pages/frontline/newswar/preview/documents.html.

10. Phelps, email, March 17, 2012.

11. Kovach, interview.

12. Darnton, interview. Peter Millones to Seymour Hersh and Martin Arnold, undated, early 1977, Rosenthal Papers, New York Public Library.

13. Hersh to David Jones, January 31, 1977, Rosenthal Papers.

14. Seymour Topping to editors, January 17, 1977. James Greenfield to A. M. Rosenthal, September 1, 1976. Sydney Schanberg to A. M. Rosenthal, August 31, 1976, Rosenthal Papers.

15. Gus Russo, *Supermob: How Sidney Korshak and His Criminal Associates Became America's Hidden Power Brokers* (New York: Bloomsbury, 2006), 519. Hersh interview with Russo, May 16, 2003. Seymour M. Hersh, "The Contrasting Lives of Sidney R. Korshak," *New York Times,* June 27, 1976, 1.

16. Jeff Gerth, telephone interview by author, April 20, 2012. Judith Exner, as told to Ovid Demaris, *My Story* (New York: Grove Press, 1977). Russo, *Supermob,* 428.

17. Hersh, *Reporter's Obligation*, 12.

18. Russo, *Supermob*, 428. Gerth, interview.

19. Russo, *Supermob*, 120-21, 428. Gerth, interview. William Moore, "Was Estes Kefauver 'Blackmailed,'" *Public Historian*, January 1983, 4-28.

20. Russo, *Supermob*, 429. Gerth said Korshak did not have their phone records.

21. Russo, *Supermob*, 429, 430. Gerth, interview.

22. Rosenthal told Hersh about Korshak and Sulzberger. Russo, *Supermob*, 430. Rosenthal to Hersh, June 24, 1976, Rosenthal Papers.

23. Seymour M. Hersh, "Korshak's Power Rooted in Ties to Labor Leaders," *New York Times*, June 28, 1976, 1. Hersh, "Major Corporations Eager to Seek Korshak's Advice," *New York Times*, June 29, 1976, 1. Hersh, "Korshak Again the Target of a Federal Investigation," *New York Times*, June 30, 1976, 1.

24. Frank Lalli, "The Korshak Series: Firecrackers, Not Dynamite," *New West*, August 2, 1976, 27. Nat Hentoff, *Village Voice*, July 19, 1976. *Congressional Record*, September 30, 1976, 17385.

25. Hersh, "Contrasting Lives"; Hersh, "Korshak's Power." See note 23.

26. Gerth, interview. Lalli, "Korshak Series," 28.

27. Lalli, "Korshak Series," 29. Seymour M. Hersh, "Korshak Leaves Hospital after Intestinal Illness," *New York Times*, July 1, 1976, 14. Russo, *Supermob*, 434-35.

28. Lalli, "Korshak Series," 30, 29. Gerth, interview. Editorial, "The Korshak Series," *New York Times*, July 1, 1976, 26.

29. Jeff Gerth, telephone interview, April 27, 2012.

20. The Big Apple Turns Sour

1. Hersh, *Reporter's Obligation*, 12.

2. Robert Sobel, *The Rise and Fall of the Conglomerate Kings* (Briarcliff Manor NY: Beard Books, 1984), 101-26.

3. Hersh to Jones, January 31, 1997; Hersh to A. M. Rosenthal, March 25, 1997, Rosenthal Papers. All subsequent letters and memos are from Rosenthal Papers. Gerth worked for the *Times* from 1978 to 2005 and has won two Pulitzer Prizes.

4. Miraldi, *Muckraking and Objectivity*.

5. Charles Davis to Seymour Topping, letter, April 25, 1977. Hersh memo to Topping, April 25, 1977.

6. Topping to Davis, April 26 and May 2, 1977. Hersh to Topping, May 2, 1977.

7. Davis to Topping, May 6, 1977. Hersh to Topping, May 9, 1977.

8. Arthur Gelb, email to author, September 30, 2011. Gelb, telephone interview by author, June 16, 2010. Sydney Schanberg, interview by author, July 26, 2005. Bill Kovach, email to author, July 8, 2011.

9. Bob Phelps, telephone interview, June 25, 2011. Bob Woodward, interview, February 8, 2012. Tom Goldstein, telephone interview by author, June 11, 2011.

10. Because of the threatening letters, Hersh reported often to Topping. Hersh to Topping, May 9 and 11, 1997. Jeff Gerth, telephone interview by author, April 20, 2012.

11. Hersh to Topping, May 12, 16, and 23, 1977.

12. John M. Lee to Topping, June 8, 1977.

13. Davis to Sulzberger, July 13, 1977.

14. Davis to James Goodale, June 7, 1997. A federal court later found that no SEC officials had leaked documents to Hersh; he had other sources.

15. Hersh to Topping, June 30 1977.

16. Seymour M. Hersh, "S.E.C. Presses Wide Investigation of Gulf and Western Conglomerate," *New York Times*, July 24, 1977, 1. Hersh, "Gulf and Western's Relationship with Banks Is Issue in S.E.C. Study," *New York Times*, July 25, 1977, 1. Hersh, "Gulf and Western Tax Practices Coming under Wide Examination," *New York Times*, July 26, 1977, 1.

17. Seymour Topping, telephone interview with author, May 4, 1997.

18. "G&W Series Tampered With?" *New York*, August 8, 1977, 8. Alexander Greenfield to A. M. Rosenthal, August 3, 1977.

19. Topping, interview. Joseph C. Goulden, *Fit to Print: A.M. Rosenthal and His Times* (Secaucus NJ: Lyle Stuart, 1998), 297.

20. Steven Brill, "The Gulf and Western-SEC fiasco," *American Lawyer*, January 1982, 8.

21. Clifton Daniel to A. M. Rosenthal, undated, circa 1976. Seymour M. Hersh, "Colby Says His Dismissal as CIA Chief Arose from His Cooperation," *New York Times*, March 14, 1978, 12.

22. Seymour M. Hersh, "The Angleton Story," *New York Times*, June 25, 1978, 13–15; Hersh, "Human Error Is Cited in '74 Glomar Failure," *New York Times*, December 9, 1978, 1; Hersh, "Participant Tells of CIA Ruses," *New York Times*, December 10, 1978, 18.

23. Goldstein, interview. Gelb, email.

24. Goulden, *Fit to Print*, 192. Hersh, email, May 7, 2012.

25. Darnton, interview. Goulden, *Fit to Print*, 192. Hersh confirmed the story.

26. Goulden, *Fit to Print*, 297, 192.

27. Denny Walsh, telephone interview by author, June 16, 2011. Russell Baker, telephone interview by author, July 18, 2011.

21. Scoop Artist versus Dr. Kissinger

1. Goulden, *Fit to Print*, 192. Walter Isaacson, *Kissinger: A Biography* (New York: Simon & Schuster, 1992), 14.

2. Bruce Manuel, "Man behind a Jolting Book on Kissinger," *Christian Science*

Monitor, June 24, 1983, B1. Seymour M. Hersh, interview by Brian Lamb, C-Span, August 11, 1983, http://www.c-spanvideo.org/program/123879-1.

3.Hersh quoted in "Letter from Washington," *National Review,* June 24, 1983, 729. Salisbury, *Without Fear or Favor,* 527.

4. I interviewed Roger Kahn for *Beyond the Boys of Summer,* ed. Rob Miraldi (New York: McGraw-Hill, 2005). Arthur Gelb, email to author, January 30, 2012. Al Siegel, telephone interview by author, February 24, 2012. Topping, interview.

5. Richard Grenier, "The Passion of Seymour Hersh," *American Spectator,* September 1983, http://www.unz.org/Pub/AmSpectator-1983sep-00010. Seymour M. Hersh, "Hanoi Asserts Ties with U.S. Were Set," *New York Times,* August 7, 1979, A1

6. Seymour M. Hersh, "2.25 Million Cambodians Are Said to Face Starvation," *New York Times,* August 8, 1979, A1. Hersh, "Exodus of Skilled Ethnic Chinese Worsens Hanoi's Plight," *New York Times,* 1979, August 9, 1979, A2. Hersh, "Black Market Makes Ho Chi Minh City Run," *New York Times,* August 10, 1979, A6. Hersh, "Vietnam Reports It Foiled a Swindle in Exit Visas," *New York Times,* August 12, 1979, 11. Hersh, "Non-communist Editor's Newspaper Is Flourishing," *New York Times,* August 13, 1979. A6. Hersh, "Everyday Life in Communist Vietnam Can Be Surprising," *New York Times,* August 14, 1979, A2. Hersh on Nguyen Co Thach, "Observer from Vietnam," *New Yorker,* October 23, 1979.

7. Jay Peterzell, "The Government Shuts Up," *Columbia Journalism Review,* July/August 1982.

8. Hersh, *Price of Power,* 15n. No document could record that scene.

9. Jay Peterzell, telephone interview by author, June 18, 2012.

10. Peterzell, interview. Hersh, *Price of Power,* 39n.

11. Seymour M. Hersh, email to author, June 22, 2012. Morton Halperin, telephone interview by author, July 3, 2012. "Ex-CIA Agent Edwin Wilson Talks about His Mysterious Allegiance to Libya," *People,* November 23, 1981.

12. Seymour M. Hersh, "The Qadaffi Connection," *New York Times,* June 14, 1981, SM1. Hersh, "Target Gadaffi," *New York Times,* February 22, 1987, SM16.

13. Seymour M. Hersh, "Exposing the Libyan," *New York Times,* June 21, SM8. Jeff Gerth, "Former Intelligence Aides Profiting from Old Ties," *New York Times,* December 6, 1981, 1. Gerth, email to author, June 20, 2012.

14. Seymour M. Hersh, "Panel in House Will Investigate Ex-CIA Agent," *New York Times,* September 19, 1981, 1; Hersh, "Rogue Elephants at Large," *New York Times,* October 19, 1981, A22.

15. "The Spy Who Stayed in the Cold," *Time,* November 8, 1982. Peter Maas, *Manhunt: The Incredible Pursuit of a CIA Agent Turned Terrorist* (New York: Random House, 1986). Richard Lloyd, *Beyond the CIA: The Frank Terpil Story* (New York: Seaver Books, 1983).

16. Kissinger wrote three memoirs: *White House Years* (Boston: Little, Brown,

1979); *For the Record: Selected Statements, 1977–1980* (Boston: Little, Brown, 1981, and *Years of Upheaval* (Boston: Little, Brown, 1982). "Kissinger Rescued in Protest at Brazil College," *New York Times*, November 19, 1981, 9.

17. Isaacson, *Kissinger*, 705–29. Seymour M. Hersh, "The Wiretaps," *Atlantic Magazine,* May 1982; quotes taken from the online article, http://www.theatlantic.com/past/docs/issues/82may/hershwh.htm. Hersh, *Price of Power*, 83–97. Hersh, "Who Did What to Whom and Why, with the Taps?" *New York Times*, June 16, 1974, 187.

18. Roger Morris, *Uncertain Greatness: Henry Kissinger and American Foreign Policy* (New York: Harper & Row, 1977). Marvin and Bernard Kalb, *Kissinger* (Boston: Little, Brown, 1974).

19. Stanley Hoffman, "The Kissinger Antimemoirs," *New York Times*, July 3, 1983, BR1.

20. Hersh, interview by Lamb. Walter LaFeber, "Henry Kissinger and the World of Diplomacy," *Washington Post*, June 12, 1983, Book World, 1.

21. Kissinger's unpublished response is Kissinger to A. M. Rosenthal, July 12, 1983, Rosenthal Papers, New York Public Library. Woodward quoted in Mallary Jean Tenore, "Bob Woodward: 'You Get the Truth at Night, the Lies during the Day,'" Poynter, March 15, 2011, http://www.poynter.org/latest-news/top-stories/123587/bob-woodward-you-get-the-truth-at-night-the-lies-during-the-day/.

22. Tom Wicker, "Haig and Watergate," *New York Times*, April 27, 1982, A23, and April 30, 1982; A23.

23. Kissinger to Rosenthal. Kissinger, *Years of Upheaval.*

24. Hersh, email to author, July 5, 2012. LaFeber, "Henry Kissinger."

25. Hersh relied heavily on depositions in Halperin's lawsuit for his "wiretaps" research. Hersh, *Price of Power*, 647. Anthony Lewis, "Mephisto's Waltz," *New York Times*, April 19, 1982, A21. Martin Tolchin, "Kissinger Issues Wiretap Apology," *New York Times*, November 13, 1992, http://www.nytimes.com/1992/11/13/us/kissinger-issues-wiretap-apology.html.

22. *The Summer's Literary Furor*

1. James Reston, "Kissinger at 60," *New York Times*, May 15, 1983, 198. See chapter 16, note 6 on Chile.

2. On Hersh's sources, see Hersh, *Price of Power*, 653–54. Walter LaFeber, "Henry Kissinger and the World of Diplomacy," *Washington Post*, June 12, 1983, Book World, 1. Seymour M. Hersh, "Kissinger, Nixon, and Chile," *Atlantic*, December 1982. http://www.theatlantic.com/past/docs/issues/82dec/hersh.htm.

3. Victor Gold, "The Great Conspiracy," *National Review,* August 19, 1983, 1021. Henry Kissinger to A. M. Rosenthal, July 12, 1983, Rosenthal Papers, New York Public Library.

4. William Safire, "Henry and Sy," *New York Times*, June 9, 1983, A23. Charlotte Curtis, "The Kissinger Aura," *New York Times*, August 30, 1983, C11.

5. Stephen Rosenfeld, "Kissinger's Faults Weren't the Worst," *Washington Post*, September 2, 1983, A21. Saul Landau, "Seymour Hersh," *Progressive,* October 1988, 33–37.

6. Hoffman, "Kissinger Antimemoirs." Jonathan Steinberg, "Rug Time," *London Review of Books,* October 30 1983, http://www.lrb.co.uk/v05/n19/jonathan-steinberg/rug-time. Anthony Lewis, "The Kissinger Lesson," *New York Times*, June 26, 1983, E21.

7. Robert Dallek, *Nixon and Kissinger* (New York: Harper Collins, 2007), x. Peter S. Prescott, "All the Presidents' Man," *Newsweek*, June 20, 1983, 74.

8. Hersh, "The Job Seeker," *Price of Power*, 11–24. Bernard Gwertzman, "Book Portrays Kissinger as a Double-Dealer in '68," *New York Times*, June 2, 1983, A14; "Kissinger Says Assertions of Double-Dealing Are 'Slimy Lies,'" *New York Times,* June 3, 1983, A3. Henry Kissinger to A. M. Rosenthal, July 12, 1983, Rosenthal Papers.

9. Kissinger to Rosenthal, July 12, 1983. Ostensibly Kissinger was writing to Rosenthal to ask him to control what the *Times* wrote about Hersh's book. But clearly his arguments were being made privately to a number of other journalists.

10. Russell Baker, "The Hissing of Hersh," *New York Times*, June 15, 1983, A27. Curtis, "Kissinger Aura."

11. Hersh, interview by Lamb. Hersh, email to author, July 2, 2012.

12. Steinberg, "Rug Time." Gold, "Great Conspiracy."

13. Bruce Manuel, "Man behind a Jolting Book on Kissinger," *Christian Science Monitor,* June 24, 1983, B1. Alan Wolfe, "Henry's Nemesis," *Nation*, July 23–30, 1983, 85.

14. Hoffman, "Kissinger Antimemoirs." Manuel, "Man behind a Jolting Book."

15. Curtis, "Kissinger Aura." Edwin McDowell, "About Books and Authors," *New York Times*, July 24, 1983, BR22.

16. James Reston, "Kissinger at 60," New York Times, May 15, 1983, p. 198. Steven Weisman, "Reagan Chooses Kissinger to Run New Latin Team," *New York Times,* July 19, 1983, 1. Hersh, interview by Lamb.

17. Wolfe, "Henry's Nemesis." Colman McCarthy, "Rushing to Judge," *Washington Post*, June 12, 1983, L6. Lewis, "Kissinger Lesson."

18. Gold, "Great Conspiracy." Safire, "Henry and Sy." Ian Davidson, "As They Were," *Financial Times*, October 8, 1983, 12.

19. Hersh, interview by Lamb. Prescott, "All the Presidents' Man."

20. Hoffman, "Kissinger Antimemoirs." Wajahat Ali, "Going 15 Rounds with Seymour Hersh," *Counterpunch*, January 15, 2008, http://www.counterpunch.org/2008/01/15/going-15-rounds-with-seymour-hersh/.

21. McCarthy, "Rushing to Judge." Sydney Schanberg, "The Kissinger Debate,"

New York Times, June 14, 1983, 23. Hersh, commencement address, Columbia University Journalism School, May 21, 2003.

22. Hersh, interview by Lamb.

23. Manuel, "Man behind a Jolting Book."

24. Wolfe, "Henry's Nemesis." LaFeber, "Henry Kissinger." Manuel, "Man behind a Jolting Book."

25. George W. Ball, "Scathing Re-examination," *Christian Science Monitor,* September 2, 1982, B5.

26. Ball, "Scathing Re-examination." Walter Isaacson, *Kissinger: A Biography* (New York: Simon & Schuster, 1992). Henry Kissinger bibliography, NNDB, http://www.nndb.com/people/357/000022291/bibliography/.

27. Christopher Hitchens, *The Trial of Henry Kissinger* (London: Verso, 2001). Hitchens cowrote the documentary film version of *The Trial of Henry Kissinger.*

28. Wolfe, "Henry's Nemesis."

29. Manuel, "Man behind a Jolting Book." Curtis, "Kissinger Aura."

23. Who Shot Down the Korean Airliner?

1. Henry Kissinger to A. M. Rosenthal, July 12, 1983, Rosenthal Papers, New York Public Library. Hersh, *Price of Power,* 450.

2. Hersh, *Price of Power,* 444–45, 447.

3. Bill Peterson, "Kissinger's Day in Court," *Washington Post,* October 2, 1989, B 1; Peterson, "Kissinger Takes the Stand," *Washington Post,* October 3, 1989, D1. John Gorman, "Hersh Libel Trial Nearing Finish," *Chicago Tribune,* October 5, 1989. Gorman, "Author Hersh Acquitted," *Chicago Tribune,* October 7, 1989, 18.

4. Gorman, "Author Hersh Acquitted."

5. Jon Bor, "The World of Kissinger according to Sy Hersh," *Post-Standard,* October 21, 1983.

6. Seymour M. Hersh, "The Pardon," *Atlantic,* August 1983, 55–62.

7. "Nixon Threatened Ford on Pardon, Story Says," *Deseret News,* July 21–22, 1983, 2A. Montgomery Brower, "Reporter Seymour Hersh Unravels the Tragic Mystery," *People,* October 6, 1986.

8. Seymour M. Hersh, "Pakistani in U.S. Sought to Ship A-bomb Trigger," *New York Times,* February 5, 1985, A1.

9. Seymour M. Hersh, *"The Target Is Destroyed": What Really Happened to Flight 007 and What America Knew about It* (New York: Random House, 1986), 170n. Garry Abrams, "Hersh's Book on Downing of Jet Called Off Course," *Los Angeles Times,* October 12, 1986.

10. George Johnson, "New and Noteworthy," *New York Times,* September 27, 1987, 50.

11. Johnson, "New and Noteworthy." Hersh, *"Target Is Destroyed,"* 19.

12. Brower, "Reporter Seymour Hersh Unravels." Abrams, "Hersh's Book on Downing of Jet."

13. Brower, "Reporter Seymour Hersh Unravels." Warren Richey, "KAL 007 Aftermath Mismanaged, Author Says," *Christian Science Monitor,* October 3, 1986.

14. Hersh, *"Target Is Destroyed,"* 273.

15. In the paperback version of *"Target Is Destroyed,"* Hersh added a preface describing the call from Casey, ix-xvii. Casey conceded the government lied about KAL. Joseph Persico, *Casey: The Lives and Secrets of William J. Casey* (New York: Viking, 1990), 356.

16. Stephen Engelberg, "U.S. Data Said to Conclude Soviet Mistook Korean Plane," *New York Times,* August 24, 1986, 1. Brower, "Reporter Seymour Hersh Unravels." Abrams, "Hersh's Book on Downing of Jet."

17. Douglas B. Feaver, "The Shot Heard round the World," *Washington Post,* September 14, 1986, X1. Thomas Powers, "Believing the Worst of Each Other," *New York Times,* September 21, 1986, BR3. Richey, "KAL 007 Aftermath Mismanaged." Fred Glaeser, "Inside Account," *Christian Science Monitor*, October 3, 1986, 22.

18. Hersh, *"Target Is Destroyed,"* xx. Glaeser, "Inside Account."

19. Edward Luttwak, "007, Licensed to Kill?," *New Republic,* October 13, 1986, 34, 36. Glaeser, "Inside Account." Brower, "Reporter Seymour Hersh Unravels."

20. Seymour M. Hersh, "Panama Strongman Said to Trade in Drugs," *New York Times,* June 12, 1986, A1. Hersh, "Panama General Said to Have Told Army to Rig Vote," *New York Times*, June 22, 1986, 1. He detailed the allegations in "The Creation of a Thug: Our Man in Panama," *Life,* March 1990, 81-93.

21. Seymour M. Hersh, "U.S. Aides in '72 Weighed Killing Officer Who Now Leads Panama," *New York Times,* June 13, 1986, A1.

22. Frederick Kempe, *Divorcing the Dictator: America's Bungled Affair with Noriega* (New York: Putnam, 1990), 178. Charles R. Babcock and Bob Woodward, "Report on Panama General Poses Predicament for U.S.," *Washington Post,* June 13, 1986, 1.

23. Margaret E. Scranton, *The Noriega Years: U.S.-Panamanian Relations, 1981-1990* (Boulder CO: Lynne Rienner, 1991). James LeMoyne, "Panamanian, Denying Charges, Says He Won't Quit," *New York Times,* June 18, 1986, A3.

24. William Arkin, telephone interview by author, August 20, 2012.

24. Reporting the Worst-Kept Secret in the World

1. "Reporter Hersh on Noriega," CBS *This Morning,* February 21, 1990."The CIA: Down and Dirty with Noriega," *Nightline,* March 1, 1990. Seymour M. Hersh, *"Our Man in Panama: The Creation of a Thug,"* Life, March 1990, 81-85.

2. Obst, *Too Good,* 248. David Obst, interview by author, July 21, 2011.

3. Obst, interview. James Riordan, *Stone: The Controversies, Excesses, and Exploits of a Radical Filmmaker* (New York: Hyperion, 1995), Stone's affairs, 572. Bob Thompson,

"The Hersh Alternative," *Washington Post*, January 28, 2001, 9–15, 20–27. Seymour M. Hersh, email interview, September 14, 2012.

4. Frankel, *Times of My Life*, 431. Seymour M. Hersh, "The Iran Contra Committees: Did They Protect Reagan?" *New York Times*, April 29 1990, 46–47.

5. Seymour M. Hersh, "Scooped by Mike Wallace," *New Yorker*, April 8, 2012, http://www.newyorker.com/online/blogs/newsdesk/2012/04/scooped-by-mike -wallace.html. Bob Woodward, *Veil: The Secret Wars of the CIA* (New York: Simon and Schuster, 1987).

6. Tim Madigan, "Mr. Hersh Goes to War," Knight-Ridder Newspapers, July 22, 2004, http://archive.truthout.org/article/tim-madigan-mr-hersh-goes-war.

7. "Jews," Encyclopedia of Chicago, http://www.encyclopedia.chicagohistory .org/pages/671.html. I am indebted to Marguerite Stein and Janet Graham Gottlieb for help on Hersh family ancestry.

8. "Q & A with Investigative Journalist Seymour Hersh," *Jewish Journal*, September 20, 2007, http://www.jewishjournal.com/community_briefs/article/q_a_with _investigative_journalist_seymour_hersh_20070921. Gerald Sorin, email to author, September 4, 2012.

9. Hersh, *Price of Power*, 84n. Joseph Pryweller, "Hersh Gets the Story," *Daily Press*, September 12, 1989. Paul Warnke, "Nuclear Israel," *Bulletin of Atomic Scientists*, March 1992, 41–42.

10. Max Friedman, telephone interview by author, August 31, 2012. Seymour M. Hersh, *The Samson Option: Israel's Nuclear Arsenal and American Foreign Policy* (New York: Random House), author's note, 92.

11. Roger Morris, "Nukes in the Negev," *Los Angeles Times*, November 10, 1991. Hersh, *Samson Option*, 109.

12. One critic was angry that Hersh got details of the Samson story wrong. David Bar-Illan, "Portrait of an Israel-Basher," *Jerusalem Post*, March 6, 1992.

13. Andrew and Leslie Cockburn, *Dangerous Liaison: The Inside Story of the U.S.-Israeli Covert Relationship* (New York: HarperCollins 1991). Victor Mallet, "Dual Loyalty," *London Review of Books*, December 1991, 6–7. Bar-Illan, "Portrait of an Israel-Basher."

14. Seymour M. Hersh, "U.S. Said to Have Allowed Israel to Sell Arms to Iran," *New York Times*, December 8, 1991, 1. Joel Brinkley, "Israeli Nuclear Arsenal Exceeds Earlier Estimates, Book Reports," *New York Times*, October 20, 1991, 1.

15. Hersh, *Samson Option*, 284–315. Steven Prokesch, "Britain Urged to Investigate Spy Allegations," *New York Times*, October 23, 1991, A9. Tom Bower, *Maxwell: The Final Verdict* (New York: HarperCollins, 1996), 263–64. Seymour M. Hersh, "The Traitor: The Case against Jonathan Pollard," *New Yorker*, January 18, 1999, 26–33.

16. Seymour M. Hersh, interview by Saul Landau, *Progressive*, October 1998, 33–37.

17. Geoffrey Stevens, "Weapons the U.S. Pretended Not to See," *Toronto Star*,

November 16, 1991, K15. William B. Quandt, "Israel's Nuclear Arsenal," *Washington Post,* November 24, 1991, X7. Curtis Wilkie, "Israel's Deadly Open Secret," *Boston Globe,* November 1, 1991, 67. Morris, "Nukes in the Negev." Warnke, "Nuclear Israel."

18. Hugh Wilson, "Timely Look at Israel's Nuclear Capability," *Montreal Gazette,* November 16, 1991, K3. Peter D. Zimmerman, "Weak Journalism, Poor Scholarship," *St. Petersburg Times,* January 5, 1992, 6D. Steven Emerson, "Inventing the Facts," *Commentary,* January 1995, 55.

19. Brian Hutchinson, "The Unbelievable Life of Ari Ben-Menashe," *National Post,* November 18, 2011. http://news.nationalpost.com/2011/11/18/the-unbelievable -life-of-ari-ben-menashe. Craig Unger, "The Trouble with Ari," *Village Voice;* July 7, 1992, 33. Hersh defended his use of Ben-Menashe in the paperback version of *Samson Option,* September 1992. Rael Jean Isaac, "The Cult of Seymour Hersh," *American Spectator,* July 26, 2004, http://www.intellectualconservative.com/article3654.html. David Bar-Illan, "Hersh: Portrait of an Israel-Basher," *Jerusalem Post,* March 6, 1992.

20. Bower, *Maxwell,* 164. Karen Davis, "Writer Labels Maxwell Story Stuff of Thrillers," *Stars and Stripes,* November 7, 1991, 9. "Editor Named as an Israeli Spy Is Dismissed," *New York Times,* October 29, 1991, A10. Lawrence Van Gelder, "U.S. Author Gets Apology in Libel Case," *New York Times,* August 19, 1994, A11.

21. Hersh as anti-Semite, see Martin Peretz, "What Explains Fashionable Hostility toward Israel?" *Tel Aviv Journal,* July 30, 2011. Micah Sifry, "Israel's Nuclear Arsenal and American Foreign Policy," *Nation,* February 3, 1992, 130.

25. Sex, Lies, and Fraud

1. Margo Hammond, "Camelot's Dirty Laundry," *St. Petersburg Times,* November 16, 1997, 5D.

2. Seymour M. Hersh, "Nixon's Last Cover-up," *New Yorker,* December 14, 1992, 76, 79–80.

3. Seymour M. Hersh, "The Spoils of the Gulf War," *New Yorker,* September 6, 1993, 70, 71, 78.

4. Josh Gitlin, "Bombshells and Brickbats," *Los Angeles Times,* November 12, 1997. Robert Sam Anson, "Secrets and Lies," *Vanity Fair,* November 1997, 110.

5. Saul Landau, "Seymour Hersh," *Progressive,* October 1998, 33–37.

6. Arthur M. Schlesinger Jr., *A Thousand Days* (New York: Houghton Mifflin, 1965). Ted Sorensen, *Kennedy* (New York: Harper & Row, 1965). Kenneth P. O'Donnell and David F. Powers, with Joe McCarthy, *"Johnny, We Hardly Knew Ye": Memories of John Fitzgerald Kennedy* (Boston: Little, Brown, 1972). Seymour M. Hersh, interview by Charlie Rose, December 2, 1997, http://www.charlierose.com/view/interview/8409.

7. Richard Reeves, *President Kennedy: Profile of Power* (New York: Simon & Schuster, 1993). Michael R. Beschloss, *The Crisis Years: Kennedy and Khrushchev,*

1960-1963 (New York: Burlingame Books, 1991). Nigel Hamilton, *JFK: Reckless Youth* (New York: Random House, 1992).

8. Max Friedman, telephone interview, September 25, 2012. Seymour M. Hersh, interview, "Darker Than We Want to Know," *Atlantic,* January 8, 1988.

9. Hammond, *Military and the Media.* Thomas Powers, "The Sins of a President," *New York Times*, November 30, 1997, BR13.

10. Seymour M. Hersh, *The Dark Side of Camelot* (Boston: Little, Brown, 1997); on Honey Fitz, chapter 3, on the election, chapter 7, 27n.

11. Chris Suellentrop, "Sy Hersh Says It's Okay to Lie (Just Not in Print),"*New York,* April 18, 2005, 38.

12. Hersh, *Dark Side*, 228, 114. Dave Saltonstall, "Ex-Prez' Aides and Bro Call Book a Fabrication," *New York Daily News,* November 9, 1991, 28. Anson, "Secrets and Lies," 114.

13. Hersh, *Dark Side,* chapter 9. Josh Getlin, "Bombshells and Brickbats," *Los Angeles Times*, November 12, 1997.

14. Eszterhas, "Reporter Who Broke,"57. Seymour M. Hersh, "Two Stories Seymour Hersh Never Wrote," *Nieman Reports*, Spring 1998, 10.

15. Hersh, *Dark Side,* 389, 18-19, 23.

16. Seymour M. Hersh at a Washington bookstore, "Book Discussion on *The Dark Side of Camelot*," December 10, 1997, http://www.c-spanvideo.org/program/ Dark. Hersh, *Dark Side*, 226. Tim Weiner, "Secret Service Tells Its Agents to Keep Quiet," *New York Times*, December 17, 1997, 22.

17. Hersh, *Dark Side*, 229-30, 241-43.

18. Exner, *My Story*. On "Judy," Hersh, *Dark Side*, 294-325.

19. Patricia Holt, "Hersh Defends His JFK Exposé," *San Francisco Chronicle*, November 11, 1997. Anson, "Secrets and Lies," 114. Mimi Alford, *Once upon a Secret* (New York: Random House, 2012).

20. Hersh quote, Melissa Katsoulis, *Literary Hoaxes* (New York: Skyhorse, 2009).

21. David Samuels, "Fakes," *New Yorker,* November 3, 1997, 68. Benjamin Weiser, "Reporter Chasing Fraudulent Source Finds Methods under Scrutiny," *New York Times*, May 3, 1999, C1.

22. Anson, "Secrets and Lies," 120. Weiser, "Reporter Chasing Fraudulent Source."

23. Lloyd Grove, "Was the Writing on the Wall?" *Washington Post*, October 27, 1997 C11. Anson, "Secrets and Lies," 110.

24. Dan Barry, "History Rewritten," *New York Times,* October 12, 1997, 1.

25. Letter from Hersh to Cusack cited in Weiser, "Reporter Chasing Fraudulent Source." Anson, "Secrets and Lies," 100.

26. Samuels, "Fakes," 68. Anson, "Secrets and Lies," 110.

27. Samuels, "Fakes," 68. Hersh, *Dark Side*, 234–37. Weiser, "Reporter Chasing Fraudulent Source."

28. Grove, "Was the Writing on the Wall?" Trust document quoted in John Reznikoff, interview by Jake Halperin, *This American Life*, National Public Radio, March 15, 2011.

29. Weiser, "Reporter Chasing Fraudulent Source." Patricia Holt, "Vidal Supports Hersh's 'Dark Side,'" *SFGate*, December 7, 1997. Gore Vidal, review, "Coached by Camelot," *New Yorker*, December 1, 1997, 85–92. Hersh, "Book Discussion," C-span video.

30. Samuels, "Fakes." Weiser, "Reporter Chasing Fraudulent Source." Anson, "Secrets and Lies."

31. "Miss Rush Wed to L.X. Cusack," *New York Times*, December 8, 1991, 80. Seymour M. Hersh, interview, "Darker Than We Want to Know," *Atlantic,* January 8, 1998, http://bztv.typepad.com/Winter/HershInterview.pdf.

32. Bill Carter, "NBC Also Questioned Book on Kennedy," *New York Times*, September 27, 1997, 10. Ed Gray, telephone interview by author, October 14, 2012.

33. Bill Carter, "ABC Says Documents on Kennedy Were Faked," *New York Times*, September 25, 1997, 26. Lloyd Grove, "Incendiary JFK Story Goes Up in Smoke," *Washington Post*, September 25, 1997.

34. Eleanor Randolph, "JFK-Monroe 'Affair' Papers Faked," *Los Angeles Times*, September 26, 1997. Grove, "Incendiary JFK Story." Weiser, "Reporter Chasing Fraudulent Source." Anson, "Secrets and Lies," 112.

35. Anson, "Secrets and Lies," 122. Hersh, interview, "Darker Than We Want."

36. "Dangerous World: The Kennedy Years," narrated by Peter Jennings, produced by Mark Obenhaus and Ed Gray for ABC, 1997, found at http://vimeo.com/17924647. Bill Carter, "A Hot-Potato Lands at ABC," *New York Times*, December 3, 1997, E8. Richard Bernstein, "Looking for the Worst and the Darkest in Kennedy," *New York Times*, November 13, 1997, E12.

26. Going after Sy Hersh

1. Maureen Dowd, "J.F.K., ABC and me," *New York Times,* September 27, 1997, 15. Anson, "Secrets and Lies," 122.

2. Patricia Holt, "Hersh Defends His JFK Exposé," *San Francisco Chronicle*, November 11, 1997. Richard Lacayo, "Smashing Camelot," *Time,* November 17, 1997, 40. Jacob Weisberg, "JFK TKO," *Slate*, November 14, 1997, http://www.slate.com/articles/news_and_politics/strange_bedfellow/1997/11/jfk_tko.html.

3. Hersh interview, "Darker Than We Want." David Usborne, "I Take on JFK and What Thanks Do I Get?" *Independent,* November 24, 1997, M5.

4. Frank Rich, "Endless Shining Moment," *New York Times*, November 15, 1997, 17.

Usborne, "I Take on JFK." Seymour M. Hersh, interview by Charlie Rose, December 2, 1997, http://www.charlierose.com/view/interview/8409.

5. Andrew Sullivan, "See No Evil, Hear No Evil in Camelot Country," *London Times,* November 23, 1997.

6. William F. Buckley Jr., "How to Handle Hersh?" *National Review,* December 22, 1997, 74. William Safire, "The President's Friend," *New York Times,* November 16, 1997, WK15. "Dark Side of History," editorial, USA *Today,* November 11, 1997, 14A.

7. Hersh interview, "Darker Than We Want." Barry Bearak, "Assault on 'Camelot,'" *New York Times,* November 9, 1997. Josh Gitlin, "Bombshells and Brickbats," *Los Angeles Times,* November 12, 1997.

8. Hersh, *Dark Side of Camelot* 4, 8, 18, 223.

9. Saltonstall, "Ex-Prez' Aides and Bro," 28. Seymour M. Hersh, interview, *Firing Line,* January 13, 1998. Weisberg, "JFK TKO."

10. "Former JFK Aide Calls Hersh's Book 'Garbage,'" *Patriot Ledger,* November 14, 1997. Anson, "Secrets and Lies," 106.

11. Garry Wills, *Nixon Agonistes: The Crisis of the Self-Made Man* (New York: New American Library, 1979). Wills, "A Second Assassination," *New York Review of Books,* December 12, 1997. Hersh, *Dark Side,* 127–39.

12. Hersh, interview by Rose, December 2, 1997. Howard Kurtz, "Reporter Hersh Hit Hard by Friendly Fire," *Washington Post,* November 17, 1997. Richard Reeves, "In the Matter of Seymour Hersh," *Baltimore Sun,* November 18, 1997.

13. Richard Bernstein, "Looking for the Worst and the Darkest in Kennedy," *New York Times,* November 13, 1997, E12. Edward Jay Epstein, "Hersh's Dark Camelot," *Los Angeles Times,* December 28, 1997, http://www.edwardjayepstein.com/archived/hersh.htm. Alan Brinkley, "The Dark Side," *Time,* November 17, 1997, 50, teacher's guide at http://www.time.com/time/classroom/archive/971117.pdf.

14. Tim Weiner, "Secret Service Tells Its Agents to Keep Quiet," *New York Times,* December 17, 1997.

15. Thomas Powers, "The Sins of a President," *New York Times,* November 30, 1997, BR13. Deborah Kisatsky, review of Hersh's *Dark Side, Presidential Studies Quarterly,* March 1999, 208.

16. Steve Weinberg, "Hersh's Critics Fail to Make Their Case," *Baltimore Sun,* November 23, 1997. Weisberg, "JFK TKO."

17. Thomas Reeves, *A Question of Character* (New York: Free Press, 1991). Roosevelt speech, "The Man with the Muck-rake," delivered April 14, 1906, American rhetoric, http://www.americanrhetoric.com/speeches/teddyrooseveltmuckrake.htm. Harrison Salisbury, "Assault on Camelot," *Philadelphia Inquirer,* November 18, 1997.

18. Steve Weinberg, telephone interview by author, July 10, 2009. Anson, "Secrets and Lies," 120.

19. Ernest R. May and Philip D. Zelikow, "Camelot Confidential," *Diplomatic History* 22, no. 4 (Fall 1998): 642-53. Seymour M. Hersh, "May-Zelikow Confidential," *Diplomatic History* 22, no. 4 (Fall 1998): 654-61. Ed Gray, telephone interview by author, October 14, 2012.

20. Evan Thomas, "Pool Parties in Camelot?" *Newsweek*, November 17, 1997, 3. Jonathan Yardley, "'Camelot': Hearsay Replaces Myth," *Washington Post*, November 12, 1997, D1.

27. *The* New Yorker *Years*

1. Bell et al., "Reporting the Darkness," 60. David Halberstam, *The Best and the Brightest* (New York: Random House, 1972). William Prochnau, *Once upon a Distant War: David Halberstam, Neil Sheehan, Peter Arnett—Young War Correspondents and Their Early Vietnam Battles* (New York: Vintage, 1995).

2. Seymour M. Hersh, *Gulf War Syndrome: The War between America's Ailing Veterans and Their Government* (New York: Ballantine, 1998), 1-4. John MacArthur, *Second Front: Censorship and Propaganda in the Gulf War* (New York: Hill and Wang, 1992). See also Alison Johnson, *Gulf War Syndrome: Legacy of a Perfect War* (Brunswick ME: MCS Information Exchange, 2001).

3. Hersh, *Gulf War Syndrome*, 8-9, 24-5, 50.

4. "Last Battle of the Gulf War: *Frontline*'s Definitive Account of What's behind the Bitter Gulf War Controversy." *Frontline*, January 1998, http://www.pbs.org/wgbh/pages/frontline/shows/syndrome/. Hersh, *Gulf War Syndrome*, 69.

5. Hersh, *Gulf War Syndrome*, 68-71, 55.

6. Seymour M. Hersh, "The Intelligence Gap," *New Yorker*, December 6, 1999. Hersh, "Saddam's Best Friend," *New Yorker*, April 5, 1999. Hersh, "The Traitor: The Case against Jonathan Pollard," *New Yorker*, January 18, 1998. See also the Seymour Hersh page at the Justice for Jonathan Pollard website, www.jonathan pollard.org/hersh.htm.

7. Arthur Allen, "Portrait of a Drug Czar," Salon.com, August 30, 2000. Seymour M. Hersh, "Overwhelming Force: What Happened in the Final Days of the Gulf War?" *New Yorker*, May 22, 2000, 48.

8. Hersh, "Overwhelming Force," 49-82. David Remnick, interview by Charlie Rose, May 18, 2000.

9. Hersh, Overwhelming Force," 49, 51. Michael Gordon and Bernard Trainor, *The Generals' War: The Inside Story of the Conflict in the Gulf* (Boston: Little, Brown, 1995).

10. Hersh, interview by Amy Goodman, "Democracy Now," May 31, 2000. Barry R. McCaffrey, email to author, December 19, 2012. McCaffrey also supplied the author with a packet of material, refuting Hersh's allegation.

11. Hersh, "Overwhelming Force," 53-56.

12. Hersh, interview, "Democracy Now," May 31, 2000. It was unclear why

McCaffrey's drug office spokesman was fielding questions regarding his war duty. McCaffrey, email to author, December 19, 2012.

13. Hersh, "Overwhelming Force," 61.

14. David Remnick said McCaffrey was offered numerous chances to speak with Hersh, but he refused. He did grant interviews to a number of reporters.

15. John Barry, "Probing a Slaughter," *Newsweek*, May 29, 2000, 28.

16. Hersh, "Overwhelming Force," 67. Rebuttal by Barry McCaffrey: James Kitfield, "McCaffrey Responds," interview of Barry McCaffrey, *National Journal*, June 3, 2000, 1762.

17. "Drug Czar Launches Pre-emptive Strike," *Chicago Tribune*, April 19, 2000. Howard Kurtz, "Media Notes," *Washington Post*, May 22, 2000, C01.

18. Martin Kettle, "Drug Tsar Accuses Veteran Journalist," *Guardian*, April 20, 2000, 19. McCaffrey statement: "Gen. McCaffrey Responds to New Yorker Article about Desert Storm," May 16, 2000, USIS Washington File, http://www.fas.org/news/iraq/2000/05/000515-iraq-usia01.htm. Bob Thompson, "The Hersh Alternative," *Washington Post*, January 28, 2001, W9.

19. Thompson, "Hersh Alternative." David Martin, TV interview by Charlie Rose. Weiner, "Democracy Now."

20. "The New Gulf War: McCaffrey vs. Hersh." *NewsMax.com, May 16,* 2000. John Pilger, "Iraqi Dead Were Untallied, *New Statesman,* June 26, 2000, 17.

21. Mark Riley, "Besieged General Fights for Reputation," *Morning Herald*, May 20, 2000, 27. Michael Ellison, "U.S. General 'Attacked Defeated Iraqi Army,'" *Guardian*, May 16, 2000, 13c.

22. Michael R. Gordon, "Report Revives Criticism of General's Attack," *New York Times*, May 15, 2000, 6.

23. NBC News Transcripts.

24. Barry R. McCaffrey, "The New Yorker's Revisionist History," *Wall Street Journal,* May 22, 2000, 38. David Remnick, "You're Right, It Is Revisionist History," *Wall Street Journal,* May 26, 2000, A23. See also Remnick, "The Long Aftermath of a Short War," *New Yorker*, May 22, 2000, 29. Gordon, "Report Revives Criticism, 436.

25. "The Last Battle of the Gulf War," *New York Times,* May 18, 2000, 30.

26. Gary Solis, *The Law of Armed Conflict* (New York: Cambridge University Press, 2010), 124.

27. Georgie Anne Geyer, "Seymour Hersh's Gulf War Misconceptions," *Chicago Tribune*, May 19, 2000. "McCaffrey Stands by Decisions in Gulf War," Associated Press, *Washington Post,* May 16, 2000.

28. BR McCaffrey Associates, www.mccaffreyassociates.com. "No Inquiry on Gulf Attack," *New York Times*, May 16, 2000, A10. David Martin, TV interview on Charlie Rose. McCaffrey, email to author, December 1, 2012.

28. *An Alternative View of the Mideast*

1. McCaffrey, email to author, December. 19, 2012. Scott Sherman, "The Avenger," *Columbia Journalism Review* July/August 2003, 36–38.

2. David Remnick, introduction to *Chain of Command: The Road from 9/11 to Abu Ghraib*, by Seymour M. Hersh (New York: HarperCollins, 2004), xiii. Hersh, interview, January 17, 2013, Investigative Reporters and Editors (IRE) conference, Phoenix, June 8, 2007.

3. Remnick, introduction to *Chain of Command*, xiii. Seymour M. Hersh, interview by ghamal, October 6, 2007, http://www.youtube.com/watch?v=vX3fog0lY70. IRE conference, June 9, 2007. Johanna Neuman, "Sy Hersh: The Reporter Is Back in the Maelstrom," *Los Angeles Times* November 19, 2001.

4. IRE Conference, Baltimore, June 13, 2009. James Bamford, *A Pretext for War: 9/11, Iraq, and the Abuse of America's Intelligence Agencies* (New York: Anchor Books, 2005).

5. Sherman, "Avenger." Remnick, introduction, *Chain of Command*, xv.

6. Seymour M. Hersh, "The Price of Oil," *New Yorker,* July 9, 2001, 48. David Rubien, "The Hardest-Working Muckraker," *Salon,* January 18, 2000, http://www.salon.com/2000/01/18/hersh_2/.

7. Tim Madigan, "Mr. Hersh Goes to War," July 22, 2004, http://archive.truthout.org/article/tim-madigan-mr-hersh-goes-war. Remnick, introduction, *Chain of Command,* xv.

8. Neuman, "Sy Hersh."

9. Seymour M. Hersh, "What Went Wrong?" *New Yorker*, October 8, 2001, 34.

10. Seymour M. Hersh, "King's Ransom," *New Yorker,* October 22, 2001, 35.

11. Michael Massing, "The Hersh Paradox," *Nation*, December 31, 2001, 5.

12. Seymour M. Hersh, "Escape and Evasion," *New Yorker*, November 1, 2001, 50. John Miller, "Sly Sy: A Journalist's Latest Tricks," *National Review*, December 3, 2001.

13. Seymour M. Hersh, interview by Bob Edwards, NPR, November 7, 2001.

14. Miller, "Sly Sy." Rubien, "Hardest-Working Muckraker." Peter Pringle, "Leader of the Pack," *Guardian*, November 12, 2001, 2.

15. Rubien, Hardest-Working Muckraker." Kurtz, "At the Front Lines on War Scandals," *Washington Post*, May 19, 2004, p.C1.

16. Seymour M. Hersh, "The Getaway," *New Yorker,* January 8, 2002, 36. Hersh, interview by Jane Wallace, PBS, February 21, 2003, http://www.pbs.org/now/transcript/transcript_hersh.html.

17. Bob Woodward, *Bush at War* (New York: Simon and Schuster, 2002), 303.

18. Seymour M. Hersh, "The Twentieth Man," *New Yorker,* September 30, 2002, 56. Hersh, "Missed Messages," *New Yorker,* June 3, 2002, 40.

19. Seymour M. Hersh, "The Iraq Hawks," *New Yorker,* December 24, 2002, 58.

Hersh, "The Cold Test," *New Yorker,* January 27, 2003, 42. Hersh, "Who Lied to Whom," *New Yorker,* March 31, 2003, 41. Hersh, interview by Wallace.

20. Seymour M. Hersh, "Selective Intelligence," *New Yorker*, May 12, 2003, 44. Max Boot, "Digging into Seymour Hersh," *Los Angeles Times,* January 27, 2005. Boot, "Think Again: Neocons," Council on Foreign Relations, January/February 2004, http://www.cfr.org/us-strategy-and-politics/think-again-neocons/p7592.

21. Seymour M. Hersh, IRE Conference, Baltimore, June 13, 2009. Remnick, introduction to *Chain of Command*, xxvi. Rael Isaac, "The Cult of Seymour Hersh," *American Spectator*, July/August, 2004.

22. Seymour M. Hersh, "Lunch with the Chairman," *New Yorker*, March 17, 2003. Eric Alterman, "Perle Interrupted," *Nation,* April 7, 2003, http://www.thenation .com/article/perle-interrupted#.

23. Hersh, "Lunch with the Chairman."

24. Stephen Labaton, "Pentagon Adviser Is Also Advising Global Crossing," *New York Times*, March 1, 2003, C1. Richard Perle, "For the Record," *Wall Street Journal,* March 31, 2003, A10. "CNN with Wolf Blitzer," March 9, 2003. Ben Withers, "The People vs. Richard Perle," *In These Times.* April 14, 2003. Alterman, "Perle Interrupted." Editorial, "Richard Perle's Conflict," *New York Times*, March 24, 2003, A14.

25. Maureen Dowd, "Perle's Plunder Blunder," *New York Times,* March 23, 2003, E13. Stephen Labaton, "After Disclosures, Pentagon Adviser Quits a Post," *New York Times,* March 28, 2003, C1. Labaton, "Report Finds No Violations," *New York Times,* November 15, 2003. David Jackson, "Hersh Uncovered Pentagon Adviser," *Chicago Tribune,* June 25, 2004.

29. Back on Top

1. Alec Russell, "Old Reporters Don't Fade Away," *Daily Telegraph*, May 22, 2004, 15. David Jackson, "Rumsfeld Pushed for FBI Probe of Hersh,". *Chicago Tribune,* June 25, 2004.

2. Hersh, "The Other War," *New Yorker,* April 12, 2004, p.40. http://www.the dailyshow.com/watch/tue-august-16-2005/seymour-hersh.

3. Rachel Cooke, "The Man Who Knows Too Much," *Observer*, October 19, 2008. Eric Umansky, "Failures of Imagination," *Columbia Journalism Review,* September/ October 2006, 16. Umansky, "Out of Sight, out of Mind," *Columbia Journalism Review,* July/August 2004, 6.

4. Heidi Benson, "Want to Get Seymour Hersh Excited?" *San Francisco Chronicle*, October 14, 2004, E1. Seymour M. Hersh, "Torture at Abu Ghraib," *New Yorker*, May 10, 2004, 42.

5. Seymour M. Hersh, interviewed by Amy Goodman, "Chain of Command," *New Yorker,* September 14, 2004, on *Democracy Now.* Hersh, "We've Been Taken

Over by a Cult," *New Yorker,* January 26, 2005, on *Democracy Now.* Joe Hagan, "Sy Hersh's News," *New York Observer*, October 25, 2004.

6. Andrew McCarthy, "Bad Press," *National Review*, October 11, 2004.

7. Seymour M. Hersh, telephone interview with author, August 3, 2004. Elana Berkowitz, "Five Minutes with Seymour Hersh," Campus Progress, March 21, 2005, http://www.campusprogress.org/articles/seymour_hersh. Sherry Ricchiardi, "Missed Signals," *American Journalism Review*, August/September 2004. Seymour M. Hersh, "Seymour Hersh's ACLU Keynote Speech," July 8, 2004, http://www .informationclearinghouse.info/article6492.htm.

8. Deborah Hastings, "Sy Hersh Doesn't Like to Talk about Himself," Associated Press, May 21, 2004. Neuman, "Sy Hersh." Hersh, *Chain of Command*, xvii.

9. Hersh, *Chain of Command*. Mark Danner, *Torture and Truth: America, Abu Ghraib, and the War on Terror* (New York: New York Review of Books, 2004). Lisa Hajjar, "The Penal Colony," *Nation*, February 7, 2005, 23.

10. Seymour M. Hersh, "Chain of Command," *New Yorker,* May 17, 2004, 38. Hersh, "The General's Report," *New Yorker,* June 25, 2004, 58. Hersh, interview by Amy Goodman, "How Gen. Taguba Was Forced to Retire," *Democracy Now,* June 19, 2007, http://www.democracynow.org/2007/6/19/seymour_hersh_reveals _rumsfeld_misled_congress.

11. Seymour M. Hersh, "The Gray Zone," *New Yorker*, May 24, 2004, 38. Jane Mayer, *The Dark Side: The Inside Story of How the War on Terror Turned into a War on American Ideals* (New York: Doubleday, 2008). David Johnston, "Rumsfeld and Aide Backed Harsh Tactics, Article Says," *New York Times*, May 16, 2004, 1.

12. News release, Department of Defense, May 15, 2004. Seymour M. Hersh, interview by Wolf Blitzer, CNN, aired May 9, 2004, http://transcripts.cnn.com/ TRANSCRIPTS/0405/09/le.00.html. Tim Harper, "Hersh, on the Record," *Toronto Star,* May 23, 2004, F3. Periscope, *Newsweek*, May 10 2004.

13. Oliver Burkeman, "Profile: Seymour Hersh," *Guardian*, October 9, 2004, 20. Peter Grier, review of *Chain of Command*, by Seymour M. Hersh, *Christian Science Monitor,* September 21, 2004. Robert Fisk, "Seymour Hersh versus the Bush Administration," *Independent,* June 6, 2010. Rick Karr, "Profile of Seymour Hersh," National Public Radio, May 18, 2004, http://www.npr.org/templates/story/ story.php?storyId=1901290. Alastair McKay, "An Investigative Reporter Reborn," *Scotsman*, September 30, 2004, 42.

14. Alec Russell, "The Man the White House Loves to Hate," *Daily Telegraph,* May 20, 2004, 21. Benson, "Want to Get Seymour Hersh Excited?"

15. "Seymour Hersh: Mario Savio Memorial Lecture," University of California– Berkeley, October 27, 2005, http://www.youtube.com/watch?v=7N-zM83DWZk. Missreporter, "[UPDATED] Hersh: 'We've Got Serious Problems Folks,'" Daily

Kos, October 27, 2005, http://www.dailykos.com/story/2005/10/27/160022/
--UPDATED-Hersh-quot-We-ve-got-serious-problems-folks-quot.

16. Tim Madigan, "Mr. Hersh Goes to War," Knight-Ridder Newspapers, July 22, 2004, http://archive.truthout.org/article/tim-madigan-mr-hersh-goes-war.

17. McCarthy, "Bad Press." Amir Taheri, "Many Sources but No Meat," *Telegraph*, September 22, 2004. Michael Rubne, review of *Chain of Command*, *Middle East Policy*, Winter 2004, 29. Rich Barlow, "Full of Detail, Lacking in Style," *Boston Globe*, November 22, 2004. Andrew J. Bacevich, review of *Chain of Command*, *Miami Herald*, October 10, 2004.

18. Michael Ignatieff, "'Chain of Command': What Geneva Conventions?" *New York Times*, October 17, 2004. Erik Harden, "Reporter Blasts 'Neocons,'" *Columbus Dispatch*, October 27, 2004, 4G.

19. Bob Woodward, *Plan of Attack: The Definitive Account of the Decision to Invade Iraq* (New York: Simon & Schuster, 2004). Medi Hasan, "Seymour Hersh—Extended Interview," http://www.newstatesman.com/media/2009/11/vietnam-war-obama -bush-story. Rachel Cooke, "The Man Who Knows Too Much," *Observer*, October 19, 2008.

20. Sherman, "Avenger," 42. Woodward, *Bush at War*. David Shaw, "Hersh, Woodward Are Still the Best in the Business," *Los Angeles Times*, May 16, 2004.

21. David Carr, "Dogged Reporter's Impact," *New York Times*, May 20, 2004, E4. Burkeman, "Profile."

22. Madigan, "Mr. Hersh Goes to War."

Epilogue

1. Seymour M. Hersh, IRE Conference, Phoenix, June 8, 2007. Hersh would not elaborate on the incident when I asked him about it. *New Yorker* website post, September 4, 2004.

2. Woodward, interview by author, February 8, 2012.

3. Robert Entman, "Cascading Activation," *Political Communication*, October–December 2003, 18. Peter Johnson, "Media Mix," USA *Today*, May 18, 2004.

4. Bob Thompson, "The Hersh Alternative," *Washington Post*, Jan. 28, 2001, W9. Howard Kurtz, "At the Front Lines," *Washington Post*, May 19, 2004; Page C1.

5. Rupert Cornwell, "The Reporter Who's the Talk of the Town," *Independent*, May 22, 2004, 40. Neuman, "Reporter Is Back." Bill Bradlee, telephone interview by author, March 1, 2012.

6. Thompson, "Hersh Alternative." Bill Arkin, telephone interview by author, August 20, 2012.

7. James Kirchick, "The Deceits of Seymour Hersh," *Commentary*, March 2012, 18. Seymour M. Hersh, "Iran and the Bomb," *New Yorker*, June 6, 2011, 30–35. Hersh, "Shifting Targets," *New Yorker*, October 8, 2007, 40. Hersh, "The Redirection,"

New Yorker, March 5, 2007, 54. Hersh, "The Next Act," *New Yorker,* November 27, 2006, 94–107. Hersh, "Last Stand," *New Yorker,* July 10, 2006, 42. Hersh, "The Iran Plans," *New Yorker,* April 17, 2005, 30.

8. Scott Shuger, "King Sy's Mistakes," *Slate,* posted Nov. 8, 2001. Kirchick, "Deceits of Seymour Hersh." Carl Suellentrop, "It's Okay to Lie (Just Not in Print)," *New York Magazine,* May 21, 2005.

9. Barry McCaffrey, email to author, December 19, 2012. Steve Weinberg, "All Things Considered," NPR, May 19, 2004. Neuman, "Sy Hersh."

10. Mehdi Hasan, "The Obama White House Can't Abide Me," *NewStatesman,* November 26, 2009. Alex Kane, "Seymour Hersh: Obama's Iran Policy Is a 'Political Game' to 'Look Tough,'" *Mondoweiss,* November 21, 2011. http://mondoweiss .net/2011/11/seymour-hersh-obamas-iran-policy-is-a-political-game-to-look-tough .html. David Remnick interview with Seymour M. Hersh, October 6, 2007, http:// www.youtube.com/watch?v=vX3fo9olY7o.

11. Seymour M. Hersh, emails to author, June 22, 2012, and January 18, 2013.

12. William Safire, "The President's Friend," *New York Times,* November 16, 1997, WK15. See, for example, Seymour M. Hersh, "Direct Quotes: Bashar Assad," blog, *New Yorker,* February 3, 2010. Woodward. Hersh, "Iraq 'Moving towards Open Civil War,'" *Democracy Now!* May 11, 2005.

13. Lakshmi Chaudhry, "Seymour Hersh: Man On Fire," October 26, 2004. http://www.alternet.org/mediaculture/20309/. Seymour M. Hersh, IRE Conference, Phoenix, June 8, 2007. Hersh, commencement address, Columbia University Journalism School, May 21, 2003.

Index

spying, 187–92, 195, 198; and *Glomar Explorer*, 201–11, 213–14
Cold War, 91, 191, 205, 264, 318
Colombia, 309, 313
Colson, Charles, 186, 242, 284
Columbia Journalism Review, 15, 152, 183, 334
Columbus GA, 8, 11, 42
Committee to Re-Elect the President, 148
Congo, 177, 196
Conrad, Charles, 71
Conyers, John, 167
CounterPunch, xv
Cowan, Geoffrey, 1
Cowan, Paul, 1
Crewdson, John, 145, 196
C-Span, 252
Cuba, 121, 181, 240, 264
Currie, Brainerd, 46
Currie, David, 46
Curtis, Charlotte, 248, 252, 253
Cusack, Lawrence X., III, 292–97, 299, 301

Daley, Richard, 65
Daniel, Clifton, 149, 153, 157, 176, 208, 211, 232
The Dark Side of Camelot (Hersh), 284–305
Darnton, John, 132, 170, 216, 233
Davies, Nick, 282
Davis, Charles, 225
Davis, Nathaniel, 172
Dayan, Moshe, 277
Dean, John, 151, 157, 158
Deep Throat, 153, 159, 272
Defense Policy Board, 325
Delta Force, 321

Department of Health, Education and Welfare, 94
Desai, Morarji, 258–60
Diplomatic History 304
Di Rita, Lawrence, 328, 329
Dispatch News Service, 17, 18, 22, 26, 31, 32, 271
Domenici, Pete, 29
Dornfeld, Arnold, 49
Dowd, Maureen, 298
Downie, Leonard, 15, 77, 151, 159, 197
Drinan, Robert, 166
Duckett, Carl, 203, 208
Dudman, Richard, 19
Dugway Proving Ground, 92–93, 120

Eagleburger, Lawrence, 177, 241, 243
Eisenhower, Dwight, 71, 92, 276, 284
Eller, Jerry, 100, 103, 106
Ellsberg, Daniel, 82, 148, 236, 237, 242
Emerson, Gloria, 35
Emerson, Steven, 280, 281
England, Lynndie, 330, 332
Epstein, Edward Jay, 301
Erlichman, John, 152, 157, 169, 237, 242, 244
Ertegun, Ahmet, 257
Eszterhas, Joe, xv, 198
Evergreen Dispatch, 56–58
Evergreen IL, 56
Ewing, Michael, 294, 304
Exner, Judith Campbell, 291, 299, 311

Federal Bureau of Investigation (FBI), 144, 151, 159, 162, 186, 190–91, 217–18, 228, 238, 241, 267, 320; investigating Hersh, 214, 267, 328
Feith, Douglas, 323
Feldstein, Mark, 157
Felt, W. Mark, 159
Finch, Robert, 237

Hearst, William Randolph, 135

Heinenman, Ben, 2

Heller, Jean, 81, 83, 85, 89

Helms, Richard, 122, 173, 188, 190–91, 194, 209

Hemingway, Ernest, 62

Hentoff, Nat, 221

Hersh, Alan, xiii, 45, 56, 274

Hersh, Dorothy Margolis, 56, 272, 274

Hersh, Elizabeth, xiii, 55, 66, 67, 185, 196, 198, 215, 216, 329, 339

Hersh, Isador (Hershowitz), 45, 56, 112, 273–74

Hersh, Matthew, 190, 216

Hersh, Melissa, 216

Hersh, Seymour Myron: Abu Ghraib, 328–35; anonymous sources, 84, 135, 138, 153–56, 185, 214, 230, 262, 268, 273, 275, 281, 312, 323–24, 334, 336, 344; anti-Semitism, 35, 51, 161–62, 279–80, 274, 279–80, 283; Associated Press, 61–87; awards, xi, xii, 19, 32, 44, 58, 83, 124–25, 132–33, 146, 147, 155, 168, 170, 180, 200–201, 216, 335, 338; chemical and biological weapons, 2, 28, 43, 85, 86, 88–97, 116–24; City News Bureau, 2, 47–54, 56, 60, 74, 234, 341; and defamation lawsuits, 220, 231, 258–60, 279–83, 326; education of, 12, 45–47, 324; and Gulf War I, 285, 306–7, 309, 310, 313, 317; Iran, 272–73, 276, 309, 318, 323, 342–43; Iraq, 330–38; military service of, 54–56; mistakes of, 131–32, 165–70, 341–42; and My Lai massacre, 1–44; *New Yorker*, 306–38; *New York Times*, 125–233; on Nixon 155, 166; on nuclear weapons, 271–83; and POWs,

128–31; as press secretary, 98–115; Pulitzer Prize, xi, 19, 32, 44, 200; and rivalry with Bob Woodward, xv, 145, 151, 154–59, 197–98, 273, 286, 293, 337–38; speechmaking, xi, xv, 125–26, 260–61, 331, 336; United Press International, 58–60; Watergate, 144–56. *See* Hersh, Alan; Hersh, Dorothy Margolis; Hersh, Elizabeth; Hersh, Isador; Hersh, Matthew; Hersh, Melissa

Hess, John L., 133, 134

Hewitt, Don, 46

Hilton, Barron, 222

Hill, Clarence A., Jr. , 77

Hirstein, Stuart, 312

Hitchens, Christopher, 256

Ho Chi Minh Trail, 165

Ho Chi Minh City, 235

Hoffa, Jimmy, 62, 217, 222

Hoffman, Dustin, 108

Hoffman, Fred, 75–79, 83–84

Hoffman, Stanley, 241, 249, 252

Hoover, J. Edgar, 144, 241

Horrock, Nicholas, 196

Hotel Metropole (Vietnam), 128

Houseman, Martin, 173

Howard Hughes Company, 206–7, 212

Hughes, Harold, 136–38, 163–64, 294

Humphrey, Hubert, 73, 117–18, 250

Hussein, Saddam, 307, 309, 331

Hyde Park (Chicago), 45, 47, 112

impeachment of Richard Nixon, 166–67, 273

India, 174, 258–59

International Telegraph and Telephone Co. (ITT), 173

Iran-Contra affair, 272–73

Isaac, Rael Jean, 281–82, 324

White, John, 125
Wicker, Tom, 138, 165; on Chile, 172, 174, 176, 178, 181; on CIA, 177, 198
Wills, Gary, 301-2
Wilson, Edwin, 238
Wilson, Hugh, 280
Wise, David, 195, 340
Witcover, Jules, 301
Wolfe, Alan, 253-54, 256
Wolfowitz, Paul, 323
Woodstock festival, 1, 3
Woodward, Bob, 18, 157-58, 213, 233, 344; CIA, 270; Hersh rival, xv, 145, 151, 154-59, 197-98, 273, 286, 293, 337-38; and David Obst, 155, 271-72; sourcing, 185, 243; and Watergate, 138, 144, 146-50, 154
World Trade Center, 319

Yardley, Jonathon, 305
Yeosock, John J., 310
Yom Kippur War, 279
yellow journalism, 49, 73, 301

Ziegler, Ronald, 29, 157, 169
Zimbrakos, Paul, 49-54, 57, 74
Zimmerman, Peter D., 280